The 2nd Fostoria PRICE WATCH

Hazel Marie Weatherman

Glassbooks

STATEMENT OF POLICY

This publication is not a price list. It is a price **guide**. It does not establish fixed prices but records price **trends**. It doesn't tell the collector what he should pay, but what he might **expect to pay** to stay within certain popular price ranges.

The price trends suggested in these pages are representative of price averages in the United States from coast to coast, allowing for price fluctuations due to regional scarcities of, or demands for, a particular piece, color or pattern.

Prices are for single pieces, not pairs.

Where crystal is listed together with colors, Crystal is always low trend. I have tried to list the colors in order of desirability and value. For example, when you see "Crystal, Amber, Green, Rose, Topaz, and Azure" you should read Crystal low trend and Azure high, and the others accordingly.

When Canary, Ruby, Regal Blue, or Ebony is in the picture, the price span will be greater to allow for its added desirability.

Few patterns introduced before 1943 were still being made in 1978, and these in short lines only. **PRICE WATCH** will note them, and tell you also which patterns are still available from the company's Matching Service, which usually involves only stemware and the 7'' and 8'' plates.

Fostoria glass was not marked until 1953. Since then FOSTORIA has been sandblasted on the bottoms of most stemware, but not on the flat pieces.

Use **PRICE WATCH** as a guide, but more importantly use your own judgement based on your knowledge of your particular area and circumstances. Remember that the price you pay must ultimately be your own.

Price Watch: What Makes It Tick?

If you've just bought **PRICE WATCH**, you're probably familiar with the big illustrated **FOSTORIA: ITS FIRST FIFTY YEARS** and the current passion for collecting Fostoria Glass Company's historic patterns in glass.

You're seeing more and more of the beautiful Fostoria colors at glass shows, and you've noticed the frequency with which it's being sought-for and sold-through the collecting publications.

Many of you have a cache of Fostoria in your glass showcase, or your own wedding service proudly preserved. Most probably, you have your eye on a special Fostoria pattern you never thought of collecting 'til now.

Now. Do you know what your Fostoria is worth today?

PRICE WATCH **is a catalogue of observations to tell you, as accurately as possible, just that. It reports the value of Fostoria glass according to present supply versus present demand, the average price a piece will actually bring on the collectors' market today.**

Just as essential as pricing—whether you buy, sell, collect or deal—is the truly comprehensive list of pieces contained only in this **PRICE WATCH**. The ''big book'' pictures each pattern and each type of piece, but despite the thousands of examples shown, more than half the number of actual pieces had to be left out for lack of space.

Here in **PRICE WATCH**, compiled for the first time, is the sum total of the Fostoria parts—piece by piece by color by pattern.

A brand new feature of this WATCH is the inclusion of those many ''blank'' or plain stems which I reported to you but never had room to print before. Voilá ! You'll find them in the last section.

Although a few of the minor patterns still have not made it to the market place, most patterns have surfaced since the Fostoria collecting buzz started five years ago. During these five years your **PRICE WATCH** has watched closely the fluctuating of a young hobby, and this second edition marks the attainment of Fostoria's first level of stabilization. The ground floor has been established. From here we watch the continuation of the rise.

Fostoria is bound to go higher than the levels you see here. But the principle I used through this work, as in all my publications, has been one of reflecting actual prices, not projecting future ones. Better prices attain their own natural rise, free of any inflation or manipulation from me. Prices will spiral upward soon enough as it is, on their own!

So welcome to the longest, the most complete, and the most official pricing guide we may ever see for any one company's glasswares.

The longest? Covering an unbroken span of 450 patterns over more than fifty years, **PRICE WATCH** prices more than 20,000 individual pieces.

The most complete? The most official? Let's consider these together.

We are lucky that Fostoria, unlike so many other glass companies, kept comprehensive files through its long years of existence. In addition to the 50 years of catalogs reprinted in the **FOSTORIA** book, every price list (except a few from the earliest 1887-1900 period, and possibly some mid-year supplements) is still on hand. In them are listed and measured all pieces to every pattern sold through the years. These price lists were graciously loaned me by the company for this publication.

Then the hard work really began. Right away I saw that a complete listing of pieces couldn't be obtained from any one price list due to the number of pieces not only added to, but dropped from any year. The company's idea was to create variety for the buyer, and depending on a pattern's popularity the outcome could be astounding. The incredible AMERICAN pattern, begun in 1915 and still being made today, boasted over 200 pieces at one point and claims over 300 in all!

Finally, after months of cross-checking each year to each year, we have the comprehensive list you see here. As we've said, we could not collect without it.

HOW TO USE PRICE WATCH? This guide corresponds logically to the **FOSTORIA** book. By using them in conjunction, you'll have no problem. The few points needing explanation will be given in the "STATEMENT OF POLICY" on the first page.

WHERE TO FIND FOSTORIA GLASS TO COLLECT? This question is often put to me by beginners. My answer: If you're in it for the good time, by all means develop the get-out-and-beat-the-bushes approach. You'll profit in fun as much as in savings. But if practicality is the order of your day; if your joy rests simply in the beauty of possessing and preserving glass; or if you're trying to finish a collection or find a difficult piece, use the collection newspapers and journals which carry sure, specific Fostoria-for-sale ads in the glass columns. You can also advertise your "wants" this way, with excellent results.

Of the many publication now offered nationally, I'm finding the most Fostoria, the most glass reportage, and the most fun in the DEPRESSION GLASS DAZE ($6.50 a year, Box 57, Otisville MI 48463). By all means try it. You'll meet all of us there! Secondly, a good deal of Fostoria is listed in the ANTIQUE TRADER WEEKLY ($12.00 a year, Box 1050, Dubuque IA 52001).

May I suggest...? Pay Fostoria Glass Company itself a visit. The factory maintains two low-priced outlet stores showcasing hundreds of new and discontinued patterns. A glassfan's delight! The first store is off Hiway 70 in Wheeling, W. Va., and the second is next to the factory in Moundsville, W. Va.

On the next four pages are partial piece listings for a few of the oldest patterns not shown in the catalog reprints in the Fostoria book.

Pictured below are three pieces of the VICTORIA pattern, the butterdish, the water bottle, and the spoon holder. The rest of the illustrations are taken from early glass trade journals researched after I published FOSTORIA. More of these early patterns may show up for future editions.

Immediately following this is the PRICE WATCH proper, corresponding page by page to the big book.

VICTORIA OR 183 WARE

Satin Finish

Sugar and Cover	30.00--40.00	Celery Tray	8.00--12.00
Cream	20.00--25.00	Custard, Hdl.	5.00----8.00
Spoon	20.00--25.00	Custard Plate	3.00----5.00
Butter and Cover	40.00--50.00	Nut Bowl	6.00----9.00
Tumbler	9.00--12.00	Canoe	8.00--12.00
Finger Bowl	4.00----6.00	Tumbler (183)	9.00--12.00
Nappy 4½", 5", deep	4.00----6.00	Flower Bowl, Large	10.00--15.00
Nappy 9", 10", deep	12.00--15.00	Flower Bowl, Ind.	6.00----9.00
Bowl 8", 9", regular	10.00--14.00	Molasses Can, Large S.P.T.	45.00--60.00
Jug, Globe ½ gal.	35.00--45.00	Molasses Can, Ind.	40.00--50.00
Shaker, Double Screw	5.00----8.00	Molasses Can, C.S.T.	40.00--50.00
Oil, 10 oz.	30.00--40.00	Ind. Cream Tank	15.00--20.00
Ice Cream Saucer	6.00----9.00	Tooth Pick	12.00--15.00
Water Bottle	20.00--25.00	Cigar Holder	20.00--25.00
Mustard and Bail	15.00--20.00	Smoker Set	25.00--35.00
Cruet Set (1 Oil, 2 Shakers, 1 Mustard)	50.00--65.00	Napkin Ring	8.00--10.00
		Pickle Jar	10.00--15.00
Olive, Hdl.	9.00--12.00	Pickle Jar and Cover	20.00--25.00
Celery, Tall	22.00--28.00	Lamp	100.00--150.00

VERONA OR 200 WARE

Sugar and Cover	8.00--10.00	Oil, 10 oz., Plain	6.00----9.00
Cream	4.00----6.00	Cruet Set (1 Tray, 1 Oil, 2	
Spoon	8.00--10.00	Shakers)	12.00--18.00
Butter and Cover	15.00--20.00	Celery, Tall	10.00--12.00
Tumbler	2.00----3.00	Custard, Hdl.	2.00----4.00
Finger Bowl	2.00----3.00	Custard Plate	1.00----2.00
Nappy 4", 4½"	2.00----3.00	Molasses Can B. T.	15.00--20.00
Bowl, H.F., 6", 7", 8", Open	8.00--10.00	Sugar Shaker	6.00----9.00
Bowl, H.F., 6", 7", 8", Cov'd.	20.00--25.00	Jelly 5"	5.00----8.00
Comport 4"	5.00----8.00	Goblet	5.00----8.00
Comport 6", 7", 8", Open	7.00--10.00	Salver 8, 9, 10	10.00--15.00
Comport 6", 7", 8", Covered	12.00--16.00	Tank Cream	9.00--10.00
Jug, ½ Gal.	20.00--25.00	Ind. Can	10.00--12.00
Shakers	2.00----3.00	Mustard and Bail	9.00--12.00
Oil, 10 oz., Cut Stopper	7.00--10.00		

No. 200, Engraved 111.

Cream.

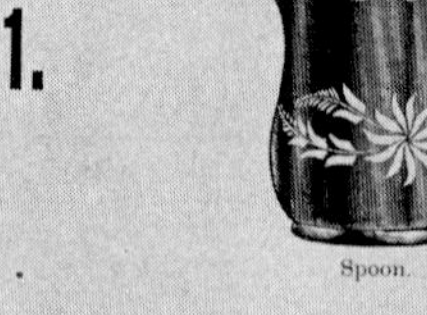

Spoon.

Butter.

Fostoria Glass Co.   Fostoria, Ohio.

Sugar.

Sugar.

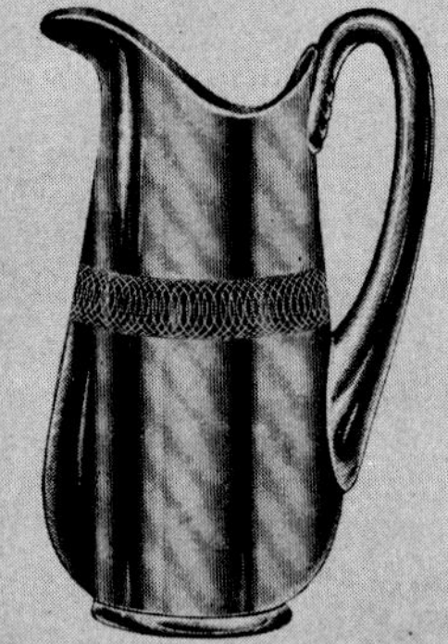

Tankard.

Butter.

Cream.

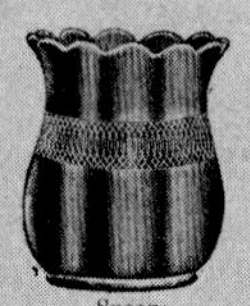

Spoon.

No. 200, Etched 32.

ENGRAVED 111 AND ETCHED 32 WARE

200 Sugar & Cover	10.00--15.00		200 Jug		25.00--35.00
200 Sugar	8.00--10.00		200 Tankard		25.00--35.00
200 Cream	8.00--10.00		200 Sugar Shaker		8.00--10.00
200 Spoon	9.00--12.00		200 Oil, Cut Stopper		10.00--15.00
200 Butter and Cover	20.00--25.00		200 Celery, Tall		10.00--15.00
127 Tumbler	3.00----4.00		200 Custard		3.00----5.00
200 Finger Bowl	3.00----4.00		200 Custard Plate		2.00----3.00
225 4½'', 4¾'' Nappy	2.00----4.00		200 Molasses Can		20.00--25.00
200 Open Bowl H.F., 6'', 7'', 8''	10.00--15.00		200 Ind. Can		10.00--15.00
200 Open Bowl L.F., 6'', 7'', 8''	6.00--10.00		200 Jelly		6.00--10.00

VALENCIA OR 205 WARE

Sugar and Cover	25.00--35.00	Bowl, H.F., Open, 7″, 8″	20.00--25.00
Cream	15.00--20.00	Bowl, H.F., Cov'd, 7″, 8″	30.00--40.00
Spoon	15.00--20.00	Bowl, L.F., Open, 7″, 8″	15.00--20.00
Butter and Cover	35.00--45.00	Bowl, L.F., Cov'd, 7″, 8″	20.00--30.00
Tumbler	8.00--11.00	Comport 4″	10.00--15.00
Finger Bowl	3.00----5.00	Salver, 9″, 10″	25.00--35.00
Nappy 4½″	4.00----6.00	Ind. Can	20.00--25.00
Bowl 7″, 8″, 9″	10.00--12.50	Mustard	15.00--20.00
Shaker	5.00----7.00	Ind. Cream	10.00--15.00
Jug ½ Gal.	30.00--40.00	Nut Bowl	8.00--12.00
Jug, Tankard	30.00--40.00	Cruet Set	50.00--60.00
Celery, Tall	20.00--25.00	Oil	30.00--35.00
Molasses Can, B.T.	35.00--45.00		

226 WARE

Sugar and Cover	8.00--12.00	Shaker, S.P.	2.00----3.00
Cream	4.00----6.00	Can (225)	10.00--12.00
Spoon	8.00--10.00	Custard	3.00----4.00
Butter and Cover	15.00--25.00	Plate 6¾''	2.00----3.00
Butter, Cut Star	20.00--25.00	Rose Bowl 3'', 4'', 5'', 7''	5.00--10.00
Nappy 4½'', 4¾''	3.00----4.00	Mustard	9.00--12.00
Nappy 7'', 8'', 9''	6.00----9.00	Oval 7'', 8'', 9''	6.00--10.00
Shaker, Nickle	2.00----3.00		

OPAL WARE (c. 1903)

524 Pen Tray	5.00----8.00	562 Pen Tray	5.00----8.00
526 Pin Tray	4.00----6.00	563 Puff and Cover	15.00--20.00
544 Box	15.00--20.00	564 Rose Bowl	20.00--25.00
545 Box	15.00--20.00	565 Puff	15.00--20.00
546 Pin Tray	4.00----6.00	566 Hair Receiver	20.00--25.00
541 Bottle	20.00--25.00	680 C and B Tray	8.00--10.00
542 Bottle	20.00--25.00	681 Pen Tray	5.00----8.00
556 Box and Cover, H.P.	20.00--25.00	682 Pin Tray	4.00----6.00
557 C and B Tray	8.00--10.00	683 Bottle	20.00--25.00
550 Box and Cover	15.00--20.00	684 Puff and Cover	15.00--20.00
553 Puff	15.00--20.00	685 Box, H.P.	20.00--25.00
554 Puff	15.00--20.00	686 Hair Receiver	20.00--25.00
555 Puff	15.00--20.00	735 Vase	15.00--20.00
552 C and B Tray	8.00--10.00	736 Vase	15.00--20.00
560 Pin Tray	4.00----6.00	696 Cologne	20.00--25.00
561 Pin Tray	4.00----6.00		

No. 2	Candelabra 4 lights	100.00--150.00
15	2 light Candelabra	75.00--100.00
737	Candlestick	15.00--20.00

FINE BLOWN & CUT VASES

736	Vase—Etched or Plain	30.00--45.00
641	Vase—Cut 91—12" high	10.00--15.00
735	Vase—Etched and Plain	20.00--25.00
466	5" Vase also 7"	9.00--12.00
625	Vase—Cut 91—8"	10.00--12.50

No. 1106	Orchid Vase Small 6½"	18.00--20.00
	Large 8"	20.00--22.00
No. 332	3-Hdle. Loving Cup Optic 6"	10.00--15.00
No. 330	3-Hdle. Loving Cup 7"	15.00--20.00

HOFFMAN HOUSE GOBLETS

No. 812	16 oz.	1.00----2.00
No. 811	14 oz.	1.00----2.00
No. 810	12 oz.	1.00----2.00
No. 809	10 oz.	1.00----2.00
No. 808	8 oz.	1.00----2.00

BLOWN SAND BLAST TUMBLERS

820	Blown Tumbler 8 oz.	.50----1.00
820	Blown Tumbler SB#1	2.00----3.00
820	Blown Tumbler SB#2	2.00----3.00
820	Blown Tumbler SB#3	2.00----3.00
820	Blown Tumbler SB#4	2.00----3.00
820	Blown Tumbler SB#5	2.00----3.00

MOST PERFECT DIPPER MADE

| Crystal Dipper | 20.00--25.00 |

PRESSED JUGS

142	3 pt. Jug	10.00--12.50
162	3 pt. Jug	12.00--15.00
618	3 pt. Jug	30.00--40.00
493	Boston Measuring Cup	2.00----3.00

VASES

272	14" Vase	10.00--12.00
272	11½" Vase	8.00--10.00
272	8" Vase	6.00----8.00
272	5½" Vase	3.00----4.00
184	14" Vase	10.00--12.00
184	9" Vase	5.00----8.00
184	11" Vase	8.00--10.00
600	11" Vase	10.00--12.50
195	5" Vase	5.00----6.00
600	9" Vase	7.00----9.00
600	7" Vase	6.00----8.00
402	7" Vase	6.00----8.00

195	9" Vase	7.00----9.00
402	8" Vase	8.00--12.00
402	10" Vase	10.00--14.00

No. 553	Butter & Cover	10.00--12.00
No. 402	8" Crushed Fruit & Cvr.	15.00--20.00
No. 444	Ice Tub & Drainer	12.00--16.00
No. 1270	6" Covered Comport	8.00--10.00
No. 1170	Wine Flat Foot	3.00----4.00
No. 677	8" Crushed Fruit & Cvr.	12.00--15.00
No. 444	12" Punch Bowl with or without foot	35.00--45.00
No. 444	Handled Lemonade	3.00----5.00
No. 402	Handled Lemonade	3.00----5.00
No. 402	15" Punch Bowl with foot separate	35.00--50.00
Burdett	11" Cake Cover	12.00--16.00
Burdett	Cake Fruit or Sandwich Cover	20.00--25.00
No. 444	Cheese & Cover made in 8 & 9" Plain	15.00--20.00
	or engraved	30.00--35.00
No. 444	9" Plate	3.00----5.00
No. 112	Mustard	5.00----6.00
No. 403	Mustard & Cover	3.00----4.00
No. 226½	6" Cheese & Cover	8.00--10.00

APPLE WINES, COCKTAILS, HOT WHISKEYS & SHERRYS

428	Cocktail 4½ oz.	2.00----3.00
435	Cocktail 4¼ oz.	2.00----3.00
438	Cocktail 4¼ oz.	2.00----3.00
415½	Cocktail 3¼ oz.	3.00----4.00
439	Cocktail 3 oz.	2.00----3.00
436	Cocktail 3½ oz.	2.00----3.00
437	Cocktail 4¼ oz.	2.00----3.00
413	Cocktail & Sherry 2¼ oz.	3.00----4.00
430	Apple Wine 4½ oz.	2.00----3.00
414½	Hot Whiskey 3¼ oz.	2.00----3.00

THREE PINT PRESSED HANDLE PITCHERS

No. 1166	P.H. Jug Panal C	100.00--150.00
No. 1166	P.H. Jug Panal B	100.00--150.00
No. 1166	P.H. Jug Panal D	100.00--150.00
No. 1166	P.H. Jug Panal A	100.00--150.00

No. 501, HARTFORD

501	Sugar & Cover	25.00--35.00
501	Cream	22.00--30.00
501	Spoon	20.00--30.00
501	Butter	35.00--45.00
501	Basket Spoon	15.00--20.00
501½	Sugar and Cover	25.00--35.00
501	5½" Olive	4.00----6.00
501	5½" Berry	3.00----5.00
501	6" Berry	4.00----6.00
501	7" Berry	5.00----8.00
501	8" Berry	8.00--10.00
501	5½" Hdld. Desert	10.00--12.50
501	Small Finger Bowl	4.00----6.00
501	Olive (star)	5.00----6.00

501	Shaker, Salt	8.00--10.00
501	Tumbler	10.00--15.00
501	Tall Celery	25.00--35.00
501	Individual Salt	6.00----8.00
501	Syrup, nickel top	35.00--50.00
501	Syrup, heavy top	35.00--50.00
501	4½" Comport	3.00----6.00
501	5½" Comport	4.00----7.00
501	6" Comport	5.00----9.00
501	7" Comport	8.00--12.00
501	8" Comport	10.00--15.00
501	7" Oblong	5.00----7.00
501	8" Oblong	7.00----9.00
501	9" Oblong	8.00--10.00

No. 600 BRAZILIAN

600	Sugar & Cover	20.00--25.00
600	Cream	15.00--17.50
600	Spoon	15.00--17.50
600	Butter & Cover	25.00--30.00
600	Jug	25.00--35.00
600	Tankard	30.00--35.00
600	Tumbler	7.00----9.00
600	7" Berry	8.00--10.00
600	8" Berry	10.00--12.50
600	4½" Nappy	3.00----4.00
600½	8" Berry	10.00--12.50
600½	4½" Nappy	4.00----5.00
600	8" Comport	15.00--18.00
600½	8" Comport	18.00--20.00
600	Cracker Jar & Cover	22.00--25.00
600	Pickle Dish	4.00----5.00
600	Handled Olive	10.00--12.50
600	Vinegar, P. S.	15.00--18.00
600	Vinegar, C. S.	16.00--20.00
600	Syrup, Heavy Top	30.00--40.00
600	Syrup, Nickel Top	30.00--40.00
600	Individual Salt	4.00----5.00
600	Shaker Salt, S.P.T.	4.00----5.00
600	Shaker Salt, N.P.C. Top,	4.00----5.00
600	Toothpick	12.00--15.00
600	Pickle Jar & Cover	20.00--25.00
600	Pickle Jar, no Cover	10.00--15.00
600	Celery, Tall	20.00--25.00
600	Celery, Tray	8.00--10.00
600	8" Oblong	4.00----6.00
600	9" Oblong	6.00----8.00
600	Water Bottle	15.00--20.00
600	Finger Bowl	4.00----5.00
600	Custard	4.00----5.00
600	Rose Bowl	12.00--15.00
600	Individual Cream	6.00----8.00
600	Individual Sugar	6.00----8.00
600	Vase, 7"	6.00----8.00
600	Vase, 9"	7.00----9.00
600	Vase, 11"	10.00--12.50

No. 601 DIANA WARE

601	Sugar & Cover	12.00--15.00
601	Creams	10.00--12.50
601	Spoons	10.00--12.50
601	Butter & Cover	15.00--18.00
601	½ gallon Jug	12.00--15.00
601	½ gallon tankard	20.00--30.00
601	Tumbler, Post	1.00----2.00
601	Celery	10.00--12.50
601	Syrup	15.00--18.00
601	4½" Berry	1.00----3.00
601	7" Berry	2.00----3.00
601	8" Berry	3.00----4.00
601	Shaker, Spun Nick. Top.	2.00----3.00
601	Vinegar or Oil, P.S.	8.00--10.00
601	7" H.F. Bowl, Open	15.00--18.00
601	8" H.F. Bowl, Open	18.00--20.00
601	7" H.F. Bowl & Cover	20.00--22.50
601	8" H.F. Bowl & Cover	22.00--25.00
601	7" L.F. Bowl, Open	9.00--12.00
601	8" L.F. Bowl, Open	10.00--15.00
601	5" Jelly	5.00----8.00
601	4" Comport	3.00----4.00
601	9" Salver	12.00--15.00
601	10" Salver	14.00--16.00

No. 603 ROBIN HOOD WARE

603	Sugar & Cover	25.00--28.00
603	Cream	15.00--20.00
603	Spoon	15.00--20.00
603	Butter & Cover	30.00--35.00
603	Jug	30.00--35.00
603	Tumbler, Post Bottom	4.00----5.00
603	9" Salver	25.00--30.00
603	10" Salver	30.00--35.00
603	Syrup, Nickel Top	25.00--30.00
603	Shaker, Spun Nickel Top	8.00--10.00
603	Pickle Dish	6.00----7.50
603	Mug	15.00--18.00
603	6" Berry	10.00--12.00
603	7" Berry	12.00--15.00
603	8" Berry	15.00--18.00
603	4½" Nappy	4.00----5.00
603	6" Nappy not polished	3.00----4.00
603	7" Nappy not polished	4.00----5.00
603	8" Nappy not polished	5.00----8.00
603	4" Nappy not polished	1.00----2.00
603	6" High Open Bowl	18.00--20.00
603	7" High Open Bowl	20.00--25.00
603	8" High Open Bowl	25.00--30.00
603	6" High Covered Bowl	25.00--30.00
603	7" High Covered Bowl	30.00--35.00
603	8" High Covered Bowl	35.00--40.00
603	Tall Celery	25.00--30.00
603	Oil, P.S.	20.00--25.00

SALVERS

601	10" Salver	11.00--14.00
603	9" Salver	25.00--30.00
603	10" Salver	30.00--35.00
444	9" Salver	15.00--20.00
677	10" Salver	12.00--15.00

BOWLS

459	9" Berry Bowl	10.00--12.00
972	8" Berry Bowl	10.00--15.00
459	5" Nappy	2.00----3.00
971	8" Berry Bowl	10.00--15.00

794	4½" Nappy	3.00----4.00
740	9" Berry Bowl	15.00--18.00
740	4½" Berry Nappy	4.00----5.00
794	8" Berry Bowl (also 7").	12.00--18.00

No. 675 EDGEWOOD WARE

675	Sugar & Cover	10.00--12.50
675	Cream	8.00--10.00
675	Spoon	8.00--10.00
675	Butter & Cover	15.00--17.50
675	Tankard	25.00--35.00
675	Tumbler	5.00----8.00
675	Oil or Vinegar, P.S.	15.00--17.00
675	Oil or Vinegar, C. S.	15.00--18.00
675	Syrup, Nickel Top	25.00--30.00
675	Syrup, Heavy Top	25.00--30.00
675	Shaker, S. P. T.	4.00----5.00
675	Shaker, N. P. Cast Top	4.00----5.00
675	Water Bottle	15.00--18.00
675	Sugar Shaker, S. P. T.	10.00--12.00
675	* 8" Berry	8.00--10.00
675	4½" Berry	2.00----3.00
675	Celery Stand	12.00--15.00
675	Celery Tray	5.00----8.00
675	9" Oval	4.00----6.00
675	Custard, Stuck Handle,	3.00----4.00
675	Finger Bowl	2.00----3.00
675	Toothpick	10.00--12.50
675	Pickle Jar & Cover	15.00--18.00
675	Pickle Jar, no Cover	8.00--10.00

Made in 1974 and 1975 in lead Crystal: List Price, $15.50 and $18.50.

No. 676 PRISCILLA
Also Gold Decorated

676	Sugar	12.00--15.00
676	Cream	12.00--15.00
676	Spoon	12.00--15.00
676	Butter	25.00--30.00
676	Jug	35.00--40.00
676	Tumbler	8.00--10.00
676	8½" Berry	20.00--25.00
676	4½" Nappy	4.00----5.00
676	Water Bottle	20.00--22.50
676	Custard—Stuck Handle	6.00----8.00
676	Finger Bowl	4.00----6.00
676	Shaker, Salt, Large, nickel top	8.00----9.00
676½	Shaker, Salt, small, Silver plated	6.00----8.00
676	Shaker, Salt, large, silver plated top	8.00--10.00
676	Syrup—nickel top	30.00--35.00
676	Vinegar or oil P.S.	25.00--28.00
676	Vinegar or Oil C. S.	25.00--30.00
676	Celery	20.00--22.50
676	Egg	4.00----6.00
676	Pickle Dishes	6.00----8.00
676	Toothpick	12.00--15.00
676	6" H. F. Bowl	20.00--25.00
676	6" H. F. Bowl & Cover	30.00--35.00

No. 789 WEDDING BELLS
Also Gold and Ruby Decorated

789	Sugar & Cover	35.00--40.00
789	Cream	25.00--30.00
789	Spoon	25.00--30.00
789	Butter & Cover	40.00--50.00
789	Jug	50.00--75.00
789	Tumbler	15.00--20.00
789	7" Berry	18.00--20.00
789	8" Berry	20.00--22.50
789	9" Berry	22.50--25.00
789	4½" Nappy	4.00----5.00
789	Celery, Tall	35.00--45.00
789	Celery, Tray	8.00--12.00
789	9" Oval	6.00----8.00
789	Pickle Dish or Olive	8.00--10.00
789	Shaker, large, Spun Nickel Top	7.00----9.00
789½	Shaker, Small, N. P. Cast	6.00----8.00
789½	Shaker, Small, S. P. T.	6.00----8.00
789	Vinegar or Oil	40.00--50.00
789	Syrup, Heavy Top	50.00--65.00
789	Syrup, Nickel Top	50.00--65.00
789	Toothpick	30.00--35.00
789	Finger Bowl	5.00----7.00
789	Water Bottle	30.00--40.00
789	Quart Decanter	50.00--65.00
789	Custard Stuck Handle	5.00----7.00
789	Tankard	50.00--65.00
789	Wine	15.00--20.00
789	Whiskey	15.00--20.00
789	Punch Bowl	40.00--60.00
789	Punch Bowl & Foot	50.00--75.00

No. 793 NIAGARA
Also Came Gold Decorated

793	Sugar & Cover	20.00--25.00
793	Cream	15.00--17.50
793	Spoon	15.00--17.50
793	Butter	25.00--35.00
793	Jug, Tankard	25.00--30.00
793	Tumbler	7.00----9.00
793	Celery Tall	15.00--20.00
793	Vinegar or Oil, P.S.	20.00--25.00
793	Vinegar or Oil, C. S.	20.00--25.00
793	Syrup, Heavy top	25.00--30.00
793	Syrup, nickel top	25.00--30.00
793	Shaker Salt, N. T.	4.00----5.00
793	7" Berry	12.00--15.00
793	8" Berry	15.00--18.00
793	9" Berry	18.00--20.00
793	4" Nappy	3.00----4.00
793	4½" Nappy	4.00----5.00

PRESSED JUGS

953	3 pt. Jug	10.00--12.50
	Fruit Jar Filler	4.00----5.00
583	Soap Slab, Opal	5.00----7.50
802	5" Covered Sweetmeat	20.00--25.00
952	3 pt. Jug	15.00--20.00
801	Butter & Cover	20.00--25.00

PRESSED WATER SETS

162	Water Set-1Jug, 6Tmblrs.	25.00--35.00
600	Water Set-1Jug, 6Tmblrs.	50.00--75.00
602	High Foot Jelly	8.00--10.00
142	Water Set-1Jug, 6Tmblrs.	20.00--25.00
601	5" Jelly	5.00----7.00

SHAKERS – NICKEL TOPS

136	Shaker	4.00----5.00
137	Shaker	4.00----5.00
112½	Shaker	3.00----4.00
112	Shaker	3.00----4.00
601	Shaker	2.00----2.50
676	Shaker	8.00----9.00
956	Shaker	8.00----9.00
603	Shaker	8.00--10.00
1000	Shaker	4.00----5.00
1000½	Shaker	4.00----5.00
1001	Shaker	4.00----5.00
732	Shaker	2.00----3.00
600	Shaker	4.00----5.00
175½	Shaker	3.00----4.00
550	Saloon Shaker	2.00----3.00
180	Shaker	1.00----2.00
187	Med. Shaker	1.00----2.00
187	Lg. Shaker	1.00----2.00
187½	Shaker	1.00----2.00
614	Shaker	1.00----2.00
518	Shaker	1.00----2.00
475	Shaker	1.00----2.00
713	Shaker	1.00----2.00

BLOWN OILS

936	Catsup, Grnd. Stopper 9oz	8.00--10.00
808	9 oz	8.00--10.00
313	Cut Stopper 9 oz	10.00--12.00
300	11 oz	10.00--12.00
517	Catsup 10 oz	8.00--10.00

TOOTHPICKS

403	Toothpick	3.00----4.00
600	Toothpick	12.00--15.00
675	Toothpick	10.00--12.50
789	Toothpick	30.00--35.00
Hat	Toothpick	7.00----9.00
1000	Toothpick	10.00--12.50

CELERY DIPS

107	Individual Butter	1.00----2.00
465	Celery Dip	4.00----5.00
515	Celery Dip	4.00----5.00
600	Celery Dip	4.00----5.00
511	Celery Dip	4.00----5.00
575	Celery Dip	5.00----7.50
112	Individual Salt	3.00----4.00
594	Individual Salt	2.00----3.00
742	Individual Salt	1.00----2.00
743	Table Salt	3.00----4.00
585	Individual Salt	2.00----3.00
93	Individual Salt	2.00----3.00
95	Individual Salt	3.00----4.00

MOLASSAS

600	Hvy Brit. Syrup top 6 oz	35.00--40.00
417	Syrup Silver Plated top & Hdle 4½ oz	25.00--30.00
444	Syrup Small Silver P.T. & H. 6 oz	30.00--35.00
726	Can Silver P.T. & H 5½ oz	30.00--35.00
675	Syrup Brit. Top 8 oz.	25.00--30.00
951	Syrup tin Top No. 1 Sand Blast 18 oz	25.00--30.00
597	Tin Top 16 oz	20.00--25.00
598	Tin Top 15 oz	20.00--25.00
601	Spun Nickel Top 14 oz.	18.00--20.00
603	Spun Nickel Top 15 oz	25.00--30.00
789	Syrup 8½ oz	50.00--60.00
956	Syrup 12 oz	25.00--30.00
1000	Syrup 10½ oz	25.00--30.00
961	Syrup Glass lid 14 oz	20.00--25.00
921	Syrup Glass lid 16 oz	20.00--25.00

HORSERADISH BOTTLES

456	Horseradish & Spoon No Handle	4.00----6.00
456	Horseradish, Handle & Spoon	6.00----8.00
963	Horseradish 10 oz	3.00----4.00
979	Horseradish 5 oz	2.00----3.00

No. 956 WARE

956	Sugar & Cover	20.00--25.00
956	Cream	18.00--20.00
956	Spoon	18.00--20.00
956	Butter & Cover	25.00--30.00
956	4½" Nappy	5.00----6.00
956	8" Berry	20.00--25.00
956	Pickle Dish	7.00----9.00
956	6" H.F. Bowl, open	25.00--30.00
956	7" H.F. Bowl, open	30.00--35.00
956	8" H.F. Bowl, open	35.00--40.00
956	6" H.F. Bowl, & cover	35.00--40.00
956	7" H.F. Bow., & cover	40.00--45.00
956	8" H.F. Bowl & cover	45.00--50.00
956	10" Salver	30.00--35.00
956	Syrup	25.00--30.00
956	Oil	20.00--25.00
956	Tankard	30.00--35.00
956	Tumbler	8.00--10.00
956	Shaker, Spun Nickel Top	7.00----9.00

No 1000 BEDFORD WARE

1000	Sugar & Cover	15.00--20.00
1000	Cream	12.00--15.00
1000	Spoon	12.00--15.00
1000	Butter & Cover	22.00--25.00
1000	Jug	30.00--35.00
1000	Tankard	30.00--35.00
1000	Tumbler	8.00--10.00
1000	4" Royal Berry	3.50----4.50
1000	4½" Royal Berry	4.00----5.00
1000	7" Royal Berry	18.00--20.00

1000	8" Royal Berry	20.00--22.50
1000	9" Royal Berry	22.50--25.00
1000	4½" Square Nappy	5.00----6.00
1000	8" Square Nappy	20.00--25.00
1000	4½" Round Nappy	3.00----4.00
1000	7" Round Nappy	15.00--17.50
1000	8" Round Nappy	18.00--20.00
1000	5" Handled Nappy	7.00----9.00
1000	6" Handled Nappy	10.00--12.50
1000	6" Bon Bon	7.00----9.00
1000	6" High Foot Bowl, open	20.00--22.50
1000	6" High Foot Bowl, Cover	25.00--30.00
1000	6" Footed Comport	18.00--20.00
1000	Celery, Tall	18.00--20.00
1000	Celery Tray	10.00--12.00
1000	8" Pickle Dish	8.00--10.00
1000	7" Oval	7.00----9.00
1000	8" Oval	8.00--10.00
1000	9" Oval	10.00--12.50
1000	10" Oval	12.00--15.00
1000	Syrup, spun top	25.00--30.00
1000	Oil	20.00--25.00
1000	Shaker, spun nickel Top	4.00----5.00
1000½	Shaker, nickel plated cast top	4.00----5.00
1000½	Shaker, Silvr. Plt. Tp	4.00----5.00
1000	Sugar Shaker	12.00--15.00
1000	Tooth Pick	10.00--12.50
1000	Finger Bowl	4.00----6.00
1000	Ind. Oval Salt	5.00----6.00
1000	Pickle Jar & Cover	20.00--25.00
1000	Pickle Jar, no cover	10.00--15.00
1000	Individual Sugar & Cover	12.00--15.00
1000	Individual Sugar, no cover	10.00--12.00
1000	Individual Cream, no cover	10.00--12.00
1000	Water Bottle	20.00--25.00
1000	Cracker Jar & Cover	25.00--30.00
1000	Cracker Jar, no cover	15.00--20.00
1000	Custard	4.00----5.00
1000	12" Punch Bowl	30.00--35.00
1000	12" Punch Bowl & Foot	40.00--45.00
1000	14" Punch Bowl & Foot	50.00--65.00
1000	14" Punch Bowl	40.00--50.00
1000	I. C. Tray	20.00--25.00
1000	Claret Jug	30.00--35.00
1000	Whiskey Jug & Stopper	25.00--30.00
1000	Whiskey Tumbler	8.00----9.00
1000	Goblet	15.00--20.00
1000	Claret	20.00--25.00
1000	Wine	15.00--20.00
1000	Bitter Bottles With Tube	15.00--18.00
1000	Bitter Bottles without Tube	12.00--15.00
1000	Horseradish & Stopper & Spoon	12.00--15.00
1000	Horseradish & Stopper, no Spoon	10.00--12.50
1000	Mug	12.00--15.00

No. 1001 BRILLIANT WARE

1001	Sugar & Cover	12.00--15.00
1001	Cream	10.00--12.50
1001	Spoon	10.00--12.50
1001	Butter & Cover	20.00--25.00
1001	Jug	25.00--30.00
1001	Tumbler	7.00----9.00
1001	Shaker, Nickel Plated Cast Top	4.00----5.00

1001	Shaker, Spun Nickel Top	4.00----5.00
1001	Oil, 8 oz	25.00--30.00
1001	4" Nappy	3.00----4.00
1001	4½" Nappy	4.00----5.00
1001	7" Berry	10.00--12.50
1001	8" Berry	12.00--15.00
1001	Pickle Dish	7.00----9.00
1001	6" H.F. Bowl	25.00--30.00
1001	6" H.F. Bowl & Cov.	30.00--40.00
1001	7" Vase	8.00--10.00
1001	9" Vase	10.00--12.50
1001	11" Vase	12.00--15.00
1001	6" Handled Olive	10.00--12.00
1001	Cracker Jar & Cover	25.00--30.00
1001	Tall Celery	15.00--20.00
1001	9" Oval	12.00--15.00
1001	Toothpick	10.00--12.50
1001	Individual Sugar	10.00--12.00
1001	Individual Cream	10.00--12.00
1001	Syrup Can	25.00--35.00
	Crystal Dipper	20.00--25.00
493	Boston Measuring Cup	2.00----3.00

PRESSED OILS & VINEGARS

1333	6 oz Oil	15.00--20.00
444½	6 oz Oil	18.00--20.00
1258	5 oz Oil	14.00--16.00
675	6 oz Vinegar	12.00--15.00
600	6 oz Vinegar	15.00--18.00
1121	6 oz Vinegar	16.00--18.00
1229	6 oz Oil	14.00--16.00
1119	6 oz Vinegar	14.00--16.00
1093	4 oz Vinegar	12.00--15.00
1299	4½ oz Oil C.S.	12.00--15.00

No. 1118 YORK WARE

1118	Sugar & Cover	25.00--27.50
1118	Butter & Cover	30.00--35.00
1118	Cream	18.00--20.00
1118	Spoon	18.00--20.00
1118	8" Berry	18.00--20.00
1118	4½" Berry	3.00----4.00
1118	Shaker Salt, No. 1118, Nickel Plated Cast Top	8.00----9.00
1118	Shaker Salt, No. 1118, Silver Plated Cast Top	8.00----9.00
1118	Shaker Salt, No. 1118½, Nickel Plated Cast Top	7.00----8.00
1118	Shaker Salt, No. 1118½, Silver Plated Cast Top.	7.00----8.00
1118	Custard	4.00----5.00
1118	Syrup, Silver Plated Top & Handle	40.00--45.00

No. 1119 SYLVAN WARE
Also Gold Decorated

1119	Sugar & Cover	20.00--25.00
1119	Butter & Cover	30.00--35.00
1119	Creams	12.00--15.00
1119	Spoons	12.00--15.00

1119	4″ Comport	4.00----6.00
1119	4½″ Comport	4.00----6.00
1119	6″ Comport	5.00----7.00
1119	7″ Comport	7.00----9.00
1119	8″ Comport	8.00--10.00
1119	10″ Comport	10.00--12.00
1119	4″ Comport, Flared	4.00----6.00
1119	4½″ Comport, Flared	6.00----8.00
1119	6″ Comport, Flared to 7″	6.00----8.00
1119	7″ Comport, Flar. to 8½″	8.00--10.00
1119	8″ Comport, Flar. to 9½″	9.00--12.00
1119	10″ Comport, Flar. to 12″	10.00--15.00
1119	4½″ Comport, Belled	6.00----8.00
1119	6″ Comport, Belled to 7″	7.00----9.00
1119	7″ Comport, Bell. to 8½″	8.00--10.00
1119	8″ Comport, Bell. to 9½″	9.00--12.00
1119	10″ Comport, Bell. to 12″	10.00--15.00
1119	10″ Comport Cupped	10.00--15.00
1119	½ gallon Pitcher	25.00--30.00
1119	½ gallon Tankard	20.00--25.00
1119	Water Bottle	15.00--20.00
1119	Finger Bowls	4.00----5.00
1119	Ice Tea Tumblers	8.00--10.00
1119	Table Tumbler	6.00----8.00
1119	Wine Tumbler	7.00----9.00
1119	Whiskey Tumbler	6.00----8.00
1119	Toothpicks	15.00--20.00
1119	Celery, Tall	15.00--20.00
1119	Celery Tray	8.00--10.00
1119	4½″ Jelly Stand	8.00--10.00
1119	5″ Jelly Stand	10.00--12.00
1119	4½″ Jelly Stand, Flared	8.00--10.00
1119	5″ Jelly Stand, Flared	10.00--12.00
1119	6″ Plate	3.00----4.00
1119	5″ Ice Cream	4.00----5.00
1119	8½″ Cabaret	6.00----8.00
1119	9½″ Cabaret	6.00----8.00
1119	11″ Cabaret	8.00--10.00
1119	14″ Cabaret	10.00--12.00
1119	5″ Handled Nappy	7.00----9.00
1119	Handled Bon Bon—3 corner	8.00--10.00
1119	Vinegar	14.00--16.00
1119	Large Syrup, Cap. 12 oz., Brittania Nickel Plat. Top Silver Plated Top	20.00--30.00
1119	Small Syrup, Capacity 5 oz. Nickel Plated Top	15.00--25.00
1119	Salt & Pepper, Nickel Plated Top	7.00----9.00
	Silver Plated Top	7.00----9.00
1119	Individual Cream	12.00--15.00
1119	3 Handled Sugar	10.00--15.00
1119	3 Handled Sugar & Cover	15.00--20.00
1119	Sugar Sifter, Silver Plated Top	16.00--18.00
1119	Cracker Jar & Cover	20.00--25.00
1119	Cracker Jar	15.00--20.00
1119	Pickle Jar & Cover	20.00--25.00
1119	Chow-Chow Jar & Ground Stopper	12.00--15.00
1119	Square Olive	5.00----7.50
1119	3 Corner Olive	4.00----5.00
1119	Salted Almond	4.00----5.00
1119	Pickle Dish	7.00----8.00
1119	14″ Punch Bowl	30.00--35.00
1119	14″ Punch Bowl & Foot	40.00--50.00
1119	Lemonade	14.00--17.00
1119	9″ Oval Tray	8.00--10.00
1119	11″ Oval Tray	10.00--12.00
1119	7″ Oval Tray	6.00----8.00
1119	13″ Oval Tray	12.00--15.00

1119	Medium Rose Bowl	8.00--12.00
1119	Large Rose Bowl	12.00--15.00
1119	Sponge Cup	2.00----3.00
1119	1 oz. Cologne, Cut Stopper	5.00----8.00
1119	2 oz. Cologne, Cut Stopper	8.00--10.00
1119	4 oz. Cologne, Cut Stopper	10.00--12.00

No. 1121 LOUISE WARE
Also Gold Decorated

1121	Sugar & Cover	25.00--30.00
1121	Butter & Cover	30.00--35.00
1121	Cream	15.00--20.00
1121	Spoon	15.00--20.00
1121	Small Butter & Cover	25.00--30.00
1121	4″ Nappy	3.00----4.00
1121	4½″ Nappy	4.00----5.00
1121	6″ Nappy	4.00----6.00
1121	7″ Nappy	5.00----7.00
1121	8″ Nappy	8.00--10.00
1121	6″ Nappy, Flared to 7″	5.00----7.00
1121	7″ Nappy, Flared to 8½″	6.00----8.00
1121	8″ Nappy, Flared to 9½″	8.00--10.00
1121	4½″ Comport	8.00--10.00
1121	5″ Comport	10.00--12.00
1121	4½″ Jelly Stand	10.00--15.00
1121	5″ High Foot Bowl	12.00--16.00
1121	6″ High Foot Bowl	15.00--18.00
1121	7″ Low Foot Bowl	15.00--20.00
1121	*8″ Low Foot Bowl	20.00--25.00
1121	4½″ Jelly, Flared	12.00--16.00
1121	5″ High Foot Bowl, Flared to 6″	12.00--15.00
1121	6″ High Foot Bowl, Flared to 7″	15.00--18.00
1121	7″ Low Foot Bowl, Flared to 8½″	18.00--20.00
1121	8″ Low Foot Bowl, Flared to 9½″	20.00--22.00
1121	4½″ Jelly & Cover	20.00--25.00
1121	5″ High Foot Bowl & Cover	25.00--30.00
1121	6″ High Foot Bowl & Cover	30.00--35.00
1121	10″ Salver	25.00--30.00
1121	11″ Salver	30.00--35.00
1121	½ gallon Pitcher	30.00--40.00
1121	Tumbler	10.00--12.50
1121	Custard	4.00----5.00
1121	Vinegar	16.00--18.00
1121	Shaker Salt, Spun Nickel Top	8.00----9.00
1121	5″ Handled Nappy	10.00--14.00
1121	Toothpick	20.00--25.00
1121	Blown Molasses Can, Nickel Top, Capacity 16 oz.	30.00--35.00
1121	Blown Molasses Can, Tin Top, Capacity 16 oz.	30.00--35.00
1121	Pickle Dish	4.00----6.00
1121	Confection	6.00----8.00
1121	9″ Oval Dish	8.00----9.00
1121	Celery Tray	10.00--12.00
1121	8½″ Cabaret	8.00--10.00
1121	9½″ Cabaret	10.00--12.00
1121	11″ Cabaret	12.00--15.00

RECENT: 9″ footed comport was made in 1974-1976 in Lead Crystal.

No. 1223 PATTERN

1223	4" Nappy, not Polished	2.00----3.00
1223	4½" Nappy, not Polished	3.00----4.00
1223	6" Nappy, not Polished	4.00----5.00
1223	7" Nappy, not Polished	5.00----6.00
1223	8" Nappy, not Polished	6.00----7.00
1223	8" Pickle, not Polished	6.00----7.00
1223	7" Oval, not Polished	4.00----6.00
1223	8" Oval, not Polished	5.00----7.00
1223	5x7 Candy Tray	4.00----6.00
1223	6x8 Candy Tray	5.00----7.00
1223	Finger Bowl	3.00----4.00
1223	8" Plate	4.00----5.00

PAGE 32 MISC.

1063	7½ oz Tumbler	7.00----9.00
1225	Butter & Cover	35.00--45.00
1225	Cream	20.00--25.00
1225	Sugar & Cover	25.00--30.00
1183	Shaker	4.00----6.00
1182	Shaker	4.00----6.00
1093	4 oz Vinegar	15.00--18.00
402	8¾ oz Tumbler	5.00----8.00
444½	8½ oz Tumbler	5.00----8.00

SHAKERS

444	Round Shaker	4.00----6.00
506	Shaker	4.00----5.00
675	Shaker	4.00----5.00
691	Shaker	3.00----4.00
676½	Small Shaker	6.00----8.00
789½	Shaker	6.00----8.00
444½	Shaker	5.00----6.00
28	Shaker	5.00----6.00
718	Shaker	5.00----6.00

EGG CUP

421	Egg Saucer foot	2.00----3.00
91	Egg Cup	1.00----2.00
432	Egg Cup	1.00----2.00
433	Egg Cup	1.00----2.00
114	Egg Cup	1.50----2.50

BLOWN CUSTARDS

480	Optic, Blown Custard	1.00----2.00
481	Optic, Blown Custard	1.00----2.00
482	Optic, Blown Custard	1.00----2.00
481	Optic, Etched 48, Blown	2.00----3.00

BAR, WHISKEYS & BITTER BOTTLES

319	1 qt Bar Bottle	2.00----3.00
319	1 qt Bar Bottle, Optic	4.00----5.00
335	1 qt Bar Bottle, Cut Neck & Flute	4.00----6.00
	Straw Jar & Cover, Optic	40.00--45.00
315	Bitter Bottle, Optic 11½ oz (cut neck) also made Plain Neck	15.00--20.00
476	4 oz Bitter Bottle; also 8 oz	16.00--20.00
103	Tumbler 2¾ oz Sham	1.00----1.50
100	Tumbler 2¾ oz light	1.00----1.50
101	Tumbler 2¼ oz Sham	1.00----1.50
104	Tumbler 2¾ oz light	1.00----1.50
105	Tumbler 2½ oz Sham	1.00----1.50
102	Tumbler 3 oz light	1.00----1.50

No. 1236 PASTE MOULD PITCHERS

1236	1 Pitcher	5.00----7.00
1236	2 Pitcher	7.00----9.00
1236	3 Pitcher	8.00--10.00
1236	4 Pitcher	10.00--12.00
1236	5 Pitcher	12.00--15.00
1236	6 Pitcher	15.00--18.00
1236	7 Pitcher	18.00--20.00

PAPER WEIGHTS

9	3" Paper Weight	3.00----4.00
35	3¼" Paper Weight	3.00----5.00
37½	5½" Star Paper Weight	10.00--12.50
32	4½" Paper Weight	4.00----5.00
33	3" Paper Weight	5.00----7.00
31	3" Paper Weight	3.00----4.00
34	4x2½" oblong Paper Weigh	4.00----5.00
36	4½x2-7/8" Paper Weight	4.00----5.00
1126	2" Paper Weight	5.00----8.00
776	3" Paper Weight	2.00----4.00
30	3" Paper Weight	2.00----4.00
16	4" Sponge Cup	2.00----4.00
112	3" Round Sponge Cup	3.00----5.00
1119	3½" Sponge Cup	7.00----9.00

SQUARE COLOGNES

209	2 oz Cologne	4.00----5.00
209	4 oz Cologne	4.00----6.00
209	8 oz Cologne	5.00----7.00

PASTE MOULD BLOWN WARE

1232	Optic Jug	12.00--15.00
1195	Small Decanter, S/S 9 oz	12.00--15.00
1195	Med. Decanter, C/S 20 oz	15.00--18.00
1195	Lg. Decanter, C/S 34 oz	18.00--22.00
1201	Bar Bottle	2.00----3.00

MISC.

582	Mucilage Cup & Brush	10.00--12.50
15	Ink & Cover	10.00--12.50
486	Safety Ink	7.00----9.00
14	Ink & Cover	8.00--10.00
308	½" Government Ink, Stoppered	5.00----8.00
	Also made in 1½", 2", 2¼", 2½", 3", 3½".	
112	No. 3. Diam. 2"	10.00--15.00
	Also made in ½", 1", 2", 2¼", 2½", 3".	
306	Ink Cut, 2" sq.	4.00----5.00
1258	Individual Cream	6.00----8.00
1258	4½" Comport	4.00----5.00
954	Pickle Dish	4.00----5.00
583	Soap Slab Opal	8.00----9.00

No. 1229 FRISCO LINE

1229	Spoon	18.00--20.00
1229	Sugar & Cover	25.00--27.50
1229	Butter	30.00--35.00
1229	Cream	18.00--20.00

1229	8" Cabarette	10.00--12.50
1229	Shaker N. T.	8.00----9.00
1229	6" Comport	8.00--10.00
1229	7" Comport	10.00--12.50
1229	9" Fruit Bowl	30.00--35.00
1229	7" Bowl & Cover	40.00--45.00
1229	4½" Comport	4.00----5.00
1229	8" Comport	12.50--15.00
1229	Tumbler	10.00--12.50
1229	3½" Vase	6.00----7.50
1229	½ Gallon Pitcher Shape "A"	25.00--30.00
1229	13" Vase	12.00--15.00
1229	6" Vase	8.00--10.00
1229	6 oz Oil	14.00--16.00
1229	½ Gal. Pitcher Shape "B"	30.00--35.00

RECENT: Milk glass pieces made 1954 to 1964 (and in aqua and peach opaque in 1957 and 1958) were:

1229	Candy Jar & Cover, List Price $4.00	
1229	Spoon Holder $2.50	
1229	Toothpick $1.50	
1229	6" Bud Vase $1.75	
1229	10" Swung Vase $3.00	

Candy Jar & Cover being made in lead crystal 1978, list price $26.50.

No. 1231 PATTERN

1231	Sugar	5.00----6.00
1231	Cream	5.00----8.00
1231	Rose Bowl	4.00----6.00
1231	4½" Nappy	2.00----3.00
1231	10" Oval Berry	10.00--15.00
1231	½ Gal. Tankard	20.00--25.00
1231	Tumbler	6.00----7.50
1231	Finger Bowl	4.00----5.00
1231	Pickle Jar & Cover	12.00--15.00
1231	Custard	4.00----5.00
1231	15" Punch Bowl & Stand	40.00--50.00
1231	Footed Sherbet 3½ oz	5.00----7.50

No. 1299 PATTERN

1299	Sugar & Cover	15.00--20.00
1299	Butter & Cover	22.00--27.50
1299	Cream	12.00--15.00
1299	Spoon	12.00--15.00
1299	4" Comport	3.00----4.00
1299	4½" Comport	4.00----5.00
1299	7" Comport	8.00----9.00
1299	8" Comport	10.00--12.50
1299	9" Comport	12.00--15.00
1299	½ Gal. Pitcher	25.00--30.00
1299	½ Gal. Tankard	20.00--25.00
1299	Tumbler Belled	7.00----8.00
1299½	Tumbler Restaurant	7.00----9.00
1299	Tumbler Ice Tea	8.00--10.00
1299	Toothpick	10.00--12.50
1299	Celery Tall	17.00--20.00
1299	Celery Tray	8.00----9.00
1299	5" Ice Cream	5.00----6.00
1299	Pickle Dish	6.00----7.00
1299	7" Oblong Dish	4.00----5.00
1299	8" Oblong Dish	5.00----6.00
1299	9" Oblong Dish	6.00----7.50
1299	10" Oblong Dish	8.00----9.00
1299	Pickle Jar & Cover	15.00--18.00
1299	Cracker Jar	10.00--15.00
1299	Cracker Jar & Cover	20.00--25.00
1299	Ind. Cream	6.00----7.50
1299	Ind. Sugar	6.00----7.50
1299	Ind. Table Salt	4.00----5.00
1299	Shaker Salt S. P. T.	6.00----7.50
1299	Shaker Salt H. N. T.	6.00----7.50
1299	Custard	4.00----5.00
1299	Oil or Vinegar C.S.	12.00--15.00
1299	Oil or Vinegar D.S.	12.00--15.00
1299	Syrup Straight Sil. P. Top	50.00--60.00
1299	Syrup, Swelled Silver Top	55.00--65.00
1299	Bouquet Holder, 14"	10.00--12.50
1299	Bouquet Holder, 17"	12.00--15.00
1299	18" Punch Bowl	30.00--40.00
1299	18" Punch Bowl, Footed	40.00--50.00

No. 1299 PATTERN CUT No. 83

1299	Sugar & Cover	20.00--25.00
1299	Butter & Cover	30.00--35.00
1299	Cream	15.00--20.00
1299	Spoon	15.00--20.00
1299	½ Gal. Ice Pitcher	25.00--35.00
1299	½ Gal. Tankard	25.00--35.00
1299	Tumbler Belled	8.00--10.00
1299½	Tumbler Restaurant	10.00--12.00
1299	Tumbler Ice Tea	10.00--12.00
1299	Toothpick	10.00--15.00
1299	Cracker Jar & Cover	25.00--30.00
1299	Shaker Salt, Sil. Plat. Top	8.00--10.00
1299	Oil C. S.	25.00--30.00
1299	Syrup, Straight Sil. Top	60.00--70.00
1299	Syrup, Swelled Sil. Top	65.00--75.00

No. 1300 PATTERN

1300	Sugar & Cover	15.00--20.00
1300	Butter & Cover	30.00--35.00
1300	Cream	12.00--15.00
1300	Spoon	12.00--15.00
1300	4" Comport	4.00----5.00
1300	4½" Comport	5.00----6.00
1300	7" Comport	8.00----9.00
1300	8" Comport	8.00--10.00
1300	9" Comport	10.00--12.50
1300	10" Comport	12.50--15.00
1300	11" Comport	15.00--17.50
1300	11" Comport, Cupped	17.00--20.00
1300	5" Plate	3.00----4.00
1300	6" Plate	4.00----5.00
1300	9" Plate	5.00----6.00
1300	5" Ice Cream	5.00----6.00
1300	5" Footed Jelly	8.00--10.00
1300	7" Footed Bowl	10.00--15.00
1300	8" Footed Bowl	12.00--16.00
1300	10½" Footed Bowl	15.00--20.00
1300	11½" Footed Bowl	20.00--25.00
1300	13" Fruit Bowl	20.00--25.00
1300	9" Salver	25.00--35.00
1300	½ Gal. Pitcher	30.00--35.00
1300	Tumbler	8.00----9.00

1300	Finger Bowl	4.00----6.00
1300	Toothpick	20.00--25.00
1300	Celery Tall	20.00--25.00
1300	5'' Handled Nappy	7.00----9.00
1300	Handled Bon Bon	7.00----9.00
1300	Nicknack	8.00--10.00
1300	Water Bottle	20.00--25.00
1300	Shaker, Pressed Spun Nickle Top	8.00----9.00
1300	Shaker, Blown, Spun Nickle Top	6.00----8.00
1300	Oil or Vinegar D.S.	25.00--35.00
1300	Molasses Can, Nickel Top	50.00--65.00
1300	Molasses Can, Tin Top	50.00--65.00
1300	Cracker Jar	15.00--20.00
1300	Cracker Jar & Cover	25.00--30.00
1300	Ind. Cream	6.00----7.50
1300	Ind. Sugar	5.00----6.00
1300	Footed Sherbet	8.00----9.00
1300	Custard	4.00----5.00
1300	16'' Punch Bowl	40.00--45.00
1300	16'' Punch Bowl & Stand	50.00--60.00
1300	Vase 14'' Light	8.00--12.00
1300	Vase 12'' Heavy	10.00--12.50
1300	Rose Bowl	8.00--10.00

RECENT: 4½'' Vase being made in 1978 in lead Crystal. List Price $13.25.

No. 1303 PATTERN

1303	Sugar & Cover	30.00--35.00
1303	Butter & Cover	40.00--45.00
1303	Cream	20.00--25.00
1303	Spoon	20.00--25.00
1303	Small Butter & Cover	30.00--35.00

No. 1333 SIDNEY PATTERN

1333	Sugar & Cover	20.00--25.00
1333	Butter & Cover	30.00--35.00
1333	Cream	15.00--20.00
1333	Spoon	15.00--20.00
1333	4'' Round Nappy	4.00----5.00
1333	4½'' Round Nappy	5.00----6.00
1333	6'' Round Nappy	6.00----7.50
1333	4½'' Square Nappy	5.00----6.00
1333	6'' Square Nappy	6.00----7.50
1333	8'' Square Nappy	8.00--10.00
1333	4½'' Comport	4.00----6.00
1333	8'' Comport, Regular	8.00--12.00
1333	9'' Comport, Regular	12.00--15.00
1333	8'' Comport, Belled	12.00--15.00
1333	9'' Comport, Belled	15.00--18.00
1333	9'' Comport, Cupped	15.00--18.00
1333	9½'' Carbarette	10.00--12.00
1333	5'' Ice Cream	5.00----7.00
1333	6'' Plate	4.00----6.00
1333	5'' Handled Nappy	7.00----9.00
1333	½ Gal. Pitcher	30.00--35.00
1333	3-Pt. Pitcher	20.00--25.00
1333	Tumbler	10.00--12.50
1333	Champagne	8.00--10.00
1333	Whiskey	7.00----9.00
1333	Custard	4.00----5.00

1333	Shaker Salt Blown with S.N. Top	8.00----9.00
1333	Shaker Salt Pressed with S.N. Top	8.00----9.00
1333	Molasses Can, Tin Top	35.00--45.00
1333	Molasses Can, Nickel Top	35.00--45.00
1333	Vinegar	15.00--20.00
1333	7'' Pickle Dish	3.00----5.00
1333	8'' Pickle Dish	5.00----7.00
1333	5x7 Tray	5.00----8.00
1333	9'' Salad	6.00----7.50
1333	Celery Tray	6.00----9.00
1333	Sweetmeat	8.00--10.00
1333	Quart Decanter	14.00--16.00
1333	Quart Decanter, Drop Stopper	16.00--18.00
1333	Quart Decanter, Ground Stopper	18.00--20.00
1333	Quart Decanter, Ground and Polished Stopper	20.00--25.00

No. 1372 ESSEX PATTERN

1372	Sugar & Cover	10.00--12.00
1372	Butter & Cover	15.00--18.00
1372	Cream	6.00----8.00
1372	Spoon	6.00----8.00
1372	5½'' Ice Cream	**3.00----4.00**
1372	5'' Nappy	1.00----2.00
1372	6'' Nappy	1.00----3.00
1372	7'' Nappy	2.00----4.00
1372	8'' Nappy	3.00----6.00
1372	4½'' Comport	2.00----3.00
1372	8'' Comport	3.00----4.00
1372	9'' Comport	4.00----5.00
1372	10'' Cabarette	3.00----4.00
1372	11'' Cabarette	4.00----6.00
1372	½ Gal. Pitcher	15.00--20.00
1372	Tumbler	4.00----5.00
1372	Ice Tea Tumbler	4.00----5.00
1372	Finger Bowl	1.00----2.00
1372	Finger Bowl Plate	1.00----2.00
1372	Shaker Salt & Pepper w/Heavy Nickle Top.	1.00----2.00
1372	w/Silver Plated Top	1.00----2.00
1372	Toothpick	4.00----6.00
1372	Olive	2.00----3.00
1372	Bon Bon	1.00----2.00
1372	Hotel Cream	5.00----7.00
1372	Hotel Sugar	5.00----7.00
1372	Celery	6.00----9.00
1372	Syrup, Brittania Top	8.00--10.00
1372	Syrup, Ewer Nickle Top	8.00--10.00
1372	Syrup, Nickle Top	8.00--10.00
1372	Pickle Dish	2.00----3.00
1372	7'' Oval Dish	2.00----3.00
1372	8'' Oval Dish	3.00----4.00
1372	9'' Oval Dish	4.00----5.00
1372	Sugar Shaker, Silver P.T.	3.00----5.00
1372	5'' Handled Nappy	3.00----5.00
1372	Sundae	2.00----3.00
1372	Custard	1.00----2.00
1372	10'' Punch Bowl	10.00--15.00
1372	10'' Punch Bowl, Footed	20.00--25.00
1372	Goblet	7.00----9.00
1372	Claret	7.00----9.00
1372	Wine	7.00----9.00
1372	Cordial	4.00----6.00

1372	Cocktail	5.00----7.00
1372	Saucer Champagne	4.00----6.00
1372	Tall Champagne	6.00----9.00
1372	Footed Tumbler	4.00----5.00
1372	Violet Bouquet Holder	4.00----6.00
1372	Oyster Cocktail & Liner	7.00----9.00

No. 1432 PURITAN PATTERN

1432	Hotel Cream	6.00----7.50
1432	Hotel Sugar	6.00----7.50
1432	Ind. Salt	2.00----3.00
1432½	Ind. Salt	2.00----3.00
1432	Tumbler	4.00----5.00
1432	Tumbler, Ice Tea	5.00----6.00
1432	Finger Bowl	1.00----2.00
1432	Molasses Can, Ewer S. T.	8.00--12.00
1432	Molasses Can, Ewer N. T.	8.00--12.00
1432	Oil, 6 oz. Drop Plain Stop.	6.00----8.00
1432	Oil, 6 oz. Ground Cut Stop.	8.00--12.00
1432	Sugar Sifter, Silver Plat. T.	4.00----6.00
1432	Shaker Salt—	
	w/Heavy Plat. Top	2.00----4.00
	w/Silver Plat. Top	2.00----4.00
	w/Non-Corrosive Top	2.00----4.00

No. 1460 OLD ENGLISH PATTERN

1460	Sugar & Cover	15.00--20.00
1460	Cream	12.00--15.00
1460	Spoon	12.00--15.00
1460	Butter	20.00--25.00
1460	Shaker N.C.T.	6.00----8.00
1460	Tumbler	6.00----8.00
1460	Sundae	4.00----5.00
1460	Custard Cup	4.00----5.00
1460	9" Bouquet Holder	12.00--15.00
1460	Molasses Can N.T. 13 oz	30.00--35.00
1460	Vinegar 6 oz	20.00--25.00
1460	½ gal. Pitcher	25.00--30.00
1460	4½" Comport	4.00----5.00
1460	8" Pickle Dish	4.00----6.00
1460	5" Handled Nappy	7.00----9.00
1460	7" Comport	7.00----9.00
1460	Olive	4.00----6.00
1460	8" Comport	10.00--12.50
1460	10" Comport	12.50--15.00
1460	11" Celery Tray	6.00----7.50
1460	10" Footed Bowl	20.00--25.00
1460	10' Comport Belled to 12"	12.00--15.00

EXTRA BOWLS

*1497	4½" Comport	4.00----5.00
*1497	8" Comport	12.00--15.00

CRYSTAL WEDDING ASSORTMENT
Gold Edge Decorated

1460	Cream	20.00--25.00
1460	Butter & Cover	40.00--50.00
1460	Sugar & Cover	30.00--35.00
1460	Spoon	20.00--25.00
1460	4½" Nappy	7.00----9.00
1460	8" Nappy	25.00--30.00
600	Tumbler	10.00--15.00
1549	Pitcher	35.00--45.00

*Pieces in No. 1497 reintroduced in 1969
(CRESAP)*

No. 1467 VIRGINIA PATTERN

1467	Sugar & Cover	18.00--22.50
1467	Butter & Cover	25.00--30.00
1467	Cream	12.00--15.00
1467	Spoon	12.00--15.00
1467	4½" Nappy	3.00----4.00
1467	5" Nappy	3.00----4.00
1467	6" Nappy	4.00----5.00
1467	7" Nappy	5.00----6.00
1467	8" Nappy	6.00----7.00
1467	9" Nappy	8.00--10.00
1467	4½" Comport, Unfinished	4.00----5.00
1467	4½" Comport	4.00----5.00
1467	8" Comport, Reg. Shape	8.00--10.00
1467	9" Comport, Reg. Shape	10.00--12.00
1467	8" Comport, Belled Shape	10.00--12.00
1467	9" Comport, Belled Shape	12.00--15.00
1467	4½" Handled Nappy	8.00--10.00
1467	5" Handled Nappy	10.00--12.00
1467	7" Shallow Bowl, Footed	15.00--18.00
1467	8" Shallow Bowl, Footed	18.00--20.00
1467	9" Shallow Bowl, Footed	20.00--22.00
1467	8" Deep Bowl, Footed	20.00--25.00
1467	9" Deep Bowl, Footed	25.00--30.00
1467	8" Deep Bowl, Footed, Be Shape	20.00--25.00
1467	9" Deep Bowl, Footed, Be Shape	25.00--30.00
1467	9" Salver	15.00--20.00
1467	10" Salver	20.00--25.00
1467	11" Salver	25.00--30.00
1467	Hotel Cream	7.00----9.00
1467	Hotel Sugar	7.00----9.00
1467	Ind. Salt	4.00----6.00
1467½	Shaker Salt	
	w/Heavy Nick. Top	7.00----9.00
	w/Silver Plat. Top	7.00----9.00
1467	Shaker Salt, Cut Shut	
	w/Heavy Nickel Plated Top	8.00--10.00
	w/Silver Plat. Top.	8.00--10.00
	w/Non-Corros. Top	8.00--10.00
1467	Sugar Shaker, Silver Plate Top	25.00--30.00
1467	Oil, 8 oz	20.00--25.00
1467	½ Gal. Pitcher	25.00--30.00
1467½	½ Gal. Ice Jug	25.00--30.00
1467	Tumbler	7.00----9.00
1467	Finger Bowl	4.00----5.00
1467	Toothpick	10.00--15.00
1467	Custard	4.00----5.00
1467	Water Bottle	16.00--18.00
1467	Wine, 3 oz	8.00--10.00
1467	Molasses Can, w/Ewer Sil. Plat. Top	30.00--40.00
	w/Ewer Nick. Plat. Top	20.00--30.00
1467	Molasses Can, Silver Plat. Top & Handle	35.00--45.00
1467	4½" Jelly Bowl	3.00----5.00
1467	Bon Bon, Club Shape	4.00----5.00
1467	Bon Bon, Heart Shape	4.00----5.00
1467	Bon Bon, Spade Shape	4.00----5.00
1467	Bon Bon, Diamond Shape	4.00----5.00
1467	Bon Bon, Square Shape	4.00----5.00
1467	3 Corner Olive	4.00----5.00
1467	Spoon Tray	4.00----6.00
1467	Salted Almond	4.00----5.00
1467	8" Round Plate	6.00----8.00
1467	8" Pickle Dish	5.00----8.00
1467	12" Celery Tray	6.00----9.00

1467 Punch Bowl, 16" 40.00--50.00
1467 Punch Bowl & Foot 16" 55.00--65.00

RECENT: Pieces made in lead crystal between 1974 and 1978.

1467 5½" Sweetmeat, list price $4.50
1467 6½" Shallow Nappy, $8.25
1467 8½" Pickle, $8.25
1467 Hostess Server w/spoon $7.50

No. 1515 LUCERE PATTERN

1515	Sugar & Cover	15.00--17.50
1515	Butter & Cover	20.00--25.00
1515	Cream	10.00--12.50
1515	Spoon	12.00--15.00
1515	4½" Comport	3.00----4.00
1515	7" Comport	4.00----6.00
1515	7" Comport, Star Shape	6.00----8.00
1515	7" Comport, Square Shape	6.00----8.00
1515	8" Comport	6.00----8.00
1515	8" Comport Star Shape	7.00----9.00
1515	8" Comport, Square Shape	7.00----9.00
1515	5" Handled Nappy	6.00----7.00
1515	5" Olive Dish	3.00----4.00
1515	7" Oval Dish	3.00----4.00
1515	8" Oval Dish	4.00----6.00
1515	9" Oval Dish	5.00----7.00
1515	10" Oval Dish	6.00----8.00
1515	Spoon Tray	6.00----8.00
1515	Pickle Dish	5.00----6.00
1515	Celery Tray	6.00----8.00
1515	½ Gal. Ice Pitcher	15.00--20.00
1515	½ Gal. Jug, "Glove Shape"	20.00--25.00
1515	Table Tumbler	3.00----4.00
1515	Ice Tea Tumbler	4.00----5.00
1515	Tumbler Plate	1.00----2.00
1515	Finger Bowl	1.00----2.00
1515	Tooth Pick	5.00----7.50
1515	Custard	3.00----4.00
1515	Footed Sherbet	2.00----3.00
1515	Sundae	2.00----3.00
1515	4" Low Ft. Jelly	5.00----6.00
1515	7" Low Ft. Bowl, Flared	6.00----9.00
1515	7" Low Ft. Bowl, Star Shape	6.00----9.00
1515	4½" High Ft. Jelly Bowl	7.00----9.00
1515	4½" High Ft. Jelly Bowl, Flared	7.00----9.00
1515	7" High Ft. Bowl, Flared	8.00--10.00
1515	7" High Ft. Bowl, Star Shape	8.00--10.00
1515	8" High Ft. Bowl, Flared	9.00--12.00
1515	8" High Ft. Bowl, Star Shape	10.00--12.00
1515	7" High Ft. Bowl & Cover	18.00--22.00
1515	8" High Ft. Bowl & Cover	20.00--25.00
1515	Large Fruit Bowl	8.00--10.00
1515	Ind. Cream	7.00----9.00
1515	Ind. Sugar	7.00----9.00
1515	Footed Ind. Salt	4.00----6.00
1515	Shaker Salt— w/Heavy Nick. Top	3.00----4.00
1515	w/Sil. Plat. Top	3.00----4.00
1515½	Shaker Salt, Cut Shut— w/Heavy Nick. Top	3.00----4.00
1515½	w/Sil. Plat. Top	3.00----4.00
1515½	w/Non-Corros. Top	3.00----4.00

1515	Molasses Can, with Brittania Tp. w/Ewer Nick. Top	15.00--17.00
1515	w/Ewer Sil. Plat. Top	15.00--17.00
1515	Syrup, Sil. Plat. Tp. & Hdl.	15.00--18.00
1515½	Syrup, Sil. Plat. Tp. & Hdl.	15.00--18.00
1515	2 oz Oil, Plain Drop Stop.	12.00--15.00
1515	4 oz Oil, Plain Drop Stop.	12.00--15.00
1515	6 oz Oil, Plain Drop Stop.	12.00--15.00
1515	2 oz Oil, Cut Stop. Ground	15.00--18.00
1515	4 oz Oil, Cut Stop. Ground	15.00--18.00
1515	6 oz Oil, Cut Stop. Ground	15.00--18.00
1515	Pickle Jar & Cover	14.00--18.00
1515	Cracker Jar	12.00--14.00
1515	Cracker Jar & Cover	16.00--18.00
1515	Crushed Ice & Plate	8.00--10.00
1515	Nut Bowl	8.00--10.00
1515	8½" Plate	4.00----6.00
1515	7½" Ice Bowl Plate	3.00----5.00
1515	9" Vase	2.00----5.00
1515	10" Vase	3.00----6.00
1515	12" Vase	5.00----8.00
1515	4 oz Cologne, Drop Stop.	4.00----6.00
1515	4 oz Cologne, Cut Stop. Ground	6.00----8.00
1515	Goblet	6.00----8.00
1515	Claret	6.00----8.00
1515	Tall Champagne	6.00----8.00
1515	Saucer Champagne	6.00----8.00
1515	3 oz Cocktail	3.00----5.00
1515	2½ oz Creme de Menthe	3.00----5.00
1515	Wine	4.00----6.00
1515	Sherry	3.00----5.00
1515	Cordial	3.00----5.00
1515	Brandy	3.00----5.00

CRYSTAL WARE—GOLD DECORATED LUCERE GOLD ASSORTMENT

1515	8" Berry	8.00--10.00
1515	4½" Berry	3.00----5.00
1515	½ Gal. Ice Jug	20.00--25.00
1515	Tumbler	4.00----6.00
1515	Tall Cider Goblet	8.00--10.00
1515	Table Tumbler	4.00----6.00
1515	Handled Nappy, 5"	8.00--10.00
1515	Berry Saucer, 4½"	2.00----3.00
1515	Square Olive Dish, 5"	4.00----6.00
1515	Handled Custard	4.00----5.00
1515	Footed Sherbet	3.00----4.00
1515	Low Foot Jelly	3.00----4.00
1515	High Foot Jelly	4.00----6.00
1515	Star Shape Nappy, 4½"	3.00----5.00
1515	Pickle Dish, 8"	7.00----8.00
1515	Spoon Tray	6.00----8.00
1515	Ind. Cream	9.00--12.00
1515	Ind. Sugar	9.00--12.00
1515	Wine Glass	6.00----8.00

No. 1578 TUXEDO PATTERN

1578	Sugar & Cover	20.00--25.00
1578	Butter & Cover	25.00--30.00
1578	Cream	15.00--17.50
1578	Spoon	15.00--17.50
1578	4½" Comport	4.00----5.00
1578	7" Comport	10.00--12.00
1578	8" Comport	12.00--15.00
1578	8" Comport, Square	10.00--12.50
1578	½ Gal. Tankard	30.00--35.00

1578½ ½ Gal. Ice Pitcher 25.00--30.00
1578   Ice Tea Tumbler 10.00--12.50
1578   Table Tumbler 8.00----9.00
1578   Wine Tumbler 10.00--12.50
1578   Finger Bowl 5.00----6.00
1578   Toothpick 12.00--15.00
1578   Custard 4.00----5.00
1578   Water Bottle 20.00--25.00
1578   6 oz Oil, Drop Stop. . . 15.00--18.00
1578   6 oz Oil, Ground Stop. . . 18.00--22.00
1578   6 oz Oil, Cut Stop. . . . 22.00--25.00
1578   4 oz Oil, Drop Stop. . . 12.00--15.00
1578   4 oz Oil, Ground Stop. . . 15.00--18.00
1578   4 oz Oil, Cut Stop. . . . 15.00--20.00
1578   Molasses Can,
           w/Spun Nick. Top . . 25.00--30.00
           w/Brittania Top . . . 25.00--30.00
           w/Ewer Nick. Top . . 30.00--35.00
           w/Ewer Sil. Plat. Top 30.00--35.00
1578   Tall Celery 20.00--25.00
1578   Celery Tray 8.00--10.00
1578   Pickle Jar & Cover . . . 20.00--25.00
1578   Pickle Dish 6.00----7.50
1578   Olive Dish 4.00----5.00
1578   Handled Nappy, 5" 6.00----8.00
1578   Shaker Salt—
           w/Heavy Nick. Top . . 6.00----7.50
           w/Sil. Plat. Top . . . 6.00----7.50
           w/Fostoria Glass Top 8.00----9.00
1578½ Shaker Salt, Cut Shut—
           w/Heavy Nick. Top . . 6.00----8.00
           w/Sil. Plat. Top . . . 6.00----8.00
           w/Non-Corros. Top . . 6.00----8.00
           w/Fostoria Glass Top 8.00--10.00
1578   7" Deep Bowl 10.00--12.00
1578   5" Deep Bowl 7.00----9.00
1578   4½" Deep Bowl 6.00----8.00
1578   4½" Jelly Stand 7.00----9.00
1578   Footed Bon Bon   . . . 15.00--18.00
1578   Footed Rose Bowl . . . 10.00--12.50
1578   Orange Bowl 10.00--13.00
1578   Fruit Bowl 10.00--12.50
1578   Footed Nut Bowl 10.00--12.50
1578   Banana Jar 10.00--12.50
1578   Biscuit Jar 10.00--12.50
1578   10" Vase 12.00--15.00
1578   8" Vase 10.00--12.50
1578   12" Plate 8.00--12.00
1578   Two Handled Nut Bowl 10.00--15.00
1578   Two Hand. Open Sugar . . 10.00--12.50
1578   Footed Hotel Sugar . . . 12.00--15.00
1578   Footed Hotel Cream   . . 12.00--15.00
1578   Footed Ind. Salt 10.00--12.00
1578   Footed Sherbet 5.00----7.00
1578   Footed Cracker Jar &
           Cover 30.00--35.00
1578   Footed Cracker Jar . . . 15.00--20.00
1578   Sundae 5.00----7.00
1578   Straw Jar & Cover . . . 40.00--45.00
1578   Straw Jar 30.00--35.00
1578   Crush Fruit & Cover   . . 30.00--35.00
1578   Crushed Fruit 20.00--25.00
1578   Crushed Fruit Spoon   . . 4.00----6.00

No. 1630 ALEXIS PATTERN

1630   Sugar & Cover 25.00--30.00
1630   Sugar, No Cover 15.00--20.00

1630   Butter & Cover 30.00--35.00
1630   Cream 18.00--22.50
1630   Spoon 18.00--22.50
1630   4½" Nappy 4.00----5.00
1630   5" Nappy 5.00----7.00
1630   7" Nappy 12.00--15.00
1630   8" Nappy 15.00--18.00
1630   9" Nappy 18.00--22.00
1630   3 qt. Ice Jug 20.00--25.00
1630   ½ Gal. Ice Jug 25.00--30.00
1630   3 pt. Ice Jug 15.00--20.00
1630   Qt. Ice Jug 10.00--15.00
1630½ ½ Gal. Pitcher, Tall . . . 30.00--35.00
1630½ Table Tumbler 3.00----5.00
1630/3 Tumbler 3.00----5.00
1630/3 Ice Tea 4.00----6.00
1630   Table Tumbler 3.00----5.00
1630   Split Tumbler 4.00----6.00
1630   Finger Bowl 6.00----8.00
1630   Ice Tea Tumbler 4.00----6.00
1630   Ice Tea Plate 3.00----4.00
1630   Wine Tumbler 5.00----7.00
1630   Whiskey Tumbler 3.00----4.00
1630   Water Bottle 15.00--20.00
1630   2 oz Oil, Drop Stop. . . 12.00--15.00
1630   4 oz Oil, Drop Stop. . . 15.00--17.00
1630   6 oz Oil, Drop Stop. . . 15.00--20.00
1630   2 oz Oil, Ground Stop. . 15.00--17.00
1630   4 oz Oil, Ground Stop. . 18.00--20.00
1630   6 oz Oil, Ground Stop. . 20.00--22.00
1630   Catsup, Ground Stop. . . 20.00--25.00
1630   Catsup, Drop Stop. . . . 18.00--22.00
1630   Mustard & Cover 30.00--35.00
1630   Horseradish Jar & Spoon 30.00--35.00
1630   Flat Table Salt 7.00----9.00
1630   Flat Ind. Salt 4.00----5.00
1630   Footed Ind. Salt 5.00----8.00
1630   Ind. Almond 5.00----8.00
1630   Shaker No. 1—
           w/Heavy Nick. Top . . 7.00----9.00
           w/Sil. Plat. Top 7.00----9.00
           w/Non-Corros. Top . . 7.00----9.00
           w/Glass Top 7.00----9.00
1630   Shaker No. 2—
           w/Heavy Nick. Top . . 7.00----9.00
           w/Sil. Plat. Top 7.00----9.00
           w/Non-Corros. Top . . 7.00----9.00
           w/Glass Top 7.00----9.00
1630   Molasses Can—
           w/Ewer Nick. Top . . 30.00--35.00
           w/Ewer Sil. Plat. Top 30.00--35.00
           w/Brittania Top 30.00--35.00
1630   Molasses Can Plate 2.00----3.00
1630   Tall Celery 20.00--25.00
1630   Celery Tray 8.00--10.00
1630   Pickle Tray 5.00----7.00
1630   Olive Tray 5.00----7.00
1630   Toothpick 8.00--10.00
1630   Sugar Sifter, Sil. Plat. Top 20.00--25.00
1630   Hotel Sugar 15.00--17.50
1630   Hotel Cream 15.00--17.50
1630   4½" High Foot Bowl   . . 10.00--15.00
1630   High Foot Ice Cream . . 4.00----5.00
1630   Low Foot Sherbet 3.00----4.00
1630½ Low Footed Sherbet . . 3.00----4.00
1630   High Foot Sherbet 4.00----5.00
1630   Custard 5.00----6.00
1630½ Custard 5.00----6.00
1630   Nut Bowl 4.00----5.00
1630   Crushed Ice & Plate 15.00--17.50
1630   Mayonnaise 4.00----6.00

1630	Mayonnaise & Plate	6.00----8.00
1630	9" Vase	10.00--12.50
1630	Sweet Pea Vase	7.00----9.00
1630	Nasturtium Vase	6.00----7.50
1630	Decanter & Ground Stop.	30.00--35.00
1630	10 oz Goblet	6.00----9.00
1630	6 oz Tall Champagne	6.00----9.00
1630	5 oz Claret	6.00----9.00
1630	3 oz Wine	6.00----9.00
1630	2 oz Wine	6.00----9.00
1630	1 oz Cordial	6.00----9.00
1630	3 oz Cocktail	6.00----9.00
1630	2½ oz Creme de Menthe	6.00----9.00
1630	¾ oz Pousse Cafe	6.00----9.00
1630	Egg	4.00----5.00
1630	10 oz Footed Ice Tea	8.00--10.00
1630	8½ oz Ft. Table Tumbler	6.00----8.00

No. 1641 PATTERN

1641	Sugar & Cover	20.00--25.00
1641	Butter & Cover	25.00--30.00
1641	Cream	15.00--17.50
1641	Spoon	15.00--17.50
1641	4" Comport	4.00----5.00
1641	4½" Comport	4.00----5.00
1641	6" Comport, Flared to 7"	5.00----7.00
1641	7" Comport, flared to 8"	6.00----8.00
1641	8" Comport, flared to 9"	7.00--10.00
1641	Quart Pitcher	25.00--30.00
1641	½ Gal. Pitcher	30.00--35.00
1641	Finger Bowl	5.00----7.00
1641	Table Tumbler	10.00--12.00
1641	Whiskey Tumbler	10.00--15.00
1641	Toothpick	15.00--20.00
1641	Celery, Tall	18.00--22.00
1641	Celery, Tray	7.00----9.00
1641	5" Ice Cream	6.00----8.00
1641	5" Handled Nappy	5.00----8.00
1641	Hdl. Bon Bon, 3-cornered	6.00----9.00
1641	Molasses Can, Pressed, S.T.	25.00--30.00
1641	Molasses Can, Pressed. B.T.	25.00--30.00
1641	Molasses Can, Blown, T.T.	30.00--35.00
1641	Molasses Can, Blown, N.T.	30.00--35.00
1641	Shaker, Tall Spun Nick. T.	8.00----9.00
1641	Shaker, Tall w/Heavy N. T.	8.00----9.00
1641	Shaker, Lrg. Cut Shut with	
	Heavy Nickel Top	8.00----9.00
	Silver Plated Top	8.00----9.00
	Glass Top	8.00----9.00
1641	Shaker, Small Cut Shut wit	
	Heavy Nickel Top	7.00----8.00
	Silver Plated Top	7.00----8.00
1641	Sugar Sifter, Sil. Plat. Top	20.00--25.00
1641	Cracker Jar & Cover	30.00--35.00
1641	Pickle Jar & Cover	20.00--25.00
1641	Square Olive	7.00----9.00
1641	Three-Cornered Olive	7.00----9.00
1641	Salted Almond	4.00----6.00
1641	Pickle Dish	5.00----7.00
1641	Oil, Drop Stopper	15.00--18.00
1641	Punch Bowl & Foot	40.00--50.00
1641	Lemonade or Custard	4.00----6.00
*1641	10" Footed Salver	25.00--30.00
1641	Large Rose Bowl	15.00--18.00

RECENT: Made from 1974-1978 in Lead Crystal.

PRINCE GOLD ASSORTMENT

1515	Ind. Cream	7.00----9.00
1515	Ind. Sugar	7.00----9.00
1515	Wine	10.00--12.00
1515	Low Foot Jelly	10.00--12.00
1641	Confection	7.00----9.00
1641	Nut	7.00----9.00
1641	Wafer	7.00----9.00
1641	Pickle Dish	7.00----9.00
1641	Lemonade	4.00----6.00
1641	4½" Comport	4.00----6.00
1641	Table Tumbler	12.00--15.00
1641	Whiskey Tumbler	15.00--17.00
1641	5" Ice Cream	6.00----7.50
1641	5" Handled Nappy	7.00----9.00
1641	Handled Bon Bon	8.00--10.00

No. 1605 PATTERN

Reintroduced as "Sherwood" in 1969

1605	Sherbet	6.00----7.50
1605	Punch Bowl & Foot	35.00--40.00
1605	Custard	4.00----5.00

PRESSED PITCHERS WITH PRESSED HANDLES

1661	½ Gal. Jug	15.00--17.00
1661	Quart Jug	10.00--12.50
1660	½ Gal. Jug	18.00--22.00
1660	Quart Jug	15.00--18.00
1693	Coaster	1.00----2.00
999	½ Gal. Blown Jug	12.00--15.00
1693½	Coaster 4"	.50----1.00
	also made in 3½"	.50----1.00

114 FIFTH AVENUE LINE—PLAIN

114	Goblet	1.00----2.00
114	Champagne	1.00----2.00
114	Claret	1.00----2.00
114	Wine	1.00----2.00
114	Cordial	1.00----2.00

114 FIFTH AVENUE LINE—ETCHED 32

114	Goblet	2.00----4.00
114	Champagne	2.00----4.00
114	Claret	2.00----4.00
114	Wine	2.00----4.00
114	Cordial	2.00----4.00

BLOWN & ETCHED WATER SETS

302	Water Jug Etched 39	25.00--30.00
302	Tumbler Etched 39	5.00----6.00
318	Water Jug Optic Etched 48	16.00--18.00
318	Tumbler Etched 48	2.00----4.00
303	Water Jug Etched 32	15.00--20.00
303	Tumbler Etched 32	2.00----4.00

OILS

1164	Etched 48 12 oz	12.00--15.00
1163	Ketcup Etched 48 14 oz	12.00--15.00
300½	Large Etched 47 9 oz	12.00--15.00
187½	Oil , Cut Stopper 4 oz	8.00--10.00
300½	Etched 70, 6½ oz	12.00--15.00
312	Etched 32, 6½ oz	12.00--15.00
312	Etched 53, 6½ oz	12.00--15.00
300½	Small etched 47, 6½ oz	12.00--15.00
312	Etched 70, 6½ oz	12.00--15.00
315	Blown Straw Jar & Cover Plain or Optic	40.00--45.00
300	Decanter, Cut Stopper, etched 70, 1 quart	12.00--15.00
1452	Quart Decanter	8.00--10.00

NEEDLE ETCHING NO. 36 "IRISH LACE" PATTERN

880	9 oz. Goblet	2.00----3.00
895	9 oz. Goblet	2.00----3.00
880	5 oz. Saucer Champagne	2.00----3.00
880	Sherbet	2.00----2.50
767	Parfait	2.00----3.00
5054	Parfait	2.00----3.00
880	4½ oz. Claret	2.00----3.00
880	2¾ Wine	2.00----3.00
880	2 oz. Sherry	2.00----3.00
880	1 oz. Cordial	2.00----3.00
880	2½ oz. Creme de Menthe	2.00----3.00
880	3½ oz. Cocktail	2.00----3.00
810	Custard	2.00----2.50
810	Finger Bowl	1.00----2.00
810	Finger Bowl Plate (200-6'')	1.00----2.00
766	9 oz. Goblet	2.00----3.00
766	5 oz. Saucer Champagne	2.00----3.00
766	Fruit	2.00----2.50
766	Sherbet	2.00----2.50
766	2¾ oz. Wine	2.00----3.00
840	5'' Sheridan Plate	1.00----2.00
837	Oyster Cocktail	2.00----2.50
766	3 oz. Cocktail	2.00----3.00
766	Almond	2.00----3.00
766	Finger Bowl	1.00----2.00
766	Finger Bowl Plate (1736-6'')	1.00----2.00
879	9 oz. Goblet	2.00----3.00
879	5 oz. Saucer Champagne	2.00----3.00
879	Fruit	2.00----2.50
879	Sherbet	2.00----2.50
5051	Large Almond	2.00----3.00
5051	Small Almond	2.00----2.50
880½	Grape Fruit	2.00----3.00
880½	Grape Fruit Liner	2.00----3.00
858	Sweetmeat	2.00----3.00
880	4½'' Bon Bon	2.00----3.00
803	5'' Comport	2.00----3.00
803	6'' Comport	2.00----3.00
803	5'', 6'', 7'' Footed Nappy	2.00----3.00
1227	4½'' Nappy	2.00----2.50
1227	8'' Nappy	3.00----4.00
820	Tumbler	2.00----2.50

833	8 oz Tumbler	2.00----2.50
833	8 oz Tumbler, ½ Sham.	2.00----2.50
4061	Ftd. Ice Tea, Handled	3.00----4.00
766	Ftd. Ice Tea, Handled	3.00----4.00
4011	12 oz Tumbler, Handled	3.00----4.00
701	5'' Tumbler Plate	1.00----2.00
701	14, 12, 10, 8 oz Tumbler	2.00----3.00
858	Table Tumbler	2.00----3.00
858	14, 12, 10, 8, 5 oz Tumbler	2.00----3.00
4011½	Table Tumbler	2.00----3.00
4011	15, 12, 10, 8, 5 oz Tumbler	2.00----3.00
4077	Table, 12, 8, 5 oz Tumbler	2.00----3.00
889	5 oz Tumbler	2.00----2.50
887	2½ oz Tumbler	2.00----2.50
300-7	Jug	12.00--15.00
724-7	Jug	18.00--22.00
318-7	Jug	15.00--20.00
303-7	Jug	15.00--18.00
1236-6	Jug	15.00--18.00
317½-7	Jug & Plain Cover	15.00--20.00
1480	Sugar	2.00----3.00
1480	Cream	2.00----3.00
300½	Large Oil	12.00--15.00
300½	Small Oil	12.00--15.00
1465	7 oz Oil, Cut Neck	14.00--16.00
300	Qt. Decanter, Cut Neck	12.00--15.00
1165½	Shaker, Pearl Top	2.00----2.50
922	Toothpick, Punty	4.00----6.00
1897	7'' Plate	2.00----3.00

NEEDLED ETCHED NO. 37

5070	10 oz Goblet, Optic Etched 37	2.00----3.00
5070	9 oz Goblet, Optic	2.00----3.00
5070	8 oz Goblet, Optic	2.00----3.00
5070	5½ oz Tall Champ., Optic	2.00----3.00
5070	6 oz Claret, Optic	2.00----3.00
5070	4½ oz Claret, Optic	2.00----3.00
5070	3 oz Wine, Optic	2.00----3.00
5070	2 oz Wine, Optic	2.00----3.00
5070	1 oz Cordial, Optic	2.00----3.00
5070	¾ oz Cordial, Optic	2.00----3.00
5070	4½ oz H.S. Champ., C.F. Optic	2.00----3.00
5070	4½ oz Rhine Wine, Optic	2.00----3.00
5070	4 oz Hot Whiskey, Optic	2.00----3.00
5070	3½ oz Cocktail, Optic	2.00----3.00
5070	3 oz Cocktail, Optic	2.00----3.00
5070	2½ oz Creme De Menthe, Optic	2.00----3.00
5070	1 oz Pousse Cafe, Optic	2.00----3.00
5070	¾ oz Pousse Cafe, Optic	2.00----3.00
5070	5½ oz Saucer Champ., Op.	2.00----3.00
5070	Sherbet, Optic	2.00----2.50
5050	11, 10, 9 oz Goblet, Optic	2.00----3.00
5050	6½ oz Claret, Optic	2.00----3.00
5050	4½ oz Claret, Optic	2.00----3.00
5050	3½ oz Wine, Optic	2.00----3.00
5050	2 oz Sherry, Optic	2.00----3.00
5050	1 oz Cordial, Optic	2.00----3.00
5050	6 oz Saucer Champ. Optic	2.00----3.00
5050	5½ oz Tall Champ., Optic	2.00----3.00
5050	4 oz Hot Whiskey, Optic	2.00----3.00
5050	3½ oz Cocktail, Optic	2.00----3.00
5050	2½ oz Creme De Menthe, Optic	2.00----3.00
5050	1 oz Pousse Cafe, Optic	2.00----3.00
5050	Egg, Optic	2.00----2.50
5050	Sherbet, Optic	2.00----2.50

No.	Description	Price
823	4½, 5″, Fruit, Optic	2.00----2.50
803	4½, 5″, Shallow, Optic	1.00----2.00
803	6, 7, 8″, Shallow, Optic	2.00----4.00
803	4½, 5, 6, 7″, Deep, Optic	2.00----4.00
803	5, 6″, Ft. Comport, Optic	3.00----5.00
300	7 Tankard, Optic Etched 37	12.00--15.00
318	7 Tankard, Optic	12.00--15.00
1236	6 Tankard, Optic	15.00--18.00
303	7 Jug, Optic	15.00--18.00
820	Tumbler, Optic	1.00----2.00
701	14 oz. Ice Tea, Optic	2.00----2.50
858	Table, 3½, 5 oz Tumbler, Op.	1.00----2.00
858	6½, 8, 10, 12, 14 oz Tumbler Optic	2.00----2.50
1478	Cream, Optic	2.00----3.00
1478	Sugar, Optic	2.00----3.00
858	Finger Bowl, Optic	1.00----2.00
858	Finger Bowl, Plate, Optic	.50----1.00
858	Custard, Optic	2.00----2.50
480	Custard, Optic	2.00----2.50
1769	Finger Bowl, Optic	1.00----2.00
1769	Finger Bowl Plate, Optic	.50----1.00
300½	Small Oil, Optic, Cut S	12.00--15.00
300	Qt. Decanter, Cut Neck, Optic	12.00--15.00
4015	14 oz Tumbler, Optic	2.00----2.50
160½	Water Bottle, Optic, C.N.	8.00--10.00
840	Sherbet, Optic	2.00----2.50
932	Saucer Champagne, Optic	2.00----3.00
858	H. S. Champagne, C. F. Op.	2.00----3.00
863	Almond, Optic	2.00----2.50
922	Toothpick, Sham. Pty. Op.	4.00----6.00
885	1¾ oz Tumbler	2.00----2.50
833	4 oz Tumbler	2.00----2.50
833	6 oz Tumbler	2.00----2.50
822	Parfeit	2.00----3.00
880	4½″ Bon Bon	2.00----3.00
880	Grape Fruit	2.00----3.00
880½	Grape Fruit	2.00----3.00
1558	Water Bottle, C. N.	10.00--12.00
5071	Cocktail, Et. 37	2.00----3.00
5068	Cocktail, Et. 37	2.00----3.00
5069	Cordial, Et. 37	2.00----3.00

NEEDLE ETCHING NO. 38

No.	Description	Price
882	11, 10, 9, 8 oz Goblet, Et. 38	2.00----3.00
882	5 oz Tall Champagne	2.00----3.00
882	6½, 4½ oz Claret	2.00----3.00
882	3½ oz Wine	2.00----3.00
882	2¾ oz Wine	2.00----3.00
882	2 oz Sherry	2.00----3.00
882	1, ¾ oz Cordial.	2.00----3.00
882	6½ oz Tall Ale	2.00----3.00
882	4½ oz Hot Whiskey	2.00----3.00
882	4 oz Rhine Wine.	2.00----3.00
882	1, ¾ oz Pousse Cafe	2.00----3.00
882	2½ oz Creme De Menthe	2.00----3.00
882	3, 3½ oz Cocktail	2.00----3.00
882	4½ oz H. S. Champ. C. F.	2.00----3.00
882	5, 7 oz Saucer Champgne	2.00----3.00
882	4½″ Bon Bon	2.00----3.00
882½	Grape Fruit	2.00----3.00
882	Grape Fruit	2.00----3.00
882	Grape Fruit Liner	1.00----2.00
882½	Grape Fruit Liner	1.00----2.00
882	Sherbet	2.00----2.50
300	7 Tankard, Cut Flute	12.00--15.00

No.	Description	Price
1558	Water Bottle, C. N.	10.00--12.00
1465	7 oz Oil, C. N. Cut S.	12.00--15.00
1478	Sugar	2.00----3.00
1478	Cream	2.00----3.00
1227	8″ Nappy	3.00----5.00
1227	4½″ Nappy	1.00----2.00
1867	Finger Bowl	1.00----2.00
1867	Finger Bowl Plate	1.00----2.00
922	Toothpick, Sham, C. F., Pty	4.00----6.00
810	Custard, Cut Flute	2.00----3.00
810	Finger Bowl, Cut Flute	2.00----3.00
858	Table, 3½ oz Tumb., Cut 19	2.00----4.00
858	5, 6½, 8, 10 oz Tumb., C. 19	2.00----4.00
858	12, 14, 16 oz Tumb., C. 19	2.00----4.00
820	Tumbler, Cut B. Punty	2.00----3.00
820½	Tumbler, Cut 19, Punty	2.00----3.00
833	8 oz Sham, Tumb., C. 19, Pty.	2.00----3.00
701	8, 10, 14 oz Tumbler, Cut B. Punty	2.00----3.00
863	Almond	2.00----3.00

NEEDLE ETCHING NO. 38½ "BLOCK"

No.	Description	Price
863	10½ oz Goblet, plain	2.00----3.00
863	9 oz Goblet	2.00----3.00
863	5½ oz Tall Champagne	2.00----3.00
863	4½ oz Claret	2.00----3.00
863	3 oz Wine	2.00----3.00
863	1 oz Cordial	2.00----3.00
863	4 oz Rhine Wine.	2.00----3.00
863	2 oz Sherry	2.00----3.00
863	5½ oz Saucer Champagne	2.00----3.00
863	3 oz Cocktail	2.00----3.00
863	2½ oz Creme De Menthe	2.00----3.00
863	1 oz Pousse Cafe	2.00----3.00
863	Fruit	2.00----2.50
840	Sherbet Plate	1.00----2.00
863	Almond	2.00----3.00
863	H. S. Champagne	2.00----3.00
899	Parfait	2.00----3.00
945	Grape Fruit	2.00----3.00
945½	Grape Fruit Liner	1.00----2.00
945½	Grape Fruit	2.00----3.00
879	9 oz Goblet	2.00----3.00
879	4½ oz Claret	2.00----3.00
879	2¾ oz Wine	2.00----3.00
879	2 oz Sherry	2.00----3.00
879	¾ oz Cordial	2.00----3.00
879	¾ oz Pousse Cafe	2.00----3.00
879	5 oz Saucer Champagne	2.00----3.00
879	3 oz Cocktail	2.00----3.00
879	2½ oz Creme de Menthe	2.00----3.00
879	Sherbet	2.00----2.50
820	Tumbler	2.00----2.50
820½	Tumbler, ½ Sham	2.00----2.50
833	8 oz Tumbler	2.00----2.50
833	8 oz Tumbler, ½ Sham	2.00----2.50
889	5 oz Tumbler	2.00----2.50
887	2½ oz Tumbler	2.00----2.50
701	14 oz Tumbler	2.00----2.50
701	Tumbler Plate	1.00----2.00
4065	16 oz Tom Collins, ½ Sham, Cut 19	3.00----4.00
4065	14 oz Ice Tea, ½ Sham, Cut 19	3.00----4.00
4065	12 oz Strained Lemonade, ½ Sham, Cut 19	3.00----4.00
4065	10 oz Beer, ½ Sham, Cut 19	3.00----4.00
4065	8 oz Gin Fizz, ½ Sham, Cut 19	3.00----4.00

4065	7 oz Split Beer, ½ Sham, Cut 19	3.00----4.00
4065	6 oz Appolinaris, ½ Sham, Cut 19	3.00----4.00
4065	5 oz Mineral, ½ Sham, Cut 19	3.00----4.00
4065	4½ oz Wine, ½ Sham, Cut 19	3.00----4.00
4065	3 oz Whiskey, ½ Sham, Cut 19	3.00----4.00
4070	12 oz Milk Punch, ½ Sham, Cut 19	3.00----4.00
4070	10 oz Table Tumbler, ½ Sham. Cut 19	2.00----3.00
4070	9 oz Old Fashioned Cocktail Cut 19	3.00----4.00
4070	8 oz Hiball, ½ Sham, Cut 19	3.00----4.00
4070	7 oz Split Beer, ½ Sham, Cut 19	3.00----4.00
4070	5½ oz Bar Water, ½ Sham, Cut 19	3.00----4.00
4070	3½, 3, 2½, 2 oz Whiskey, ½ Sham, Cut 19	3.00----4.00
1478	Sugar	2.00----3.00
1478	Cream	2.00----3.00
300½	Large Oil	10.00--14.00
300½	Small Oil	10.00--14.00
1465	Large Oil, C. N.	14.00--16.00
300	Qt. Decanter, C. N.	10.00--12.00
1165	Shaker, S. P. Top	1.00----2.00
922	Toothpick, Cut 19	5.00----8.00
4061	Lemonade	2.00----3.00
1769	Finger Bowl	1.00----2.00
200	6" Finger Bowl Plate	1.00----2.00
1598	Custard	2.00----3.00
200	5" Custard Plate	1.00----2.00
803	8" Nappy, Footed	4.00----6.00
803	7, 6, 5, 4½" Deep Nappy, Footed	2.00----5.00
803	6" Comport	2.00----4.00
803	5" Comport	2.00----4.00
1227	8" Nappy	2.00----4.00
1227	4½" Nappy	1.00----2.00
300-7	Tankard	12.00--15.00
724-7	Tankard	18.00--22.00
1787-6	Tankard	15.00--18.00
303-7	Jug	15.00--18.00
160½	Water Bottle, C. N.	8.00--10.00
1558	Small Water Bottle, C. N.	8.00--10.00
858	Table, 14, 12, 10, 8, 5 oz Tumbler	2.00----2.50
1236-6	Jug	15.00--18.00

5054	Parfait	2.00----3.00
481	Custard	2.00----3.00
1769	Finger Bowl	1.00----2.00
1769	F. Finger bowl (200-6")	1.00----2.00
858	Sweetmeat	2.00----3.00
880	4½" Bon Bon	2.00----3.00
803	5" Comport	2.00----2.50
803	6" Comport	2.00----3.00
803	5" Footed Nappy	2.00----3.00
803	6" Footed Nappy	2.00----3.00
803	7" Footed Nappy	3.00----4.00
1227	4½" Nappy	2.00----2.50
1227	8" Nappy	4.00----5.00
820	Table Tumbler	2.00----2.50
833	8 oz Tumbler	2.00----2.50
833	8 oz Tumbler, ½ Sham	2.00----2.50
766	Ftd. Ice Tea, Handled	2.00----3.00
4011	12 oz Tumbler, Handled	2.00----3.00
701	5" Tumbler Plate	1.00----2.00
701	14 oz Tumbler	2.00----2.50
701	12 oz Tumbler	2.00----2.50
858	Table, 14, 12, 10, 8, 5 oz Tumbler	2.00----2.50
4011½	Table Tumbler	2.00----2.50
4011	12 oz Tumbler	2.00----2.50
4011	8 oz Tumbler	2.00----2.50
889	5 oz Tumbler	2.00----2.50
887	2 oz Tumbler	2.00----3.00
300-7	Jug	12.00--15.00
318-7	Jug	12.00--15.00
303-7	Jug	15.00--18.00
1236-6	Jug	15.00--18.00
1478	Sugar	2.00----3.00
1478	Cream	2.00----3.00
300½	Small Oil	12.00--15.00
300	Qt. Decanter, Cut Neck	10.00--12.00

NEEDLE ETCHING NO. 42
"CHAIN" PATTERN

863	10 oz Goblet	2.00----3.00
863	9 oz Goblet	2.00----3.00
862	5½ oz Saucer Champagne	2.00----3.00
863	Fruit	2.00----2.50
863	3 oz Wine	2.00----3.00
863	2 oz Sherry	2.00----3.00
863	1 oz Cordial	2.00----3.00
863	2½ oz Creme de Menthe	2.00----3.00
863	3½ oz Cocktail	2.00----3.00
766	9 oz Goblet	2.00----3.00
766	5 oz Saucer Champagne	2.00----3.00
766	4½ oz Claret	2.00----3.00
766	Cocktail	2.00----3.00
766	Fruit	2.00----2.50
1736	6" Fruit Plate	1.00----2.00

NEEDLE ETCHING NO. 44
"GARTER" PATTERN

805	9 oz Goblet	2.00----3.00
805	Saucer Champagne	2.00----3.00
805	Sherbet	2.00----2.50
837	Oyster Cocktail	2.00----2.50
805	Parfait	2.00----2.50
805	4½ oz Claret	2.00----3.00
805	2¾ oz Wine	2.00----3.00
805	2 oz Sherry	2.00----3.00
805	Cordial	2.00----3.00
805	Cocktail	2.00----3.00
863	Almond	2.00----3.00
766	Finger Bowl	1.00----2.00
766	F. Bowl Plate (1736-6")	1.00----2.00
858	Sweetmeat	2.00----3.00
880	4½" Bon Bon	2.00----3.00
803	5" Comport	2.00----3.00
803	6" Comport	2.00----3.00
803	5" Footed Nappy	2.00----3.00
803	6" Footed Nappy	2.00----3.00
803	7" Footed Nappy	3.00----4.00
820	Table Tumbler	2.00----2.50
833	8 oz Tumbler	2.00----2.50
833	8 oz Tumbler, ½ Sham	2.00----2.50
766	Ftd. Ice Tea, Handled	2.00----3.00
4011	12 oz Tumbler, Handled	2.00----3.00
701	5" Tumbler, Plate	1.00----2.00
701	14 oz Tumbler	2.00----2.50
858	Table, 14, 12, 8, 5, 3 oz Tumbler	2.00----2.50
889	5 oz Tumbler	2.00----2.50

300-7	Jug	12.00--15.00
318-7	Jug	15.00--18.00
303-7	Jug	15.00--18.00
1236-6	Jug	15.00--18.00
1478	Sugar	2.00----3.00
1478	Cream	2.00----3.00
300½	Small Oil	12.00--15.00

NEEDLE ETCHING NO. 45

5050	11, 10, 9 oz Goblet, Optic	2.00----3.00
5050	6½ oz Claret, Optic	2.00----3.00
5050	4½ oz Claret, Optic	2.00----3.00
5050	3½ oz Wine, Optic	2.00----3.00
5050	2 oz Sherry, Optic	2.00----3.00
5050	1 oz Cordial, Optic	2.00----3.00
5050	6 oz Saucer Champ. Optic	2.00----3.00
5050	5½ oz Tall Champ., Optic	2.00----3.00
5050	4 oz Hot Whiskey, Optic	2.00----3.00
5050	3½ oz Cocktail, Optic	2.00----3.00
5050	2½ oz Creme de Menthe, O.	2.00----3.00
5050	1 oz Pousse Cafe, Optic	2.00----3.00
5050	Egg, Optic	2.00----2.50
5050	Sherbet, Optic	2.00----2.50
5025	10, 8, 9 oz Goblet	2.00----3.00
5025	6½, 5½ oz Champagne	2.00----3.00
5025	5, 4¾ oz Claret	2.00----3.00
5025	2¾ oz Wine	2.00----3.00
5025	2 oz Wine	2.00----3.00
5025	¾ oz Pousse Cafe	2.00----3.00
5025	1 oz Cordial	2.00----3.00
5025	¾ oz Cordial	2.00----3.00
801	11 oz Goblet	2.00----3.00
801	5, 4 oz Claret	2.00----3.00
801	1 oz Cordial	2.00----3.00
801	¾ oz Brandy	2.00----3.00
825	Saucer Champagne	2.00----3.00
932	Saucer Champagne	2.00----3.00
858	Sweetmeat	2.00----3.00
902	5 oz Wine	2.00----3.00
952	Cocktail	2.00----3.00
953	Cocktail	2.00----3.00
846	Sherry	2.00----3.00
840	Sherbet	2.00----2.50
5008	Sherbet	2.00----2.50
863	Almond	2.00----3.00
863	Fruit	2.00----2.50
858	H. S. Champagne C. F.	2.00----3.00
300	1, 2, 3, 3½, 4, 5, 6, 7, 8, Claret Tankard	10.00--20.00
300½	7 Tankard	15.00--18.00
724	7 Tankard	18.00--20.00
303	7 Jug	15.00--18.00
318	7 Jug, Optic	15.00--18.00
1232	Jug, Optic	15.00--18.00
1236	3, 6, 7 Jug	12.00--18.00
1227	7 Jug	15.00--18.00
160½	Water Bottle, C. N.	8.00--10.00
1558	Water Bottle, C. N.	8.00--10.00
315	Finger Bowl	1.00----2.00
1478	Sugar	2.00----3.00
1478	Cream	2.00----3.00
300½	Small Oil	10.00--15.00
312	Oil	10.00--15.00
1465	Oil, Cut Neck	12.00--15.00
481	Custard	2.00----2.50
481	Custard Plate	1.00----2.00
1755	Custard	2.00----2.50
1277	8" Nappy	4.00----5.00
1227	4½" Nappy	1.00----2.00

315	4, 4½, 5, 6, 7, 8, 9, 10" Nappy	1.00----5.00
1227	Punch Bowl & Stand	20.00--25.00
300	Pt. Decanter, C. N.	10.00--15.00
300	Qt. Decanter, C. N.	10.00--15.00
863	H. S. Champagne C. F.	2.00----3.00
1499	Finger Bowl	1.00----2.00
1449	Finger Bowl Plate	1.00----2.00
1769	Finger Bowl	1.00----2.00
1769	Finger Bowl Plate	1.00----2.00
1111	6 Jug, Optic	15.00--18.00
1111	7 Jug, Optic	15.00--18.00
480	Custard	2.00----2.50
480	Custard Plate	1.00----2.00
300½	Large Oil, Cut S	12.00--15.00
840	Sherbet Plate	1.00----2.00
858	Table, 3½, 5, 6½, 8. 10, 12, 14, 16 oz Tumbler, Et. 45	2.00----2.50
858	Tumbler Plate	1.00----2.00
858	Custard	2.00----2.50
858	Custard Plate	1.00----2.00
858	Finger Bowl	1.00----2.00
858	Finger Bowl Plate	1.00----2.00
820	Tumbler	2.00----2.50
820½	Tumbler, ½ Sham	2.00----2.50
833	8 oz Tumbler	2.00----2.50
833	8 oz Tumbler, ½ Sham	2.00----2.50
887	3, 5, 2½ oz Tumbler	2.00----2.50
701	8, 10, 12 oz Tumbler	2.00----2.50
160½	Water Bottle	8.00--10.00
803	5" Comport	2.00----2.50
803	6" Comport	2.00----2.50
803	4½, 5, 6, 7" Footed Nappy, Deep	2.00----5.00
803	4½, 5, 6, 7, 8" Footed Nappy, Shallow	2.00----5.00
823	4½, 5" Fruit	2.00----2.50
880	11, 10, 9, 8 oz Goblet, Et. 45	2.00----3.00
880	5 oz Tall Champagne	2.00----3.00
880	6½ oz Claret	2.00----3.00
880	4½ oz Claret	2.00----3.00
880	3½ oz Wine	2.00----3.00
880	2¾ oz Wine	2.00----3.00
880	2 oz Sherry	2.00----3.00
880	1 oz Cordial	2.00----3.00
880	¾ oz Cordial	2.00----3.00
880	6½ oz Tall Ale	2.00----3.00
880	4½ oz Hot Whiskey	2.00----3.00
880	4 oz Rhine Wine	2.00----3.00
880	1 oz Pousse Cafe	2.00----3.00
880	¾ oz Pousse Cafe	2.00----3.00
880	7½ oz Creme De Menthe	2.00----3.00
880	3 oz Cocktail	2.00----3.00
880	3½ oz Cocktail	2.00----3.00
880	4½ oz H. S. Champagne C.F	2.00----3.00
880	5 oz Saucer Champagne	2.00----3.00
880	7 oz Saucer Champagne	2.00----3.00
880	4½" Bon Bon	2.00----3.00
880½	Grape Fruit	2.00----3.00
880	Grape Fruit	2.00----3.00
880	Grape Fruit Liner	2.00----3.00
880½	Grape Fruit Liner	2.00----3.00
880	Sherbet	2.00----2.50
945	Grape Fruit	2.00----3.00
945½	Grape Fruit	2.00----3.00
945½	Grape Fruit Liner	2.00----3.00
300	Pt. Decanter, C. N.	10.00--12.00
300	Qt. Decanter, C. N.	12.00--15.00
1491	Decanter, Optic, C.N.	12.00--15.00
1464	18 oz Decanter, C.N.	15.00--18.00

NEEDLE ETCHING NO. 45
GREEK DESIGN

Also made in Rose, Green and Amber Bowl
With Crystal Foot

5297½	Grape Fruit	2.00----3.00
945½	Grape Fruit Liner	2.00----3.00
5000	12, 9, 5, 2½ oz Ftd. Tumbler	2.00----3.00
5000	7 Footed Jug	10.00--12.00
5297	Goblet	3.00----5.00
5297	High Sherbet	3.00----5.00
5297	Low Sherbet	2.00----3.00
5297	Parfait	2.00----3.00
5297	Claret	2.00----3.00
5297	Wine	2.00----3.00
5297	Cocktail	3.00----4.00
5297	Cordial	3.00----4.00
5200	Oyster Cocktail	2.00----3.00
5097	Goblet	3.00----4.00
5097	High Sherbet	3.00----4.00
5097	Low Sherbet	2.00----3.00
5097	Parfait	2.00----3.00
5097	Claret	2.00----3.00
5097	Wine	2.00----3.00
5097	Cocktail	3.00----4.00
5097	Cordial	3.00----4.00
5000	Oyster Cocktail	2.00----3.00
869	Finger Bowl	1.00----2.00
2283	6" Plate, Reg. Optic	1.00----2.00
5000	12, 9, 5, 2½ oz Ftd. Tumbler	2.00----3.00
2283	7" Plate	1.00----2.00
2283	8" Plate	2.00----3.00

NEEDLE ETCHING NO. 47
"LARGE CLOVERLEAF" PATTERN

Not Illustrated in Fostoria Book

858	9 oz Goblet	2.00----3.00
858	5½ oz Saucer Champagne	2.00----3.00
858	Fruit	2.00----2.50
1736	6" Fruit Plate	1.00----2.00
858	2¾ oz Wine	2.00----3.00
858	Finger Bowl	1.00----2.00
837	Oyster Cocktail	2.00----2.50
822	Parfait	2.00----3.00
805	Parfait	2.00----3.00
801	10, 9 oz Goblet	2.00----3.00
801	5½ oz Saucer Champagne	2.00----3.00
801	5 oz Claret	2.00----3.00
801	4, 3, 2 oz Wine	2.00----3.00
801	1 oz Cordial	2.00----3.00
5025	10, 9, 8 oz Goblet	2.00----3.00
5025	6½, 5½ oz Champagne	2.00----3.00
5025	4¾ oz Claret	2.00----3.00
5025	2¾, 2 oz Wine	2.00----3.00
5025	1 oz Cordial	2.00----3.00
481	Custard	2.00----2.50
1769	Finger Bowl	1.00----2.00
1769	F. Finger Bowl Plate (200-6")	1.00----2.00
826	9 oz Goblet	2.00----3.00
991	Goblet (Pressed)	4.00----5.00
114	Goblet (Pressed)	4.00----5.00
932	Saucer Champagne	2.00----3.00
932	Champagne Plate (932-6")	1.00----2.00
840	Sherbet	2.00----2.50
840	5" Sherbet Plate	1.00----2.00

841	Sherbet	2.00----2.50
1478	Sugar	2.00----3.00
1478	Cream	2.00----3.00
300½	Large Oil	12.00--15.00
300½	Small Oil	12.00--15.00
300	Qt. Decanter, Cut Neck	12.00--15.00
160½	Water Bottle, Cut Neck	8.00--10.00
979	Horseradish	3.00----4.00
1733	Marmalade & Cover	4.00----6.00
1697	Carafe	8.00--10.00
1697	Carafe Tumbler (4023-6 oz)	2.00----2.50
1697	Carafe Whiskey (981-2½ oz)	2.00----2.50
801	¾ oz Cordial	2.00----3.00
801	¾ oz Liquor	2.00----3.00
5001	11, 8¾, 7½ oz Goblet	2.00----3.00
5001	5¾ oz Tall Champagne	2.00----3.00
5001	5½ oz Claret	2.00----3.00
5001	4¾ oz Claret	2.00----3.00
5001	5 oz Hot Whiskey	2.00----3.00
5001	5 oz Saucer Champagne	2.00----3.00
5001	4, 3, 2½ oz Cocktail	2.00----3.00
5001	4 oz Rhine Wine	2.00----3.00
5001	Large Wine	2.00----3.00
5001	Small Wine	2.00----3.00
5001	1½ oz Sherry	2.00----3.00
5001	2 oz Sherry	2.00----3.00
5001	1, ¾ oz Cordial	2.00----3.00
5001	¾ oz Brandy	2.00----3.00
1227	1, 2, 3, 4, 5, 6 Pitcher	10.00--15.00
952	Cocktail	2.00----3.00
953	Cocktail	2.00----3.00
846	2 oz Sherry	2.00----3.00
315	Finger Bowl	1.00----2.00
1192	Finger Bowl (Pressed)	1.00----2.00
945½	Grape Fruit	2.00----3.00
945½	Grape Fruit Liner	2.00----3.00
315	4, 4½, 5, 6, 7, 8" Nappy	1.00----5.00
1227	4½" Nappy	1.00----2.00
1227	8" Nappy	4.00----5.00
858	Sweetmeat	2.00----3.00
820	Table Tumbler	2.00----2.50
833	8 oz Tumbler	2.00----2.50
833	8 oz Tumbler, ½ Sham	2.00----2.50
4061	Ftd. Ice Tea, Handled	2.00----3.00
701	5" Tumbler Plate	1.00----2.00
701	14, 12, 10, 8, 7 oz Tumbler	2.00----2.50
4011	12 oz Tumbler	2.00----2.50
4011½	Table Tumbler	2.00----2.50
858	Table Tumbler	2.00----2.50
858	14 oz Tumbler	2.00----2.50
858	8 oz Tumbler	2.00----2.50
889	5 oz Tumbler	2.00----2.50
887	2½ oz Tumbler	2.00----2.50
300	8, 7, 6, 5, 4, 3, 2, 1 Jug	12.00--16.00
300½	7 Jug	12.00--16.00
318	7, 6, 5, 4 Jug	12.00--16.00
303	8, 7, 6, 5, 4 Jug	12.00--16.00
1236	7, 6 Jug	12.00--16.00
2018	Jug	15.00--18.00
1227	7 Jug	15.00--18.00
316	7 Jug	15.00--18.00
317½	7 Jug	15.00--18.00
826	9 oz Goblet, Et. 47	2.00----3.00
825	Saucer Champagne	2.00----3.00
932	Saucer Champagne	2.00----3.00
791	Hollow Stem Champ. C.F.	2.00----4.00
863	Hollow Stem Champ. C.F.	2.00----4.00
953	Cocktail	2.00----3.00
952	Cocktail	2.00----3.00
902	5, 4, 3 oz Wine	2.00----3.00
845	Hot Whiskey	2.00----3.00

846	Sherry	2.00----3.00
849	Sherry	2.00----3.00
847	Wine	2.00----3.00
945	Grape Fruit	2.00----3.00
945½	Grape Fruit	2.00----3.00
945½	Grape Fruit Liner	2.00----3.00
701	16 oz. Straight	2.00----3.00
883	4, 5, 6, 7, 8, 9, 10 oz. Bell Top	2.00----3.00
724	6, 7 Tankard	12.00--15.00
1236	1, 2, 3, 4, 5 Pitcher	8.00--10.00
1389	Oyster Cocktail	2.00----2.50
820	Tumbler,	2.00----2.50
4023	6 oz. Tumbler	2.00----2.50
901	8 oz. Tumbler	2.00----2.50
889	5 oz. Tumbler	2.00----2.50
887	3, 2½, 2 oz. Tumbler	2.00----2.50
701	3, 4, 4½, 5, 6, 6½, 9, 9½, 10 7½ oz. Straight Tumbler	2.00----2.50
5025	¾ oz. Pousse Cafe	2.00----3.00
5025	¾ oz. Cordial	2.00----3.00
114	Goblet	2.00----3.00
114	Champagne	2.00----3.00
114	Claret	2.00----3.00
114	Wine	2.00----3.00
114	Cordial	2.00----3.00
991	Goblet	2.00----3.00
315	Finger Bowl	1.00----2.00
315	Finger Bowl Plate	1.00----2.00
1449	Finger Bowl	1.00----2.00
1449	Finger Bowl Plate	1.00----2.00
1769	Finger Bowl	1.00----2.00
470	Finger Bowl	1.00----2.00
1192	Finger Bowl	1.00----2.00
1349	Finger Bowl	1.00----2.00
480	Custard, Etched 47	2.00----2.50
481	Custard	2.00----2.50
858	Custard	2.00----2.50
1227	Custard	2.00----2.50
1239	Custard	2.00----2.50
1241	Custard	2.00----2.50
1598	Custard	2.00----2.50
	Custard Plate	1.00----2.00
1227	Sugar	2.00----3.00
1227	Cream	2.00----3.00
1478	Sugar	2.00----3.00
1478	Cream	2.00----3.00
1480	Sugar	2.00----3.00
1480	Cream	2.00----3.00
1558	Water Bottle, C. N.	8.00--10.00
1697	Water Bottle	8.00--10.00
444	9″, 8″ Cheese & Cover	12.00--15.00
1686	9″, 8″ Cheese & Cover	12.00--15.00
312	Oil, Cut Stopper	12.00--15.00
304	Water Bottle, C. N.	8.00--10.00
300	Pt. Decanter, C. N.	12.00--16.00
1195	Large Decanter, C. N.	14.00--18.00
1195	Medium Decanter, C. N.	12.00--15.00
1195	Small Decanter, C. N.	10.00--12.00

NEEDLE ETCHING NO. 53
"PARISIAN" PATTERN

867	10 oz. Goblet	2.00----3.00
867	Saucer Champagne	2.00----3.00
867	Fruit	2.00----2.50
867	Sherbet	2.00----2.50
840	5″ Sherbet Plate	1.00----2.00
822	Parfait	2.00----3.00

867	5 oz. Claret	2.00----3.00
867	2¾ oz. Wine	2.00----3.00
867	2 oz. Sherry	2.00----3.00
867	Cordial	2.00----3.00
867	Cocktail	2.00----3.00
863	Almond	2.00----3.00
858	Custard	2.00----2.50
858	Finger Bowl	1.00----2.00
858	F. Bowl Plate (1499-6″)	1.00----2.00
858	Sweet meat	2.00----3.00
880	4½″ Bon Bon	2.00----3.00
803	5″, 6″ Comport	3.00----4.00
803	5″, 6″, 7″ Footed Nappy	4.00----5.00
820	Table Tumbler	2.00----2.50
833	8 oz. Tumbler	2.00----2.50
833	8 oz. Tumbler, ½ Sham	2.00----2.50
766	Footed Ice Tea, Handled	2.00----3.00
701	5″ Tumbler Plate	1.00----2.00
701	14 oz. Tumbler	2.00----2.50
701	8 oz. Tumbler	2.00----2.50
858	Table Tumbler	2.00----2.50
858	14, 8, 5 oz. Tumbler	2.00----2.50
4011½	Table Tumbler	2.00----2.50
4011	12, 8, 5 oz. Tumbler	2.00----2.50
889	5 oz. Tumbler	2.00----2.50
887	2½ oz. Tumbler	2.00----2.50
300	7 Jug	12.00--15.00
318	7 Jug	15.00--18.00
303	7 Jug	15.00--18.00
1236	6 Jug	15.00--18.00
303	Sugar	2.00----3.00
303	Cream	2.00----3.00
300½	Large Oil	12.00--15.00
300½	Small Oil	12.00--15.00

NEEDLE ETCHING NO. 54
"LUNAR" PATTERN
PLAIN, NOT OPTIC
Not Illustrated in Fostoria Book

863	9 oz. Goblet	2.00----3.00
863	5½ oz. Saucer Champagne	2.00----3.00
863	Fruit	2.00----2.50
863	4½ oz. Claret	2.00----3.00
863	3 oz. Wine	2.00----3.00
863	3½ oz. Cocktail	2.00----3.00
767	Parfait	2.00----3.00
837	Oyster Cocktail	2.00----2.50
481	Custard	2.00----2.50
858	Finger Bowl	1.00----2.00
1736	6″ Plate	1.00----2.00
945½	Grape Fruit	2.00----3.00
945½	Grape Fruit Liner	2.00----3.00
858	Sweetmeat	2.00----3.00
880	4½″ Bon Bon	2.00----3.00
803	5″ Comport	2.00----3.00
803	6″ Comport	2.00----4.00
803	5″, 6″, 7″ Footed Nappy	2.00----4.00
820	Table Tumbler	2.00----2.50
833	8 oz. Tumbler	2.00----2.50
833	8 oz. Tumbler, ½ Sham	2.00----2.50
4011	12 oz. Tumbler, Handled	2.00----3.00
701	5″ Plate	1.00----2.00
4011½	Table Tumbler	2.00----2.50
701	14, 12 oz. Tumbler	2.00----2.50
4011	12, 8, 5 oz. Tumbler	2.00----2.50
300	7 Tankard	12.00--15.00
303	7 Jug	15.00--18.00

1236	6 Jug	15.00--18.00
1478	Sugar	2.00----3.00
1478	Cream	2.00----3.00
300½	Small Oil	12.00--15.00

NEEDLE ETCHING NO. 67 "SMALL CLOVERLEAF"
Not Illustrated in Fostoria Book

863	10, 9 oz Goblet	2.00----3.00
863	5½ oz. Saucer Champagne	2.00----3.00
863	Fruit	2.00----2.50
1736	6'' Fruit Plate	1.00----2.00
810	9 oz. Goblet	2.00----3.00
810	5½, 7 oz. Saucer Champag.	2.00----3.00
932	6'' Champagne Plate	1.00----2.00
810	Sherbet	2.00----2.50
840	5'' Fruit Plate	1.00----2.00
810	6 oz. Tall Champagne	2.00----3.00
810	4½ oz. Claret	2.00----3.00
810	3 oz. Wine	2.00----3.00
810	2 oz. Sherry	2.00----3.00
810	1 oz. Cordial	2.00----3.00
810	1 oz. Brandy	2.00----3.00
810	2½ oz. Creme de Menthe	2.00----3.00
810	3½ oz. Cocktail	2.00----3.00
810	Custard	2.00----2.50
810	Finger Bowl	1.00----2.00
810	F. Bowl Plate (200-6'')	1.00----2.00
843	Sherbet	2.00----2.50
842	Sherbet	2.00----2.50
858	Sweetmeat	2.00----3.00
880	4½'' Bon Bon	2.00----3.00
803	5'', 6'' Comport	2.00----4.00
803	5'', 6'', 7'' Footed Nappy	2.00----4.00
820	Table Tumbler	2.00----2.50
701	14 oz. Tumbler	2.00----2.50
701	5'' Tumbler Plate	2.00----2.50
810	9'' Tumbler	2.00----2.50
810	10, 8, 5 oz. Tall Tumbler	2.00----2.50
810	5½, 3½ oz. Claret	2.00----3.00
863	10½ oz. Goblet, Etched 67	2.00----3.00
863½	9 oz. Goblet, S. S.	2.00----3.00
863½	7 oz. Goblet, L. S.	2.00----3.00
863	7, 5½ oz. Goblet	2.00----3.00
863	5½ oz. Tall Champagne	2.00----3.00
863	4½ oz. Claret	2.00----3.00
863	3 oz. Wine	2.00----3.00
863	1¼ oz. Cordial	2.00----3.00
863½	¾ oz. Cordial	2.00----3.00
863	4½ oz. Rhine Wine	2.00----3.00
863	2 oz. Sherry	2.00----3.00
863	5½ oz. Saucer Cham.	2.00----3.00
863	3½, 3 oz. Cocktail	2.00----3.00
863	2½ oz. Creme De M.	2.00----3.00
863	1½ oz. Pousse Cafe	2.00----3.00
863½	¾ oz. Pousse Cafe	2.00----3.00
863	Fruit	2.00----2.50
863	Individual Almond	2.00----2.50
863	Hollow Stem Cham., C. F.	2.00----4.00
803	4½,5,6,7,8'', Shal. Nappy	1.00----4.00
803	4½, 5, 6, 7'', Deep Nappy	1.00----5.00
803	5'', Footed Comport	2.00----3.00
803	6'', Footed Comport	2.00----3.00

DEEP PLATE ETCHING—NO. 201 LACE WORK

315	9'' Nappy Etched 201	6.00----8.00
315	8'' Nappy	4.00----6.00

315	7'' Nappy	4.00----5.00
315	6'' Nappy	3.00----5.00
315	5'' Nappy	2.00----3.00
315	4½'' Nappy	2.00----3.00
315	4'' Nappy	2.00----3.00
1281	5'' Ice Cream	2.00----3.00
480	Custard	2.00----4.00
481	Custard	2.00----4.00
1227	Custard	2.00----4.00
1239	Custard	2.00----4.00
1241	Custard	2.00----4.00
315	Finger Bowl	2.00----3.00
820	Tumbler	3.00----4.00
820½	Tumbler, Half Sham	3.00----4.00

ETCHING NO. 202 "THISTLE WITH BAND."

300	7 Jug Etched 202	15.00--20.00
1227	7 Jug	20.00--25.00
820	Tumbler	2.00----4.00
820½	Tumbler, Half Sham	2.00----4.00

ETCHING NO. 202½ "THISTLE WITHOUT BAND."

303	7 Jug Etched 202½	15.00--20.00
300	7 Jug	15.00--20.00
1227	7 Jug	15.00--20.00
1227	7 Jug, Cut Neck	20.00--25.00
820	Tumbler	2.00----4.00
820½	Tumbler, Half Sham	2.00----3.00
315	Finger Bowl	2.00----3.00
160½	Water Bottle, Cut Neck	10.00--15.00
1227	Punch Bowl	20.00--30.00
1227	Punch Bowl and Foot	25.00--35.00
481	Custard	3.00----4.00
1227	Custard	3.00----4.00

DEEP PLATE ETCHING—NO. 203 "PERSIAN SCROLL"

300	7, 6, 5, 4, 3½, 3, 2, 1, Jug Etched 203	5.00--10.00
303	7, 6 Jug	10.00--20.00
318	7 Jug	15.00--18.00
724	7 Jug	15.00--20.00
724	6 Jug	20.00--25.00
1227	7 Jug	20.00--25.00
1227	7 Jug, Cut Neck	18.00--22.00
820	Tumbler	20.00--25.00
820½	Tumbler, Half Sham	2.00----3.00
833	10 oz. Sham Tumbler	2.00----3.00
833	7 oz. Sham Tumbler	2.00----3.00
889	5 oz. Tumbler	2.00----3.00
887	3 oz. Tumbler	2.00----3.00
801	11, 10, 9, 5, 4, 2, 1, ¾ oz. Stemware	2.00----3.00
902	5, 4, 3 oz. Stemware	2.00----4.00
931	5 oz. Stemware	2.00----4.00
952	Stemware, 3 oz.	2.00----3.00
932	Saucer Champagne	2.00----4.00
480	Custard	2.00----4.00
481	Custard	2.00----3.00
1227	Custard	2.00----3.00
1241	Custard	2.00----3.00
	Custard Plate	2.00----3.00
160½	Water Bottle, Cut Neck	10.00--14.00
1061	Cracker Jar & Cover, Optic	10.00--15.00
315	Finger Bowl	2.00----3.00
315	Finger Bowl Plate	2.00----3.00
1163	Catsup, C. S.	15.00--18.00

1164	Oil, C. S.	15.00--18.00
300½	Small Oil, C. S.	15.00--18.00
300½	Large Oil, C. S.	15.00--18.00
312	Oil, C. S.	15.00--18.00
1227	Sugar & Cover	8.00--12.00
1227	Cream	5.00----8.00
1227	8" Nappy	5.00----8.00
1227	4½" Nappy	2.00----3.00
444	8" Cheese & Cover	10.00--15.00
444	9" Cheese & Cover	10.00--15.00
226	Cheese & Cover	10.00--12.50
701	16 oz. Tumbler	2.00----3.00
701	14 oz. Tumbler	2.00----3.00
	Ice Tea Plate	1.00----2.00

DEEP PLATE ETCHING NO. 204
VINE AND GRAPES
Vintage Pattern

858	11, 10, 9 oz Goblet	2.00----3.00
858	6½ oz. Claret	2.00----3.00
858	4½ oz. Claret	2.00----3.00
858	3½ oz. Wine	2.00----3.00
858	2¾ oz. Wine	2.00----3.00
858	2 oz. Sherry	2.00----3.00
858	1 oz. Cordial	2.00----3.00
858	7 oz. Saucer Champagne	2.00----3.00
858	Hollow Stem Chapagne, C. F	2.00----3.00
858	5½ oz. Tall Champagne	2.00----3.00
858	4 oz. Hot Whiskey	2.00----3.00
858	1 oz. Brandy	2.00----3.00
858	3½ oz. Cocktail	2.00----3.00
858	2½ oz. Creme de Menthe	2.00----3.00
858	Sherbet	2.00----2.50
858	Fruit Salad	2.00----3.00
858	Oyster Cocktail	2.00----3.00
858	4½" Ice Cream	2.00----3.00
858	Long Stem Champagne	3.00----4.00
858	Long Stem Champ'ne, C. R.	3.00----4.00
858	Custard	2.00----3.00
858	Custard Plate	1.00----2.00
858	Finger Bowl	1.00----2.00
858	Finger Bowl Plate	1.00----2.00
858	3½ oz. Tumbler	2.00----2.50
858	5 oz. Tumbler	2.00----2.50
858	6½ oz. Tumbler	2.00----2.50
858	8 oz. Tumbler	2.00----2.50
858	Table Tumbler	2.00----2.50
858	10, 12, 14, 16 oz. Tumbler	1.00----3.00
858	Tumbler Plate	1.00----3.00
858	8 oz. Tumbler, Handled	2.00----3.00
858	10 oz. Tumbler, Handled	2.00----3.00
840	Sherbet	2.00----3.00
840	Sherbet Plate	1.00----2.00
842	Sherbet	2.00----3.00
1389	Oyster Cocktail	2.00----3.00
1542	Oyster Cocktail	2.00----3.00
5039	Oyster Cocktail	2.00----3.00
5039	Liner	1.00----2.00
932	Saucer Champagne	2.00----3.00
932	6" Plate	1.00----2.00
826	9, 7 oz. Goblet	2.00----3.00
952	Cocktail	2.00----3.00
846	Sherry	2.00----3.00
847	Wine	2.00----3.00
315	Finger Bowl	2.00----3.00
1349	Finger Bowl	1.00----2.00
	Finger Bowl Plate	1.00----2.00
1499	Finger Bowl	1.00----2.00
1499	Finger Bowl Plate	1.00----2.00

1061	Cracker Jar & Cover, Optic	15.00--18.00
160½	Water Bottle, Cut Neck	12.00--15.00
820	Tumbler	2.00----2.50
833	10 oz. Tumbler, Sham	2.00----2.50
833	8 oz. Tumbler, Sham.	2.00----2.50
833	7 oz. Sham	2.00----2.50
833	5 oz. Light	2.00----2.50
889	5 oz. Tumbler	2.00----2.50
889	8 oz. Tumbler	2.00----2.50
887	3 oz. Tumbler	2.00----2.50
701	16 oz. Ice Tea	2.00----3.00
	Ice Tea Plate	1.00----2.00
480	Custard	2.00----3.00
481	Custard	2.00----3.00
482	Custard	2.00----3.00
1227	Custard	2.00----3.00
1239	Custard	2.00----3.00
1240	Custard	2.00----3.00
1241	Custard	2.00----3.00
	Custard Plate	1.00----2.00
1227	Punch Bowl & Foot	30.00--35.00
863	10½, 9, 7 oz. Goblet	2.00----4.00
863	5½ oz. Tall Champagne	2.00----4.00
863	4½ oz. Claret	2.00----4.00
863	3 oz. Wine	2.00----4.00
863	1 oz. Cordial	2.00----4.00
863	4½ oz. Rhine Wine	2.00----4.00
863	2 oz. Sherry	2.00----4.00
863	5½ oz. Saucer Champagne	2.00----4.00
863	3½ oz. Cocktail	2.00----4.00
863	2½ oz. Creme de Menthe	2.00----4.00
863	¾ oz. Pousse Cafe	2.00----4.00
863	Fruit	2.00----3.00
863	Individual Almond	2.00----3.00
863	H.S. Champ'ne, Cut Flute	3.00----4.00
837	1 oz. Brandy	2.00----4.00
837	1 oz. Cordial	2.00----4.00
837	2 oz. Sherry	2.00----4.00
837	2½ oz. Creme de Menthe	2.00----4.00
837	3½ oz. Wine	2.00----4.00
837	4 oz. Cocktail	2.00----4.00
837	4½ oz. Claret	2.00----4.00
837	6½ oz. Claret	2.00----4.00
837	5½ oz. Tall Champagne	2.00----4.00
837	7 oz. Saucer Champagne	2.00----4.00
837	9 oz. Goblet	2.00----4.00
837½	10 oz. Goblet	2.00----4.00
873½	8 oz. Goblet	2.00----4.00
837½	Footed Tumbler	2.00----2.50
837	Sherbet	2.00----3.00
837	3, 5, 9 oz. Tumbler, Optic	2.00----2.50
791	Hollow Stem Champ'ne C.F.	3.00----4.00
792	Hollow Stem Champ'ne C.F.	3.00----4.00
793	Hollow Stem Champ'ne C.F.	3.00----4.00
840	Sherbet, Handled	2.00----3.00
923	Tumbler, Handled	2.00----3.00
945	Grape Fruit	2.00----3.00
945½	Grape Fruit	2.00----3.00
945½	Grape Fruit Liner	1.00----2.00
822	Cafe Parfait	2.00----3.00
1897	7" Plate	1.00----2.00
1733	Marmalade & Cover	6.00----9.00
1831	Mustard & Cover	8.00--10.00
823	4½" Fruit	1.00----2.00
823	5" Fruit	1.00----2.00
803	5", 6" Footed Comport	2.00----4.00
803	7" Footed Nappy, Deep	3.00----5.00
803	4½" Ftd. Nappy, Shallow.	3.00----5.00
803	5", 6", 7", Ftd. Nappy, Sh'w.	3.00----5.00
725	6" Vase	3.00----4.00
725	8" Vase	4.00----6.00

300½	Small Oil, C. S.	12.00--15.00
300½	Large Oil, C. S.	12.00--15.00
312	Oil, Cut Neck, C. S.	15.00--18.00
1465	Oil, Cut Neck, C. S.	15.00--18.00
1164	Oil, C. S.	12.00--15.00
1163	Catsup, C. S.	15.00--18.00
1227	Cream	3.00----5.00
1227	Sugar & Cover	5.00----8.00
1478	Cream	2.00----3.00
1478	Sugar, Two Handles	2.00----3.00
1480	Cream	3.00----5.00
1480	Sugar, Two Handles	3.00----5.00
1720	Cream	3.00----5.00
1720	Sugar	3.00----5.00
1759	Cream	3.00----5.00
1759	Sugar	3.00----5.00
300	Qt. Decanter, Cut Neck	10.00--12.00
300	Pt. Decanter, Cut Neck	10.00--12.00
1195	Large Decanter, Cut Neck	10.00--12.00
1195	Med. Decanter, Cut Neck	10.00--12.00
1195	Small Decanter, Cut Neck	10.00--12.00
1491	25 oz. Decanter, C.N., Optic	10.00--15.00
1464	18 oz. Decanter, Cut Neck	10.00--12.00
1464	10 oz. Decanter, Cut Neck	10.00--12.00
1464	10 oz. Decanter, C. N., C. F.	10.00--12.00
1464	18 oz. Decanter, C. N., C. F.	10.00--15.00
1227	Punch Bowl and Foot	30.00--35.00
300	1, 2, 3, 3½, 4, 5, 6, 7 Tankard	10.00--17.00
300	Claret Tankard	20.00--25.00
724	6 Tankard	15.00--17.50
724	7 Tankard	15.00--17.50
303	7 Jug	15.00--17.50
318	7 Jug, Optic	15.00--17.50
1236	6 Jug	15.00--17.50
1761	Tankard	15.00--18.00
300	7 Tankard, Cut Flute	14.00--20.00
803	8" Ftd. Nappy, Shallow	6.00----8.00
315	4" Nappy	2.00----3.00
315	4½" Nappy	2.00----3.00
315	5" Nappy	2.00----3.00
315	6" Nappy	2.00----4.00
315	7" Nappy	2.00----4.00
315	8" Nappy	4.00----6.00
315	9" Nappy	5.00----7.00
315	10" Nappy	6.00----8.00
1227	4½" Nappy	2.00----3.00
1227	8" Nappy	6.00----8.00
1281	5" Ice Cream	2.00----3.00
826	9 oz., 7 oz. Goblet	2.00----3.00
826	9 oz., 7 oz., Goblet, C. S.	3.00----4.00
952	Cocktail	10.00--12.00
1132	Horseradish	4.00----6.00
1165	Shaker, Silver Plated Top	3.00----5.00
1483	Individual Decanter	8.00--10.00
1483	Individual Decanter, C. N.	9.00--11.00
922	Toothpick, Sham Punty	6.00----8.00
403	Mustard & Cover	6.00----8.00
403	Toothpick	4.00----6.00
1931	Cream & Cover	3.00----5.00
1931	Sugar & Cover	3.00----5.00
725	10" Vase	6.00----8.00
725	12" Vase	8.00--10.00
1558	Water Bottle, Cut Neck	12.00--15.00
820	Tumbler	2.00----3.00
823	4" Fruit	1.00----2.00
803	4½" Footed Nappy, Deep	2.00----3.00
863	1 oz. Brandy	2.00----3.00
863	Parfait	2.00----3.00
863	4: oz. Roemer	2.00----3.00
863	5 oz. Roemer	2.00----3.00

863	Almond	2.00----3.00
858	5½ oz. Saucer Champagne	3.00----4.00

DEEP PLATE ETCHING NO. 205
"BLACKBERRY"

858	Custard	4.00----5.00
858	Custard Plate	1.00----2.00
858	Finger Bowl	2.00----3.00
858	Finger Bowl Plate	1.00----2.00
858	3½ oz. Whiskey	3.00----4.00
858	5 oz. Mineral	3.00----4.00
858	Table Tumbler	2.00----3.00
858	8 oz. Split Beer	2.00----3.00
858	10 oz. Strained Lemonade	3.00----4.00
858	16 oz. Lemonade	3.00----4.00
858	Lemonade Plate	2.00----3.00
858	11 oz. Goblet	3.00----5.00
858	10 oz. Goblet	3.00----4.00
858	9 oz. Goblet	3.00----4.00
858	6½ oz. Claret	3.00----4.00
858	4½ oz. Claret	3.00----4.00
858	3½ oz. Wine	3.00----4.00
858	2 oz. Sherry	3.00----4.00
858	1 oz. Cordial	3.00----4.00
858	7 oz. Saucer Champagne	3.00----4.00
858	Hollow Stem Champ'ne C.F.	4.00----5.00
858	5½ oz. Tall Champagne	3.00----4.00
858	4 oz. Hot Whiskey	3.00----4.00
858	1 oz. Brandy	3.00----4.00
858	3½ oz. Cocktail	3.00----4.00
858	2½ oz. Creme de Menthe	3.00----4.00
858	Sherbet	2.00----3.00
858	4½" Ice Cream	2.00----3.00
5008	11 oz. Goblet	3.00----4.00
5008	10 oz. Goblet	3.00----4.00
5008	9 oz. Goblet	3.00----4.00
5008	6½ oz. Claret	3.00----4.00
5008	4½ oz. Claret	3.00----4.00
5008	3½ oz. Wine	3.00----4.00
5008	2 oz. Sherry	3.00----4.00
5008	1 oz. Cordial	3.00----4.00
5008	6 oz. Saucer Champagne	3.00----4.00
5008	5½ oz. Tall Champagne	3.00----4.00
5008	4 oz. Hot Whiskey	3.00----4.00
5008	3½ oz. Cocktail	3.00----4.00
5008	2½ oz. Creme de Menthe	3.00----4.00
5008	1 oz. Pousse Cafe	3.00----4.00
5008	Egg	3.00----4.00
5008	Sherbet	3.00----4.00
300	5, 6, 7 Tankard	18.00--22.00
303	5, 6, 7 Jug	18.00--22.00
318	7 Jug, Optic	17.00--20.00
1236	5 Jug	15.00--18.00
1236	6 Jug	15.00--18.00
1236	7 Jug	17.00--20.00
820	Tumbler	2.00----3.00
820½	Tumbler, Half Sham	2.00----3.00
833	8 oz. Sham.	2.00----3.00
1478	Cream	3.00----5.00
1478	Sugar	3.00----5.00
1480	Cream	3.00----5.00
1480	Sugar	3.00----5.00
300½	Small Oil, C. S.	18.00--20.00
300½	Large Oil, C. S.	18.00--22.00
315	Finger Bowl	2.00----3.00
1165	Shaker, Silver Plated Top	4.00----5.00
840	Sherbet	2.00----3.00
932	Saucer Champagne	3.00----4.00

1227	Punch Bowl & Foot	30.00--40.00
315	4'', 4½'', 5'', 6'', 7'', 8''	
	9'' Nappy	2.00----8.00
300	Pt. Decanter, Cut Neck . .	15.00--20.00
300	Qt. Decanter, Cut Neck . .	15.00--20.00
1464	10 oz. Decanter, Cut Neck	15.00--20.00
1464	18 oz. Decanter, Cut Neck	15.00--20.00
1464	10 oz. Decanter, C. N. &	
	C. F.	18.00--20.00
1464	18 oz. Decanter, C. N. &	
	C. F.	18.00--20.00

SHAKERS

475	Shaker	1.00----2.00
614	Shaker	1.00----2.00
713	Shaker	1.00----2.00
1577	Shaker	2.00----3.00
1314	Shaker w/German Silver	
	S. P. Top	2.00----3.00
1685	Shaker Pressed C. S. . .	2.00----3.00
800	Shaker Etched B	2.00----3.00
713	Shaker Etched B	2.00----3.00
187	Shaker Large	1.00----2.00
187	Shaker Medium	1.00----2.00
180	Shaker	1.00----2.00
187½	Shaker	1.00----2.00
518	Shaker	1.00----2.00
1056	Shaker	1.00----2.00
505	Shaket Et. Intaglio Cut 1.	2.00----3.00
504	Shaker Et. Intaglio Cut 1.	2.00----3.00
800	Shaker Cut 1	1.00----2.00
800	Shaker Cut 5	2.00----3.00
800	Shaker Cut 4	2.00----3.00
800	Shaker Cut 2	2.00----3.00
713	Shaker Cut 5	2.00----3.00
713	Shaker Cut 2	2.00----3.00
713	Shaker Cut 4	2.00----3.00

MISC.

300½	Cut S < > and Fan	
	Capacity 6½ oz.	12.00--15.00
300½	Small Cut 42, Capacity	
	6½oz.	12.00--15.00
300½	Small Cut 20, Capacity	
	6½ oz.	12.00--15.00
1711	Cigar Jar, Cut 77, Cut Star	15.00--20.00
1711	Cigar Jar, Cut 36, Cut Star	15.00--20.00
1128	Decanter Cut Stopper, Cut	
	50, Capacity 37 oz. . .	20.00--25.00

BLOWN JUGS

127	Tumbler Cut 36	2.00----3.00
300	No. 7 Tankard Cut 36 w/	
	Fan Star	20.00--25.00
724	No. 7 Jug, Cut 36, w/Fan	
	Star	20.00--25.00
300	No. 7 Tankard, Cut Straw-	
	berry Diamond & Fan	20.00--25.00

MISC.

1137	Decanter Cut Stopper, Cut	
	51, Capacity 50 oz. . .	20.00--30.00
1136	Decanter Cut Stopper, Cut	
	53, Capacity 40 oz. . .	20.00--30.00
1135	Decanter Cut Stopper, Cut	
	52, Capacity 48 oz. . .	20.00--30.00

CUT NO. 11 SMALL SUNBURST STAR

No. 7	Cut 11	15.00--17.50
No. 6	Tankard	15.00--17.00
No. 5	Tankard	14.00--16.00
No. 4	Tankard	12.00--15.00
No. 3½	Tankard	12.00--14.00
No. 3	Tankard	10.00--12.00
No. 2	Tankard	9.00--12.00
No. 1	Tankard	8.00--10.00
300	Claret	20.00--30.00
820	Tumbler	2.00----4.00
820½	Sham. Tumbler	2.00----4.00
889	8 oz. Tumbler	2.00----4.00
833	8 oz. ½ Sh. Tumbler, Bell	2.00----4.00
981	2½ oz. Sham. Tumbler, Bell	2.00----4.00
315	Blown Finger Bowl	2.00----3.00
200	6'' Finger Bowl Plate . .	2.00----3.00
Any	Blown Custard	2.00----3.00
200	5'' Custard Plate	2.00----3.00
300½	Large Oil, Cut Stopper . .	12.00--15.00
300½	Small Oil, Cut Stopper . .	12.00--15.00
1465	Oil, Cut N'k & Stopper . .	12.00--15.00
1480	Sugar	3.00----5.00
1480	Cream	3.00----5.00
160½	Water Bottle, Cut Neck . .	12.00--15.00
1332	Water Bottle, Cut Neck . .	12.00--15.00
319	Bar Bottle	3.00----5.00
319	Bar Bottle, Cut Neck . . .	4.00----6.00
315	10'' Nappy	6.00----8.00
315	9'' Nappy	5.00----8.00
315	8'' Nappy	5.00----7.00
315	7'' Nappy	5.00----7.00
315	6'' Nappy	4.00----5.00
315	5'' Nappy	3.00----4.00
315	4½'' Nappy	2.00----3.00
315	4'' Nappy	2.00----3.00
1195	Large Decanter, Cut N'k .	18.00--20.00
300	Quart Decanter, Cut N'k .	18.00--20.00
1132	Horseradish	8.00--10.00
1165	Shaker, S. P. Top	4.00----6.00
810	Sherbet	2.00----3.00
840	Sherbet	2.00----3.00
841	Sherbet	2.00----3.00
840	Sherbet	2.00----3.00
841	Sherbet	2.00----3.00
826	Goblet	3.00----4.00
810	9 oz. Goblet	3.00----4.00
810	9 oz. Goblet	3.00----4.00
801	10 oz. Goblet	3.00----4.00
801	10 oz. Goblet	3.00----4.00
801	9 oz. Goblet	3.00----4.00
801	9 oz. Goblet	3.00----4.00
932	Saucer Champagne	3.00----4.00
825	Saucer Champagne	3.00----4.00
801	3 oz. Wine	3.00----4.00
952	Cocktail	3.00----4.00
1227	8'' Nappy	6.00----8.00
1227	4½'' Nappy	2.00----4.00
845	Hot Whiskey	3.00----4.00
837	2 oz. Wine	3.00----4.00
858	Hollow Stem Champagne	3.00----4.00
858	7 oz. Champagne	3.00----4.00
481	Custard	2.00----3.00
315	Finger Bowl Plate	2.00----3.00

CUTTING NO. 77

300	7, 6, 5, 4 Tankard	12.00--20.00
300	3½, 3, 2, 1 Tankard	8.00--10.00

300	Claret	20.00--25.00
724	7, 6 Tankard	18.00--22.00
1236	7 Tankard	18.00--20.00
303	7 Tankard	18.00--20.00
1743	5 Cover Tankard	18.00--22.00
160½	Water Bottle, C. N.	12.00--15.00
300	Quart Decanter, C. N.	15.00--20.00
801	11 oz, 10 oz, 9 oz, 5 oz, 4 oz, 3 oz, 2 oz, 1 oz, Stemware	3.00----4.00
801	¾ oz. Cordial	3.00----4.00
801	¾ oz. Liquor	3.00----4.00
858	11 oz, 10 oz, 9 oz. Goblet	3.00----4.00
858	6½ oz. Claret	3.00----4.00
858	4½ oz. Claret	3.00----4.00
858	3½ oz. Wine	3.00----4.00
858	2¾ oz. Wine	3.00----4.00
858	2 oz. Sherry	3.00----4.00
858	1 oz. Cordial	3.00----4.00
858	7 oz. Saucer Champagne	3.00----4.00
858	Hollow Stem Champ'ne, C.F.	3.00----4.00
858	5½ oz. Tall Champagne	3.00----4.00
858	4 oz. Hot Whiskey	3.00----4.00
858	1 oz. Brandy	3.00----4.00
858	3½ oz. Cocktail	3.00----4.00
858	2½ oz. Creme de Menthe	3.00----4.00
858	Sherbet	2.00----3.00
858	Fruit Salad	2.00----3.00
858	4½" Ice Cream	2.00----3.00
858	Long Stem Champagne	4.00----6.00
932	Saucer Champagne	3.00----4.00
952	3 oz. Cocktail	3.00----4.00
840	Sherbet	2.00----3.00
843	Sherbet	2.00----3.00
846	Sherry	3.00----4.00
863	Fruit	2.00----3.00
820	Tumbler	2.00----3.00
833	10 oz, 7 oz Tumbler, Sham	2.00----3.00
889	5 oz. Tumbler	2.00----3.00
887	3 oz. Tumbler	2.00----3.00
858	Finger Bowl	2.00----3.00
315	Finger Bowl	2.00----3.00
315	Finger Bowl Plate	1.00----2.00
315	7" Nappy	4.00----6.00
315	8" Nappy	4.00----6.00
300½	Large Oil, C. S.	12.00--15.00
1465	Oil C. N.	12.00--15.00
1227	Punch Bowl & Foot	30.00--40.00
1227	Custard	2.00----3.00
1227	8" Nappy	4.00----6.00
1227	Sugar & Cover	5.00----8.00
1227	Cream	3.00----5.00
725	8", 10", 12" Vase	10.00--15.00
1120	12" Vase	12.00--15.00
1711	Cigar Jar & Cover, Cut 77	15.00--20.00
1711	Cigar Jar & Cover, Cut 36	15.00--20.00

ENGRAVED NO. 23

	No. 7, 6, 5, 4 Jug, Engraved No. 23	15.00--20.00
	No. 3½, 3, 2, 1 Jug	10.00--15.00
300	Claret Jug	20.00--25.00
160½	Water Bottle, C. N.	12.00--15.00
300½	Large Oil, Cut Stopper	12.00--15.00
480	Custard	3.00----4.00
1136	Decanter, Cut Stopper	20.00--25.00
315	Finger Bowl	1.00----2.00
820	Tumbler	2.00----3.00
833	10, 8, 7 oz. Tumbler, Sham	2.00----3.00
889	5 oz. Tumbler	2.00----3.00

887	3 oz. Tumbler	2.00----3.00
801	10, 9, 5, 4, 3, 2, 1 oz.	2.00----3.00
801	¾ oz. Liquor	3.00----4.00
801	¾ oz. Cordial	3.00----4.00
932	Saucer Champagne	3.00----4.00
952	3 oz. Cocktail	3.00----4.00
840	Sherbet	2.00----3.00
845	Hot Whiskey	3.00----4.00
846	Sherry	3.00----4.00
847	Wine	3.00----4.00
481	Custard	2.00----3.00
1227	Cream	3.00----5.00
1227	Sugar & Cover	5.00----8.00
1478	Cream	3.00----4.00
1478	Sugar	3.00----4.00

CUTTING NO. 81
LARGE SUNBURST STAR

863	10 oz. Goblet	3.00----4.00
863	9 oz. Goblet	3.00----4.00
863	5½ oz. Saucer Champagne	3.00----4.00
863	Fruit	3.00----4.00
1736	6" Fruit Plate	2.00----3.00
766½	Parfait	3.00----4.00
863	4½ oz. Claret	3.00----4.00
863	3 oz. Wine	3.00----4.00
863	1 oz. Cordial	3.00----4.00
863	3½ oz. Cocktail	3.00----4.00
863	Almond	3.00----4.00
858	Custard	2.00----3.00
858	Finger Bowl	2.00----3.00
858	F. Bowl Plate (1499-6)	1.00----2.00
315	Finger Bowl	2.00----3.00
481	Custard	2.00----3.00
826	9 oz. Goblet	3.00----4.00
932	Saucer Champagne	3.00----4.00
840	Sherbet	2.00----3.00
842	Sherbet	2.00----3.00
952	Cocktail	3.00----4.00
846	2 oz. Sherry	3.00----4.00
945½	Grape Fruit	3.00----4.00
945½	Grape Fruit Liner	3.00----4.00
858	Sweet Meat	3.00----4.00
880	4½ Bon Bon	3.00----4.00
825	Saucer Champagne	3.00----4.00
825	Jelly & Cover	5.00----8.00
803	5" Footed Nappy & Cover	6.00----9.00
803	5" Fted. Comport & Cover	6.00----9.00
803	5" Comport	2.00----4.00
803	6" Comport	2.00----4.00
803	4½" Footed Nappy	2.00----3.00
803	5" Footed Nappy	2.00----3.00
803	6" Footed Nappy	3.00----5.00
803	7" Footed Nappy	6.00----8.00
315	4½" Nappy	2.00----3.00
315	8" Nappy	8.00--10.00
1227	4½" Nappy	2.00----3.00
1227	8" Nappy	8.00--10.00
820	Table Tumbler	2.00----3.00
820	Table Tumbler, ½ Sham.	2.00----3.00
833	8 oz. Tumbler, ½ Sham	2.00----3.00
701	14 oz. Tumbler	2.00----3.00
701	5" Tumbler Plate	2.00----3.00
858	Table Tumbler	2.00----3.00
858	8 oz. Tumbler	2.00----3.00
858	14 oz. Tumbler	2.00----3.00
858	16 oz. Tumbler	2.00----4.00
4011	12 oz. Tumbler, Punty	2.00----3.00
4011	12 oz. Handld. Tumbler, Post	3.00----5.00

No.	Description	Price
4011½	Table Tumbler, Punty	2.00----3.00
889	5 oz. Tumbler, Punty	2.00----3.00
	All Tumblers Cut 81 are Puntied.	
880	11, 10, 9, 8 oz. Goblet	3.00----4.00
880	5 oz. Tall Champagne	3.00----4.00
880	6½ oz. Claret	3.00----4.00
880	4½ oz. Claret	3.00----4.00
880	3½ oz. Wine	3.00----4.00
880	2¾ oz. Wine	3.00----4.00
880	2 oz Sherry	3.00----4.00
880	1 oz Cordial	3.00----4.00
880	¾ oz Cordial	3.00----4.00
880	6½ oz Tall Ale	3.00----4.00
880	4½ oz Hot Whiskey	3.00----4.00
880	4 oz Rhine Wine	3.00----4.00
880	1 oz Pousse Cafe	3.00----4.00
880	¾ oz Pousse Cafe	3.00----4.00
880	2½ oz Creme de Menthe	3.00----4.00
880	3 oz Cocktail	3.00----4.00
880	3½ oz Cocktail	3.00----4.00
880	4½ oz H. S. Champgn. C.F.	4.00----6.00
880	5 oz Saucer Champagne	3.00----4.00
880	7 oz Saucer Champagne	3.00----4.00
880	4½" Bon Bon	3.00----4.00
880½	Grape Fruit	2.00----3.00
880	Grape Fruit	2.00----3.00
880½	Grape Fruit Liner	2.00----3.00
880	Grape Fruit Liner	2.00----3.00
880	Sherbet	2.00----3.00
1163	Catsup, C.S.	15.00--18.00
801	11, 10, 9, 5, 4, 3, 2, 1 oz. Goblet	3.00----4.00
801	¾ oz Cordial	3.00----4.00
801	¾ oz. Liquor	3.00----4.00
858	11, 10, 9 oz Goblet	3.00----4.00
858	6½, 4½ oz. Claret	3.00----4.00
858	3½, 2¾ oz. Wine	3.00----4.00
858	2 oz. Sherry	3.00----4.00
858	1 oz. Cordial	3.00----4.00
858	7 oz. Saucer Champagne	3.00----4.00
858	H. S. Champ'ne, C. F.	4.00----6.00
858	5½ oz. Tall Champagne	3.00----4.00
858	4 oz. Hot Whiskey	3.00----4.00
858	1 oz. Brandy	3.00----4.00
858	3½ oz. Cocktail	3.00----4.00
858	2½ oz. Creme de Menthe	3.00----4.00
858	Sherbet	2.00----3.00
858	Fruit Salad	2.00----3.00
858	4½" Ice Cream	2.00----3.00
858	Long Stem Champagne	3.00----5.00
858	Long Stem Champ. C.R.	4.00----6.00
863	10½ oz. Goblet	3.00----4.00
1227	Sugar, No Cover	3.00----4.00
1227	Sugar, Plain Cover	4.00----5.00
1227	Sugar & Cover	5.00----8.00
1227	Cream	3.00----5.00
1478	Sugar, Two Handles	3.00----4.00
1478	Cream	3.00----4.00
1480	Sugar Two Handles	3.00----5.00
1480	Cream	3.00----5.00
1712	Cream	3.00----5.00
1712	Sugar	3.00----5.00
1720	Cream	3.00----5.00
1720	Sugar	3.00----5.00
1759	Cream	3.00----5.00
1759	Sugar	3.00----5.00
1132	Horseradish	10.00--12.00
930	5 oz. Tall Sherbet	3.00----4.00
932	Champagne	3.00----4.00
932	Champagne	3.00----4.00
825	Champagne	3.00----4.00
952	Cocktail	3.00----4.00
844	Hot Whiskey	3.00----4.00
845	Hot Whiskey	3.00----4.00
846	Sherry	3.00----4.00
847	Wine	3.00----4.00
863	¾ oz. Pousse Cafe	3.00----4.00
724	7 Jug, Large Stars	25.00-30.00
724	7 Jug, Small Stars	25.00-30.00
303	7 Jug, Large Stars	20.00-25.00
303	7 Jug, Small Stars	20.00-25.00
1236	6 Jug, Large Stars	20.00-25.00
315	4" Nappy	2.00----3.00
820½	Tumbler, Half Sham, puntied	2.00----3.00
833	Bell, 3, 6, 8, 10 oz. Half Sham, puntied	2.00----3.00
981	2½ oz. Sham, puntied	2.00----3.00
981	12 oz. Half Sham, puntied	2.00----3.00
923	Handled Tumbler	3.00----4.00
858	3½ oz. Whiskey	4.00----5.00
858	5 oz. Mineral	2.00----3.00
858	Table Tumbler	2.00----3.00
858	6½, 8, 10, 12, 14, 16 oz. Tall	2.00----4.00
858	Tumbler Plate	2.00----3.00
300	1, 2, 3, 3½, 4, 5, Tankard	10.00--15.00
300	6, 7 Tankard, Lg. Stars	15.00--20.00
300	6, 7 Tankard, Med. Stars	15.00--20.00
300	7, 1, 2 Tankard	10.00--15.00
300	3, 3½, 4, 5 Tankard	10.00--15.00
300	6, 7, 8 Tankard	15.00--20.00
300	Claret	20.00--25.00
303	2 Jug	8.00--10.00
303	3, 4, 5, 6, 7, 8 Jug	10.00--15.00
724	6, 7 Tankard	10.00--15.00
1227	7 Jug	15.00--20.00
1227	7 Jug, C. N.	20.00--25.00
1227	7 Jug 2 Stars on Neck, 5 Stars around body of Jug	20.00--25.00
160½	Water Bottle, C. N.	12.00--15.00
160½	Water Bottle, C. N.	12.00--15.00
304	Water Bottle, C. N.	12.00--15.00
1558	Water Bottle, C. N.	12.00--15.00
1558	Water Bottle, C. N.	12.00--15.00
810	9 oz. Goblet	3.00----4.00
810	7 oz. Saucer Champagne	3.00----4.00
810	5½ oz. Saucer Champagne	3.00----4.00
810	6 oz. Champagne	3.00----4.00
810	5½ oz. Claret	3.00----4.00
810	4½ oz. Claret	3.00----4.00
810	3 oz. Wine	3.00----4.00
810	3½ oz. Cocktail	3.00----4.00
810	2½ oz. Creme de Menthe	3.00----4.00
810	2 oz. Sherry	3.00----4.00
810	1 oz. Cordial	3.00----4.00
810	1 oz. Brandy	3.00----4.00
810	Sherbet	2.00----3.00
810	Finger Bowl	2.00----3.00
810	Finger Bowl	2.00----3.00
810	Custard	2.00----3.00
5008	11, 10, 9 oz. Goblet	3.00----4.00
5008	6½, 4½ oz. Claret	3.00----4.00
5008	3½ oz. Wine	3.00----4.00
5008	2 oz. Sherry	3.00----4.00
5008	1 oz. Cordial	3.00----4.00
5008	6 oz. Saucer Champagne	3.00----4.00
5008	5½ oz. Tall Champagne	3.00----4.00
5008	4 oz. Hot Whiskey	3.00----4.00
5008	3½ oz. Cocktail	3.00----4.00
5008	2½ oz. Creme de Menthe	3.00----4.00
5008	1 oz. Pousse Cafe	3.00----4.00
5008	Egg	3.00----4.00

5008	Sherbet	2.00----3.00
823	4½" Fruit	2.00----3.00
823	5" Fruit	2.00----3.00
803	4½" Ftd. Nappy Deep	2.00----4.00
403	Toothpick	8.00--10.00
1227	Punch Bowl & Foot	35.00--45.00
300	Qt. Decanter, C. N.	25.00-30.00
2194	8 oz. Syrup, N. T.	12.00--15.00
2194	12 oz. Syrup, N. T.	12.00--15.00
4069	9" Vase	8.00--10.00
1697	Caraffe	8.00--10.00
1697	Caraffe Tumbler (4023-6 oz)	3.00----4.00
1165½	Shaker, Pearl Top	4.00----6.00
614	Shaker, Pearl Top	4.00----6.00
2263	Individual Salt	4.00----6.00
922	Toothpick Punty C/19	8.00--10.00
1733	Marmalade & Cover	10.00--12.00
1831	Mustard & Cover	8.00--10.00
1227	9" Nappy	8.00--10.00
1694	8" Vase	6.00----8.00
1120	12" Vase	8.00--10.00
1120	15" Vase	10.00--14.00
725	6, 8, 10, 12" Vase	8.00--12.00
725	6, 8, 10, 12" Vase	10.00--15.00
1061	Cracker Jar & Cover	20.00--25.00
315	Straw Jar & Cover, plain	20.00--25.00
922	Toothpick, Cut Flute, Pty.	8.00--10.00
403	Toothpick	6.00----8.00
403	Mustard & Cover	8.00--10.00
1483	Individual Decanter	10.00--15.00
1483	Individual Decanter, C. N.	15.00--20.00
1165	Shaker, Silver-plated Top	2.00----3.00
1195	Lg. Decanter, C.N., C.S.	20.00--25.00
1195	Med. Decanter, C.N., C.S.	20.00--25.00
1195	Sm. Decanter, C.N., C.S.	15.00--20.00
300	Qt. Decanter, C.N., C.S.	20.00--25.00
300	Pt. Decanter, C.N., C.S.	20.00--25.00
1136	Decanter, Cut Stopper	20.00--25.00
1464	18 oz. Decanter, C.N., C.S.	25.00--30.00
1464	10 oz. Decanter, C.N., C.S.	20.00--25.00
1491	25 oz. Decanter, Optic C.N	25.00--30.00
858	Finger Bowl Plate	2.00----3.00
315	Finger Bowl	2.00----3.00
315	Finger Bowl Plate	1.00----2.00
1349	Finger Bowl	2.00----3.00
1499	Finger Bowl	2.00----3.00
1499	Finger Bowl Plate	1.00----2.00
601	Shaker, S.P.T.	4.00----5.00
1227	5, 6, 7" Nappy	2.00----3.00
843	Sherbet	2.00----3.00
840	Sherbet Plate	2.00----3.00
1389	Oyster Cocktail	2.00----3.00
1542	Oyster Cocktail	2.00----3.00
791	Hollow Stem Champagne C.F.	3.00----5.00
792	Hollow Stem Champagne, C.F.	3.00----5.00
793	Hollow Stem Champagne, C.F.	3.00----5.00
4025	Hiball Cut Flute	3.00----5.00
5013	Gin Rickey	2.00----4.00
945	Grape Fruit	2.00----3.00
453	4, 4½, 5, 6" Hdl. Nappy	2.00----4.00
803	6, 7, 8" Ftd. Nap., Shallow	4.00----6.00
863	H. S. Champagne, C.F.	3.00----5.00
858	Custard Plate	2.00----3.00
858	Finger Bowl	2.00----3.00
300½	Small Oil	12.00--15.00
1465	7 oz. Oil, Cut Neck	12.00--15.00
863	7 oz. Goblet	3.00----4.00
200	Custard Plate	1.00----2.00

312	Oil, C.S.	12.00--15.00
1164	Oil, C.S.	12.00--15.00
863	4½ oz. Rhine Wine	3.00----4.00
863	2 oz. Sherry	3.00----4.00
863	5½ oz. Tall Champagne	3.00----4.00
863	2½ oz. Creme de Menthe	3.00----4.00
315	9" Nappy	6.00----8.00
315	10" Nappy	7.00----9.00
315	5, 6, 7" Nappy	5.00----7.00

CUTTING NO. 104
DESIGN PATENT 39, 156

300	1, 2, 3, 3½ Tankard	10.00--15.00
300	4, 5, 6, 7 Tankard	15.00--20.00
300	Claret	25.00--30.00
318	7 Jug	15.00--20.00
724	7 Tankard	15.00--20.00
1227	7 Jug, Cut Neck	15.00--20.00
303	7 Jug	15.00--20.00
300½	7 Jug	20.00--25.00
160½	Water Bottle, C. N.	12.00--15.00
1558	Water Bottle, C. N.	12.00--15.00
481	Custard	2.00----3.00
1241	Custard	2.00----3.00
1598	Custard	2.00----3.00
200	Custard Plate	1.00----2.00
315	Finger Bowl	2.00----3.00
315	Finger Bowl Plate	1.00----2.00
300½	Small Oil, C. Stop	12.00--15.00
300½	Large Oil, C. Stop	12.00--15.00
312	Oil, Cut Stopper	12.00--15.00
1465	Oil, C.N. C.S.	12.00--15.00
1465	Oil Not C.N. C.S.	12.00--15.00
1227	Sugar, Cover Plain	3.00----5.00
1227	Cream	2.00----3.00
1478	Sugar	2.00----3.00
1478	Cream	2.00----3.00
1480	Sugar	2.00----3.00
1480	Cream	2.00----3.00
1759	Sugar	2.00----3.00
1759	Cream	2.00----3.00
453	4½, 5, 6" Hdl. Nappy	5.00----8.00
1666	Puff & Cut Cover	10.00--15.00
1904	Bon Bon & Cut Cover	12.00--15.00
1132	Horseradish	12.00--15.00
820	Tumbler	2.00----3.00
820½	Tumbler, Half Sham	2.00----3.00
887	3½ oz. Half Sham	2.00----3.00
887	5 oz. Half Sham	2.00----3.00
889	5 oz.	2.00----3.00
858	Custard	2.00----3.00
858	Finger Bowl	2.00----3.00
858	Finger Bowl Plate	1.00----2.00
858	3½, 5, 6½, 8, 10, 12, 14, 16 oz. Tumbler	2.00----3.00
858	Table Tumbler	2.00----3.00
858	Table Tumbler, Cut 19, 3, 5, 6½, 8, 10, 12, 14, 16 oz.	2.00----4.00
858	Tumbler Plate	1.00----2.00
858	11, 10, 9 oz. Goblet	3.00----4.00
858	6½, 4½ oz. Claret	3.00----4.00
858	3½, 2¾ oz. Wine	3.00----4.00
858	2 oz. Sherry	3.00----4.00
858	1 oz. Cordial	3.00----4.00
858	7 oz. Saucer Champagne	3.00----4.00
858	Hollow Stem Champ'ne C.F.	4.00----5.00
858	5½ oz. Tall Champagne	3.00----4.00
858	4 oz. Hot Whiskey	3.00----4.00
858	1 oz. Brandy	3.00----4.00

858	3½ oz. Cocktail	3.00----4.00
858	2½ oz. Creme de Menthe	3.00----4.00
858	Sherbet	2.00----3.00
858	Fruit Salad	2.00----3.00
858	4½" Ice Cream	2.00----3.00
833	6 oz. Half Sham	2.00----3.00
833	8 oz. Tumbler, ½ Sham	2.00----3.00
701	12 oz. Tumbler	2.00----3.00
220	2½ oz. Cut C.	2.00----3.00
230	2½ oz. Cut F.	2.00----3.00
74	Toddy Glass	3.00----4.00
5048	Hiball, Cut Flute	3.00----4.00
315	4", 4½", 5", 6" Nappy	2.00----4.00
315	7", 8", 9", 10" Nappy	5.00----8.00
1227	4½" Nappy	1.00----2.00
1227	8" Nappy	4.00----6.00
725	8", 10", 12" Vase,	6.00--10.00
315	Bitter, Cut Neck	15.00--18.00
725	8", 10", 12", Vase, Top and Bottom cut	8.00--15.00
1227	Punch Bowl & Foot	25.00--35.00
945½	Grape Fruit	2.00----3.00
945	Grape Fruit	2.00----3.00
945½	Grape Fruit Lining	2.00----3.00
823	4" Fruit	2.00----3.00
823	5" Fruit	2.00----3.00
803	4", 5", 6", 7" Footed Nappy Deep	3.00----4.00
803	4", 5", 6", 7" Footed Nappy, Shallow	3.00----4.00
1165	Shaker, Silver Plated Top	2.00----3.00
300	Pint Decanter, Cut Neck	20.00--25.00
300	Quart Decanter, Cut Neck	25.00--30.00

MISC.

No. 1	Round Floating Island Flower Tray	4.00----6.00
No. 2048	Blown Stein 17 oz.	4.00----6.00
No. 2049	Blown Stein Capacity 16 oz.	4.00----5.00
No. 840	6 oz. Sherbet & Plate 5¼"	2.00----3.00
No. 1735	4 oz. Oyster Cocktail	3.00----4.00
No. 5051	Cheese & Cracker Plate	3.00----4.00
No. 863	Fruit & Plate 5½ oz.	2.00----3.00
No. 701	14 oz. Ice Tea Cracquelled Glass	1.00----2.00
No. 303	No. 8 Jug 84 oz. Cracquelled Glass	15.00--17.50

No. 1704 ROSBY PATTERN
Also Gold Decorated

1704	Sugar & Cover	15.00--20.00
1704	Butter & Cover	20.00--25.00
1704	Cream	12.00--15.00
1704	Spoon	12.00--15.00
1704	½ Gal. Pitcher	20.00--25.00
1704	Tumbler	5.00----7.50
1704	Finger Bowl	4.00----5.00
1704	8" Berry, Regular	10.00--12.50
1704	7" Berry, Regular	10.00--12.50
1704	4½" Berry	4.00----5.00
1704	8" Comport, Regular	10.00--12.50
1704	8" Comport, Belled	10.00--12.50
1704	8" Comport Star	10.00--12.50
1704	10" Berry, Regular	12.00--15.00
1704	10" Berry, Belled	12.00--15.00
1704	10" Berry, Cupped	12.00--15.00
1704	4½" Dp. Hld. Nappy, Reg.	7.00----8.00
1704	4½" Dp. Hld. Nappy, Sq.	8.00--10.00
1704	4½" Dp. Hld. Nappy, 3 c'n'r	8.00----9.00

1704	7" Square Nappy	5.00----6.00
1704	7" sq. Nappy, partitioned	6.00----8.00
1704	8" Pickle Dish	5.00----6.00
1704	6" Olive Tray	4.00----5.00
1704	Celery Tray	7.00----8.00
1704	7" Oval Dish	4.00----6.00
1704	8" Oval Dish	5.00----7.00
1704	9" Oval Dish	6.00----8.00
1704	Toothpick	8.00----9.00
1704	Cracker Jar, No Cover	15.00--20.00
1704	Cracker Jar & Cover	20.00--25.00
1704	Pickle Jar & Cover	15.00--20.00
1704	6 oz. Vinegar, Drop Stop.	15.00--17.50
1704	6 oz. Vinegar, Cut Stop.	15.00--18.00
1704	Mayonnaise	6.00----8.00
1704	12" Oval Salad	8.00--12.00
1704	Flower Bowl & N. Mesh	6.00----8.00
1704	Molasses can, Large—	
	With Brittania Top	20.00--25.00
	With Ewer Nickel Top	20.00--25.00
	With Ewer S.P. Top	20.00--25.00
1704	5" Plate	3.00----4.00
1704	Syrup, S.P. Top & Handle	25.00--30.00
1704	Shaker, "Tall"	
	With Fostoria Glass top	5.00----7.50
	With Heavy Nickel Top	5.00----7.50
	With Silver Plate Top	5.00----7.50
1704½	Shaker, Cut Shut, w/Fostoria Glass, Heavy Nickel, Silver Plate Top	4.00----5.00
1704	4½" High Ft. Jelly, Reg.	10.00--12.00
1704	4½" High Ft. Jelly, Star	10.00--12.00
1704	4½" High Ft. Jelly, Sq.	10.00--12.00
1704	5" Low Ft. Jelly, Reg.	10.00--12.00
1704	5" Low Ft. Jelly, Star	10.00--12.00
1704	5" Low Ft. Jelly, Sq.	10.00--12.00
1704	Custard P.H.	4.00----5.00
1704	15" Punch Bowl, No Ft.	20.00--25.00
1704	15" Punch Bowl & Foot	30.00--35.00
1704	10" Punch Bowl, No Ft.	15.00--20.00
1704	10" Punch Bowl & Foot	20.00--30.00
1704	16" Punch Bowl, No Ft.	25.00--30.00
1704	16" Punch Bowl & Foot	35.00--40.00

New Pieces made between 1974-78.   List Price

1704	10" Serving Plate	$23.75
1704	Footed Preserve	11.50
1704	10¼" Relish Tray	15.25
1704	7½" Bowl	21.00
1704	Sugar & Cover	12.50
1704	Cream	10.00
1704	16" Punch Bowl	30.00
	Punch Bowl Foot	13.50
1704	Punch Cups	4.50
1704	Handled Nappy, Regular	8.50

No. 1819 I. C. PATTERN

1819	Sugar & Cover	20.00--25.00
1819	Butter & Cover	30.00--35.00
1819	Cream	15.00--20.00
1819	Spoon	15.00--20.00
1819½	½ Gal. Pitcher	30.00--35.00
1819	½ Gal. Ice Jug	30.00--35.00
1819	Tumbler	10.00--12.50
1819	Ice Tea Tumbler	10.00--12.50
1819	Finger Bowl	5.00----6.00
1819	Finger Bowl Plate	2.00----3.00
1819	4½" Berry	4.00----5.00

1819	4¾" Berry	4.00----5.00
1819	5" Deep Nappy	5.00----6.00
1819	6" Deep Nappy	10.00--12.00
1819	7" Deep Nappy	12.00--15.00
1819	8" Deep Nappy	15.00--20.00
1819	10" Deep Nappy	20.00--25.00
1819	5" Nappy, flared to 6"	5.00----6.00
1819	6" Nappy, flared to 8"	10.00--12.00
1819	7" Nappy, flared to 9"	12.00--15.00
1819	8" Nappy, flared to 10"	15.00--20.00
1819	10" Nappy, flared to 12"	20.00--25.00
1819	Celery Tray	8.00----9.00
1819	Olive	4.00----5.00
1819	Pickle	6.00----7.50
1819	Toothpick	12.00--15.00
1819	8 oz. Oil & Stop. ground	20.00--25.00
1819	6 oz. Oil & Stop. ground	18.00--22.00
1819	4 oz. Oil & Stop. ground	18.00--20.00
1819	8 oz. Oil & Stop., drop	20.00--25.00
1819	6 oz. Oil & Stop., drop	18.00--22.00
1819	4 oz. Oil & Stop., drop	18.00--20.00
1819	Shaker No. 1—	
	With Heavy Nickel Top	8.00--10.00
	With Silver Plated Top	8.00--10.00
	With Non-Corrosive Top	8.00--10.00
	With Pearl Top	8.00--10.00
	With Glass Top	8.00--10.00
1819	Shaker No. 2—	
	With Heavy Nickel Top	8.00--10.00
	With Silver Plated Top	8.00--10.00
	With Non-Corrosive Top	8.00--10.00
	With Pearl Top	8.00--10.00
	With Glass Top	8.00--10.00
1819	Molasses Can—	
	With Ewer Nickel Top	30.00--35.00
	With Ewer Silver Top	30.00--35.00
1819	Molasses Can Plate	3.00----5.00
1819	Syrup w/Metal Top & Handle	
	Nickel Plated	30.00--35.00
	Silver Plated	30.00--35.00
1819	Sugar Shaker—	
	Nickel Top	20.00--25.00
	Silver Plated Top	20.00--25.00
1819	Hotel Cream	15.00--17.50
1819	Hotel Sugar, two handles	15.00--17.50
1819	Footed Jelly	20.00--22.00
1819	Footed Sherbet	6.00----7.50
1819	10" Deep Punch Bowl & Stand	40.00--50.00
1819	10" Punch Bowl & Stand flared to 12"	50.00--60.00
1819	Custard	5.00----6.00

No. 1827 RAMBLER PATTERN

1827	4½" Berry	4.00----5.00
1827	4¾" Berry	4.00----5.00
1827	8" Deep Nappy	12.00--15.00
1827	10" Deep Nappy	15.00--20.00
1827	8" Nappy, flared to 10"	15.00--18.00
1827	10" Nappy, flared to 12"	20.00--25.00
1827½—½ Gal. Pitcher		20.00--25.00
1827	Tumbler	10.00--12.50
1827	Custard	5.00----6.00
1827	10" Dp. Punch Bowl & St.	40.00--50.00
1827	10" Punch Bowl & Stand, flared to 12"	50.00--60.00
1827	13" Vase	15.00--20.00
1827	7" Vase	10.00--15.00
1827	9" Vase	12.00--15.00

No. 1861 LINCOLN PATTERN

1861	Sugar & Cover	8.00--10.00
1861	Butter & Cover	12.00--15.00
1861	Cream	8.00----9.00
1861	Spoon	8.00----9.00
1861½—2 handled Sugar & Cover		10.00--12.50
1861½—2 handled Spoon		8.00--10.00
1861	½ Gal. Pitcher	12.00--15.00
1861	Tumbler	2.00----2.50
1861	14 oz. Tea Tumbler	2.00----3.00
1861	5" Ice Tea Plate	1.00----2.00
1861	17 oz. Ice Tea Tumbler	3.00----4.00
1861	6" Finger Bowl Plate	1.00----2.00
1861	Finger Bowl	2.00----3.00
1861	Water Bottle	8.00--10.00
1861	4" Comport	1.00----2.00
1861	4½" Comport	2.00----2.50
1861	6" Comport	2.00----3.00
1861	6" Comport & Cover	10.00--12.00
1861	7" Comport	3.00----4.00
1861	8" Comport	4.00----5.00
1861	8" Comport, Reg. & Cover	12.00--14.00
1861	8" Comport, Dp. & Cover	14.00--16.00
1861	4½" Comport & Cover	6.00----8.00
1861	7" Oval Dish	2.00----2.50
1861	8" Oval Dish	2.00----3.00
1861	9" Oval Dish	3.00----4.00
1861	10" Oval Dish	4.00----5.00
1861	Olive Tray	1.00----2.00
1861	Pickle Tray	2.00----3.00
1861	Celery Tray	3.00----4.00
1861	Celery, Tall	8.00--10.00
1861½—Celery Dip, Small		2.00----3.00
1861	Celery Dip, Small	2.00----3.00
1861	Footed Ind. Nut	1.00----2.00
1861	Nut Bowl	2.00----3.00
1861	Mustard & Cover	10.00--12.00
1861½—Mustard & Cover, Small		8.00--10.00
1861	Horseradish & Ground Stop.	8.00--10.00
1861	Chow Chow & Ground Stop.	7.00----9.00
1861	Catsup & Ground Stop.	10.00--14.00
1861	6 oz. Tall Oil & Gr. Stop.	10.00--12.00
1861	6 oz. Squat Oil & Gr. Stop.	12.00--15.00
1861	Shaker, Large, No. 1— w/Heavy Nickel, Silver Plated, "G" & "R" top	2.00----3.00
1861	Shaker, Small, No. 2— w/Heavy Nickel, Silver Plated, Non-corrosive, & "P" Top	2.00----3.00
1861	Shaker, No. 5— w/Heavy Nickel, Silver Plated, "W", & Star Glass Top	2.00----3.00
1861	Syrup Can, w/Metal Handle	
	Screw Top, Nickel Plat.	20.00--25.00
	Screw Top, Silver Plat.	20.00--25.00
1861	Molasses Can— Ewer Nickel, Ewer Silver, Top.	20.00--22.00
1861	Sugar Sifter—Silver Top	8.00----9.00
	Nickel Top	8.00----9.00
1861	Individual Sugar	4.00----5.00
1861	Individual Cream	4.00----5.00
1861	Toothpick	4.00----6.00
1861	High Ft. Sherbet, Reg.	3.00----4.00
1861	High Ft. Sherbet, Flared	3.00----4.00
1861	Low Ft. Sundae, Reg.	2.00----3.00
1861	Low Ft. Sundae, Flared	2.00----3.00
1861	Custard	2.00----3.00
1861	Wine	3.00----4.00
1861	Goblet	3.00----4.00

1861	Jelly, No Cover	5.00----6.00
1861	Jelly and Cover	8.00----9.00
1861	Cracker Jar, No Cover . .	10.00--12.00
1861	Cracker Jar and Cover . .	12.00--15.00
1861	8" High Footed Bowl . .	8.00--10.00
1861	8" High Footed Bowl & Cover	12.00--15.00
1861	10" Fruit Bowl	8.00--10.00
1861	10" Salver	10.00--15.00
1861	Fruit Salad (Two Piece)	6.00----8.00
1861	Marmalade, No Cover . .	3.00----4.00
1861	Marmalade and Cover . .	8.00--10.00
1861	Punch Bowl, No Foot . .	6.00----8.00
1861	Punch Bowl and Foot . .	10.00--12.00

NO. 1871 BRILLIANT PATTERN

1871	Sugar and Cover	18.00--20.00
1871	Butter and Cover . . .	20.00--25.00
1871	Cream	10.00--15.00
1871	Spoon	10.00--15.00
1871	4½" Nappy	4.00----5.00
1871	8" Nappy	10.00--12.50
1871	Qt. Jug	20.00--25.00
1871	3-Pt. Jug	20.00--25.00
1871	Tumbler	6.00----7.50

New pieces made in 1973 called
HERITAGE COLLECTION

1871	Candy Box & Cover	8.00--12.00
1871	Quart Jug	12.00--15.00
1871	8-3/8" Bowl	8.00--10.00
1871	Torte Plate	8.00--12.00
1871	3-Piece Tid Bit Set	10.00--15.00
1871	Covered Sugar & Creamer Set	8.00--12.00
1871	7" Plate (Boxed set of four)	8.00--10.00
1871	4½" Nappy (Boxed set of four)	8.00--12.00
1871	14 oz. Highball (Boxed set of four)	8.00--12.00
1871	Double Old Fashioned (Boxed set of four) . .	8.00--12.00

RECENT: 1871 Shaker w/chrome top made in 1974-75. $4.50

BERRY NAPPIES

453	4½" Handled Nappy (Also without handle) . . .	2.00----3.00
453	5" Handled Nappy (Also without handle)	3.00----4.00
453	6" Handled Nappy (Also without handle) . . .	4.00----5.00
453	7" Nappy	1.00----2.00
1636	5" Nappy	1.00----2.00
1857	4½" Nappy	2.00----3.00
1857	9" Nappy	6.00----9.00
1870	8" Nappy	8.00--10.00
1870	4½" Nappy	3.00----4.00
1763	6" Show Case Tray	20.00--25.00

PRESSED PITCHERS & HANDLES

1988	½ Gal. Jug	15.00--18.00
1988	3 Pt. Jug	12.00--15.00
1800	Saftey Ink	5.00----6.00
1270	6" Covered Comport . .	7.00----9.00
486	Practical Ink	5.00----7.00

NO. 1913 FLEMISH PATTERN

1913	Sugar & Cover	4.00----5.00
1913	Butter & Cover	8.00--10.00
1913	Cream	3.00----3.50
1913	Spoon	3.00----3.50
1913	4" Nappy	1.00----2.00
1913	4½" Nappy	1.00----2.00
1913	7" Nappy	2.00----3.00
1913	8" Nappy	3.00----4.00
1913	9" Nappy	3.00----4.00
1913	Qt. Hall Boy Jug . . .	6.00----7.50
1913	½ Gal. Ice Jug	8.00--10.00
1913	Table Tumbler	1.00----2.00
1913	Ice Tea Tumbler	1.00----2.00
1913	2 oz. Whiskey Tumbler . .	2.00----3.00
1913	4½ oz. Wine Tumbler . .	1.00----2.00
1913½	6 oz. Tumbler	1.00----2.00
1913	8 oz. Split Tumbler . . .	1.00----2.00
1913	11 oz. Milk Tumbler . .	1.00----2.00
1913	9 oz. Goblet	2.00----3.00
1913	2 oz. Sherry	2.00----3.00
1913	Toothpick	2.00----3.00
1913	Celery Tray	3.00----4.00
1913	Pickle	2.00----3.00
1913	Molasses Can. With Ewer Nickle Top	10.00--12.50
	With Ewer Silver Top	10.00--12.50.
1913	Syrup with Metal Handle. W/Screw Top—N. plated	12.00--15.00
	W/Screw Top—S. plated	12.00--15.00
1913	Sugar Sifter W/Nickle Plated Top . .	6.00----7.50
	W/Silver Plated Top . .	6.00----7.50
1913	Shaker, No. 1 with Heavy Nickle, Silver Plated, "K", "W" & Glass Top	1.00----2.00
1913½	Shaker, No. 2, Cut Shut with Heavy Nickle, Silver Plated, Non-Corossive, "P" & Glass Top	1.00----2.00
1913	Shaker, No. 3 with Heavy Nickel, Silver Plated & Glass top	1.00----2.00
1913½	Restaurant Salt or Pepper with Heavy Nickel, & Silver Plated Top	1.00----2.00
1913½	Syrup Can with Metal Handle with Screw Top, Nickel Plated	10.00--15.00
	with Screw Top, Silver Plated	10.00--15.00
1913	Large Celery Dip	2.00----3.00
1913	½ Small Celery Dip	1.00----2.00
1913	Custard	1.00----2.00
1913	Finger Bowl	1.00----2.00
1913	Finger Bowl Plate . . .	1.00----2.00
1913	Individual Cream . . .	2.00----3.00
1913	Individual Sugar	2.00----3.00
1913	Pickle Jar & Cover . . .	8.00----9.00
1913	Tall Celery	4.00----6.00
1913	Jelly Bowl	6.00----9.00
1913	Jelly Bowl & Cover	10.00--12.00
1913	Cracker Jar	6.00----9.00
1913	Cracker Jar & Cover . .	10.00--12.00
1913	5 oz. Squat Oil, Ground Stopper	10.00--12.50
	Drop Stopper	10.00--12.50
1913	7 oz. Tall Oil, Ground Stop	12.00--15.00
	Drop Stopper	12.00--15.00
1913	1 Low Sherbet	1.00----2.00
1913	2 Medium Sherbet	1.00----2.00
1913	3 Tall Sherbet	2.00----3.00
1913	14" Punch Bowl	8.00--10.00
1913	14" Punch Bowl & Stand	12.00--15.00

1913	11" Fruit Bowl	6.00----9.00
1913	9" Orange Bowl	4.00----6.00
1913	11" Basket	8.00--10.00
1913	6" Bud Vase	3.00----5.00
1913	6" Vase	3.00----5.00
1913	8" Vase	4.00----6.00
1913	10" Vase	4.00----6.00
1913	Match or Pick Box	2.00----4.00
1913	3 Bottle Ind. Caster	6.00----8.00

NO. 2000 "REGAL" PATTERN

2000	Hotel Sugar	4.00----5.00
2000	Hotel Cream	4.00----5.00
2000	4½" Berry	1.00----2.00
2000	4¾" Berry	1.00----2.00
2000	5" Deep Nappy	2.00----3.00
2000	6" Deep Nappy	2.00----3.00
2000	7" Deep Nappy	3.00----4.00
2000	8" Deep Nappy	3.00----4.00
2000	10" Deep Nappy	4.00----6.00
2000	5" Nappy, flared to 6½"	3.00----4.00
2000	6" Nappy, flared to 8"	4.00----6.00
2000	7" Nappy, flared to 9"	5.00----7.00
2000	8" Nappy, flared to 10"	6.00----8.00
2000	10" Nappy, flared to 12"	6.00----8.00
2000-2	½ Gal. Jug	12.00--15.00
2000	½ Gal. Ice Jug	10.00--12.00
2000	3 Pt. Jug	8.00--10.00
2000	Table Tumbler	1.00----2.00
2000	3½ oz. Whiskey	2.00----3.00
2000	Ice Tea Tumbler	1.00----2.00
2000	Ice Tea Plate	1.00----2.00
2000-2	Table Tumbler	1.00----2.00
2000-2	Ice Tea Tumbler	1.00----2.00
2000-2	Split Tumbler	1.00----2.00
2000-2	Whiskey Tumbler	2.00----3.00
2000-3	Table Tumbler	1.00----2.00
2000-3	Ice Tea Tumbler	1.00----2.00
2000-3	Split Tumbler	1.00----2.00
2000-3	Wine Tumbler	1.00----2.00
2000-3	Whiskey Tumbler	2.00----3.00
2000-3	Table Tumbler, Optic	1.00----2.00
2000-3	Ice Tea Tumbler, Optic	1.00----2.00
2000-3	Split Tumbler, Optic	1.00----2.00
2000-3	Wine Tumbler, Optic	1.00----2.00
2000-3	Whiskey Tumbler, Optic	2.00----3.00
2000-3	Table Tumbler	1.00----2.00
2000-3	Ice Tea Tumbler	1.00----2.00
2000	Water Bottle	7.00----9.00
2000	Footed Tumbler	2.00----3.00
2000	9 oz. Goblet	3.00----4.00
2000	11 oz. Goblet	3.00----4.00
2000	13 oz. Goblet	3.00----4.00
2000	Finger Bowl	1.00----2.00
2000-2	Finger Bowl	1.00----2.00
2000	Finger Bowl Plate	1.00----2.00
2000-2	Large Ft. Sherbet, 6½ oz.	1.00----2.00
2000	Tall Footed Sherbet, 7 oz.	2.00----3.00
2000	Condiment Set, 5 pieces	20.00--25.00
2000	Condiment Tray, 5x7	2.00----3.00
*2000	Toothpick	3.00----4.00
2000	6, 8 oz. Oil, Ground Stop.	12.00--15.00
2000	4 oz. Oil, Ground Stopper	10.00--12.00
2000	8 oz. Oil, Drop Stopper	10.00--12.00
2000	4, 6 oz. Oil, Drop Stopper	8.00--10.00
2000	Olive, Pickle	2.00----3.00

Made between 1974 & 1978 in Lead Crystal: List Price $5.25.

2000	Celery Tray	3.00----4.00
2000	Low Footed Jelly	2.00----3.00
2000	High Footed Jelly	3.00----4.00
2000	8" Fruit Salad Bowl on Stand flared to 10"	12.00--16.00
2000	10" Punch Bowl & Stand	18.00--20.00
2000	10" Punch Bowl & Stand, fl to 12"	20.00--25.00
2000	Butter & Cover	12.00--15.00
2000	Sugar & Cover	6.00----8.00
2000	Cream	4.00----6.00
2000	Spoon	4.00----6.00
2000	Small Butter & Cover	10.00--12.50
2000	Shaker, No. 1 with Heavy Nickel, Silver Plated, non-corrosive, Pearl, & Fostoria Glass Top.	1.00----2.00
2000	Shaker, No. 2 with Heavy Nickel, Silver Plated, non-corrosive, Pearl, & Fostoria Glass Top.	1.00----2.00
2000	Shaker, No. 3 with Heavy Nickel, Silver Plated, "K", "W", & Fostoria Glass Top.	1.00----2.00
2000	Molasses Can Ewer Nickel Top	10.00--12.00
	Ewer Silver Top	10.00--12.00
2000	Syrup Can, with Metal Handle. Screw Top, Nickel Plat.	12.00--15.00
	Screw Top, Silver Plat.	12.00--15.00
2000	Sugar Shaker. Nickel Plated Top	7.00----9.00
	Silver Plated Top	7.00----9.00
2000	Ind. Salt, or Celery Dip	2.00----3.00
2000	Footed Salt, Individual	3.00----4.00
2000	Footed Almond	3.00----4.00
2000	Footed Mint	3.00----4.00
2000	Mustard & Cover	3.00----4.00
2000	Custard	1.00----2.00
2000	Footed Oyster Cocktail & Liner	4.00----6.00
2000	Sweetmeat	3.00----4.00
2000	Footed Liner	1.00----2.00
2000-2	Oyster Cocktail & Liner	3.00----5.00
2000-2	Loaf Sugar	3.00----4.00
2000-2	Oyster Cocktail Liner	1.00----2.00
2000-3	Oyster Cocktail Plate & Footed Liner	3.00----4.00
2000	Mayonnaise & Plate	5.00----6.00
2000	Mayonnaise Plate	2.00----3.00
2000	Lemon Dish	2.00----3.00
2000	Footed Sherbet, 6 oz.	1.00----2.00
2000-2	Small Footed Sherbet, 5	1.00----2.00

NO. 2056 AMERICAN PATTERN

Pieces being made in 1978.

2056	Almond Dish small, oval	5.00
2056	Almond oval 3¾"	5.00
2056	Individual appetizer	4.00
2056	Ash tray & match stand.	9.00
2056	Ash tray oval	6.00
2056	Ash tray square	4.00
2056	Banana Split	9.00
2056	Basket reed handle	18.00
*2056	Boat 8½"	6.50
*2056	Boat 12"	8.25
2056	Bottle Catsup & Cover	18.00
2056	Bottle bitters & stopper & handle	25.00
2056	Bottle Cologne & Stopper, 8 oz.	30.00

No.	Description	Price
2056	Bottle Cologne & Stopper 4½ oz.	20.00
2056	Bottle Cologne & Stopper 6 oz.	25.00
2056	Bottle cordial & stopper	18.00
2056	Bon Bon	6.00
*2056	Bon Bon 3-toed	6.00
2056	Boudoir Set	50.00
2056	Bowl 3½", 5" rose	9.00
2056	Bowl finger	4.00
2056	Bowl rolled edge 11½"	12.00
2056	Bowl 12" Ftd. fruit	30.00
2056	Bowl lily pond 12"	12.00
2056	Bowl 12" ftd. fruit flared to 16"	35.00
2056	Bowl floating garden 10"	10.00
2056	Bowl floating garden 11½'	12.50
2056	Bowl 16" ftd. fruit	40.00
2056	Bowl 13" shallow	15.00
2056	Bowl 8" ftd. & handled	20.00
2056	Bowl 8½" handled	10.00
2056	Bowl, 2-part Veg. 10"	11.00
*2056	Bowl 10½", 3-toed	12.50
2056	Box glove & cover	17.50
2056	Box hairpin & cover	10.00
2056	Box hair receiver & cover	20.00
2056	Box hankerchief & cover	15.00
2056	Box jewel & cover	14.00
2056	Box pomade & cover	15.00
2056	Box puff & cover, Square	15.00
2056	Box puff & cover, round	12.50
*2056	Butter & cover, oblong	10.00
2056	Butter & cover	25.00
*2056	Cake Plate, 12" ftd.	12.00
2056	Candelabra 2 light UDP	40.00
*2056	Candle 3"	8.00
2056	Candle 2056½ 7"	15.00
*2056	Candlestick twin	14.00
*2056	Candlestick 6"	11.00
2056	Candlestick duo	18.00
2056	Can, Molasses large	25.00
2056	Can, Molasses small	20.00
*2056	Candy Jar & Cover	10.00
*2056	Celery, 10"	7.00
2056	Celery, Tall	18.00
2056	Celery, Tray	9.00
*2056	Centerpiece, 9½"	12.00
*2056	Centerpiece, 11" 3-Cor.	12.50
2056	Centerpiece 15"	40.00
2056	Cheese, Footed	8.00
2056	Chiffonier	17.50
*2056	Coaster	2.00
*2056	Comport, 5" & Cover	14.00
2056	Comport, 8½"	12.00
2056	Comport, 9½"	15.00
2056	Condiment Set	50.00
2056	Cookie Jar & Cover	30.00
2056	Crab Meat Liner 4 oz. Blown	1.00
2056	Cracker & Cheese	20.00
2056	Cracker Jar & Cover	30.00
2056	Cracker Plate 11"	12.00
*2056	Cream	4.00
*2056	Cream, individual	3.00
2056	Cream, Soup	8.00
2056	Cream, Soup Plate	2.00
2056	Cream, Tea	3.00
2056	Crush Fruit, Cover & Spoon	35.00
*2056	Cup, Footed	3.50
2056	Custard, regular	5.00
2056	Custard, flared	5.00
2056	Decanter & stopper	35.00
2056	Fruit stand 16"	30.00
2056	Fruit Cocktail & liner	7.50
*2056	Goblet 10 oz.	5.00
*2056	Goblet, low 9 oz.	5.00
2056	Goblet, 3½ oz. Claret	5.00
*2056	Goblet, 7 oz. Claret	5.00
*2056	Goblet, 2½ oz. Wine	5.00
2056	Goblet, 1 oz. Cordial	8.00
2056	Hotel Cracked Ice	20.00
2056	Hurrican Lamp	20.00
2056	Ice Cream 5½"	6.00
2056	Ice Cream, square 3½"	5.00
2056	Ice Cream Saucer 5¼"	3.00
2056	Ice Cream Set (6 ice creams & 10 or 10½" tray	35.00
2056	Ice Cream Oval Tray	12.00
2056	Jam Jar & Cover	15.00
*2056	Jelly Ftd. & Cover, Reg.	12.00
*2056	Jelly, Ftd., Reg.	7.00
2056	Jelly Ftd., Flared	8.50
2056	Jelly, Deep, Reg.	8.50
2056	Jelly, Deep, Flared	8.50
*2056	Jug ½ Gal. Ice Lip	18.00
2056	Jug ½ Gal. Ice (2056½)	25.00
2056	Jug, Quart	18.50
2056	Jug, ½ Gal.	25.00
*2056	Jug, 3 pints	15.00
2056	Jug, 1 pint cereal	10.00
2056	Lemon Dish & Cover	15.00
2056	Marmalade, Cover & Spoon	15.00
2056	Mayo., 2-part—2 ladles	12.00
2056	Mayonnaise, Plate & ladle	10.00
2056	Mug, Beer	8.00
2056	Mug, Tom & Jerry	5.50
2056	Mustard, & Cov. & Spoon	12.00
*2056	Napkin Ring	2.00
*2056	Nappy 4¼", Reg.	3.00
*2056	Nappy 4¾" (fruit)	4.00
*2056	Nappy 5", 6", Reg.	4.00
*2056	Nappy 5" Reg. & Cover	9.00
*2056	Nappy 7", 8", Reg.	8.50
*2056	Nappy 8", 10" Deep	12.00
2056	Nappy 8", 2 handles	10.00
2056	Nappy 4½", Flared to 4¾"	6.00
2056	Nappy 5", Flared to 6¼"	7.00
2056	Nappy 6", Flared	8.00
2056	Nappy 7", Flared to 8¼"	12.50
2056	Nappy 8", Flared to 9¼"	15.00
2056	Nappy 8", Dp. Flared to 9"	15.00
2056	Nappy 8", Flared	12.00
2056	Nappy 8" Dp. Flared to 10	15.00
2056	Nappy 7" Flared	10.00
2056	Nappy 7" Shallow	8.00
2056	Nappy 8" Shallow	9.00
*2056	Nappy, Handled 4½", Reg.	4.00
*2056	Nappy, handled 4½" Sq.	4.00
2056	Nappy, hdld. 4½", 3-Cor.	5.00
*2056	Nappy, 5", 3-cornered	4.00
2056	Nappy 5¼" Flared, hdld.	6.00
2056	Nappy 9" Flared	12.00
2056	Nappy 10" Shallow	12.00
2056	Nappy 10", Flared	13.00
2056	Nappy 5" handled	6.00
*2056	Nappy 9", Tab. Hdld.	11.50
2056	Oil 5, 7 oz. drop stopper	15.00
2056	Oil 5, 7 oz. ground stopper	20.00
*2056	Oil & Stopper, 5 oz.	12.00
*2056	Olive 6"	4.00
2056	Oval 3¾", 4½"	6.00
2056	Oval 10", 11"	12.00

*2056	Oval 9", 11¾"	10.00
*2056	Pickle Dish 8"	5.00
2056	Pickle Jar & Cover	25.00
2056	Plate, Ice Tea	3.00
2056	Plate, Finger Bowl	3.00
*2056	Plate Handled Cake	10.00
2056	Plate, Crescent Salad . .	9.00
*2056	Plate 14" Torte	15.50
*2056	Plate 18" Torte	30.00
*2056	Plate 7" Salad	4.00
2056	Plate 8" Salad	5.00
*2056	Plate 8½" Salad	5.00
2056	Plate 9" Dinner	6.00
*2056	Plate 9½" Dinner	6.00
2056	Plate, Ftd. Dessert	8.00
*2056	Plate 6" Bread & Butter . .	4.00
2056	Plate 9" Sandwich	7.50
*2056	Plate 10½" Sandwich . .	9.00
2056	Plate, Sandwich 11½" . .	12.50
2056	Plate, Square 10"	10.00
2056	Plate 20"	35.00
2056	Plate, crushed Ice	4.00
2056	Plate 24"	40.00
2056	Platter 10½", 12", Oval .	15.00
2056	Pot & Cover, Flower . .	25.00
2056	Preserve, 2 handles, Cover	15.00
2056	Pretzel Jar & Cover	25.00
*2056	Punch Bowl & Foot 14"	40.00
2056	Punch Bowl 14" & H.F.	60.00
*2056	Punch Bowl, Foot	10.00
*2056	Punch Bowl 18" & Foot	75.00
*2056	Punch Bowl 18" no Foot	65.00
*2056	Punch Bowl 14" no Foot	30.00
2056	Punch Cup, Reg.	5.00
*2056	Punch Cup, Ftd.	3.00
*2056	Relish, 2 & 3 part 7.00 &	10.00
2056	Relish, 4 part	15.00
*2056	Salt, Individual	3.00
2056	Salt, Table Shaker	5.00
*2056	Salver, Round Cake Stand	20.00
*2056	Salver, Square Cake Stand	25.00
2056	Sauce Boat	19.00
2056	Sauce Boat Plate	6.00
*2056	Saucer	2.00
2056	Shaker, Resturant H.N.T.	6.00
2056	Shaker No. 1 "w" top . .	9.50
2056	Shaker No. 2 Cut Shut . .	9.00
2056½	Shaker H.N.T.	8.00
*2056	Shaker H.S.T.	3.00
*2056	Shaker Chrome top	3.00
2056	Shaker Set, 3 Piece Ind.	12.00
*2056	Sherbet, 5 oz. Low, Reg.	4.00
*2056	Sherbet, 5 oz. Low, Flared	4.00
2056	Sherbet, Ftd.	5.00
*2056	Sherbet, High 4½ oz., Reg.	4.00
2056	Sherbet, Ftd. & Handled	6.00
*2056	Sherbet 4½ oz. High Flared	4.00
*2056	Sherbet, High Reg.	4.00
*2056	Sherbet 4½ oz. (Hex. Base)	4.00
2056	Sherbet, High, Ftd.	6.00
2056	Sherbet, Low Reg.	5.00
2056	Sherbet, Oyster Cocktail, 4½ oz.	5.00
2056	Spoon	15.00
2056	Straw Jar & Cover	50.00
2056	Sugar & Cover	17.50
2056	Sugar, Hdld.	6.50
*2056	Sugar, Handled & Cover . .	8.00
*2056	Sugar, Individual	3.00
2056	Sugar Shaker H.N.T. . . .	17.50

2056	Sugar & Cream Tray 6¾".	5.25
2056	Sugar, Tea	5.00
*2056	Sundae, Footed	4.00
*2056	Syrup, Dripcut	10.00
2056	Syrup & Cover	25.00
2056	Syrup Plate, 6"	4.00
*2056	Tankard, 12 oz.	6.00
2056	Tea Set	20.00
*2056	Tid Bit, 3-toed	4.00
*2056	Toothpick	3.00
2056	Topper 2¼", 3", 4"	8.00
2056	Topper, Ash Tray	8.00
2056	Tray, Candy	6.00
2056	Tray, Condiment 9" . . .	9.00
2056	Tray, 5½.. Ice Cream . .	6.00
2056	Tray, 13½", 14" Ice Cream	18.00
2056	Tray, 10½"x7½" Oval . .	15.00
2056	Tray, 10½" oval, Comb & Brush	15.00
2056	Tray, 10½" oblong	12.00
2056	Tray, 10" oblong, Comb & Brush	12.00
2056	Tray, Pin	5.00
2056	Tray, 5", 6" Oval, Pin . .	8.00
2056	Tray, 5" oblong pin	6.00
2056	Tray 11½" Oval	15.00
2056	Tray 12" Oval 8½" wide	16.00
2056	Tray 5½" Oval 4¼" wide	7.00
2056	Tray 12" round	15.00
2056	Tray, Utility, Hdld., 9" . .	11.75
2056	Tub, crushed ice	17.50
2056	Tub, Hotel	20.00
2056	Tub, Large Ice & 9" Plate	25.00
2056	Tub, Small Ice & 8" Plate	22.00
*2056	Tumbler, table	5.00
2056	Tumbler, Ftd. 9 oz, 12 oz.	8.00
2056	Tumbler, table (2056½). .	6.00
2056	Tumbler, ice tea	8.00
*2056	Tumbler, ice tea 12 oz. Fl.	5.00
*2056	Tumbler, ice tea (2056½)	5.00
2056	Tumbler, O. F. 6 oz. . .	6.00
2056	Tumb., Ice tea Ftd. & Hdld.	10.00
2056	Tumbler, table 8 oz. Flared	6.00
*2056	Tumbler, 5 oz. Ftd.	5.00
*2056	Tumbler, table 5 oz. . . .	4.00
2056	Tumbler, 3 oz. Ftd. Cocktail	8.00
2056	Tumbler, 2 oz. Whiskey. .	5.00
2056	Urn, 6", 7½" Square . .	15.00
*2056	Vase, 6", 8½" bud, Flared 4.00 &	6.00
*2056	Vase, 6", 8½" bud, cupped 4.00 &	6.00
2056	Vase, 6", 8"	10.00
2056	Vase 9" square Ftd.	15.00
2056	Vase 10", 12"	14.00
*2056	Vase, 8" Flared	8.00
2056	Vase, 15"	18.00
2056	Vase, 7", Flared	10.00
2056	Vase, 20"	25.00
2056	Vase, 25"	30.00
2056	Vase, small porch	12.00
2056	Vase, large porch	15.00
2056	Vase, 12" square foot . .	15.00
2056	Vase, 10" bagged	12.00
2056	Vase, 10" cupped	12.00
2056	Vase, Sweetpea	12.00
2056	Vase, Swung, 9" to 12" .	10.00
2056	Water Bottle	25.00
2056	Water cress	10.00
2056	Water cress & plate	16.00

NO. 2106 "VOGUE" PATTERN

Item		Price
2106	Butter & Cover	6.00----8.00
2106	Sugar & Cover	3.00----4.00
2106	Cream	2.00----3.00
2106	Spoon	2.00----3.00
2106	Squat Sugar	2.00----3.00
2106	Squat Sugar & Cover	3.00----4.00
2106	English Sugar, footed	1.00----2.00
2106	Oval Butter	3.00----4.00
2106	Oval Butter & Cover	4.00----5.00
2106½—Hotel Cream		3.00----4.00
2106	3¾" Nappy	1.00----2.00
2106	4¼" Nappy	1.00----2.00
2106	4¾" Nappy	1.00----2.00
2106½—4¾" Nappy		1.00----2.00
2106	5¾" Nappy	1.00----2.00
2106	6¾" Nappy	1.00----2.00
2106	7¾" Nappy	2.00----3.00
2106	8¾" Nappy	2.00----3.00
2106	5½" 2 Handled Nappy Crimped	1.00----2.00
2106	6½" Nappy, Crimped	1.00----2.00
2106	7½" Nappy, Crimped	1.00----2.00
2106	5" Handled Nappy Flared	1.00----2.00
2106	4½" Handled Nappy & Cover	2.00----3.00
2106	4¾" Nappy & Cover	2.00----3.00
2106	5½" Nappy & Cover	2.00----3.00
2106	5½" Shallow Nappy	1.00----2.00
2106	7¼" Shallow Nappy	2.00----3.00
2106	3 Quart Jug	7.00----9.00
2106	½ Gal. Jug	8.00--10.00
2106	Quart Jug	4.00----5.00
2106	3 Qt. Jug & Cover	10.00--12.00
2106	½ Gal. Jug & Cover	10.00--15.00
2106	Table Tumbler, Flared	1.00----2.00
2106	Ice Tea Tumbler, 13 oz. Flared	1.00----2.00
2106-2—Table Tumbler, straight		1.00----2.00
2106-2—13 oz. Ice Tea Tumbler, Straight		1.00----2.00
2106-4—12 oz. Bell Tumbler		1.00----2.00
2106-4—10 oz. Bell Tumbler		1.00----2.00
2106-4—8 oz. Bell Tumbler		1.00----2.00
2106-4—5 oz. Bell Tumbler		1.00----2.00
2106-5—13 oz. Ice Tea Tumbler taper		1.00----2.00
2106	Finger Bowl	1.00----2.00
2106	6¼" Finger Bowl Plate	.50----1.00
2106-2—Finger Bowl		1.00----2.00
2106-2—6" Finger Bowl Plate		.50----1.00
2106	4 oz. Footed Soda	1.00----2.00
2106	6 oz. Footed Soda	1.00----2.00
2106	8 oz. Footed Soda	2.00----3.00
2106	10 oz. Footed Soda	2.00----3.00
2106	12 oz. Footed Soda	2.00----3.00
2106-2—Parfait		1.00----2.00
2106	6 oz. Parfait	1.00----2.00
2106	Coca Cola	1.00----2.00
2106	Footed Banana Split	1.00----2.00
2106	Sauce Bowl	4.00----5.00
2106	Sauce Bowl Plate	1.00----2.00
2106	Relish Dish, no partitions	1.00----2.00
2106	Relish Dish, with partitions	2.00----3.00
2106	Sauce Ladle	1.00----2.00
2106	Match Box & Cover	1.00----2.00
2106	Cigarette Box & Cover, Sm.	1.00----2.00
2106	Cigarette Box & Cover, Lg.	1.00----2.00
2106	Handled Candle	2.00----4.00
2106	10" Tray	3.00----4.00
2106	Pear Pickle	3.00----4.00
2106	Buffet Tray	2.00----4.00
2106	5 oz. Low Sherbet	1.00----2.00
2106	Ice Tea Tumbler 15 oz.	1.00----2.00
2106	Ash Tray	2.00----3.00
2106	Celery Dip	3.00----4.00
2106	Tall Celery	3.00----4.00
2106	4½" Square Nut Bowl	1.00----2.00
2106	Toothpick, Handled	3.00----4.00
2106	Mustard & Cover	3.00----5.00
2106	Mustard & Cover & Spoon	5.00----6.00
2106	5 oz. Mustard & Cover	4.00----6.00
2106	5 oz. H. F. Sherbet	1.00----2.00
2106	3 oz. Sherbet	1.00----2.00
2106	5 oz. Sherbet	1.00----2.00
2106	4 oz. Sundae	1.00----2.00
2106	6 oz. Parfait	1.00----2.00
2106	Goblet	2.00----3.00
2106	2 oz. Wine	2.00----3.00
2106	Egg	1.00----2.00
2106	Celery Tray	2.00----3.00
2106	8" Pickle Dish	2.00----3.00
2106	5-5/8" Olive Dish	1.00----2.00
2106	Shaker, Heavy Nickel Top	1.00----2.00
2106	Fostoria Glass Top	2.00----3.00
2106	6 oz. Oil, Drop Stopper	10.00--12.00
2106	4 oz. Oil, Drop Stopper	8.00--10.00
2106	6 oz. Oil, Ground Stopper	10.00--12.00
2106	4 oz. Oil Ground Stopper	8.00--10.00
2106	Sugar Sifter, Heavy Nickel Top	4.00----5.00
2106	Syrup, Metal Handle N. P.	15.00--18.00
2106	Molasses Can, Ewer Nickel Top	10.00--12.00
2106	Ewer Silver Top	10.00--12.00
2106	5" Molasses Can Plate	1.00----2.00
2106	Cigar Jar & Cover	4.00----6.00
2106	4" High Footed Jelly	2.00----4.00
2106	4" High Ftd. Jelly & Cover	5.00----6.00
2106	4¾" High Footed Jelly	2.00----3.00
2106	4¾" High Ftd. Jelly & Cover	3.00----5.00
2106	5½" Low Footed Bowl	1.00----2.00
2106	6" Low Footed Bowl, Crimped	2.00----3.00
2106	5½" Low Ftd. Bowl & Cover	3.00----5.00
2106	5½" Footed Bon Bon	1.00----2.00
2106	Cheese & Plate	8.00--10.00
2106	Fruit Bowl	2.00----3.00
2106	Ice Tub	3.00----5.00
2106	9" Ice Tub Plate	1.00----2.00
2106	4¾" Ice Tea Plate	.50----1.00
2106	Lemon Dish, flared to 6"	2.00----3.00
2106	Lemon Dish & Cover	3.00----5.00
2106	4½" Small Tub	2.00----4.00
2106	2 Hdl. Preserve, flared to 5¼"	1.00----2.00
2106	2 Hdl. Preserve & Cover	2.00----4.00
2106	12 oz. Ftd., Hdl. Lemonade	2.00----3.00
2106	3-3/8" Coaster	.25---- .50
2106	6¾" Plate	.50----1.00
2106	6" Ice Cream	1.00----2.00
2106	8" Oval	2.00----3.00
2106	9" Oval	2.00----4.00
2106	10" Oval	3.00----5.00
2106	Honey Jar, No Cover	2.00----3.00
2106	Honey Jar & Cover	3.00----5.00
2106	Ind. Sugar & Cover	2.00----4.00
2106	Individual Sugar	1.00----2.00
2106	Individual Cream	1.00----2.00
2106	Individual Butter	1.00----2.00
2106	Salt Dip	1.00----2.00

2106	Mug	2.00----3.00
2106	Custard	1.00----2.00
2106	Punch Bowl	6.00----8.00
2106	Punch Bowl & Foot	12.00--15.00
2106½—Punch Bowl & High Foot		18.00--22.00
2106½—Punch Bowl High Foot only		4.00----5.00
2106	Nasturtium Vase	2.00----4.00
2106	9" Vase	2.00----3.00
2106	Hotel Cream	2.00----3.00
2106	Hotel Sugar	2.00----3.00
2106	Hotel Sugar & Cover	3.00----4.00
2106½—Sugar Server, Aut.		10.00--15.00

NO. 2183 "COLONIAL PRISM" PATTERN

2183	Sugar & Cover	10.00--12.50
2183	Butter & Cover	18.00--20.00
2183	Cream	8.00--10.00
2183	Spoon	8.00--10.00
2183	Squat Sugar	3.00----4.00
2183	Squat Sugar & Cover	6.00----8.00
2183	Hotel Sugar & Cover	8.00----9.00
2183	Hotel Sugar	4.00----6.00
2183	Hotel Cream	4.00----6.00
2183	Milk Pitcher, 10 oz.	10.00--12.00
2183	3¼" Nappy	1.00----2.00
2183	4½" Nappy, Reg.	1.00----2.00
2183	5" Nappy, Reg.	1.00----2.00
2183	6" Nappy, Reg.	1.00----2.00
2183	7" Nappy, Reg.	2.00----3.00
2183	8" Nappy, Reg.	3.00----4.00
2183	4½" Nappy, Flared to 4¾"	1.00----2.00
2183	5" Nappy, Flared to 6"	1.00----2.00
2183	6" Nappy, Flared to 7"	2.00----3.00
2183	7" Nappy, Flared to 8"	3.00----4.00
2183	8" Nappy, Flared to 9"	5.00----7.00
2183	7" Shallow Nappy	2.00----3.00
2183	8" Shallow Nappy	2.00----4.00
2183	8" Deep Nappy, Reg.	4.00----5.00
2183	8" Deep Nappy, Flared to 10"	4.00----6.00
2183	5½" 2 Handled Preserve.	8.00--10.00
2183	5½" 2 Hld. Preserve & Cover	12.00--15.00
2183	4½" Handled Nappy	2.00----3.00
2183	5" Handled Nappy, 3 cornered	3.00----4.00
2183	4¼" Hld. Nappy, square	3.00----4.00
2183	5" Hld. Nappy, Flared	3.00----4.00
2183½—3 Quart Ice Pitcher		15.00--17.00
2183½—½Gal. Ice Pitcher		15.00--17.00
2183	½Gal. Pitcher	15.00--17.00
2183	Quart Pitcher	12.00--15.00
2183	Table Tumbler	1.00----2.00
2183	Ice Tea	1.00----2.00
2183	12 oz. Hld. Tumbler	2.00----3.00
2183-2—Table Tumbler		1.00----2.00
2183-2—Ice Tea		1.00----2.00
2183	Finger Bowl	1.00----2.00
2183	Finger Bowl Plate	.50----1.00
2183	Toothpick	6.00----8.00
2183	Lemon Dish	1.00----2.00
2183	Lemon Dish & Cover	7.00----9.00
2183	6" Oval Dish	1.00----2.00
2183	7½" Oval Dish	2.00----3.00
2183	9" Oval Dish	3.00----4.00
2183	10½" Oval Dish	4.00----5.00
2183	12" Cabarette	4.00----5.00
2183	Combination Bowl	20.00--25.00
2183	5½" Comport	6.00----8.00

2183	5½" Comport & Cover	10.00--15.00
2183	4" Ice Tub	4.00----6.00
2183	Footed Jar & Cover	10.00--12.00
2183½—Butter & Cover, 2 Hdls.		20.00--25.00
2183½—Sugar & Cover, 2 Hlds.		8.00--10.00
2183½—Cream		7.00----8.00
2183	Condiment Tray	4.00----6.00
2183	Condiment Set — 2 6-oz. Oils D.S., 2 Shakers, HNT., 1 Tray	20.00--25.00
2183	Small Boat, 8½"	2.00----4.00
2183	Large Boat, 11"	3.00----5.00
2183	Olive, 5¾"	2.00----3.00
2183	Pickle, 8"	2.00----3.00
2183	Celery Tray, 10"	3.00----5.00
2183	Tall Celery	4.00----6.00
2183½—Celery Tray, 12"		4.00----6.00
2183½—Pickle Tray, 10"		3.00----4.00
2183	Shaker: Heavy Nickel Top	2.00----3.00
	Heavy Silver Top	2.00----3.00
	Pearl Top	2.00----3.00
	Fostoria Glass Top	2.00----3.00
2183	5½ oz. Oil, Drop Stop.	8.00--10.00
2183	6½ oz. Drop Stop.	8.00--10.00
2183	5½ oz. Oil, Ground Stop.	10.00--12.00
2183	6½ oz. Oil, Ground Stop.	10.00--12.00
2183	5" Footed Jelly	4.00----5.00
2183	4½" Ftd. Jelly & Cover	10.00--12.00
2183	Pickel Jar & Cover	5.00----7.00
2183	Ftd. Sherbet, Reg.	1.00----2.00
2183	Ftd. Sherbet, Flared	1.00----2.00
2183	Fruit Salad	1.00----2.00
2183	Custard	2.00----3.00
2183	Custard, Flared	2.00----3.00
2183	Grape Fruit Plate	2.00----3.00
2183	Grape Fruit, Footed	2.00----3.00
2183	Grape Fruit Liner Plain	1.00----2.00
2183	9¼" Plate	2.00----3.00
2183	Ice Tub	6.00----8.00
2183	Ice Tub Plate, 8"	3.00----4.00
2183	Crushed Ice, Hotel	8.00--10.00
2183	Nut Bowl	3.00----4.00
2183	14¾" Fruit Bowl	4.00----6.00
2183	12¼" Fruit Bowl	3.00----5.00
2183½—13 Swung Vase		3.00----4.00
2183	8" Vase	2.00----3.00
2183	10" Vase	2.00----3.00
2183	12" Vase	3.00----4.00
2183	Punch Bowl & Foot	15.00--20.00
2183	Punch Bowl Foot, only	3.00----4.00
2183	Footed Tankard	20.00--25.00
2183	Footed Bowl Flared	4.00----6.00
2183	Footed Bowls, Crimp	4.00----6.00
2183	4½" Ice Tea Plate	.50----1.00
2183	8½" Orange Bowl, Sq.	4.00----6.00

New pieces made recently in lead crystal.

		List Price
2183	Covered Server (looks like Butter & Cover). '74-'77	12.50
2183	Marmalade (looks like spooner). '74-'75	9.50
2183	5" Nappy. '74	8.50

DEEP PLATE ETCHING NO. 210

863	10½ oz. Goblet	2.00----3.00
863	9 oz. Goblet	2.00----3.00
863	7 oz. Goblet	2.00----3.00
863	5½ oz. Tall Champagne	2.00----3.00
863	4½ oz. Claret	2.00----3.00

863	3 oz. Wine	2.00----3.00
863	1 oz. Cordial	2.00----3.00
863	4½ oz. Rhine Wine	2.00----3.00
863	2 oz. Sherry	2.00----3.00
863	5½ oz. Saucer Champagne	2.00----3.00
863	3½ oz. Cocktail	2.00----3.00
863	2½ oz. Creme de Menthe	2.00----3.00
863	¾ oz. Pousse Cafe	2.00----3.00
863	Fruit	2.00----2.50
863	Individual Almond	2.00----3.00
863	H. S. Champagne, C.F.	2.00----3.00
858	Table, 3½, 5, 6½, 8, 10, 12, 14, 16 oz. Tumbler	1.00----2.00
858	Tumbler Plate	1.00----2.00
858	Custard	2.00----3.00
858	Custard Plate	1.00----2.00
858	Finger Bowl	1.00----2.00
858	Finger Bowl Plate	1.00----2.00
858	Table, 3½, 5, 6½, 8, 10, 12, 14, 16 oz. Tumbler, Cut 19	1.00----2.00
820	Tumbler	1.00----2.00
820½—Tumbler, half sham		1.00----2.00
833	7, 8 oz. Tumbler	1.00----2.00
833	7, 8 oz. Tumbler ½ Sham	1.00----2.00
887	3 oz. Tumbler	1.00----2.00
889	5 oz. Tumbler	1.00----2.00
303	7, 6 Jug	15.00--18.00
1227	7, 6 Jug	15.00--18.00
317	7 Jug	15.00--18.00
300	7, 2 Tankard	15.00--18.00
300	5, 3, 1 Tankard	8.00--10.00
300	Claret	20.00--22.00
724	7, 6 Tankard	15.00--18.00
481	Custard	2.00----3.00
1241	Custard	2.00----3.00
1598	Custard	2.00----3.00
1558	Water Bottle, Cut Neck	8.00--12.00
932	Saucer Champagne	2.00----3.00
793	H. S. Champagne, C.F.	3.00----4.00
810	Sherbet	2.00----2.50
840	Sherbet	2.00----2.50
840	Sherbet Plate	1.00----2.00
846	Sherry	2.00----3.00
1165	Shaker, Silver Plated Top	2.00----3.00
1132	Horseradish	6.00----8.00
945	Grape Fruit	2.00----3.00
945½—Grape Fruit Liner		2.00----3.00
5039	Oyster Cocktail	2.00----3.00
5039	Liner	1.00----2.00
315	8" Nappy	4.00----6.00
315	4½" Nappy	1.00----2.00
823	4½" Fruit	1.00----2.00
823	5" Fruit	1.00----2.00
803	5" Comport	2.00----3.00
803	6" Comport	3.00----4.00
803	4½", 5", 6", 7" Ftd. Nappy, deep	2.00--5.00
803	4½", 5", 6", 7" Ftd. Nappy, shallow	2.00----5.00
300½—Small Oil, C.S.		10.00--12.00
300½—Large Oil, C.S.		10.00--12.00
1465	Oil, Cut Neck, C.S.	12.00--15.00
1478	Cream	2.00----3.00
1478	Sugar	2.00----3.00
1480	Cream	2.00----3.00
1480	Sugar	2.00----3.00
300	Quart Decanter, C. N.	12.00--14.00
1464	18 oz. Decanter, C.N., C.F.	16.00--18.00
1464	10 oz. Decanter, C.N., C.F.	16.00--18.00
1491	25 oz. Decanter, Optic, C.N.	16.00--18.00

DEEP PLATE ETCHING NO. 212

300	7 Tankard	15.00--18.00
300	7 Tankard Cut Flute	15.00--20.00
300	2 Tankard	8.00--10.00
724	7, 6 Tankard	15.00--18.00
303	7 Jug	15.00--18.00
1236	6 Jug	14.00--16.00
318	7 Jug, Optic	14.00--16.00
1743	5 Jug & Cover	15.00--18.00
1558	Water Bottle, C.N.	10.00--12.00
315	Finger Bowl	1.00----2.00
315	Finger Bowl Plate	1.00----2.00
1349	Finger Bowl	2.00----3.00
1227	8" Nappy	4.00----6.00
1227	4½" Nappy	1.00----2.00
315	8" Nappy	4.00----6.00
315	5" Nappy	2.00----3.00
315	4½" Nappy	1.00----2.00
315	4" Nappy	1.00----2.00
1686	9" Cheese & Cover	12.00--15.00
945½—Grape Fruit		2.00----3.00
945½—Grape Fruit Liner		2.00----3.00
793	H.S. Champagne, C.F.	3.00----4.00
825	Saucer Champagne	2.00----3.00
932	Saucer Champagne	2.00----3.00
932	Plate	3.00----4.00
952	Cocktail	2.00----3.00
846	2 oz. Sherry	2.00----3.00
5036	Sherbet	2.00----2.50
840	Sherbet	2.00----2.50
840	Sherbet Plate	1.00----2.00
480	Custard	2.00----3.00
480	Custard Plate	1.00----2.00
481	Custard	2.00----3.00
1598	Custard	2.00----3.00
1132	Horseradish	8.00--12.00
1518	8 oz. Syrup	20.00--25.00
823	4½" Fruit	1.00----2.00
823	5" Fruit	1.00----2.00
803	5" Comport	2.00----3.00
803	6" Comport	2.00----3.00
803	4½", 5", 6", 7" Ftd. Nappy, deep	2.00----5.00
803	4½", 5", 6", 7" Ftd. Nappy, shallow	2.00----5.00
300½—Small Oil, C.S.		12.00--15.00
300½—Large Oil, C.S.		12.00--15.00
312	Oil, C.S.	12.00--15.00
1465	Oil, Cut Neck, C.S.	12.00--15.00
1478	Cream	2.00----4.00
1478	Sugar	2.00----4.00
1480	Cream	2.00----4.00
1480	Sugar	2.00----4.00
1759	Cream	2.00----4.00
1759	Sugar	2.00----4.00
1733	Marmalade & Cover	6.00----9.00
1831	Mustard & Cover	8.00--10.00
858	Oyster Cocktail	2.00----3.00
5054	Parfait	2.00----3.00
1719	Sandwich Plate	3.00----4.00
5013	Gin Rickey	2.00----3.00
300	Quart Decanter, C.N.	14.00--16.00
1464	18 oz. Decanter, C.N.	16.00--18.00
1227	Punch Bowl & Foot	30.00--35.00
863	10½ oz. Goblet	2.00----3.00
863	9 oz. Goblet	2.00----3.00
863	7 oz. Goblet	2.00----3.00
863	5½ oz. Tall Champagne	2.00----3.00
863	4½ oz. Claret	2.00----3.00
863	3 oz. Wine	2.00----3.00

863	1 oz. Cordial	2.00----3.00
863	4½ oz. Rhine Wine	2.00----3.00
863	2 oz. Sherry	2.00----3.00
863	5½ oz. Saucer Champagne	2.00----3.00
863	3½ oz. Cocktail	2.00----3.00
863	2½ oz. Creme de Menthe	2.00----3.00
863	Fruit	2.00----3.00
863	¾ oz. Pousse Cafe	2.00----3.00
863	Individual Almond	2.00----3.00
863	H.S. Champagne, Cut Flute	3.00----4.00
858	Sweetmeat	2.00----4.00
858	Table Tumbler	1.00----2.00
858	3½, 5, 6½, 8, 10, 12, 14, 16 oz. Tumbler	1.00----3.00
858	Tumbler Plate	1.00----2.00
858	Custard	2.00----3.00
858	Custard Plate	1.00----2.00
858	Finger Bowl	2.00----3.00
858	Finger Bowl Plate	1.00----2.00
858	Table Tumbler, Cut 19	1.00----2.00
858	3½, 5, 6½, 8, 10, 12, 14, 16 oz. Tumbler, Cut 19	1.00----2.00
820	Tumbler	1.00----2.00
820	Tumbler, Half sham	1.00----2.00
1462	Tumbler	1.00----2.00
885	2½ oz. Tumbler	1.00----2.00
887	3 oz. Tumbler	1.00----2.00
889	5 oz. Tumbler	1.00----2.00
833	6, 7, 8, 10 oz. Tumbler, Half sham	1.00----2.00
837	9 oz. Tumbler	1.00----2.00
701	7, 14 oz. Tumbler	1.00----2.00
701	Tumbler plate	1.00----2.00

DEEP PLATE ETCHING NO. 214

863	10½ oz. Goblet	2.00----3.00
863	9 oz. Goblet	2.00----3.00
863	7 oz. Goblet	2.00----3.00
863	5½ oz. Tall Champagne	2.00----3.00
863	4½ oz. Claret	2.00----3.00
863	3 oz. Wine	2.00----3.00
863	1 oz. Cordial	2.00----3.00
863	4½ oz. Rhine Wine	2.00----3.00
863	2 oz. Sherry	2.00----3.00
863	5½ oz. Saucer Champagne	2.00----3.00
863	3½ oz. Cocktail	2.00----3.00
863	2½ oz. Creme de Menthe	2.00----3.00
863	¾ oz. Pousse Cafe	2.00----3.00
863	Fruit	2.00----2.50
863	Individual Almond	2.00----3.00
863	Hol. Stem Champ., Cut Flute	3.00----4.00
846	Sherry	2.00----3.00
826	9 oz. Goblet	2.00----3.00
858	Table Tumbler	1.00----2.00
858	3½, 5, 6½, 8, 10, 12, 14, 16 oz. Tumbler	1.00----3.00
858	Tumbler Plate	1.00----2.00
858	Custard	2.00----3.00
858	Custard Plate	1.00----2.00
858	Finger Bowl	1.00----2.00
858	Finger Bowl Plate	1.00----2.00
858	Table Tumbler, Cut 19	1.00----2.00
858	3½, 5, 6½, 8, 10, 12, 14, 16 oz. Tumbler, Cut 19	1.00----2.00
820	Tumbler	1.00----2.00
820½	Tumbler, Half Sham	1.00----2.00
885	2, 3 oz. Tumbler	1.00----2.00
887	2, 3 oz. Tumbler	1.00----2.00
889	5, 8 oz. Tumbler	1.00----2.00

833	5, 7, 8, 9 oz. Tumbler, Half Sham.	1.00----2.00
300	6, 7 Tankard	15.00--18.00
300½	7 Tankard	15.00--20.00
724	7 Tankard	18.00--20.00
1236	6 Jug	18.00--20.00
1236	7 Jug	18.00--20.00
1558	Water Bottle, C.N.	12.00--15.00
1499	Finger Bowl	1.00----2.00
1499	Finger Bowl Plate	1.00----2.00
315	Finger Bowl	1.00----2.00
315	Finger Bowl Plate	1.00----2.00
480	Custard	2.00----3.00
481	Custard	2.00----3.00
481	Custard Plate	1.00----2.00
840	Sherbet	1.00----2.00
840	Sherbet Plate	1.00----2.00
932	Saucer Champagne	2.00----3.00
932	Plate	1.00----2.00
945	Grape Fruit	2.00----3.00
945½	Grape Fruit	2.00----3.00
945½	Grape Fruit Liner	2.00----3.00
793	H.S. Champagne, C.F.	3.00----4.00
794	H.S. Champagne, C.F.	3.00----4.00
300½	Small Oil, C.S.	12.00--15.00
312	Oil C.S.	12.00--15.00
1465	Oil, C. Neck, C.S.	12.00--15.00
1132	Horseradish	10.00--12.00
403	Mustard & Cover	8.00--10.00
1165	Shaker, S.P. Top	2.00----3.00
1759	Sugar	2.00----4.00
1759	Cream	2.00----4.00
1478	Sugar	2.00----4.00
1478	Cream	2.00----4.00
823	4½", 5" Fruit	1.00----2.00
803	4½", 5", 6", 7" Ftd. Nappy, deep	2.00----6.00
803	4½", 5", 6", 7", 8" Ftd. Nappy, shallow	2.00----6.00
803	5", 6" Footed Comport	4.00----6.00
1227	8" Nappy	5.00----7.00
1227	4½" Nappy	1.00----2.00
300	Pint, Quart Decanter, C.N.	14.00--16.00
1464	18 oz. Decanter, C.N.	16.00--18.00

DEEP PLATE ETCHING NO. 215

858	11 oz. Goblet	2.00----3.00
858	10 oz. Goblet	2.00----3.00
858	9 oz. Goblet	2.00----3.00
858	6½ oz. Claret	2.00----3.00
858	4½ oz. Claret	2.00----3.00
858	3½ oz. Wine	2.00----3.00
858	2¾ oz. Wine	2.00----3.00
858	2 oz. Sherry	2.00----3.00
858	1 oz. Cordial	2.00----3.00
858	7 oz. Saucer Champagne	2.00----3.00
858	H.S. Champagne, C.F.	3.00----4.00
858	5½ oz. Tall Champagne	2.00----3.00
858	4 oz. Hot Whiskey	2.00----3.00
858	1 oz. Brandy	2.00----3.00
858	3½ oz. Cocktail	2.00----3.00
858	2½ oz. Creme de Menthe	2.00----3.00
858	Sherbet	2.00----3.00
858	Fruit Salad	2.00----2.50
858	Sweet Meat	3.00----4.00
858	L.S. Champagne, Cut R	4.00----5.00
858	Table Tumbler	1.00----2.00
858	3½, 5, 6½, 8, 10, 12, 14, oz. Tumbler	1.00----2.00

858	Tumbler Plate	1.00----2.00
858	Custard	2.00----3.00
858	Custard Plate	1.00----2.00
858	Finger Bowl	1.00----2.00
858	Finger Bowl Plate	1.00----2.00
1499	Finger Bowl	1.00----2.00
1499	Finger Bowl Plate	1.00----2.00
315	Finger Bowl	1.00----2.00
315	Finger Bowl Plate	1.00----2.00
1733	Marmalade & Cover	6.00----9.00
1831	Mustard & Cover	8.00--10.00
820	Tumbler	1.00----2.00
820½	Tumbler, Half Sham	1.00----2.00
1462	Tumbler	1.00----2.00
833	7, 8 oz. Tumbler	1.00----2.00
887	3 oz. Tumbler	1.00----2.00
889	5 oz. Tumbler	1.00----2.00
892	13 oz. Tumbler	1.00----2.00
701	14 oz. Tumbler	1.00----2.00
701	Tumbler Plate	1.00----2.00
300	6, 7 Tankard	15.00--18.00
724	7 Tankard	18.00--20.00
303	7 Jug	18.00--20.00
1111	6 Jug, Optic	15.00--18.00
1558	Water Bottle, Cut Neck	12.00--15.00
160½	Water Bottle, Cut Neck	12.00--15.00
1465	Oil, Cut Neck	12.00--15.00
312	Oil	12.00--15.00
480	Custard	2.00----3.00
480	Custard Plate	1.00----2.00
481	Custard	2.00----3.00
945	Grape Fruit	2.00----3.00
945½	Grape Fruit	2.00----3.00
945½	Grape Fruit Liner	2.00----3.00
825	Saucer Champagne	2.00----3.00
932	Saucer Champagne	2.00----3.00
932	Plate	3.00----4.00
5036	Parfait	2.00----3.00
5054	Parfait	2.00----3.00
863	Almond	2.00----2.50
840	Sherbet	2.00----2.50
840	Sherbet Plate	1.00----2.00
863	Fruit	2.00----2.50
863	Fruit Plate	1.00----2.00
846	Sherry	2.00----3.00
1132	Horseradish	10.00--12.00
1165	Shaker	2.00----3.00
1478	Sugar	2.00----4.00
1478	Cream	2.00----4.00
1480	Sugar	2.00----4.00
1480	Cream	2.00----4.00
1759	Sugar	2.00----4.00
1759	Cream	2.00----4.00
823	4½", 5" Fruit	1.00----2.00
803	5", 6" Comport	3.00----4.00
803	5½", 5", 6", 7" Ftd. Nappy, deep	2.00----5.00
803	4½", 5", 6", 7" Ftd. Nappy, shallow	2.00----5.00
1227	8" Nappy	4.00----6.00
1227	4½" Nappy	1.00----2.00
1464	18 oz. Decanter, Cut Neck	16.00--18.00
300	Quart Decanter, Cut Neck	16.00--18.00

MISC.

1314	Shaker Cut & Etched 218	2.00----3.00
1432	Shaker Cut & Etched 219	2.00----3.00
800	Shaker Cut & Etched 220	2.00----3.00
1851	Sugar Etched 217	2.00----3.00
1851	Cream Etched 217	2.00----3.00
1453	11" Candle Etched F	15.00--18.00
1485	11" Candle Etched B	15.00--18.00
1485	9½" Candle Etched B	12.00--15.00
1478	Lavender Salt & Stopper Etched 221	8.00--10.00
1741	Tea Caddy & Cover Etched 221	9.00--12.00
1712	Sugar Etched 224	2.00----3.00
1712½	Cream Etched 224	3.00----4.00
840	Sherbet & Plate Et. 225	2.00----4.00
1904	Bon Bon & Cover Et. 221	15.00--18.00
1666	Puff & Cover Et. 221	12.00--15.00
803	5" Deep Nappy, Et. 222	2.00----3.00
803	5" Comport Etched 222	3.00----4.00
863	Almond, Etched 222	2.00----2.50
1632	8" Candle Stick Et. D	12.00--15.00
1204	8½" Candle Stick Et. D	12.00--15.00
701	10 oz. Tumbler Optic Et. 22	2.00----3.00
318-7	Jug Optic Et. 228	20.00--22.50

BLOWN CRYSTAL VASES

1895	12" Vase Etched 223	12.00--15.00
1895	10" Vase Etched 223	10.00--12.00
1895	8" Vase Etched 223	8.00--10.00
1895	6" Vase Etched 223	6.00----8.00
300	12" Vase Deep Etched	12.00--15.00
300	18" Vase Deep Etched	18.00--20.00
300	24" Vase Deep Etched	20.00--25.00

DEEP ETCHING NO. 227
NEW VINTAGE

858	Custard	2.00----3.00
858	Custard Plate	1.00----2.00
858	Finger Bowl	1.00----2.00
858	Finger Bowl Plate	1.00----2.00
803	5" Comport	3.00----4.00
803	6" Comport	3.00----4.00
803	4½", 5", 6", 7" Ftd. Nappy, deep	2.00----4.00
803	4½", 5", 6", 7", 8" Ftd. Nappy, shallow	2.00----6.00
1227	9", 8", 7", 6", 5", 4½" Nappy	2.00----8.00
1227	Punch Bowl & Foot	25.00--35.00
863	10½ oz. Goblet	2.00----3.00
863	9 oz. Goblet,	2.00----3.00
863½	9 oz. Goblet, S.S.	2.00----3.00
863	7½ oz. Goblet, L.S.	2.00----3.00
863	7 oz. Goblet	2.00----3.00
863	5½ oz. Goblet	2.00----3.00
863	5½ oz. Tall Champagne	2.00----3.00
863	4½ oz. Claret	2.00----3.00
863	3 oz. Wine	2.00----3.00
863	1¼ oz. Cordial	2.00----3.00
863½	¾ oz. Cordial	2.00----3.00
863	4½ oz. Rhine Wine	2.00----3.00
863	2 oz. Sherry	2.00----3.00
863	5½ oz. Saucer Champagne	2.00----3.00
863	3½ oz. Cocktail	2.00----3.00
863	3 oz. Cocktail	2.00----3.00
863	2½ oz. Creme De Menthe	2.00----3.00
863	1½ oz. Pousse Cafe	2.00----3.00
863½	¾ oz. Pousse Cafe	2.00----3.00
863	Fruit	2.00----2.50
863	Individual Almond	2.00----2.50
863	Hollow Stem Champagne C.F.	3.00----4.00

863	4½ oz. Roemer	2.00----3.00
863	5½ oz. Roemer	2.00----3.00
880	11, 10, 9, 8 oz. Goblet	2.00----3.00
880	5 oz. Tall Champagne	2.00----3.00
880	6½ oz. Claret	2.00----3.00
880	4½ oz. Claret	2.00----3.00
880	3½ oz. Wine	2.00----3.00
880	2¾ oz. Wine	2.00----3.00
880	2 oz. Sherry	2.00----3.00
880	1 oz. Cordial	2.00----3.00
880	¾ oz. Cordial	2.00----3.00
880	6½ oz. Tall Ale	2.00----3.00
880	4½ oz. Hot Whiskey	2.00----3.00
880	4 oz. Rhine Wine	2.00----3.00
880	1 oz. Pousse Cafe	2.00----3.00
880	¾ oz. Pousse Cafe	2.00----3.00
880	2½ oz. Creme De Menthe	2.00----3.00
880	3 oz. Cocktail	2.00----3.00
880	3½ oz. Cocktail	2.00----3.00
880	4½ oz. H.S. Champagne C.F	3.00----4.00
880	5 oz. Saucer Champagne	2.00----3.00
880	7 oz. Saucer Champagne	2.00----3.00
880	4½" Bon Bon	2.00----3.00
880½—Grape Fruit		2.00----3.00
880	Grape Fruit	2.00----3.00
880	Grape Fruit Liner	2.00----3.00
880½—Grape Fruit Liner		2.00----3.00
880	Sherbet	2.00----2.50
1061	Cracker Jar & Cover	18.00--20.00
1897	7" Plate	2.00----4.00
1848	9" Sandwich Plate	4.00----6.00
1719	10½" Sandwich Plate	6.00----8.00
2238	8¼" Salad Plate	2.00----3.00
2238	11" Salad Plate	4.00----6.00
2228	½ lb. Candy Jar & Cover	10.00--15.00
2219	¼, ½, 1 lb. Candy Jar & Cover	10.00--15.00
300	6, 7 Tankard	15.00--18.00
724	7 Tankard	18.00--20.00
303	7 Jug	15.00--18.00
1111	6 Jug	15.00--18.00
1558	Water Bottle C.N.	12.00--15.00
160½	Water Bottle, C.N.	12.00--15.00
1465	Oil, C.N.	10.00--12.50
312	Oil	10.00--12.50
480	Custard	2.00----3.00
	Custard Plate	1.00----2.00
481	Custard	2.00----3.00
945	Grape Fruit	2.00----3.00
945½—Grape Fruit		2.00----3.00
945½—Grape Fruit Liner		2.00----3.00
825	Saucer Champagne	2.00----3.00
932	Saucer Champagne	2.00----3.00
840	Sherbet	2.00----2.50
840	Sherbet Plate	1.00----2.00
846	Sherry	2.00----3.00
864	Peach Champagne	2.00----3.00
5036	Parfait	2.00----3.00
1132	Horseradish	10.00--12.00
1165	Shaker	2.00----3.00
1478	Sugar	2.00----3.00
1478	Cream	2.00----3.00
1480	Sugar	2.00----3.00
1480	Cream	2.00----3.00
1759	Sugar	2.00----3.00
1759	Cream	2.00----3.00
820	Tumbler	1.00----2.00
820	Tumbler, half sham	1.00----2.00
1462	Tumbler	1.00----2.00
885	2½ oz. Tumbler	1.00----2.00
887	3 oz. Tumbler	1.00----2.00

889	5 oz. Tumbler	1.00----2.00
833	6, 7, 8, 10 oz. Tumbler, half sham	1.00----2.00
701	14 oz. Tumbler	1.00----2.00
	Tumbler Plate	1.00----2.00
1491	Decanter, Cut neck	20.00--25.00
858	11, 10, 9, 8 oz. Goblet	2.00----3.00
858	7 oz. Bass Ale	2.00----3.00
858	6½ oz. Claret	2.00----3.00
858	4½ oz. Claret	2.00----3.00
858	3½ oz. Wine	2.00----3.00
858	2¾ oz. Wine	2.00----3.00
858	2 oz. Sherry	2.00----3.00
858	1 oz. Cordial	2.00----3.00
858	7 oz. Saucer Champagne	2.00----3.00
858	5½ oz. Saucer Champagne	2.00----3.00
858	H.S. Champagne C.F.	2.00----4.00
858	5½ oz. Tall Champagne	2.00----3.00
858	4 oz. Hot Whiskey	2.00----3.00
858	1 oz. Brandy	2.00----3.00
858	3½ oz. Cocktail	2.00----3.00
858	2½ oz. Creme De Menthe	2.00----3.00
858	Sherbet	2.00----2.50
858	Fruit Salad	2.00----2.50
858	Oyster Cocktail	2.00----3.00
858	Short Cake	2.00----3.00
858	4½" Ice Cream	2.00----2.50
858	L.S. Champagne	2.00----3.00
858	Table Tumbler, Cut 19	1.00----2.00
858	3½, 5, 6½, 8, 10, 12, 14, 16 oz. Tumbler, Cut 19	2.00----4.00
858	3½, 5, 6½, 8, Table, 10, 12, 14, 16 oz. Tumbler	2.00----4.00
858	Tumbler Plate	1.00----2.00

ETCHING NO. 231 "POUPEE"

300	7 Tankard	18.00--20.00
724	6 Tankard	15.00--18.00
724	7 Tankard	18.00--20.00
303	7 Jug	15.00--18.00
820	Tumbler	1.00----2.00
887	3 oz. Tumbler	1.00----2.00
889	5, 8, 9, 10,14 oz. Tumbler	2.00----3.00
701	3, 5, 8, 10, 12, 14 oz. Tumbler	2.00----3.00
4015	14 oz. Tumbler	2.00----3.00
1499	Finger Bowl	2.00----3.00
1499	Finger Bowl Plate	1.00----2.00
1769	Finger Bowl	2.00----3.00
1769	Finger Bowl Plate	1.00----2.00
300½—Oil		12.00--15.00
1465	Oil, C.N.	12.00--15.00
863	Almond	2.00----3.00
803	5", 6", 7" Deep Nappy	4.00----6.00
803	5", 6" Comport	4.00----6.00
858	Sweetmeat	3.00----4.00
945	Grape Fruit	2.00----3.00
945½—Grape Fruit Liner		2.00----3.00
1719	Sandwich Plate	5.00----8.00
1848	Sandwich Plate	4.00----6.00
1195	Large Decanter, C.N.	18.00--22.00
1491	Decanter, C.N., Optic	18.00--22.00
300	Qt. Decanter, Handled	20.00--22.00
300	Qt. Decanter, Hld. C.N.	20.00--25.00
481	Custard	2.00----3.00
840	Plate	1.00----2.00
5070	10, 9, 8 oz. Goblet	2.00----4.00
5070	5½ oz. Tall Champagne	2.00----4.00
5070	6 oz. Claret	2.00----4.00

5070	4½ oz. Claret	2.00----4.00
5070	3 oz. Wine	2.00----4.00
5070	2 oz. Sherry	2.00----4.00
5070	1 oz. Cordial	2.00----4.00
5070	¾ oz. Cordial	2.00----4.00
5070	4½ oz. H.S. Champ'ne C.F.	3.00----4.00
5070	4½ oz. Rhine Wine	2.00----4.00
5070	4 oz. Hot Whiskey	2.00----4.00
5070	3½ oz. Cocktail	2.00----4.00
5070	3 oz. Cocktail	2.00----4.00
5070	2½ oz. Creme de Menthe	2.00----4.00
5070	1 oz. Posse Cafe	2.00----4.00
5070	¾ oz. Pousse Cafe	2.00----4.00
5070	Sherbet	2.00----3.00
932	6" Plate	1.00----2.00
1769	Finger Bowl	2.00----3.00
1769	F. Bowl Plate (200-6")	1.00----2.00
945½	—Grape Fruit	2.00----3.00
840	5" Sherbet Plate	1.00----2.00
822	Parfait	2.00----4.00
863	Almond	2.00----4.00
1478	Sugar	3.00----4.00
1478	Cream	3.00----4.00

ETCHING NO. 232 "LOTUS"

300	7, 4 Tankard	15.00--20.00
300	Claret Tankard	20.00--25.00
318	7 Tankard, Optic	18.00--20.00
303	7 Jug	15.00--18.00
820	Tumbler	1.00----2.00
858	Table Tumbler	1.00----2.00
887	3 oz. Tumbler	1.00----2.00
889	5, 7, 8, 10 oz. Tumbler	1.00----3.00
4015	14 oz. Tumbler	2.00----3.00
858	Plate	2.00----3.00
1769	Finger Bowl	2.00----3.00
1769	Finger Bowl Plate	1.00----2.00
1499	Finger Bowl	2.00----3.00
1499	Finger Bowl Plate	1.00----2.00
840	Sherbet	2.00----3.00
840	Sherbet Plate	1.00----2.00
822	Parfait	2.00----4.00
858	Sweetmeat	2.00----4.00
300½	—Small Oil, C.N.	12.00--15.00
312	Oil	12.00--15.00
1465	Oil, C.N.	12.00--15.00
481	Custard	2.00----3.00
1165½	—Shaker, S.P.T.	3.00----4.00
922	Toothpick	6.00----8.00
1733	Marmalade & Cov. Notch.	8.00--12.00
1478	Sugar	3.00----4.00
1478	Cream	3.00----4.00
863	Almond	2.00----3.00
803	5", 6", 7" Deep, Nappy	3.00----5.00
803	8" Nappy	5.00----8.00
803	5" Comport	3.00----4.00
1227	4½" Nappy	2.00----3.00
1227	8" Nappy	5.00----8.00
160½	—Water Bottle, C.N.	12.00--15.00
1558	Water Bottle, C.N.	12.00--15.00
5070	10, 9, 8 oz. Goblet	2.00----4.00
5070	5½ oz. Tall Champagne	2.00----4.00
5070	6 oz. Claret	2.00----4.00
5070	4½ oz. Claret	2.00----4.00
5070	3 oz. Wine	2.00----4.00
5070	2 oz. Sherry	2.00----4.00
5070	1 oz. Cordial	2.00----4.00
5070	¾ oz. Cordial	2.00----4.00
5070	4½ oz. Champ'ne C.F.	2.00----4.00

5070	4½ oz. Rhine Wine	2.00----4.00
5070	4 oz. Hot Whiskey	2.00----4.00
5070	3½ oz. Cocktail	2.00----4.00
5070	3 oz. Cocktail	2.00----4.00
5070	2½ oz. Creme de Menthe	2.00----4.00
5070	1 oz. Posse Cafe	2.00----4.00
5070	¾ oz. Pousse Cafe	2.00----4.00
5070	5½ oz. Saucer Champagne	2.00----4.00
5070	Sherbet	2.00----3.00
945½	—Grape Fruit	2.00----3.00
945½	—Grape Fruit Liner	2.00----3.00
1195	Large Decanter, C.N.	18.00--22.00
1452	Handled Decanter, H.M.S.	22.00--25.00
1490	Candlestick	12.00--15.00
1948	5", 8", 10", 12½" Vase	4.00--12.00
858	14 oz. Tumbler	2.00----3.00
858	14 oz. Tumbler Plate	2.00----3.00
1895	8" Vase	6.00----9.00
766	5", 6" Comport	3.00----4.00
766	4½", 5", 6", 7" Ftd. Nappy	3.00----5.00
766	Parfait	2.00----4.00
766	4½ oz. Claret	2.00----4.00
766	2¾ oz. Wine	2.00----4.00
766	2 oz. Sherry	2.00----4.00
766	¾ oz. Cordial	2.00----4.00
766	3 oz. Cocktail	2.00----4.00
766	Almond	2.00----4.00
766	Custard	2.00----3.00
766	Finger Bowl	2.00----3.00
766	F. Bowl Plate (1736-6")	1.00----2.00
766	9 oz. Goblet	2.00----4.00
766	5 oz. Saucer Champagne	2.00----4.00
766	Fruit	2.00----2.50
766	Sherbet	2.00----2.50
803	6" Comport	3.00----4.00
803	5", 6", 7" Ftd. Nappy	2.00----4.00
837	Oyster Cocktail	2.00----3.00
766½	—Parfait	2.00----4.00
4061	Ftd. Ice Tea, Handled	3.00----4.00
766	Ftd. Ice Tea, Handled	3.00----4.00
701	5" Tumbler Plate	1.00----2.00
766	Grape Fruit	2.00----3.00
766	Grape Fruit Liner	2.00----3.00
766	Bon Bon	2.00----4.00
858	14 oz. Tumbler	2.00----3.00
4011½	—Table Tumbler	2.00----3.00
4011	15, 12, 10, 8, 5, 3 oz. Tumbler	1.00----3.00

ETCHING NO. 234 "KORNFLOWER"

880	11, 10, 9, 8 oz. Goblet	2.00----3.00
880	5 oz. Tall Champagne	2.00----3.00
880	6½ oz. Claret	2.00----3.00
880	4½ oz. Claret	2.00----3.00
880	3½ oz. Wine	2.00----3.00
880	2¾ oz. Wine	2.00----3.00
880	2 oz. Sherry	2.00----3.00
880	1 oz. Cordial	2.00----3.00
880	¾ oz. Cordial	2.00----3.00
880	6½ oz. Tall Ale	2.00----3.00
880	4½ oz. Hot Whiskey	2.00----3.00
880	4 oz. Rhine Wine	2.00----3.00
880	1 oz. Pousse Cafe	2.00----3.00
880	¾ oz. Pousse Cafe	2.00----3.00
880	2½ oz. Creme de Menthe	2.00----3.00
880	3 oz. Cocktail	2.00----3.00
880	3½ oz. Cocktail	2.00----3.00
880	4½ oz. H.S. Champagne C.F.	2.00----3.00
880	5 oz. Saucer Champagne	2.00----3.00

880	7 oz. Saucer Champagne	2.00----3.00
880	4½" Bon Bon	2.00----3.00
880½	—Grape Fruit	2.00----3.00
880	Grape Fruit	2.00----3.00
880	Grape Fruit Liner	2.00----3.00
880½	—Grape Fruit Liner	2.00----3.00
880	Sherbet	2.00----2.50
810	Sherbet	2.00----2.50
863	Fruit	2.00----2.50
840	Plate	1.00----2.00
1499	Finger Bowl	1.00----2.00
1499	Finger Bowl Plate	1.00----2.00
1769	Finger Bowl	1.00----2.00
1769	Finger Bowl Plate	1.00----2.00
1867	Finger Bowl	1.00----2.00
1867	Finger Bowl Plate	1.00----2.00
803	5", 6" Comport	2.00----3.00
803	5", 6", 7" Nappy, Deep	2.00----4.00
858	Sweetmeat	2.00----3.00
1478	Sugar	2.00----3.00
1478	Cream	2.00----3.00
300	Qt. Decanter, C.N.	18.00--20.00
1236	6 Pitcher	15.00--18.00
303	7, 6 Jug	15.00--18.00
820	Tumbler	1.00----2.00
885	3 oz. Tumbler	1.00----2.00
701	5, 8, 10 oz. Tumbler	1.00----2.00
858	Table Tumbler	1.00----2.00
858	3½, 5, 6½, 8, 10, 12, 14, 16 oz. Tumbler	1.00----3.00
863	Almond	2.00----3.00

ETCHING NO. 235 "IVY"

882	11, 10, 9, 8 oz. Goblet	2.00----3.00
882	5 oz. Tall Champagne	2.00----3.00
882	6½, 4½ oz. Claret	2.00----3.00
882	3½, 2¾ oz. Wine	2.00----3.00
882	2 oz. Sherry	2.00----3.00
882	1, ¾ oz. Cordial	2.00----3.00
882	6½ oz. Tall Ale	2.00----3.00
882	4½ oz. Hot Whiskey	2.00----3.00
882	4 oz. Rhine Wine	2.00----3.00
882	1 oz. Pousse Cafe	2.00----3.00
882	¾ oz. Pousse Cafe	2.00----3.00
882	2½ oz. Creme de Menthe	2.00----3.00
882	3, 3½ oz. Cocktail	2.00----3.00
882	4½ oz. H.S. Champagne C.F	2.00----3.00
882	5, 7 oz. Saucer Champagne	2.00----3.00
882	4½" Bon Bon	2.00----3.00
882½	—Grape Fruit	2.00----3.00
882	Grape Fruit	2.00----3.00
882	Grape Fruit Liner	2.00----3.00
882½	—Grape Fruit Liner	2.00----3.00
882	Sherbet	2.00----2.50
882	Custard, Cut Flute	3.00----4.00
882	Finger Bowl, Cut Flute	2.00----3.00
887	3 oz. Tumbler, Cut B.	1.00----2.00
858	Table Tumbler, Cut 19	1.00----2.00
858	3, 4, 6, 7½, 9, 11, 13, 15 oz. Tumbler, Cut 19	1.00----4.00
701	5, 8, 10 oz. Tumbler, Cut B.	1.00----3.00
300	7 oz. Tankard Cut Flute	18.00--20.00
300	Qt. Decanter C.N.	18.00--20.00
1464	18 oz. Decanter, C.N.	18.00--20.00
1558	Water Bottle, Cut Neck	10.00--14.00
1465	Oil, Cut Neck	12.00--15.00

ETCHING NO. 236 "GRILLE"

882	11, 10, 9, 8 oz. Goblet	2.00----4.00
882	5 oz. Tall Champagne	2.00----4.00
882	6½, 4½ oz. Claret	2.00----4.00
882	3½, 2¾ oz. Wine	2.00----4.00
882	2 oz. Sherry	2.00----4.00
882	1, ¾ oz. Cordial	2.00----4.00
882	6½ oz. Tall Ale	2.00----4.00
882	4½ oz. Hot Whiskey	2.00----4.00
882	4 oz. Rhine Wine	2.00----4.00
882	1 oz. Pousse Cafe	2.00----4.00
882	¾ oz. Pousse Cafe	2.00----4.00
882	2½ oz. Creme de Menthe	2.00----4.00
882	3 oz. Cocktail	2.00----4.00
882	3½ oz. Cocktail	2.00----4.00
882	4½ oz. H.S. Champagne C.F	2.00----4.00
882	5, 7 oz. Saucer Champagne	2.00----4.00
882	4½" Bon Bon	2.00----4.00
882½	—Grape Fruit	2.00----3.00
882	Grape Fruit	2.00----3.00
882	Grape Fruit Liner	2.00----3.00
882½	— Grape Fruit Liner	2.00----3.00
882	Sherbet	2.00----3.00
	Sherbet Plate	1.00----2.00
882	Custard, Cut Flute	2.00----3.00
882	Finger Bowl, Cut Flute	2.00----3.00
300	7 Tankard, Cut Flute	20.00--22.00
820	Tumbler, Cut B, Pty.	2.00----2.50
887	3 oz. Tumbler, Cut B, Pty.	2.00----3.00
833	8 oz. Tumbler, Cut B, Pty.	2.00----2.50
701	14 oz. Tumbler, Cut B, Pty.	2.00----3.00
	Tumbler Plate	1.00----2.00
300½	Small Oil	12.00--15.00
1465	7 oz. Oil, C.N.	12.00--15.00
810	Oyster Cocktail	2.00----3.00
863	Almond	2.00----2.50
803	5" Deep Nappy	3.00----4.00
803	7" Deep Nappy	4.00----6.00
803	5" Comport	3.00----4.00
1499	Finger Bowl	2.00----3.00
1499	Finger Bowl Plate	2.00----3.00
1769	Finger Bowl	2.00----3.00
1769	Finger Bowl Plate	2.00----3.00
300	Qt. Decanter, C.N.	18.00--20.00
300	Qt. Decanter Hdl., C.N.	20.00--22.00
1464	18 oz. Decanter, C.N.	20.00--25.00

DEEP PLATE ETCHING No. 237 "GARLAND"

1968	Marmalade & Cover	6.00----8.00
1831	Mustard & Cover	6.00----8.00
979	Horseradish	6.00----8.00
1719	Sandwich Plate	3.00----5.00
1848	Sandwich Plate	3.00----5.00
1918	Bar Bottle, C.N.	18.00--20.00
1918	Decanter, C.N.	18.00--20.00
1918	Bitter Bottle & Tube, C.N.	15.00--18.00
1918	Cherry Jar, C.N.	15.00--18.00
1227	Punch Bowl & Foot	25.00--35.00
701	8 oz. Tumbler	1.00----2.00
701	14 oz. Tumbler	2.00----3.00
701	Tumbler Plate	1.00----2.00
889	5 oz. Tumbler	1.00----2.00
887	3 oz. Tumbler	3.00----4.00
870	2½ oz. Tumbler, Sham, Puntied	3.00----4.00
4065	14 oz. Tumbler, Cut 19	2.00----3.00
4065	8 oz. Tumbler, Cut 19	1.00----2.00
4077	15 oz. Tumbler	2.00----3.00

No.	Description	Price
4077	9½ oz. Tumbler	1.00----2.00
1769	Finger Bowl	1.00----2.00
	Finger Bowl Plate	1.00----2.00
481	Custard	2.00----3.00
	Custard Plate	1.00----2.00
803	7", 6", 5", 4½" Nappy, Dp	2.00----5.00
160½—	Water Bottle, Cut Neck	12.00--15.00
2022	Shaker, F. Glass Top	2.00----3.00
2223	Shaker, F. Glass Top	2.00----3.00
1165½—	Shaker, Pearl Top	2.00----3.00
300	7 Tankard	15.00--18.00
724	7 Tankard	15.00--18.00
1787	6 Tankard	15.00--18.00
303	7 Jug	15.00--18.00
1236	6 Jug	15.00--18.00
2018	Jug, C.N.	15.00--18.00
1761	Claret Tankard	20.00--25.00
160½—	Water Bottle, C.N.	10.00--14.00
1465	Large Oil, C.N.	12.00--15.00
1465	Small Oil	10.00--12.00
1478	Sugar	2.00----3.00
1478	Cream	2.00----3.00
300	Qt. Decanter, C.N.	18.00--20.00
1165	Shaker, S. P. Top	2.00----3.00
922	Toothpick, Cut 19	6.00----8.00
4061	Handled Lemonade	3.00----4.00
2017	Molasses Can, Metal Hdl.	22.00--28.00
2017	Sugar Duster	6.00----8.00
880	10 oz. Goblet	2.00----3.00
880	5 oz. Tall Champagne	2.00----3.00
880	4½ oz. Claret	2.00----3.00
880	2¾ oz. Wine	2.00----3.00
880	2 oz. Sherry	2.00----3.00
880	1 oz. Cordial	2.00----3.00
880	4 oz. Rhine Wine	2.00----3.00
880	1 oz. Pousse Cafe	2.00----3.00
880	2½ oz. Creme de Menthe	2.00----3.00
880	3½ oz. Cocktail	2.00----3.00
880	5 oz. Saucer Champagne	2.00----3.00
880	4½ oz. H.S. Champagne	2.00----3.00
880	4½ " Bon Bon	2.00----3.00
880½—	Grape Fruit	2.00----3.00
880½—	Grape Fruit Liner	2.00----3.00
880	Grape Fruit	2.00----3.00
880	Grape Fruit Liner	2.00----3.00
880	Sherbet	2.00----2.50
5051	Large Almond	2.00----3.00
5051	Small Almond	2.00----3.00
899	Parfait	2.00----3.00
863	10½ oz. Goblet	2.00----3.00
863	9 oz. Goblet	2.00----3.00
863	5½ oz. Tall Champagne	2.00----3.00
863	4½ oz. Claret	2.00----3.00
863	3 oz. Wine	2.00----3.00
863	2 oz. Sherry	2.00----3.00
863	¾ oz. Cordial	2.00----3.00
863	4 oz. Rhine Wine	2.00----3.00
863	¾ oz. Pousse Cafe	2.00----3.00
863	2½ oz. Creme de Menthe	2.00----3.00
863	3½ oz. Cocktail	2.00----3.00
863	H. S. Champagne, C.F.	3.00----4.00
863	5½ oz. Saucer Champagne	2.00----3.00
863	Almond	2.00----3.00
863	Sherbet	2.00----2.50
840	Sherbet	2.00----2.50
840	Sherbet Plate	1.00----2.00
952	Cocktail	2.00----3.00
932	Saucer Champagne	2.00----3.00
932	Saucer Champagne Plate	1.00----2.00
820	Tumbler	1.00----2.00
820½—	Tumbler, Cut 19	1.00----2.00

No.	Description	Price
833	8 oz. Tumbler	1.00----2.00
833	8 oz. Tumbler, Sham	1.00----2.00
880	Footed Salt	4.00----6.00
825	Saucer Champagne	2.00----3.00
825	Jelly & Cover	4.00----6.00
803	5" Ftd. Nappy & Cover	4.00----6.00
803	5" Ftd. Comport & Cover	4.00----6.00
766	5", 6" Comport	3.00----5.00
766	5", 6", 7" Footed Nappy	3.00----6.00
803	5", 6" Comport	3.00----5.00
803	4½", 5", 6", 7" Ftd. Nappy	3.00----6.00
1227	4½", 8" Nappy	2.00----5.00
4011½—	Table Tumbler	1.00----2.00
4011	15, 12, 8, 5, 3 oz. Tumbler	1.00----3.00
2138	Mayonnaise Bowl	8.00--10.00
2138	Mayonnaise Plate	2.00----3.00
2138	Mayonnaise Ladle	1.00----2.00
1227	Punch Bowl & Foot	25.00--35.00
1897	7" Plate	1.00----2.00
1848	9" Sandwich Plate	2.00----4.00
300	7 Jug	15.00--17.00
300	7 Jug, Cut Flute	15.00--20.00
724	7 Jug	18.00--20.00
1761	Claret Jug	20.00--25.00
318	7 Jug	18.00--20.00
1697	Carafe	8.00--10.00
1697	Carafe Tumbler (4023-6 oz)	3.00----4.00
1697	Carafe Whiskey (981-2½ oz)	3.00----4.00
2194	8 oz. Syrup, Nickel Top	20.00--25.00
2194	12 oz. Syrup, Nickel Top	20.00--25.00
1480	Sugar	2.00----3.00
1480	Cream	2.00----3.00
2083	Salad Dressing Bottle	5.00----8.00
2169	Salad Dressing Bottle	5.00----8.00
1465	7, 5 oz. Oil, Cut Neck	12.00--15.00
1236	7 Jug	15.00--18.00
1236	6 Jug	15.00--18.00
2018	7 Jug, Cut Neck	15.00--18.00
317½—	Jug & Cover	18.00--22.00
2104	Jug & Tumbler, Pty.	20.00--25.00
2238	8¼" Salad Plate	2.00----3.00
2238	11" Salad Plate	3.00----4.00
2219	¼, ½, 1 lb. Candy Jar & Cover	10.00--15.00
701	14 oz. Tumbler, Handled	2.00----3.00
4061	Ftd. Ice Tea, Handled	3.00----4.00
766	Ftd. Ice Tea, Handled	3.00----4.00
4011	12 oz. Tumbler, Handled	2.00----3.00

DEEP PLATE ETCHING NO. 238
"EMPIRE" PATTERN

No.	Description	Price
858	10, 9 oz. Goblet	2.00----3.00
858	5½ oz. Saucer Champagne	2.00----3.00
858	Fruit	2.00----2.50
822	Parfait	2.00----3.00
863	Almond	2.00----3.00
858	Finger Bowl	1.00----2.00
858	F. Bowl Plate (1499-6")	1.00----2.00
858	Custard	2.00----3.00
840	Sherbet	2.00----2.50
840	5" Sherbet Plate	1.00----2.00
945½—	Grape Fruit	2.00----3.00
945½—	Grape Fruit Liner	2.00----3.00
858	Sweetmeat	2.00----3.00
803	5", 6" Comport	3.00----4.00
803	5", 6", 7" Footed Nappy	3.00----6.00
1227	4½" Nappy	1.00----2.00
1227	8" Nappy	5.00----7.00

820	Table Tumbler	1.00----2.00
833	8 oz. Tumbler	1.00----2.00
4061	Ftd. Ice Tea, Handled	3.00----4.00
701	14 oz. Tumbler	1.00----2.00
858	Table, 14, 12, 10, 8, 5 oz. Tumbler	1.00----2.00
300	7 Jug	15.00--18.00
318	7 Jug	15.00--18.00
303	7 Jug	15.00--18.00
1480	Sugar	2.00----3.00
1480	Cream	2.00----3.00
300½—Small Oil		10.00--12.00
1465	7 oz. Oil, Cut Neck	12.00--15.00
1968	Marmalade & Cover	6.00----8.00
1831	Mustard & Cover	6.00----8.00
1848	9" Sandwich Plate	2.00----3.00

DEEP PLATE ETHCING NO. 241 "LILY OF THE VALLEY"

1227	8" Nappy	5.00----8.00
1227	4½" Nappy	1.00----2.00
300	7 Tankard	18.00--20.00
724	7 Tankard	18.00--20.00
303	7 Jug	18.00--20.00
318	7 Jug, Optic	18.00--20.00
1558	Water Bottle, C.N.	12.00--15.00
1480	Sugar	2.00----3.00
1480	Cream	2.00----3.00
300½—Large Oil		12.00--15.00
300½—Small Oil		12.00--15.00
1465	Large Oil, C.N.	12.00--15.00
300	Quart Decanter, C.N.	18.00--20.00
1464	18 oz. Decanter, C.N.	18.00--20.00
1165	Shaker	2.00----3.00
922	Toothpick	6.00----8.00
4061	Lemonade	2.00----3.00
1831	Mustard & Cover	6.00----8.00
1968	Marmalade & Cover	6.00----8.00
1848	9" Sandwich Plate	2.00----4.00
1719	10½" Sandwich Plate	3.00----5.00
858	5, 6½, 8, 10, 12, 14, 16 oz. Tumbler	1.00----3.00
858	8, 14 oz. Tumbler, Cut 19	2.00----3.00
858	Tumbler Plate	1.00----2.00
4065	14, 10, 8, 5, 2½ oz. Tumble ½ Sham C 19	2.00----3.00
4077	15 oz. Ice Tea Tumbler	2.00----3.00
4077	11 oz. Grape Juice	2.00----3.00
4077	9½ oz. Table Tumbler	1.00----2.00
4077	5½ oz. Mineral	1.00----2.00
4077	3 oz. Whiskey	2.00----3.00
820	Tumbler	1.00----2.00
820½—Tumbler, Puntied		1.00----2.00
833	8 oz. Tumbler	1.00----2.00
701	14 oz. Tumbler	1.00----2.00
	Tumbler Plate	1.00----2.00
889	5 oz. Tumbler	1.00----2.00
887	3 oz. Tumbler	2.00----3.00
810	Finger Bowl	2.00----3.00
	Finger Bowl Plate	1.00----2.00
858	Finger Bowl	2.00----3.00
	Finger Bowl Plate	1.00----2.00
810	Custard	2.00----3.00
	Custard Plate	1.00----2.00
858	Custard	2.00----3.00
	Custard Plate	1.00----2.00
803	8" Nappy, Footed	5.00----8.00
803	7", 6", 5", 4½" Nappy Dp.	5.00----8.00
803	6", 5" Comport	3.00----4.00

879	9 oz. Goblet	2.00----3.00
879	4½ oz. Claret	2.00----3.00
879	2¾ oz. Wine	2.00----3.00
879	2 oz. Sherry	2.00----3.00
879	¾ oz. Cordial	2.00----3.00
879	¾ oz. Pousse Cafe	2.00----3.00
879	5 oz. Saucer Champagne	2.00----3.00
879	3 oz. Cocktail	2.00----3.00
879	2½ oz. Creme de Menthe	2.00----3.00
879	Sherbet	2.00----2.50
863	Almond	2.00----3.00
945	Grape Fruit	2.00----3.00
945½—Grape Fruit		2.00----3.00
945½—Grape Fruit Liner		2.00----3.00
858	10 oz. Goblet	2.00----3.00
858	4½ oz. Claret	2.00----3.00
858	2¾ oz. Wine	2.00----3.00
858	2 oz. Sherry	2.00----3.00
858	1 oz. Cordial	2.00----3.00
858	5½ oz. Saucer Champagne	2.00----3.00
858	H. S. Champagne	2.00----3.00
858	5½ oz. Tall Champagne	2.00----3.00
858	1 oz. Pousse Cafe	2.00----3.00
858	3½ oz. Cocktail	2.00----3.00
858	2½ oz. Creme de Menthe	2.00----3.00
858	Fruit Salad	2.00----3.00
858	Short Cake	2.00----3.00
858	Sweetmeat	2.00----3.00
858	Table Tumbler	1.00----2.00
858	3½ oz. Tumbler	1.00----2.00
803	5", 6", 7" Ftd. Nappy	4.00----6.00
1697	Carafe	8.00--10.00
1697	Carafe Tumbler (4023-6 oz.	3.00----4.00
858	Sherbet	2.00----2.50
840	5" Sherbet Plate	1.00----2.00
822	Parfait	2.00----3.00
2083	Salad Dressing Bottle	5.00----8.00
858	3 oz. Tumbler	1.00----2.00
4061	Ftd. Ice Tea, Handled	2.00----3.00

DEEP PLATE ETCHING NO. 249 "ROSILYN" PATTERN

880	9 oz. Goblet	2.00----3.00
880	5 oz. Saucer Champagne	2.00----3.00
880	Sherbet	2.00----2.50
840	5" Sherbet Plate	1.00----2.00
837	Oyster Cocktail	2.00----3.00
822	Parfait	2.00----3.00
880	4½ oz. Claret	2.00----3.00
880	2¾ oz. Wine	2.00----3.00
880	2 oz. Sherry	2.00----3.00
880	1 oz. Cordial	2.00----3.00
880	3½ oz. Cocktail	2.00----3.00
802	10 oz. Goblet	2.00----3.00
802	5½ oz. Saucer Champagne	2.00----3.00
802	Oyster Cocktail	2.00----3.00
802	4½ oz. Claret	2.00----3.00
802	3½ oz. Wine	2.00----3.00
802	2 oz. Sherry	2.00----3.00
802	¾ oz. Cordial	2.00----3.00
802	3½ oz. Cocktail	2.00----3.00
802	Sherbet	2.00----2.50
801	Rhine Wine	2.00----3.00
481	Custard	2.00----3.00
1769	Finger Bowl	1.00----2.00
1769	Finger Bowl Plate (200-6")	1.00----2.00
945½—Grape Fruit		2.00----3.00
945½—Grape Fruit Liner		2.00----3.00
880	4½" Bon Bon	2.00----3.00

No.	Item	Price
803	5" Comport	3.00----4.00
803	6" Comport	3.00----4.00
803	5", 6", 7" Footed Nappy	3.00----5.00
5051	Large Almond	2.00----3.00
5051	Small Almond	2.00----3.00
820	Table Tumbler	1.00----2.00
833	8 oz. Tumbler	1.00----2.00
4061	Ftd. Ice Tea, Handled	2.00----3.00
701	14 oz. Tumbler, Handled	2.00----3.00
701	5" Tumbler Plate	1.00----2.00
701	14 oz. Tumbler	1.00----2.00
701	8 oz. Tumbler	1.00----2.00
4011½—Table Tumbler		1.00----2.00
4011	12 oz. Tumbler	1.00----2.00
4011	8 oz. Tumbler	1.00----2.00
889	5 oz. Tumbler	1.00----2.00
300	7 Jug	18.00--20.00
724	7 Jug	18.00--20.00
318	7 Jug	18.00--20.00
303	7 Jug	18.00--20.00
1480	Sugar	2.00----3.00
1480	Cream	2.00----3.00
2083	Salad Dressing Bottle	8.00--12.00
1465	7 oz. Oil, Cut Neck	12.00--15.00
1733	Marmalade & Cover	6.00----8.00
1697	Carafe	8.00--10.00
1697	Carafe Tumbler (4023-6)	3.00----4.00
1697	Carafe Whiskey (981-2½ oz)	3.00----4.00
1848	9" Sandwich Plate	2.00----5.00
1806	Water Bottle, C.N., Cut 112	10.00--15.00

No.	Item	Price
887	3 oz. Tumbler	2.00----3.00
300	7 Jug	18.00--20.00
724	7 Jug	18.00--20.00
1761	Claret Jug	20.00--30.00
303	7 Jug	18.00--20.00
317½—Jug & Cover		22.00--25.00
2104	Jug & Tumbler, Pty..	30.00--35.00
2133	Sugar	3.00----4.00
2133	Cream	3.00----4.00
1851	Sugar	3.00----4.00
1851	Cream	3.00----4.00
2083	Salad Dressing Bottle	10.00--14.00
2169	Salad Dressing Bottle	10.00--14.00
1465	7 oz. Oil, Cut Neck	15.00--18.00
1465	5 oz. Oil, Cut Neck	15.00--18.00
300	Qt. Decanter C/U	18.00--20.00
2022	Shaker, F. Glass Top	3.00----4.00
979	Horseradish	9.00--12.00
1968	Marmalade & Cover	8.00--10.00
1831	Mustard & Cover	8.00--10.00
1697	Carafe	8.00--10.00
1697	Carafe Tumbler (4023-6 oz)	3.00----4.00
1691	Carafe Whiskey (981-2½ oz)	3.00----4.00
2138	Mayonnaise Bowl	8.00--10.00
2138	Mayonnaise Plate	2.00----3.00
2138	Mayonnaise Ladle	1.00----2.00
1227	Punch Bowl & Foot	30.00--40.00
1897	7" Salad Plate	2.00----3.00
1848	9" Sandwich Plate	4.00----6.00
1719	10½" Sandwich Plate	5.00----8.00

DEEP PLATE ETCHING NO. 250
"ORIENTAL" PATTERN

No.	Item	Price
766	9 oz. Goblet	2.00----4.00
766	5 oz. Saucer Champagne	2.00----4.00
766	Fruit	2.00----2.50
766	Sherbet	2.00----2.50
840	5" Sherbet Plate	1.00----2.00
837	Oyster Cocktail	2.00----3.00
766	Parfait	2.00----3.00
766½—Parfait		2.00----3.00
766	4½ oz. Claret	2.00----4.00
766	2¾ oz. Wine	2.00----4.00
766	2 oz. Sherry	2.00----4.00
766	¾ oz. Cordial	2.00----4.00
766	¾ oz. Brandy	2.00----4.00
766	3 oz. Cocktail	2.00----4.00
766	Almond	2.00----3.00
766	Custard	2.00----3.00
766	Finger Bowl	1.00----2.00
766	F. Bowl Plate (1736-6")	1.00----2.00
945½—Grape Fruit		2.00----3.00
945½—Grape Fruit Liner		2.00----3.00
858	Sweetmeat	2.00----3.00
880	4½" Bon Bon	2.00----3.00
803	5" Comport	2.00----4.00
803	6" Comport	3.00----4.00
803	5", 6", 7" Footed Nappy	3.00----5.00
1227	4½" Nappy	1.00----2.00
1227	8" Nappy	5.00----8.00
820	Table Tumbler	2.00----3.00
4061	Ftd. Ice Tea, Handled	3.00----4.00
766	Ftd. Ice Tea, Handled	3.00----4.00
701	14 oz. Tumbler, Handled	2.00----3.00
701	5" Tumbler, Plate	1.00----2.00
701	14, 8 oz. Tumbler	1.00----2.00
4011½—Table Tumbler		1.00----2.00
4011	15, 12, 8, 5, 3, oz. Tumbler	1.00----3.00
889	5 oz. Tumbler	1.00----2.00

DEEP PLATE ETCHING NO. 252
"NEW ADAM" PATTERN
Also Gold Trim

No.	Item	Price
858	9 oz. Goblet	2.00----4.00
858	5½ oz. Saucer Champagne	2.00----4.00
858	Fruit	2.00----2.50
840	5" Sherbet Plate	1.00----2.00
1736	6" Sherbet Plate	1.00----2.00
837	Oyster Cocktail	2.00----3.00
822	Parfait	2.00----3.00
858	4½ oz Claret	2.00----4.00
858	2¾ oz. Wine	2.00----4.00
858	2 oz. Sherry	2.00----4.00
858	1 oz. Cordial	2.00----4.00
858	3½ oz. Cocktail	2.00----4.00
858	Custard	2.00----3.00
858	Finger Bowl	2.00----3.00
858	F. Bowl Plate (1499-6")	1.00----2.00
863	Almond	2.00----3.00
945½—Grape Fruit		2.00----3.00
945½—Grape Fruit Liner		2.00----3.00
858	Sweetmeat	2.00----3.00
880	4½" Bon Bon	2.00----3.00
803	5", 6" Comport	3.00----4.00
803	5", 6", 7" Ftd. Nappy	3.00----6.00
896	Bowl & Cover	6.00----9.00
1227	4½" Nappy	2.00----3.00
1227	8" Nappy	5.00----6.00
820	Table Tumbler	1.00----3.00
833	8 oz. Tumbler	1.00----3.00
4061	Ftd. Ice Tea, Handled	2.00----3.00
766	Ftd. Ice Tea, Handled	3.00----4.00
701	14 oz. Tumbler, Handled	2.00----3.00
701	5" Tumbler Plate	1.00----2.00
701	14 oz. Tumbler	2.00----3.00
701	8 oz. Tumbler	1.00----2.00
858	Table Tumbler	1.00----2.00
858	14, 12, 10, 8, 5 oz. Tumbler	1.00----3.00

300	7 Jug	15.00--18.00
724	7 Jug	15.00--18.00
300½—5 Jug		20.00--22.00
318	7 Jug	18.00--20.00
303	7 Jug	18.00--20.00
1236	6 Jug	18.00--20.00
2104	Jug & Tumbler, Pty.	28.00--32.00
2133	Sugar	3.00----4.00
2133	Cream	3.00----4.00
2083	Salad Dressing Bottle	5.00----8.00
1465	7 oz. Oil, Cut Neck	12.00--15.00
1465	5 oz. Oil, Cut Neck	12.00--15.00
300	Qt. Decanter, Cut Neck	18.00--20.00
160½—Water Bottle, Cut Neck		12.00--15.00
2022	Shaker, F. Glass Top	2.00----3.00
922	Toothpick	6.00----8.00
979	Horseradish	8.00--10.00
1968	Marmadale & Cover	8.00--10.00
1831	Mustard & Cover	6.00----8.00
1697	Carafe	8.00--10.00
1697	Carafe Tumbler (4023-6 oz)	3.00----4.00
1691	Carafe Whiskey (981-2½ oz)	3.00----4.00
2194	8 oz. Syrup, Nickel Top	20.00--25.00
2194	12 oz. Syrup, Nickel Top	20.00--25.00
2138	Mayonnaise Bowl	8.00--10.00
2138	Mayonnaise Plate	2.00----3.00
2138	Mayonnaise Ladle	1.00----2.00
2015	Spoon Tray	4.00----6.00
1897	7″ Salad Plate	2.00----3.00
1848	9″ Sandwich Plate	3.00----4.00
1719	10½″ Sandwich Plate	4.00----5.00

CUTTING NO. 110

300	1, 2, 4, 5 Tankard	8.00--10.00
300	6, 7, 8 Tankard	10.00--15.00
300	Claret	15.00--20.00
303	2, 3, 4, 5 Jug	5.00----8.00
303	6, 7, 8 Jug	8.00--10.00
724	6, 7 Tankard	12.00--15.00
330½—7 Tankard		12.00--15.00
317	7 Jug, C.N.	10.00--15.00
1236	6, 6, 7 Jug	15.00--20.00
1227	7 Jug, C.N.	15.00--20.00
1227	7 Jug, 2 stars on Neck, 6 st. around body of Jug	15.00--20.00
160½—Water Bottle, C.N.		12.00--15.00
1558	Water Bottle, C.N.	12.00--15.00
481	Custard	2.00----3.00
1755	Custard	2.00----3.00
1241	Custard	2.00----3.00
300	3½, 3 Tankard	8.00--10.00
315	Finger Bowl	1.00----2.00
315	Finger Bowl Plate	.50----1.00
1349	Finger Bowl	1.00----2.00
1499	Finger Bowl	1.00----2.00
1499	Finger Bowl Plate	.50----1.00
1769	Finger Bowl	1.00----2.00
1769	Finger Bowl Plate	.50----1.00
300½—Small Oil, C.S.		12.00--15.00
312	Oil, C.S.	12.00--15.00
1164	Oil, C.S.	12.00--15.00
1465	Oil, C.S. C.N.	10.00--12.50
1163	Catsup, C.S.	15.00--18.00
1478	Sugar	2.00----3.00
1480	Sugar	2.00----3.00
1480	Cream	2.00----3.00
863	Individual Almond	2.00----2.50
1478	Cream	2.00----3.00

1720	Sugar	2.00----3.00
1720	Cream	2.00----3.00
1759	Sugar	2.00----3.00
1759	Cream	2.00----3.00
1664	Horseradish	4.00----6.00
820	Tumbler	1.00----2.00
820½—Tumbler, ½ Sham.		1.00----2.00
833	8 oz. Tumbler, ½ Sham	1.00----2.00
833	8 oz. Tumbler	1.00----2.00
889	5, 8, 9 oz. Tumbler	1.00----2.00
887	3 oz. Tumbler	2.00----3.00
701	14 oz. Tumbler	1.00----2.00
954½—Grape Fruit		2.00----3.00
863	10½ oz. Goblet	2.00----3.00
863	H.S. Champ. C.F.	2.00----3.00
863	9 oz. Goblet	2.00----3.00
863	7 oz. Goblet	2.00----3.00
863	5½ oz. Tall Champagne	2.00----3.00
863	4½ oz. Claret	2.00----3.00
863	3 oz. Wine	2.00----3.00
863	1 oz. Cordial	2.00----3.00
863	4½ oz. Rhine Wine	2.00----3.00
863	2 oz. Sherry	2.00----3.00
863	5½ oz. Saucer Champagne	2.00----3.00
863	2½ oz. Creme de Menthe	2.00----3.00
863	3½ oz. Cocktail	2.00----3.00
863	¾ oz. Pousse Cafe	2.00----3.00
863	Fruit	2.00----2.50
858	Tumbler Plate	1.00----2.00
858	Table Tumbler, 3½, 5, 6½, 8, 10, 12, 14, 16 oz. Tumbler, Cut 19	1.00----2.00
1165	Shaker, S.P. Top	2.00----3.00
614	Shaker, S.P. Top	2.00----3.00
315	4″, 4½″, 5″, 6″ Nappy	1.00----2.00
315	7″, 8″, 9″, 10″ Nappy	2.00----3.00
1227	8″ Nappy	2.00----3.00
1227	4½″ Nappy	1.00----1.50
300	Qt. Decanter, C.N.	18.00--20.00
1464	18 oz. Decanter, C.N.	18.00--22.00
725	8″ Vase	6.00----8.00
858	Ice Cream	2.00----3.00
825	Saucer Champagne	2.00----3.00
932	Saucer Champagne	2.00----3.00
932	Saucer Champagne	2.00----3.00
840	Sherbet	2.00----2.50
840	Sherbet	2.00----2.50
840	Sherbet Plate	1.00----2.00
843	Sherbet	2.00----2.50
846	Sherry	2.00----3.00
826	9 oz. Goblet	2.00----3.00
801	3 oz. Wine	2.00----3.00
952	Cocktail	2.00----3.00
794	H.S. Champagne, C.F.	2.00----3.00
793	H.S. Champagne, C.F.	2.00----3.00
823	4½″ Fruit	2.00----2.50
823	5″ Fruit	2.00----2.50
803	4½″, 5″, 6″, 7″ Ftd. Nap. Deep	2.00----3.00
803	4½″, 5″, 6″, 7″ Ftd. Nap. Shallow	2.00----3.00
803	5″ Comport	2.00----3.00
803	6″ Comport	2.00----3.00
1227	Punch Bowl & Foot	25.00--30.00
858	Custard	2.00----3.00
858	Custard Plate	2.00----3.00
858	Finger Bowl	1.00----2.00
858	Finger Bowl Plate	1.00----2.00
858	3½, 5, 6½, 8, 10, 12, 14 oz. Tumbler	1.00----2.00

CUTTING NO. 116
"MISSION" PATTERN

863	10 oz. Goblet	2.00----3.00
863	9 oz. Goblet	2.00----3.00
863	5½ oz. Saucer Champagne	2.00----3.00
863	Fruit	2.00----2.50
840	5" Fruit Plate	1.00----2.00
1736	6" Fruit Plate	1.00----2.00
822	Parfait	2.00----3.00
863	4½ oz. Claret	2.00----3.00
863	3 oz. Wine	2.00----3.00
863	1 oz. Cordial	2.00----3.00
863	3½ oz. Cocktail	2.00----3.00
863	Almond	2.00----3.00
1558	Water Bottle, Cut Neck	12.00--15.00
300	Qt. Decanter, Cut Neck	12.00--15.00
2022	Shaker, F. Glass Top	2.00--3.00
1165½	Shaker, Pearl Top	2.00----3.00
922	Toothpick, Cut 19	4.00---6.00
1733	Marmalade & Cover	3.00----4.00
1831	Mustard & Cover	3.00----4.00
1132	Horseradish	10.00--12.00
2194	8 oz. Syrup, Nickel Top	8.00--10.00
2194	12 oz. Syrup, Nickel Top	8.00--10.00
48	3 Piece Flower Set	12.00--15.00
1848	9" (Sandwich) Plate, C/S	3.00----4.00
481	Custard	2.00----3.00
1769	Finger Bowl	1.00----2.00
1769	Finger Bowl Plate (200-6")	1.00----2.00
858	9 oz. Goblet	2.00----3.00
858	5½ oz. Saucer Champagne	2.00----3.00
858	Fruit	2.00----2.50
858	Finger Bowl	1.00----2.00
858	Finger Bowl Plate (1499-6"	1.00----2.00
945½	Grape Fruit	2.00----3.00
945½	Grape Fruit Liner	2.00----3.00
858	Sweetmeat	2.00----3.00
880	4½" Bon Bon	2.00----3.00
803	5", 6" Comport	3.00----4.00
803	5", 6", 7" Ftd. Nappy	2.00----4.00
1227	4½" Nappy	1.00----2.00
1227	8" Nappy	3.00----4.00
820	Table Tumbler	1.00----2.00
820	Tumbler, ½ Sham, Punty.	1.00----2.00
833	8 oz. Tumbler, ½ Sham, Punty.	1.00----2.00
4061	Footed Ice Tea, Handled	2.00----3.00
701	5" Tumbler Plate	.50----1.00
701	14, 12, 8 oz. Tumbler	1.00----2.00
858	Table Tumbler	1.00----2.00
858	14, 12, 8, 5 oz. Tumbler	1.00----2.00
858	Table, 14, 10, 8 oz. Tumbler. Sham, C/19	1.00----2.00
889	5 oz. Tumbler	1.00----2.00
887	3 oz. Tumbler	2.00----3.00
300	7 Jug, 2 Bands	15.00--18.00
724	7 Jug, 2 Bands	15.00--18.00
303	7 Jug, 1 Band	8.00--10.00
303	7 Jug, 2 Bands	8.00--10.00
1851	8 Jug, 2 Bands	15.00--18.00
1478	Sugar	2.00----3.00
1478	Cream	2.00----3.00
1480	Sugar	2.00----3.00
1480	Cream	2.00----3.00
1759	Sugar	2.00----3.00
1759	Cream	4.00----5.00
1851	Sugar	2.00----3.00
1851	Cream	2.00----3.00
300½	Small Oil	10.00--12.50
1465	7 oz. Cut Neck	12.00--15.00

CUTTING NO. 116
ALSO CUTTING NO. 118 "BILLOW"

858	11, 10, 9, 8 oz. Goblet	2.00----3.00
858	7 oz. Bass Ale	2.00----3.00
858	6½ oz. Claret	2.00----3.00
858	4½ oz. Claret	2.00----3.00
858	3½ oz. Wine	2.00----3.00
858	2¾ oz. Wine	2.00----3.00
858	2 oz. Sherry	2.00----3.00
858	1 oz. Cordial	2.00----3.00
858	7 oz. Saucer Champagne	2.00----3.00
858	5½ oz. Saucer Champagne	2.00----3.00
858	H.S. Champagne, C.F.	2.00----3.00
858	5½ oz. Tall Champagne	2.00----3.00
858	4 oz. Hot Whiskey	2.00----3.00
858	1 oz. Brandy	2.00----3.00
858	3½ oz. Cocktail	2.00----3.00
858	2½ oz. Creme de Menthe	2.00----3.00
858	Sherbet	2.00----3.00
858	Fruit Salad	2.00----2.50
858	Oyster Cocktail	2.00----3.00
858	Short Cake	1.00----2.00
858	4½" Ice Cream	2.00----2.50
858	L.S. Champagne	2.00----3.00
858	3, 4, 6, 7½, 8½, 11, 13, 15 oz. Tumbler, sham, C.19	1.00----2.00
858	8½ oz. Table Tumbler, Sham C. 19	1.00----2.00
858	3½ oz. Tumbler, light	1.00----2.00
820	Tumbler	1.00----2.00
820	½ Tumbler, ½ sham	1.00----2.00
833	8 oz. Tumbler, ½ sham.	1.00----2.00
887	3 oz. Tumbler	1.00----2.00
889	5 oz. Tumbler	1.00----2.00
1297	7 oz. Tumbler	1.00----2.00
701	12, 14 oz. Tumbler	1.00----2.00
701	Tumbler Plate	.50----1.00
481	Custard	2.00----3.00
858	Custard	2.00----3.00
1598	Custard	2.00----3.00
	Custard Plate	1.00----2.00
840	Sherbet	2.00----2.50
840	Sherbet Plate	1.00----2.00
842	Sherbet	2.00----2.50
932	Saucer Champagne	2.00----3.00
932	Plate	2.00----3.00
825	Saucer Champagne	2.00----3.00
952	Cocktail	2.00----3.00
846	Sherry	2.00----3.00
826	9 oz. Goblet	2.00----3.00
793	H.S. Champagne, C.F.	2.00----3.00
792	H.S. Champagne, C.F.	2.00----3.00
945	Grape Fruit	2.00----3.00
945½	Grape Fruit	2.00----3.00
945½	Grape Fruit Liner	2.00----3.00
802	10, 7 oz. Goblet	2.00----3.00
802	4½ oz. Claret	2.00----3.00
902	3 oz. Wine	2.00----3.00
1389	Oyster Cocktail	2.00----3.00
5058	Brandy	2.00----3.00
1132	Horseradish	10.00--12.00
5049	Cheese	2.00----3.00
5049	Plate	2.00----3.00
1741	Tea Caddy & Cover	8.00--10.00
1718	6" Ice Tub	5.00----8.00
1478	Lavender Salts, Cut star stopper	8.00--10.00
1478	Lavender Salts, stoppered	6.00----8.00
1666	Puff, cut star on cover	10.00--12.00
1904	Bon Bon & Cut Star Cover	12.00--15.00

No.	Description	Price
1904	Bon Bon & Cover	10.00--12.00
1227	Punch Bowl & Stand	25.00--30.00
1195	Large Decanter, Cut Neck	15.00--20.00
1464	10 oz. Decanter, C.N. C.F.	15.00--20.00
1464	18 oz. Decanter, C.N. C.F.	15.00--20.00
300	Pt. Decanter, cut neck	15.00--20.00
300	Qt. Decanter, cut neck	15.00--20.00
858	5, 6½, Table, 8, 10, 12, 14, 16 oz. Tumbler light	1.00----2.00
858	Tumbler Plate	1.00----2.00
1719	Sandwich Plate	3.00----4.00
1848	Sandwich Plate	3.00----4.00
300	6 Tankard, 2 bands	15.00--20.00
300	7 Tankard, 2 bands	15.00--20.00
303	7 Jug, 1 band	8.00--10.00
724	6 Jug, 1 band	15.00--18.00
724	7 Tankard, 2 bands	15.00--20.00
724	6 Tankard, 2 bands	15.00--20.00
1852	8 Tankard, 2 bands	15.00--20.00
1761	Tankard, 2 bands	15.00--20.00
1787	Tankard, 2 bands	15.00--20.00
1743	5 Tankard & Cover, 2 bands	20.00--25.00
1697	Water Bottle, Flatted	10.00--15.00
4023	7 Tumbler	1.00----2.00
160½—Water Bottle, C.N.		12.00--15.00
1558	Water Bottle C.N.	12.00--15.00
1851	Cream	2.00----3.00
1851	Sugar	2.00----3.00
1759	Cream	2.00----3.00
1759	Sugar	3.00----4.00
1480	Cream	2.00----3.00
1480	Sugar	2.00----3.00
1478	Cream	2.00----3.00
1478	Sugar	2.00----3.00
1712½—Cream		2.00----3.00
1712½—Sugar		2.00----3.00
1931	Covered Cream	3.00----4.00
1931	Covered Sugar	3.00----4.00
863	10½, 9 oz. Goblet	2.00----3.00
863½—9 oz. Goblet, S.S.		2.00----3.00
863½—7 oz. Goblet, L.S.		2.00----3.00
863	7 oz. Goblet	2.00----3.00
863	5½ oz. Goblet	2.00----3.00
863	5½ oz. Tall Champagne	2.00----3.00
863	4½ oz. Claret	2.00----3.00
863	3 oz. Wine	2.00----3.00
863	1¼ oz. Cordial	2.00----3.00
863½—¾ oz. Cordial		2.00----3.00
863	4½ oz. Rhine Wine	2.00----3.00
863	2 oz. Sherry	2.00----3.00
863	5½ oz. Saucer Champagne	2.00----3.00
863	3½ oz. Cocktail	2.00----3.00
863	3 oz. Cocktail	2.00----3.00
863	2½ oz. Creme de Menthe	2.00----3.00
863	1½ oz. Pousse Cafe	2.00----3.00
863½—¾ oz. Pousse Cafe		2.00----3.00
863	Fruit	2.00----2.50
863	Individual Almond	2.00----3.00
863	H.S. Champagne, C.F.	2.00----3.00
863	4½, 5½ oz. Roemer	2.00----3.00
315	4½", 5", 6", 7", 8", 9", 10" Nappy	1.00----4.00
1227	4½", 5", 6", 7", 8" Nappy	1.00----4.00
1848	7" Deep Nappy	2.00----3.00
453	4½", 5", 6" Hdl. Nappy	3.00----4.00
803	4½", 5", 6", 7", 8" Nappy	1.00----3.00
803	5", 6" Comport	2.00----3.00
300½—Large — Small Oil		10.00--12.50
1465	Oil, C.N.	10.00--12.50
1465	Small Oil	10.00--12.50
1894	8 oz. Oil	10.00--12.50

No.	Description	Price
1165	Shaker, S.P.T.	2.00----3.00
315	Finger Bowl	1.00----2.00
315	Finger Bowl Plate	.50----1.00
858	Finger Bowl	1.00----2.00
858	Finger Bowl Plate	.50----1.00
1499	Finger Bowl	1.00----2.00
1499	Finger Bowl Plate	.50----1.00
1769	Finger Bowl	1.00----2.00
1769	Finger Bowl Plate	.50----1.00
1895	10" Vase, 2 bands	8.00--10.00
725	8" Vase, one Band	4.00----6.00
725	10" Vase, one Band	6.00----8.00
1733	Marmalade, Notch Cover	3.00----4.00
1831	Mustard, Notch Cover	3.00----4.00
1281	Lemon Dish	1.00----2.00
922	Tooth Pick, Cut Flute	4.00----6.00
701	8 oz. Tumbler	1.00----2.00
981	2½ oz. Tumbler, ½ Sham	2.00----3.00
833	6 oz. Tumbler, ½ Sham	1.00----2.00

CUTTING NO. 125

No.	Description	Price
4065	16 oz. Tom Collins, Cut 19	2.00----3.00
4065	14 oz. Ice Tea, Cut 19	1.00----2.00
4065	12 oz. Strained Lemonade, Cut 19	1.00----2.00
4065	10 oz. Beer, Cut 19	1.00----2.00
4065	8 oz. Gin Fizz, Cut 19	1.00----2.00
4065	7 oz. Split Beer, Cut 19	1.00----2.00
4065	6 oz. Appolinaris, Cut 19	1.00----2.00
4065	5 oz. Mineral, Cut 19	1.00----2.00
4065	4½ oz. Wine, Cut 19	1.00----2.00
4065	3 oz. Whiskey, Cut 19	1.00----2.00
4070	12 oz. Milk Punch, Cut 19	1.00----2.00
4070	10 oz. Table Tumbler, Cut 19	1.00----2.00
4070	9 oz. Old Fashioned Cocktail Cut 19	1.00----2.00
4070	8 oz. Hiball, Cut 19	1.00----2.00
4070	7 oz. Split Beer, Cut 19	1.00----2.00
4070	5½ oz. Bar Water, Cut 19	1.00----2.00
4070	3½ oz. Whiskey, Cut 19	2.00----3.00
4075	3 oz. Whiskey, Cut 19	2.00----3.00
4070	2½ oz. Whiskey, Cut 19	2.00----3.00
4070	2 oz. Whiskey, Cut 19	2.00----3.00
4061	Lemonade	1.00----2.00
300	7 Tankard	15.00--18.00
303	7 Jug	10.00--15.00
160½—Water Bottle, C.N.		10.00--15.00
1769	Finger Bowl	1.00----2.00
	Finger Bowl Plate	.50----1.00
1478	Sugar	2.00----3.00
1478	Cream	2.00----3.00
300½—Small Oil		10.00--12.50
481	Custard	2.00----3.00
	Custard Plate	1.00----2.00
1227	8" Nappy	3.00----4.00
1227	4½" Nappy	1.00----2.00
922	Toothpicks, C. F.	6.00----8.00
1165	Shaker, S.P. Top	2.00----3.00
766	9 oz. Goblet	2.00----3.00
766	5 oz. Saucer Champagne	2.00----3.00
766	Fruit	2.00----2.50
863	Fruit	2.00----2.50
840	5" Fruit Plate	1.00----2.00
766	Ftd. Ice Tea, Handled	2.00----3.00
4077	12 oz. Tumbler	1.00----2.00
4077	8 oz. Tumbler	1.00----2.00
2022	Shaker, F. Glass Top	2.00----3.00
863	10½, 9 oz. Goblet	2.00----3.00

863	5½ oz. Tall Champagne . .	2.00----3.00
863	4½ oz. Claret	2.00----3.00
863	3 oz. Wine	2.00----3.00
863	2 oz. Sherry	2.00----3.00
863	¾ oz. Cordial	2.00----3.00
863	4 oz. Rhine Wine	2.00----3.00
863	¾ oz. Pousse Cafe	2.00----3.00
863	2½ oz. Creme de Menthe	2.00----3.00
863	3½ oz. Cocktail	2.00----3.00
863	H.S. Champagne, C.F. . .	2.00----3.00
863	5½ oz. Saucer Champagne	2.00----3.00
863	Almond	2.00----3.00
863	Sherbet	2.00----2.50
899	Parfait	2.00----3.00
945½—Grape Fruit	2.00----3.00
945½—Grape Fruit Liner . . .	2.00----3.00
300	Quart Decanter, C.N. . .	15.00--20.00
803	5″, 6″, 7″ Deep Nappy . .	3.00----4.00
803	5″, 6″ Footed Comport. .	3.00----4.00
823	4½″, 5″ Fruit	1.00----2.00
932	Saucer Champagne	2.00----3.00
846	Sherry	2.00----3.00
840	Sherbet	2.00----2.50
840	Sherbet Plate	1.00----2.00
701	5, 8, 14 oz. Tumbler . .	1.00----2.00
701	Tumbler Plate	.50----1.00
820	Tumbler	1.00----2.00
820½—Tumbler, ½ Sham . . .	1.00----2.00
833	8 oz. Tumbler, ½ Sham . .	1.00----2.00
887	3 oz. Tumbler	1.00----2.00
889	5 oz. Tumbler	1.00----2.00

CUTTING NO. 129

1480	Sugar	2.00----3.00
1480	Cream	2.00----3.00
303	Sugar	2.00----3.00
303	Sugar & Cover	3.00----4.00
303	Cream	2.00----3.00
1712	Sugar	2.00----3.00
1712½—Cream	2.00----3.00
300½—Small Oil	12.00--15.00
1465	7 oz. Oil, Cut Neck	12.00--15.00
2022	Shaker, F. Glass Top . .	2.00----3.00
2263	Individual Salt	2.00----3.00
922	Toothpick, Punty	6.00----8.00
1968	Marmalade & Cover	3.00----4.00
1831	Mustard & Cover	3.00----4.00
1697	Carafe	8.00--10.00
1697	Carafe Tumbler (4023-6 oz)	3.00----4.00
2194	8 oz. Syrup, Nickel Top .	18.00--22.00
2194	12 oz. Syrup, Nickel Top .	20.00--25.00
2138	Mayonnaise Bowl	8.00--10.00
2138	Mayonnaise Plate	1.00----2.00
2138	Mayonnaise Ladel	1.00----2.00
2219	¼ lb. Candy Jar & Cover .	10.00--15.00
2219	½ lb. Candy Jar & Cover .	10.00--15.00
2219	1 lb. Candy Jar & Cover .	10.00--15.00
1848	9″ Sandwich Plate	3.00----4.00
4069	9″ Vase	6.00----8.00
4069	9″ Vase, 129½	8.00--10.00
2194	8 oz. Syrup, Cut 129½ . .	18.00--20.00
2194	12 oz. Syrup, Cut 129½ .	20.00--22.00
2241	Cologne & Stopper	6.00----8.00
2242	Cologne & Stopper	6.00----8.00
863	9 oz. Goblet	2.00----3.00
853	5½ oz. Saucer Champagne	2.00----3.00
863	Fruit	2.00----2.50
1736	6″ Fruit Plate	.50----1.00

822	Parfait	2.00----3.00
805	Parfait	2.00----3.00
766½—Parfait	2.00----3.00
863	4½ oz. Claret	2.00----3.00
863	3 oz. Wine	2.00----3.00
863	3½ oz. Cocktail	2.00----3.00
863	Almond	2.00----3.00
837	Oyster Cocktail	2.00----3.00
858	Finger Bowl	1.00----2.00
858	F. Finger Plate (1499-6″)	1.00----2.00
1598	Custard	2.00----3.00
1499	Finger Bowl	1.00----2.00
840	Sherbet	2.00----2.50
840	5″ Sherbet Plate	1.00----2.00
880	Almond	2.00----3.00
5051	Footed Cheese, small . .	2.00----3.00
825	Saucer Champagne	2.00----3.00
945½—Grape Fruit	2.00----3.00
945½—Grape Fruit Liner . . .	2.00----3.00
858	Sweetmeat	2.00----3.00
880	4½″ Bon Bon	2.00----3.00
803	5″, 6″ Comport	2.00----3.00
803	5″, 6″, 7″ Footed Nappy	3.00----4.00
803	5″ Ftd. Nappy & Cover .	5.00----7.00
803	5″ Ftd. Comport & Cover	6.00----8.00
825	Jelly & Cover	5.00----7.00
1227	4½″ Nappy	1.00----2.00
1227	8″ Nappy	4.00----5.00
1590	4½″ Nappy	1.00----2.00
820	Table Tumbler	1.00----2.00
820	Tumbler, ½ Sham. Punty .	1.00----2.00
833	8 oz. Tumbler	1.00----2.00
833	8 oz. Tumbler, ½ Sham. Punty	1.00----2.00
4061	Ftd. Ice Tea, Handled . .	2.00----3.00
766	Ftd. Ice Tea, Handled . .	2.00----3.00
4011	12 oz. Tumbler, Handled	1.00----3.00
701	5″ Tumbler Plate	1.00----2.00
701	14 oz. Tumbler	1.00----2.00
701	14 oz. Tumbler, ½ Sham. Punty	1.00----2.00
858	14 oz. Tumbler	1.00----2.00
4011½—Table Tumbler	1.00----2.00
4011	12 oz. Tumbler	1.00----2.00
889	5 oz. Tumbler	1.00----2.00
300	7 Jug	15.00--20.00
1743	7 Jug & Cover	18.00--22.00
1124	7 Jug	15.00--20.00
303	7 Jug	15.00--20.00
1236	6 Jug	10.00--15.00
2040	3 Jug	8.00--10.00
2100	7 Jug	15.00--20.00
2104	Jug & Tumbler, Punty . .	22.00--25.00

CUTTING NO. 130 "PRISCILLA PATTERN"

766	9 oz. Goblet	2.00----3.00
766	4½ oz. Claret	2.00----3.00
766	2¾ oz. Wine	2.00----3.00
766	2 oz. Burgundy	2.00----3.00
766	2 oz. Sherry	2.00----3.00
766	¾ oz. Cordial	2.00----3.00
766	¾ oz. Pousse Cafe	2.00----3.00
766	3 oz. Cocktail	2.00----3.00
766	2½ oz. Creme de Menthe .	2.00----3.00
766	4 oz. Rhine Wine	2.00----3.00
766	5 oz. Saucer Champagne	2.00----3.00
766	Fruit	2.00----2.50
766	Sherbet	2.00----2.50
766	Sherbet	2.00----2.50

766	Almond	2.00----3.00
766	Parfait	2.00----3.00
766	Footed Ice Tea, Handled	2.00----3.00
766	Bon Bon	2.00----3.00
766	Grape Fruit	2.00----3.00
766	Grape Fruit Liner	2.00----3.00
766	Hol'w Stem Champ'ne (795)	2.00----3.00
766	5'' Footed Comport	2.00----3.00
766	6'' Footed Comport	2.00----3.00
766	4½'' Footed Nappy	2.00----3.00
766	5'' Footed Nappy	2.00----3.00
766	6'' Footed Nappy	2.00----3.00
766	7'' Footed Nappy	3.00----4.00
766	Custard	2.00----3.00
766	Custard Plate, (200-5)	1.00----2.00
766	Finger Bowl	1.00----2.00
766	Finger Bowl Plate (840)	.50----1.00
4011	15, 12, 8, 5½, 3 oz. Tumbler	1.00----2.00
820	Table Tumbler	1.00----2.00
833	8 oz. Tumbler	1.00----2.00
833	8 oz. Tumbler, ½ Sham	1.00----2.00
2022	Shaker, F.G. Top	2.00----3.00
922	Toothpick	6.00----8.00
2084	Sugar	2.00----3.00
2084	Cream	2.00----3.00
300½—Small Oil		10.00--12.50
160½—Water Bottle, Cut Neck		12.00--15.00
300	7 Tankard	15.00--20.00
1236	6 Jug	15.00--20.00
303	7 Jug	15.00--20.00
1165	Shaker, Silver P. Top	2.00----3.00
2238	8¼'' Salad Plate	2.00----3.00

889	5 oz. Tumbler	1.00----2.00
1124	7 Jug	15.00--20.00
1793	Jug	15.00--20.00
2082	5 Jug	15.00--20.00
303	7 Jug	15.00--20.00
1236	6 Jug	15.00--20.00
2040	3 Jug	10.00--12.00
2104	Jug & Tumbler, Punty	25.00--30.00
303	Sugar	2.00----3.00
303	Sugar & Cover	3.00----4.00
303	Cream	2.00----3.00
1712	Sugar	2.00----3.00
1712½—Cream		2.00----3.00
300½—Small Oil		10.00--12.50
1465	7 oz. Oil, Cut Neck	10.00--12.50
2022	Shaker, F. Glass Top	2.00----3.00
2263	Individual Salt	3.00----4.00
922	Toothpick, Punty	6.00----8.00
1733	Marmalade & Cover	3.00----4.00
1831	Mustard & Cover	3.00----4.00
1697	Carafe	8.00--10.00
1697	Carafe Tumbler (4023-6 oz	3.00----4.00
2194	8 oz. Syrup, Nickel Top	10.00--12.00
2104	12 oz. Syrup, Nickel Top	10.00--12.00
2138	Mayonnaise Bowl	8.00--10.00
2138	Mayonnaise Plate	1.00----2.00
2138	Mayonnaise Ladle	1.00----2.00
2219	¼ lb. Candy Jar & Cover	10.00--15.00
2219	½ lb. Candy Jar & Cover	10.00--15.00
2219	1 lb. Candy Jar & Cover	10.00--15.00
2208	Sweet Pea Vase	9.00--12.00
4069	9'' Vase	3.00----5.00

CUTTING NO. 132
"CLOVER" PATTERN

863	9 oz. Goblet	2.00----3.00
863	5½ oz. Saucer Champagne	2.00----3.00
863	Fruit	2.00----2.50
1736	6'' Fruit Plate	1.00----2.00
805	Parfait	2.00----3.00
863	3 oz. Wine	2.00----3.00
863	4½ oz. Claret	2.00----3.00
863	3½ oz. Cocktail	2.00----3.00
863	2 oz. Sherry	2.00----3.00
863	Almond	2.00----3.00
481	Custard	2.00----2.50
766	Finger Bowl	1.00----2.00
1769	Finger Bowl	1.00----2.00
1769	Finger Bowl Plate (200-6'')	.50----1.00
880	Salt Dip	2.00----3.00
837	Oyster Cocktail	2.00----3.00
825	Jelly & Cover	5.00----7.00
880	4½'' Bon Bon	2.00----3.00
803	5'' Comport	2.00----3.00
803	6'' Comport	2.00----3.00
803	5'' Footed Nappy	2.00----3.00
803	6'' Footed Nappy	2.00----3.00
803	7'' Footed Nappy	2.00----3.00
1227	4½'' Nappy	1.00----2.00
1227	8'' Nappy	3.00----4.00
820	Table Tumbler	1.00----2.00
833	8 oz. Tumbler	1.00----2.00
833	8 oz. Tumbler, ½ Sham, Punty	1.00----2.00
4011	12 oz. Tumbler, Handled	1.00----3.00
701	5 oz. Tumbler Plate	1.00----2.00
701	14 oz. Tumbler	1.00----2.00
4011½—Table Tumbler		1.00----2.00
4011	12 oz. Tumbler	1.00----2.00

CUTTING NO. 133
"CHRYSANTHEMUM" PATTERN

863	9 oz. Goblet	2.00----3.00
863	5½ oz. Saucer Champagne	2.00----3.00
863	Fruit	2.00----2.50
840	5'' Fruit Plate	1.00----2.00
863	3 oz. Wine	2.00----3.00
863	3½ oz. Cocktail	2.00----3.00
863	Almond	2.00----3.00
481	Custard	2.00----2.50
1769	Finger Bowl	1.00----2.00
1769	F. Bowl Plate (200-6'')	.50----1.00
880	4½'' Bon Bon	2.00----3.00
803	5'' Comport	2.00----3.00
803	6'' Comport	2.00----3.00
803	5'' Footed Nappy	2.00----3.00
803	6'' Footed Nappy	2.00----3.00
803	7'' Footed Nappy	2.00----3.00
1227	4½'' Nappy	1.00----2.00
1227	8'' Nappy	3.00----4.00
820	Table Tumbler	1.00----2.00
833	8 oz. Tumbler	1.00----2.00
833	8 oz. Tumbler, ½ Sham, Punty	1.00----2.00
4061	Ftd. Ice Tea, Handled	2.00----3.00
701	5'' Tumbler Plate	1.00----2.00
701	14 oz. Tumbler	1.00----2.00
889	5 oz. Tumbler	1.00----2.00
300	7 Jug	15.00--20.00
303	7 Jug	12.00--15.00
2100	7 Jug	10.00--15.00
1480	Sugar	2.00----3.00
1480	Cream	2.00----3.00
1465	7 oz. Oil	10.00--12.50
2022	Shaker F. Glass Top	2.00----3.00

1733	Marmalade & Cover	3.00----4.00
1831	Mustard & Cover	3.00----4.00
2194	8 oz. Syrup, Nickel Top	10.00--12.00
2194	12 oz. Syrup, Nickel Top	10.00--12.00
4069	9" Vase	3.00----5.00
1694½—Vase	. . . .	3.00----5.00
1798	Vase	3.00----5.00

CUTTING NO. 135
"GENEVA" PATTERN

863	9 oz. Goblet	2.00----3.00
863	5½ oz. Saucer Champagne	2.00----3.00
863	Fruit	2.00----2.50
880	9 oz. Goblet	2.00----3.00
880	5 oz. Saucer Champagne	2.00----3.00
880	5½ oz. Sherbet	2.00----3.00
880	3½ oz. Cocktail	2.00----3.00
880	Footed Salt Dip	3.00----4.00
822	Parfait	2.00----3.00
1769	Finger Bowl	1.00----2.00
1769	F. Bowl Plate (200-6") . .	.50----1.00
481	Custard	2.00----2.50
880	4½" Bon Bon	2.00----3.00
803	5" Comport	2.00----3.00
803	6" Comport	2.00----3.00
803	5" Footed Nappy . . .	2.00----3.00
803	6" Footed Nappy . . .	2.00----3.00
803	7" Footed Nappy . . .	2.00----3.00
1227	4½" Nappy	1.00----2.00
1227	8" Nappy	3.00----4.00
820	Table Tumbler	1.00----2.00
833	8 oz. Tumbler ½ Sham Pty	1.00----2.00
4061	Ftd. Ice Tea, Handled . .	2.00----3.00
701	5" Tumbler Plate . . .	1.00----2.00
701	14 oz. Tumbler	1.00----2.00
4011½—Table Tumbler	. . . .	1.00----2.00
4011	12 oz. Tumbler	1.00----2.00
724	7 Jug	15.00--18.00
303	7 Jug	12.00--15.00
2133	Sugar	2.00----3.00
2133	Cream	2.00----3.00
1465	7 oz. Oil, Cut Neck . . .	10.00--12.50
2022	Shaker, F. Glass Top . .	2.00----3.00
922	Toothpick, Punty . . .	6.00----8.00
1968	Marmalade & Cover . . .	3.00----4.00
1831	Mustard & Cover . . .	3.00----4.00
2138	Mayonnaise Bowl . . .	8.00--10.00
2138	Mayonnaise Plate . . .	1.00----2.00
2138	Mayonnaise Ladle . . .	1.00----2.00
4069	9" Vase	3.00----5.00
1848	9" Sandwich Plate . . .	3.00----4.00

CUTTING NO. 138
"APPLE BLOSSOM" PATTERN

863	9 oz. Goblet	2.00----3.00
863	5½ oz. Saucer Champagne	2.00----3.00
863	Fruit	2.00----2.50
1736	6" Fruit Plate	2.00----3.00
863	3 oz. Wine	2.00----3.00
863	3½ oz. Cocktail	2.00----3.00
863	Almond	2.00----3.00
1769	Finger Bowl	1.00----2.00
1769	F. Bowl Plate (200-6") . .	.50----1.00
805	9 oz. Goblet	2.00----3.00
805	Saucer Champagne	2.00----3.00
805	Sherbet	2.00----3.00
805	Parfait	2.00----3.00

805	Cocktail	2.00----3.00
1598	Custard	2.00----2.50
880	Footed Salt Dip	3.00----4.00
945½—Grape Fruit		2.00----3.00
945½—Grape Fruit Liner		2.00----3.00
858	Sweetmeat	2.00----3.00
880	4" Bon Bon	2.00----3.00
803	5" Comport	2.00----3.00
803	6" Comport	2.00----3.00
803	5" Footed Nappy	2.00----3.00
803	6" Footed Nappy	2.00----3.00
803	7" Footed Nappy	3.00----4.00
1227	4½" Nappy	1.00----2.00
1227	8" Nappy	3.00----4.00
453	4½" Handled Nappy . .	2.00----3.00
5051	Footed Cheese	2.00----3.00
5051	Cheese Plate (1737-5") . .	1.00----2.00
1590	4½" Cheese	2.00----3.00
1590	4½" Cheese Plate (2050-9")	2.00----3.00
896	Bowl & Cover	5.00----7.00
1281	5" Lemon Dish	1.00----2.00
820	Table Tumbler	1.00----2.00
833	8 oz. Tumbler	1.00----2.00
833	8 oz. Tumbler, ½ Sham Pt	1.00----2.00
766	Ftd. Ice Tea, Handled . .	2.00----3.00
127	Table Tumbler, Handled	1.00----2.00
858	14 oz. Tumbler, Handled	2.00----3.00
4011	12 oz. Tumbler, Handled	2.00----3.00
701	5" Tumbler Plate . . .	1.00----2.00
701	14 oz. Tumbler	1.00----2.00
858	Table Tumbler	1.00----2.00
858	14 oz. Tumbler	1.00----2.00
4011½—Table Tumbler	. . . .	1.00----2.00
4011	12 oz. Tumbler	1.00----2.00
889	5 oz. Tumbler	1.00----2.00
300	7 Jug	15.00--20.00
1743	7 Jug & Cover	15.00--20.00
303	7 Jug	12.00--15.00
1236	6 Jug	12.00--15.00
2040	3 Jug	10.00--12.00
2104	Jug & Tumbler Punty . .	20.00--25.00
2100	7 Jug Cut 138½	12.00--15.00
1480	Sugar	2.00----3.00
1480	Cream	2.00----3.00
1712	Sugar	2.00----3.00
1712½—Cream	. . . .	2.00----3.00
1465	7 oz. Oil, Cut Neck . . .	10.00--12.50
1465	5 oz. Oil	10.00--12.50
2022	Shaker, F. Glass Top . .	2.00----3.00
922	Toothpick Punty . . .	6.00----8.00
1733	Marmalade & Cover	3.00----4.00
1831	Mustard & Cover	3.00----4.00
1697	Carafe	8.00--10.00
1697	Carafe Tumbler (4023-6 oz)	3.00----4.00
2194	8 oz. Syrup, Nickel Top .	10.00--12.00
2194	12 oz. Syrup, Nickel Top .	10.00--12.00
2138	Mayonnaise Bowl . .	8.00--10.00
2138	Mayonnaise Plate	1.00----2.00
2138	Mayonnaise Ladle . . .	1.00----2.00
4069	9" Vase	3.00----5.00
864	7½" Vase	2.00----4.00
1761	10½" Vase, Cut Star . .	4.00----6.00
2137	Tooth Brush Vase . . .	5.00----8.00
2135	Puff & Cover	8.00--10.00
1904	Bon Bon & Cover	10.00--12.00
2136	Bon Bon & Cover	10.00--12.00
2118	Cologne	8.00--10.00
840	5" Sherbet Plate	1.00----2.00
1897	7" Salad Plate	2.00----3.00
1848	9" Sandwich Plate	3.00----5.00
1719	10½" Sandwich Plate . .	4.00----6.00

2219	¼ lb. Candy Jar & Cover	10.00--15.00
2219	½ lb. Candy Jar & Cover	10.00--15.00
2219	1 lb. Candy Jar & Cover	10.00--15.00
2241	Cologne & Stopper	8.00--10.00
803	5" Footed Nappy & Cover	5.00----7.00
803	5" Ftd. Comport & Cover	6.00----8.00

CUTTING NO. 141
"PLUME" PATTERN

802	10 oz. Goblet	2.00----3.00
802½—Saucer Champagne		2.00----3.00
802½—Fruit		2.00----2.50
1736	6" Fruit Plate	1.00----2.00
802	Cocktail	2.00----3.00
899	Parfait	2.00----3.00
1769	Finger Bowl	1.00----2.00
1769	F. Bowl Plate (200-6")	.50----1.00
880	4½" Bon Bon	2.00----3.00
803	5" Comport	2.00----3.00
803	6" Comport	2.00----3.00
803	5" Footed Nappy	2.00----3.00
803	6" Footed Nappy	2.00----3.00
803	7" Footed Nappy	2.00----3.00
820	Table Tumbler	1.00----2.00
833	8 oz. Tumbler	1.00----2.00
833	8 oz. Tumbler, ½ Sham, Pty.	1.00----2.00
4011	12 oz. Tumbler, Handled	1.00----3.00
701	5" Tumbler Plate	1.00----2.00
701	14 oz. Tumbler	1.00----2.00
4011½—Table Tumbler		1.00----2.00
4011	12 oz. Tumbler	1.00----2.00
300	7 Jug	15.00--20.00
1236	6 Jug	12.00--15.00
2040	3 Jug	10.00--12.00
1480	Sugar	2.00----3.00
1480	Cream	2.00----3.00
1712	Sugar	2.00----3.00
1712½—Cream		2.00----3.00
2214	Sugar & Cover	3.00----4.00
2214	Cream & Cover	3.00----4.00
300½—Small Oil		10.00--12.50
2022	Shaker, F. Glass Top	2.00----3.00
1968	Marmalade & Cover	3.00----5.00
1831	Mustard & Cover	3.00----4.00
1697	Carafe	8.00--10.00
1697	Carafe Tumbler (4023-6 oz)	3.00----4.00
2194	8 oz. Syrup, Nickel Top	10.00--12.00
2194	12 oz. Syrup, Nickel Top	10.00--12.00
2138	Mayonnaise Bowl	8.00--10.00
2138	Mayonnaise Plate	1.00----2.00
2138	Mayonnaise Ladle	1.00----2.00
2219	¼ lb. Candy Jar & Cover	10.00--15.00
2219	½ lb. Candy Jar & Cover	10.00--15.00
2219	1 lb. Candy Jar & Cover	10.00--15.00
4069	9 Vase	3.00----5.00
2118	Cologne	8.00--10.00

CUTTING NO. 142
"ARROW" PATTERN

766	9 oz. Goblet	2.00----3.00
766	5 oz. Saucer Champagne	2.00----3.00
766	Fruit	2.00----2.50
766	Parfait	2.00----3.00
766½—Parfait		2.00----3.00
766	3 oz. Cocktail	2.00----3.00
766	Finger Bowl	1.00----2.00
766	Finger Bowl Plate (1736-6")	.50----1.00

766	Bon Bon	2.00----3.00
766	5" Comport	2.00----3.00
766	6" Comport	2.00----3.00
766	5" Footed Nappy	2.00----3.00
766	6" Footed Nappy	2.00----3.00
766	7" Footed Nappy	3.00----4.00
453	4½" Nappy, Handled	3.00----4.00
820	Table Tumbler	1.00----2.00
766	Ftd. Ice Tea, Handled	2.00----3.00
4011	12 oz. Tumbler, Handled	1.00----3.00
701	5" Tumbler Plate	1.00----2.00
701	14 oz. Tumbler	1.00----2.00
4011½—Table Tumbler		1.00----2.00
4011	12 oz. Tumbler	1.00----2.00
300	7 Jug	15.00--20.00
1734	7 Jug & Plain Cover	15.00--20.00
303	7 Jug	12.00--15.00
2100	7 Jug	12.00--15.00
2104	Jug & Tumbler, Punty	20.00--25.00
2133	Sugar	2.00----3.00
2133	Cream	2.00----3.00
2214	Sugar & Cover	3.00----4.00
2214	Cream & Cover	3.00----4.00
1465	7 oz. Oil, Cut Neck	10.00--12.50
1464	5 oz. Oil, Cut Neck	10.00--12.50
2022	Shaker, F. Glass Top	2.00----3.00
1733	Marmalade & Cover	3.00----4.00
1831	Mustard & Cover	3.00----4.00
1697	Carafe	8.00--10.00
1697	Carafe Tumbler (4023-6 oz)	3.00----4.00
2194	8 oz. Syrup, Nickel Top	10.00--12.00
2194	12 oz. Syrup, Nickel Top	10.00--12.00
2138	Mayonnaise Bowl	8.00--10.00
2138	Mayonnaise Plate	1.00----2.00
2138	Mayonnaise Ladle	1.00----2.00
4069	9" Vase	5.00----7.00
2135	Puff & Cover	8.00--10.00
1719	10½" Plate	2.00----3.00
2219	¼ lb. Candy Jar & Cover	10.00--15.00
2219	½ lb. Candy Jar & Cover	10.00--15.00
2219	1 lb. Candy Jar & Cover	10.00--15.00
2241	Cologne & Stopper	8.00--10.00

ROCK CRYSTAL NO. 4

5061	9 oz. Goblet, Optic	2.00----3.00
5061	Saucer Champagne	2.00----3.00
5061	Cocktail, Optic	2.00----3.00
5061	Sherbet, Optic	2.00----2.50
858	Table Tumbler, Cut 19	1.00----2.00
803	5" Deep Nappy, Optic	3.00----5.00
863	Almond, Optic	2.00----3.00
858	Custard	2.00----2.50
1478	Sugar Optic Cut Star	2.00----3.00
1478	Cream Optic Cut Star	2.00----3.00
303	7 Jug	12.00--15.00

COIN GOLD BAND NO. 2

858	10 oz. Goblet	2.00----3.00
858	4½ oz. Claret	2.00----3.00
858	7 oz. Saucer Champagne	2.00----3.00
858	3½ oz. Cocktail	2.00----3.00
858	Custard	2.00----2.50
863	Almond	2.00----3.00
1499	Finger Bowl & Plate	2.00----3.00
858	Table Tumbler	1.00----2.00
303	7 Jug 2 Bands	9.00--12.00

NO. 2222 COLONIAL PATTERN

2222	Butter & Cover	10.00--12.00
2222	Sugar & Cover	6.00----8.00
2222	Cream	4.00----6.00
2222	Spoon	4.00----6.00
2222½—	Sugar & Cover	4.00----6.00
2222	Hotel Cream	2.00----3.00
2222	Hotel Sugar	2.00----3.00
2222	Hotel Sugar & Cover	3.00----4.00
2222	Ind. or Toy Cream	3.00----4.00
2222	4", 4½", 5", 6", 7" Nappy	1.00----3.00
2222	7" Nappy, Shallow	2.00----3.00
2222	8" Nappy	3.00----4.00
2222	4½" Handled Nappy	2.00----3.00
2222	5" Handled Nappy	2.00----3.00
2222	½ gal. Pitcher	5.00----8.00
2222	3 qt. Ice Pitcher	6.00----9.00
2222½—	½ gal. Jug, Globe Shape	4.00----6.00
2222	3 qt. Ice Pitcher, Special	5.00----8.00
2222	Hall Boy Jug	4.00----6.00
2222	Pint Jug	3.00----4.00
2222	Table Tumbler	1.00----2.00
2222	5 oz. Wine Tumbler	1.00----2.00
2222	12 oz. Ice Tea	1.00----2.00
2222½—	Table Tumbler	1.00----2.00
2222½—	14 oz. Ice Tea	1.00----2.00
2222	5" Ice Tea Plate	.50----1.00
2222	7" Salad Plate	1.00----2.00
2222	8" Salad Plate	1.00----2.00
2222½—	Goblet	2.00----3.00
2222	Goblet	2.00----3.00
2222	Wine	2.00----3.00
2222	Footed Oyster Cocktail	2.00----3.00
2222	Cafe Parfait	2.00----3.00
2222	4½ oz. High Foot Sherbet	2.00----3.00
2222	4½ oz. Low Foot Sherbet	1.00----2.00
2222½—	3 oz. Low Foot Sherbet	1.00----2.00
2222	Footed Fruit Salad	1.00----2.00
2222	Footed Salt	3.00----4.00
2222	Custard	1.00----2.00
2222	4 oz. Oil, Drop Stopper	8.00--10.00
2222	6 oz. Oil, Drop Stopper	8.00--10.00
2222	8 oz. Oil, Drop Stopper "Squat"	8.00--10.00
2222	4 oz. Oil, Ground Stopper	10.00--12.00
2222	6 oz. Oil, Ground Stopper	10.00--12.00
2222	8 oz. Oil, Ground Stopper, "Squat"	10.00--12.00
2222	Ketchup, Drop Stopper	10.00--12.00
2222	Ketchup, Ground Stopper	12.00--14.00
2222	Mustard & Cover	2.00----3.00
2222	Mustard & Cover & Spoon	3.00----4.00
2222	4½" Ftd. Preserve	2.00----3.00
2222	4½" Ftd. Preserve & Cover	4.00----6.00
2222	4½" High Ft. Jelly	2.00----4.00
2222	4½" High Ft. Jelly & Cover	4.00----6.00
2222	6" Bowl, Flared	1.00----2.00
2222	6" Bowl & Cover	3.00----5.00
2222	Lemon Dish	1.00----2.00
2222	Lemon Dish & Cover	4.00----6.00
2222	Olive Tray	1.00----2.00
2222	Pickle Tray	1.00----2.00
2222	Celery Tray	2.00----3.00
2222	Blown Water Bottle	4.00----6.00
2222½—	Pressed Water Bottle	6.00----9.00
2222	Toothpick	3.00----4.00
2222	4", 5", 7" Ice Tub	2.00----6.00
2222	10" Ice Tub Plate	3.00----5.00
2222	Mayonnaise	3.00----4.00
2222	Mayonnaise Plate	1.00----2.00
2222	Mayonnaise Ladle	1.00----2.00
2222	Cheese & Cover	8.00--10.00
2222	Finger Bowl	1.00----2.00
2222	6" Finger Bowl Plate	.50----1.00
2222	Loaf Sugar	1.00----2.00
2222½—	Oyster Cocktail & Liner	2.00----3.00
2222	8½" Vase	2.00----4.00
2222	10" Vase	3.00----4.00
2222	12" Vase	3.00----5.00

New Piece made in 1973 in lead crystal.

2222	Olive or Pickle	4.00

*MISCELLANEOUS

Made in Crystal, Amber, Green, Blue & Canary.

2297	7" Candlestick	5.00----8.00
2288	"Tut" Vase	15.00--25.00
2311	7" Candlestick	5.00----8.00
2250	½ lb. Candy Jar & Cover	10.00--15.00
2245	8" Candlestick	5.00----8.00
2275	9" Candlestick	5.00----9.00
2267	10" Deep Ftd. Bowl Rolled Edge	10.00--12.00
2297	10½" Deep Bowl "C" Rolled Edge	12.00--15.00
2297	10¼" Shallow Bowl "A" Flared	10.00--12.00
2297	7½" Shal. Bowl "D", Reg.	10.00--12.00
2297	10½" Dp. Bowl "B" Cupped	10.00--15.00

Made in Crystal, Amber, Canary & Green

2290	8¼" Plate Deep Salad	2.00----4.00
2290	13" Plate Deep Salad	5.00----7.00
4095	Large Vase	20.00--25.00
2287	Lunch Tray "Fleur-de-lis"	10.00--15.00
4095	Large Vase Rolled Edge	20.00--25.00

Bases & Vases Ebony

2297½—	7½" Dp. Bowl "D" Reg. & Ebony base	10.00--15.00
1491	6" Vase Ebony	4.00----6.00
2297½—	9¼" Shal. Bowl "C" Rolled Edge Ebony base	12.00--15.00
2312	10" Vase Ebony	4.00----6.00
2297½—	9¼" Shal. Bowl "B" Cupped w/Ebony base	12.00--15.00
1491	8½" Vase Ebony	4.00----6.00
2297½—	12" Dp. Bowl "A" Flared w/Ebony base	12.00--18.00

Made in Crystal, Amber, Blue, Canary & Green

2815	Grape Fruit	6.00--10.00
2815	Mayonnaise	6.00--10.00
2815	Sugar	4.00----8.00
2815	Cream	4.00----8.00
2815	10½" Bowl "A" Flared	12.00--20.00
2815	10½" Bowl "C" Rolled Edge	12.00--20.00
2320	10" Nappy "B" Cupped & Ebony base	15.00--20.00
2255	Sugar (made in Amber, Blue, Gr.)	3.00----5.00
2255	Cream (made Am., Blue, Gr.)	3.00----5.00
2320	12" Nappy "A" Flared	12.00--15.00
2330	Sherbet & Plate (one piece) made in Gr., Am.)	3.00----5.00
2315	11½" Bowl "B" Shape	10.00--15.00
2315	8¾" Bowl "D" Shape	8.00--12.00

NOTE: Canary color is highest price, then blue, green and amber lowest.

2341	8" Plate	2.00----4.00
2342	8" Plate	1.00----3.00
2316	8" Soup Plate (made in Cry., Am., Blue, Gr.)	2.00----4.00
2333	11" Candle (made in Cry.,, Blue, Gr., Am.)	8.00--15.00
2333	11" Console Bowl (made in Cry., Blue, Gr., Am.)	15.00--20.00
2333	8" Candle (made in Cry., Blue, Gr., Am.)	6.00--10.00
2324	4" Candle	4.00----7.00
2329	11" Centerpiece	8.00--12.00
2324	9" Candle	8.00--10.00
2324	Small Urn, Top Diameter 7"	10.00--15.00

AMERICAN PATTERN
Made in amber, blue and canary

2056	Hair Receiver	20.00--30.00
2056	6" Bon Bon	10.00--15.00
2056	Puff & Cover	15.00--20.00
2056	Small Cigarette & Cover .	15.00--20.00
2056	Cologne	15.00--25.00
2056	Square Puff & Cover . .	15.00--20.00
2056	Confection & Cover	15.00--20.00
2056	5" Pin Tray	8.00--10.00
2056	Large Cigarette & Cover .	15.00--25.00
2056½—10" Comb & Brush Tray		10.00--15.00

*MISCELLANEOUS
Made in Crystal, Amber, Green, Blue and Canary.

2297	8" Vase Sq. top,	10.00--20.00
1861½—6" Jelly Flared		6.00----8.00
2297½—8" Vase Rolled Edge . .		10.00--20.00
2269	6" Candlestick	5.00----7.00
2267	7" Console Bowl	7.00----9.00
2327	7" Comport Regular . .	8.00--12.00
2300	12" Vase	10.00--15.00
2327	7" Comport Salver Shape	10.00--15.00
2328	7" Oblong Box & Cover .	12.00--16.00
2331	7" Rd. Candy Box & Cover (3 compartments) . .	15.00--20.00
2306	Smoker Set (4 ash trays nested) (made in Crys., Ebony)	5.00--10.00
1681	Wall Vase (made in Cry., Eb.).	5.00----8.00
2321	Mah Jongg Set (Sherbet & Plate)	4.00----6.00
2292	8" Vase, Regular (made in Cry., GR.)	6.00----8.00
2326	7" Vase	8.00--12.00
2292	8" Vase Flared (made in Cry., Gr.)	8.00--10.00
2324½—4" Candle (made in Eb.)		4.00----6.00
2329	14" Centerpiece (made in Gr., Am., Blue, & Eb. only)	15.00--20.00
2297	10½" Shal. Bowl Flared "A" (Eb.)	15.00--20.00
2320	11" Nappy Cupped "B" (Eb) (on 3½" Ebony base)	15.00--20.00

CIGARETTES, PUFFS & COLOGNES
Made in Crystal, Amber, Green, Blue and Ebony.

2322	Cologne	9.00--12.00
2347	Puff & Cover	9.00--12.00
2323	Cologne	8.00--10.00
2347½—Puff & Cover		8.00--10.00

2106	Large Cigarette & Cover (not made in Eb.)	8.00--10.00
2338	Puff & Cover (not made in Eb.)	4.00----6.00
2359½—Puff & Cover		5.00----8.00
2349	Cigarette	5.00----9.00
2351	Cigarette (made in solid colors, also w/colored foot)	5.00----9.00
2354	Cigarette (made in solid colors, also w/colored foot) (also in Orchid)	5.00----9.00
5092	Cigarette (made in solid colors, also w/colored foot) (not in Eb.)	5.00----9.00

PLATES
Made in Amber, Green, Blue.

2348	8" Plate	2.00----3.00
2283	7" Plate, Spiral Optic . . also made in 6, 7, 8, 13" also made in Orchid . .	2.00----3.00 / 2.00----5.00
2356	8" Plate also made in Orchid	2.00----3.00
2283	6" Plate, Reg. Optic (also made in Orchid) . . . . . 6", 7", & 8" made in Am., Blue, Green	1.00----2.00 / 2.00----3.00
2287	11" Hdl. Sandwich tray, (also made in Orchid)	8.00--10.00
2342	7" Plate made in 7", 8", 13" (also made in Orchid)	2.00----5.00
2276	Cheese & Cover	8.00--12.00
2276	11" Cracker Plate (not made in Blue)	8.00--10.00
2272	Coaster (also made in Orchid)	.50----1.00
2106	Coaster	.50----1.00
2342	12" Sandwich Tray (also made in Orchid)	8.00--10.00
2283	8" Plate (made in 6", 7", 8" & 13") (also made in Orchid) (5" made in Amber & Green)	2.00----5.00

CANDY JARS — PRESSED & BLOWN
Made in Crystal, Amber, Green, & Blue.

5084	Candy Jar & Cover —made in solid Am., Blue, Gr., Cry., Reg. Optic . . . . made in Amber Ft. Loop Optic made in Green Ft. Spiral Optic made in Blue Ft. Reg. Optic	10.00--15.00
2219	½ lb. Candy Jar & Cover	10.00--12.00
2380	Confection & Cover (made in Plain or Spiral Optic) (made in Orchid)	12.00--18.00
2331	3 Candy Box & Cover (3 partitions) (also made in Eb., Orch.)	15.00--20.00
2250	½ lb. Candy Jar & Cover (also made in Eb.)	8.00--12.00
4095½—Candy Jar & Cover Spiral Optic made in solid green . . (also green ft.) made in Loop Optic Solid Amber also Am. ft. made in Reg. Optic solid Blue also blue ft.		8.00--12.00

VASES
Made in Crystal, Amber, Green, Blue & Orchid.

1479	6" Vase not made in Blue; Orchid	6.00----8.00

2367	7" Bulb Bowl made in 8", also made in Eb. (not made in Orchid)	4.00----8.00	
4100	6" Vase Reg. Optic made in 6" 8", 10" & 12" made in Reg. or Loop Optic	6.00--15.00	
5086	9" Vase Spiral Optic	4.00----6.00	
5087	8" Vase Spiral Optic	4.00----6.00	
5085	8" Vase Spiral Optic	4.00----6.00	
4095½—8" Vase Spiral Optic (not made in Orchid)		6.00----8.00	
4095	7" Vase Spiral Optic	4.00----6.00	
2369	5" Vase Optic made in 5", 7", 9" & 11"—5" & 11" not made in Cry.	8.00--15.00	
1681	8" Wall Vase made in Eb., not made in Orchid	5.00----8.00	
2292	8" Vase Spiral Optic made Plain or Spiral Optic made in Eb., & Cry., Plain only	8.00--10.00	
2060	8" Vase Optic made in 8" & 10"— not made in Cry.	8.00--12.00	
4095	8" Vase Spiral Optic made in 8", 9" 10"—not made in Orch.	6.00--10.00	
2369	7" Vase Optic (made in 5", 7", 9" & 11") 5" & 11" not made in Cry.	8.00--15.00	

CONSOLE SET & BOWL

Made in Amber, Green, Blue & Orchid

2342	12" Salad Bowl	8.00--12.00
2362	9" Candle—made in 3" & 9"	9.00--12.00
2362	11" Comport (also made in Cry.)	10.00--18.00

FLOWER SETS

Made in Crystal, Amber, Green, Blue, Orchid

2372	2" Candle Block (also made in Spiral Optic	3.00----5.00
2371	13" Centerpiece (oval)	10.00--15.00
2371	Flower Holder	3.00----4.00
2362	3" Candle (made in 3" & 9")	4.00----6.00
2362	12" Bowl (not made in Cry.)	8.00--12.00
2309	3¾" Flower Block	1.00----3.00

BLOWN GLASSWARE

Made in solid crystal reg. Optic—solid green spiral optic—Also made Blue foot reg. optic— Green foot spiral optic—Amber foot loop optic.

4095	6 oz. parfait loop optic—not made in solid green.	3.00----5.00
4095	4 oz. Oyster Cocktail loop optic	2.00----4.00
4095	Loop optic 2½ oz. footed Tumbler	2.00----4.00
4095	5" Nappy loop optic—made in 4½", 5", 6" & 7"	4.00----8.00
4095	Ind. Almond loop optic—made in solid gr., reg. optic	2.00----4.00
4095	Ind. Salt loop optic—made in solid gr. reg. optic	2.00----4.00
4095	5 oz. Ftd. Tumbler loop optic	2.00----4.00
4095	10 oz. Ftd. Tumbler loop op	2.00----5.00
4095	13 oz. Ftd. Tumbler loop op.	3.00----6.00
4095	No. 7 Jug loop Optic Made in solid green spiral optic	15.00--25.00

1697	Carafe	6.00----8.00
4023	6 oz. Carafe Tumbler Spiral Optic	2.00----4.00
945½—Grape Fruit		2.00----4.00
945½—Grape Fruit Liner—reg. optic— Also made in Am., Blue		1.00----3.00
1769	Finger Bowl	1.00----3.00
2283	6" Finger Bowl Plate Spiral Optic	1.00----2.00
889	5 oz. Tumbler Spiral Optic	1.00----2.00
820	Tumbler Spiral Optic	1.00----2.00
701	13 oz. Tumbler Spiral Optic	2.00----3.00
2082	No. 7 Jug Spiral Optic	12.00--15.00

BOWLS, CENTERPIECES & CANDLESTICKS

2372	2" Candlestick, S/O Ro-Gr-Am-Cry.	3.00----5.00
2372	2" Candlestick, Gr-Am-Cry.	3.00----5.00
2329	11" Centerpiece S/O, Ro-Gr-Am-Cry.	4.00----6.00
2329	11" Centerpiece, Ro-Az-Gr-Am-Eb-Cry.	6.00--10.00
2390	3" Candlestick, Ro-Az-Gr-Am.	4.00----7.00
2390	12" Ftd. Bowl, Ro-Az-Gr-Am.	8.00--12.00

CONSOLE SET

Made in Crystal, Amber, Green & Orchid.

2324	12" Candle—made in 2", 4", 6", 9" 12"—12" not made in Orchid	8.00--12.00
2324	13" Console Bowl—also made in 10", 13" not made in Orch.	15.00--25.00

NO. 2321 LUNCHEON SET "Priscilla" Pattern
Made in Amber, Green & Blue.

2321	9 oz. Goblet	5.00--10.00
2321½—7 oz. Luncheon Goblet		6.00----8.00
2321	High Sherbet	3.00----5.00
2321	Footed Handled Tumbler	6.00----8.00
2321½—Footed Ice Tea		4.00----7.00
2321	3 Pint Jug	25.00--35.00
2321	Footed Handled Custard	3.00----5.00
2321	Sherbet	2.00----3.00
2321	Cup	2.00----4.00
2321	Saucer	1.00----2.00
2321	Cream Soup (Mayonnaise)	3.00----5.00
2321	Bouillon	3.00----5.00
	Also made in Rose & Azure	
2321	Cream	5.00----7.00
	Also made in Rose & Azure	
2321	Sugar	5.00----7.00
2321	8" Luncheon Plate	2.00----3.00

NO. 2350 DINNERWARE "Pioneer" Pattern
Made in Crystal, Amber, Green & Blue.

*2350	6" Bread & Butter Plate	1.00----2.00
*2350	7" Salad Plate	2.00----3.00
*2350	8" Salad Plate	3.00----4.00
*2350	9" Dinner Plate	3.00----4.00
*2350	10" Dinner Plate	3.00----5.00
2350	12" Chop Plate	5.00----8.00
2350	13" Chop Plate	6.00----9.00
2350	15" Round Plate	8.00--10.00

2350	5" Fruit		2.00----3.00
2350	6" Cereal		3.00----4.00
2350	7" Soup		4.00----5.00
2350	Cup		2.00----4.00
@*†2350½	Footed Cup		2.00----4.00
@*†2350	Saucer		1.00----2.00
@*†2350	After Dinner Cup		2.00----4.00
@*†2350	After Dinner Saucer		1.00----2.00
2350	Bouillon		2.00----4.00
2350½	Footed Bouillon		2.00----4.00
2350	Cream Soup		2.00----4.00
2350½	Footed Cream Soup		2.00----4.00
2350	Cream Soup Plate		1.00----2.00
2350	9" Oval Baker		8.00--12.00
2350	10½" Oval Baker		10.00--15.00
2350	8" Nappy		6.00----8.00
2350	9" Nappy		8.00--10.00
2350	10" Salad Bowl		10.00--12.00
2350	10½" Oval Platter		8.00--10.00
2350	12" Oval Platter		9.00--12.00
2350	15" Oval Platter		10.00--15.00
2350	Sauce Boat		8.00--12.00
2350	Sauce Boat Plate		2.00----4.00
2350	8" Pickle		3.00----4.00
2350	11" Celery		4.00----6.00
2350	Butter & Cover		20.00--30.00
2350	Sugar & Cover		10.00--15.00
2350	Sugar		3.00----5.00
2350	Cream		3.00----5.00
2350½	Footed Sugar & Cover		10.00--15.00
@*2350½	Footed Sugar		3.00----5.00
	Also made in Rose		
@*2350½	Footed Cream		3.00----5.00
	Also made in Rose		
2350	Egg Cup		3.00----5.00
	Also made in Rose & Azure		
2350	8" Comport		8.00--12.00
*2350	Small Ash Tray		3.00----5.00
	Also made in Rose & Azure		
*2350	Large Ash Tray		5.00----8.00
	Also made in Rose & Azure		
2350	3 Compartment Relish		6.00--10.00
	Also made in Rose & Azure		
2350	Grape Fruit		2.00----4.00
2350	Grape Fruit Liner		1.00----2.00

*Made in Ebony
†Made in Regal Blue, Empire green & Burgundy
@Made in Ruby

NO. 2375 DINNERWARE "Fairfax" Pattern
Made in Crystal, Amber, Green, Rose, Azure & Orchid.

2375	6" Bread & Butter Plate		1.00----2.00
2375	7" Salad Plate		1.00----3.00
2375	8" Salad Plate		2.00----3.00
2375	9" Dinner Plate		2.00----4.00
2375	10" Dinner Plate		3.00----5.00
2375	13" Chop Plate		6.00----8.00
2375	10" Grill Plate		3.00----5.00
2375	Fruit		2.00----3.00
2375	Cereal		2.00----4.00
2375	Soup		2.00----4.00
2375	Cup		2.00----3.00
2375½	Footed Cup		2.00----4.00
2375	Saucer		1.00----2.00
2375	After Dinner Cup		2.00----3.00
2375	After Dinner Saucer		1.00----2.00
2375	Footed Bouillon		2.00----3.00
2375	Footed Cream Soup		2.00----3.00
2375	Cream Soup Plate		1.00----2.00
2375	9" Oval Baker		6.00--10.00
2375	10½" Oval Baker		8.00--12.00
2375	8" Round Nappy		5.00----8.00
2375	10½" Oval Platter		5.00----7.00
2375	12" Oval Platter		7.00--10.00
2375	15" Oval Platter		9.00--12.00
2375	8½" Pickle		3.00----5.00
2375	11½" Celery		4.00----6.00
2375	8½" Relish		3.00----5.00
2375	11½" Relish		4.00----6.00
2375	Sauce Boat		12.00--15.00
2375	Sauce Boat Plate		3.00----5.00
2375	Butter & Cover		30.00--35.00
2375	Sugar		4.00----6.00
	Not made in Rose, Topaz or Azure		
2375	Cream		4.00----6.00
	Not made in Rose, Topaz or Azure		
2375½	Footed Sugar & Cover		15.00--20.00
2375½	Footed Sugar		4.00----6.00
2375½	Footed Cream		4.00----6.00
*2375½	Tea Sugar		4.00----7.00
	Also made in Ebony & Ruby		
*2375½	Tea Cream		4.00----7.00
	Also made in Ebony & Ruby		
2375	Footed Shaker		5.00----8.00
2375	Mayonnaise		3.00----5.00
2375	Mayonnaise Plate		2.00----3.00
2375	Mayonnaise Ladle		1.00----2.00
*2375	7" Comport		4.00----7.00
2375	11" Hdl. Lunch Tray		6.00----8.00
*2375	Footed Cheese		2.00----4.00
*2375	Cracker Plate		4.00----6.00
*2375	Cheese & Cracker		6.00--10.00
*2375	Sweetmeat		3.00----5.00
*2375	Whipped Cream		3.00----5.00
*2375	Lemon Dish—Also made in Ebony		3.00----6.00
2375	12" Bread Plate		6.00----9.00
*2375	Bon Bon—Also made in Eb.		3.00----6.00
*2375	10" Cake Plate, 2 Hdles.		6.00----9.00
	Also made in Ebony		
*2375	Large Dessert, 2 Hdles.		4.00----6.00
*2375	Ice Bucket, N.P. Hdle.		12.00--15.00
*2375	Footed Oil		15.00--20.00
2375	Canape Plate—also made in Ebony		1.00----3.00
2375	Ash Tray		3.00----5.00
2375	12" Bowl		8.00--12.00
2375	3" Candlestick		3.00----5.00
2375	12" Centerpiece		10.00--12.00
2375	15" Centerpiece		12.00--15.00
2375½	Candlestick		3.00----5.00
2375½	Oval Centerpiece		12.00--16.00
2371	Oval Flower Holder		2.00----3.00
*2375	7" Round Nappy		4.00----6.00
*2375	Salad Dressing Bottle		14.00--18.00
2427	Cigarette Box & Cover		8.00--12.00
2429	Service Tray		6.00----8.00
2429	Lemon Dish		2.00----3.00

Not made in Orchid

NO. 2222 TEA ROOM SERVICE
Made in Amber & Green.

2222	Goblet		4.00----6.00
2222	4½ oz. High Sherbet		3.00----5.00
2222	4½ oz. Low Sherbet		2.00----3.00
2222	3 oz. Low Sherbet		2.00----3.00
2222	3 oz. Fruit Cocktail		2.00----3.00

2222	Cocktail	4.00----6.00
2222	Claret	4.00----6.00
2222	5 oz. Parfait	3.00----5.00
2222	Finger Bowl	2.00----3.00
2222	6" Finger Bowl Plate	1.00----2.00
2222½	Sugar & Cover	4.00----6.00
2222	Individual Cream, No Hdl.	2.00----3.00
2222	4 oz. Oil, G.S.	12.00--15.00
2222	6 oz. Oil, G.S.	12.00--15.00
2222½	14 oz. Ice Tea	3.00----4.00
2222½	8 oz. Table Tumbler	2.00----3.00
2222½	5 oz. Tumbler	2.00----3.00
1372	Oyster Cocktail	2.00----3.00
1372	Oyster Cocktail Liner	1.00----2.00
713½	Shaker, Glass Top	3.00----4.00
2222½	Water Bottle	10.00--15.00
2391	Lg. Cigarette & Cover Ro-Az-Gr-Am-Eb-Cry.	6.00----9.00
2391	Sm. Cigarette & Cover Ro-Az-Gr-Am-Eb-Cry.	5.00----8.00
2306	4 Pce. Smoker Set Ro-Az-Gr-Am-Eb-Cry.	4.00----6.00
5092	Cigarette Holder Ro-Az-Gr-Am.	4.00----6.00
5000	Ftd. Shaker—Gr-Am-Cry.	3.00----5.00
2111	Shaker—Ro-Az-Gr-Am-Tz-Cry.	2.00----3.00
2128	Shaker—Gr-Am-Cry.	2.00----3.00
2127	Shaker—Gr-Am-Cry.	2.00----3.00
2327	7" Comport—Ro-Gr-Am-Cry	5.00----9.00
2106	Coaster—Gr-Am-Cry.	.50----1.00
2272	Coaster—Ro-Az-Gr-Am-Cry.	.50----1.00
1861½	Jelly—Ro-Az-Gr-Am-Cry.	4.00----6.00
2378	Ice Bucket, S/O—Ro-Az-Gr-Am.	8.00--12.00
2378	Ice Bucket—Ro-Az-Gr-Am-Cry.	8.00--12.00
2378	Whipped Cream Pail S/O Ro-Az-Gr-Am-	8.00--12.00
2378	Whipped Cream Pail Ro-Az-Gr-Am-Tz-Cry.	8.00--12.00
2378	Sugar Pail, S/O Ro-Az-Gr-Am.	8.00--12.00
2378	Sugar Pail—Ro-Az-Gr-Am-Tz-Cry.	8.00--12.00
2378	Ice Tongs N.P.	1.00----2.00
2378	Sugar Tongs S.F.	1.00----2.00
4101	2½ oz. Ftd. Tumbler—Tz-Ro-Az-Gr-Am-Wist	2.00----3.00
4101	Qt. Decanter—Ro-Az-Gr-Am-Wist-Tz	15.00--20.00
4101	Jug—Ro-Az-Gr-Am.	15.00--20.00
4101	9, 13 oz. Tumbler—Ro-Az-Gr-Am-Tz.	3.00----5.00
4101	6½ oz. Sherbet—Ro-Az-Gr-Am-Tz.	2.00----3.00
2297	10½" Deep Bowl "B", S/O Gr-Am.	7.00--10.00
2297	10½" Deep Bowl "B", Ro-Gr-Am-Cry.	7.00--10.00
2297	10½" Deep Bowl "C", S/O Ro-Gr-Am.	7.00--10.00
2297	10½ Deep Bowl "C" Ro-Gr-Am-Cry.	7.00--10.00
2297	12" Deep Bowl "A", S/O Ro-Gr-Am.	8.00--10.00
2297	12" Deep Bowl "A", Ro-Az-Gr-Am-Eb-Cry.	8.00--10.00
2324	4" Candlestick Ro-Az-Gr-Am-Eb-Cry.	3.00----5.00

NO. 2412 "QUEEN ANNE" PATTERN
Made in Crystal, Amber, Green & Blue.

2412	12" Vase	15.00--18.00
2412	14" Vase	16.00--20.00
2412	9" Candle	8.00--12.00
2412	11" Centerpiece	10.00--15.00
2412	9" Shal. Bowl, Low Ft.	15.00--18.00
2412	9" Shal. Bowl, Hg. Ft.	18.00--20.00
2412	9" Shal. Bowl, Hg. Ft. w/Crystal Bowl & Amber, Blue or Green Ft.	15.00--20.00
2412	14½" Lustre Amber, Blue or Green Pedestal w/Crystal Bobache & Candleholder Complete w/U.D. Prisms	25.00--35.00
2412	2 Light Candelabra w/Amber, Blue or Green Pedestal, Crystal Arms & Bobache Complete w/U.D. Prisms	50.00--75.00

BOWLS & CANDLESTICKS

2425	2" Candlestick Ro-Az-Gr-Am-Eb-Cry -Tz.	4.00----6.00
2425	13" Oblong Bowl Ro-Az-Gr-Am-Eb-Cry-Tz	6.00--10.00
2309	4½" Oval Flower Block Ro-Gr-Am-Cry.	2.00----3.00
2393	2" Candlestick Ro-Az-Gr-Am.	3.00----5.00
2393	12" Centerpiece Also 15" size, Ro-Az-Gr-Am.	7.00--10.00
2309	3¾" Flower Block	2.00----3.00
2418	10" Oval Ftd. Bowl Ro-Az-Gr-Am.	8.00--10.00
2395½	5" Candlestick Ro-Az-Gr-Am-Tz-Eb-Cry.	4.00----6.00
2402	Mint, Ro-Az-Gr-Am-Tz.	2.00----3.00
2402	9" Bowl Ro-Az-Gr-Am-Tz-Eb.	6.00----9.00

NO. 2430 LINE "DIADEM" PATTERN
Made in Cry-Am-Gr-Ro-Tz-Az-Eb.

2430	7" Jelly	3.00----5.00
2430	½ lb. Candy Jar & Cover	10.00--15.00
2430	5½" Mint	2.00----4.00
2430	8" Vase	6.00----9.00
2430	11" Bowl	7.00--12.00

NEEDLE ETCHING NO. 73 "LENORE PATTERN"
Optic Only

858	9 oz. Goblet	2.00----4.00
858	5½ oz. Saucer Champagne	2.00----4.00
858	Fruit	1.00----2.00
858	4½ oz. Claret	2.00----4.00
858	2¾ oz. Wine	2.00----4.00
858	1 oz. Cordial	2.00----4.00
858	3½ oz. Cocktail	2.00----4.00
858	Parfait	2.00----3.00
858	Sherbet (Oyster Cocktail)	2.00----3.00
858	Finger Bowl	1.00----2.00
2283	6" Finger Bowl Plate	1.00----2.00
858	Mayonnaise Set—3 piece	3.00----5.00
945½	Grape Fruit	2.00----3.00
945½	Grape Fruit Liner	2.00----3.00

858	Sweetmeat	2.00----4.00
880	Sweetmeat	2.00----4.00
5078	5" Compote	3.00----4.00
5078	6" Compote	3.00----4.00
5078	5" Nappy	1.00----2.00
5078	6" Nappy	2.00----3.00
5078	7" Nappy	3.00----4.00
820	Table Tumbler	1.00----2.00
701	12 oz. Ice Tea	2.00----3.00
701	5" Tumbler Plate	1.00----2.00
858	Table Tumbler	1.00----2.00
858	14 oz. Tumbler	2.00----3.00
858	12 oz. Tumbler	2.00----3.00
858	8 oz. Tumbler	1.00----2.00
858	5½ oz. Tumbler	1.00----2.00
858	3 oz. Tumbler	1.00----2.00
869	12 oz. Hdld. Tumbler (837)	2.00----4.00
2283	5" Plate	1.00----2.00
300	7 Tankard	15.00--18.00
303	7 Jug	15.00--18.00
318	7 Jug	15.00--18.00
1236	6 Jug	15.00--18.00
2270	Jug & Cover	15.00--20.00
2133	Sugar	2.00----4.00
2133	Cream	2.00----4.00
312	Oil	12.00--15.00

RICHMOND PATTERN
NEEDLE ETCHING NO. 74

5082	9 oz. Goblet	2.00----4.00
5082	Saucer Champagne	2.00----4.00
5082	Fruit	1.00----2.00
5082	Parfait	2.00----4.00
5082	Claret	2.00----4.00
5082	Wine	2.00----4.00
5082	Cocktail	2.00----4.00
5082	Cordial	2.00----4.00
4095	Oyster Cocktail	2.00----3.00
837	Oyster Cocktail	2.00----3.00
1769	Finger Bowl	1.00----2.00
2283	6" Plate	1.00----2.00
858	Sweetmeat	3.00----4.00
945½	Grape Fruit	2.00----3.00
945½	Grape Fruit Liner	1.00----2.00
5039	Liner, tumbler shape, not etched	1.00----2.00
5078	5" Compote	3.00----4.00
5078	5" Nappy	1.00----2.00
5078	6" Nappy	2.00----3.00
820	Tumbler	1.00----2.00
701	13 oz. Tumbler	2.00----3.00
701	8 oz. Tumbler	1.00----2.00
701	5" Plate	1.00----2.00
889	5 oz. Tumbler	1.00----2.00
887	2½ oz. Tumbler	2.00----3.00
869	12 oz. Hdld. Tum. (837)	3.00----4.00
4095	13 oz. Ftd. Tumbler	2.00----3.00
4095	10 oz. Ftd. Tumbler	2.00----3.00
4095	5 oz. Ftd. Tumbler	2.00----3.00
4095	2½ oz. Ftd. Tumbler	2.00----3.00
2270	Jug & Cover	15.00--20.00
2270	7 Jug	15.00--18.00
303	7 Jug	15.00--18.00
318	7 Jug	15.00--18.00
2283	7" Plate	2.00----3.00

Also presented as Richmond Pattern Needle Etching No. 74. Gold Band No. 43.

NEEDLE ETCHING NO. 77
"SHERMAN" PATTERN

869	Goblet	2.00----4.00
869	Saucer, Champagne	2.00----4.00
869	Fruit	1.00----2.00
869	Parfait	2.00----3.00
869	Cocktail	2.00----4.00
869	Wine	2.00----4.00
4095	Oyster Cocktail	2.00----3.00
766	Finger Bowl	2.00----3.00
2283	6" Plate	1.00----2.00
945½	Grape Fruit	2.00----3.00
4095	5" Nappy	2.00----3.00
4095	6" Nappy	2.00----3.00
4095	7" Nappy	2.00----4.00
5078	5" Compote	2.00----4.00
4095	13 oz. Ftd. Tumbler	2.00----3.00
4095	10 oz. Ftd. Tumbler	2.00----3.00
4095	5 oz. Ftd. Tumbler	2.00----3.00
4095	2½ oz. Ftd. Tumbler	2.00----3.00
5100	12 oz. Ftd. Tumbler	2.00----3.00
5100	9 oz. Ftd. Tumbler	2.00----3.00
5100	5 oz. Ftd. Tumbler	2.00----3.00
5100	2½ oz. Ftd. Tumbler	2.00----3.00
869	12 oz. Hdld. Tumbler	3.00----4.00
869	Table Tumbler	1.00----2.00
869	12 oz. Tumbler	1.00----2.00
869	5 oz. Tumbler	1.00----2.00
869	2 oz. Tumbler	1.00----2.00
4095	7 Jug	15.00--18.00
2270	7 Jug & Cover	15.00--20.00
2283	7" Plate	1.00----2.00
2283	8" Plate	2.00----3.00

DECORATION No. 54 "ALASKA" White Gold
NEEDLE ETCHING No. 77

869	Goblet	4.00----5.00
869	Saucer Champagne	4.00----5.00
869	Fruit	2.00----3.00
869	Parfait	4.00----5.00
869	Wine	4.00----5.00
869	Cocktail	4.00----5.00
4095	Oyster Cocktail	3.00----4.00
766	Finger Bowl	2.00----4.00
2283	6" Plate	2.00----3.00
945½	Grape Fruit	2.00----4.00
945½	Grape Fruit Liner (Gold Edge Only)	1.00----2.00
5078	5" Comport	4.00----6.00
4095	13 oz. Ftd. Tumbler	2.00----4.00
4095	10 oz. Ftd. Tumbler	2.00----4.00
4095	5 oz. Ftd. Tumbler	2.00----4.00
4095	2½ oz. Ftd. Tumbler	2.00----4.00
869	12 oz. Hdld. Tumbler	3.00----5.00
869	Table Tumbler	2.00----3.00
869	12 oz. Tumbler	2.00----4.00
869	8 oz. Tumbler	2.00----3.00
869	5 oz. Tumbler	2.00----3.00
4095	7 Jug	20.00--25.00
2270	7 Jug	15.00--20.00
2270	7 Jug & Cover	20.00--25.00
2283	7" Plate	2.00----3.00
2283	8" Plate	2.00----4.00

NEEDLE ETCHING NO. 78
"FRESNO" PATTERN

| 867½ | Goblet | 2.00----4.00 |

867½—Saucer Champagne . . 2.00----3.00
867½—Fruit 1.00----2.00
867½—Cocktail 2.00----4.00
867½—Wine 2.00----4.00
4095　10 oz. Tumbler 1.00----2.00
820　Tumbler 1.00----2.00
701　13 oz. Tumbler 1.00----2.00
316　7 Jug 18.00--20.00

NEEDLE ETCHING NO. 79
"BRUNSWICK" PATTERN
Made in Crystal, Amber, Green and Blue.

870　Goblet 5.00----8.00
870　High Sherbet 5.00----8.00
870　Low Sherbet 2.00----4.00
870　Parfait 4.00----6.00
870　Cocktail 5.00----8.00
870　Wine 5.00----8.00
870　Cordial 5.00----8.00
870　Oyster Cocktail (5084) . . 4.00----6.00
870　Claret 5.00----8.00
869　Finger Bowl 2.00----3.00
2283　6" Plate 2.00----3.00
5084　12 oz. Ftd. Tumbler . . . 3.00----5.00
5084　9 oz. Ftd. Tumbler . . . 3.00----5.00
5084　5 oz. Ftd. Tumbler . . . 3.00----5.00
5084　2½ oz. Ftd. Tumbler . . 3.00----5.00
5084　7 Footed Jug 20.00----35.00
869　Table Tumbler 2.00----4.00
869　12 oz. Tumbler 2.00----4.00
869　5 oz. Tumbler 2.00----4.00
869　2 oz. Tumbler 2.00----4.00
2270　7 Jug 20.00--25.00
2283　7" Plate 1.00----3.00
2283　8" Plate 2.00----4.00
870　Saucer Champagne 5.00----8.00
870　Fruit 2.00----3.00

DECORATION NO. 60
"MONARCH" PATTERN
Needle Etching No. 79 Yellow Gold

870　Goblet 5.00----7.00
870　Saucer Champagne 4.00----6.00
870　Fruit 2.00----4.00
870　Parfait 3.00----4.00
870　Wine 5.00----7.00
870　Cordial 5.00----7.00
870　Cocktail 5.00----7.00
870　Oyster Cocktail (5084) . . 4.00----6.00
869　Finger Bowl 3.00----4.00
2283　6" Plate 2.00----3.00
945½—Grape Fruit 3.00----4.00
945½—Grape Fruit Liner, Gold
　　　　Edge Only 1.00----2.00
5084　12 oz. Ftd. Tumbler . . 2.00----3.00
5084　9 oz. Ftd. Tumbler 2.00----3.00
5084　5 oz. Ftd. Tumbler 2.00----3.00
5084　2½ oz. Ftd. Tumbler . . 2.00----3.00
5084　7 Ftd. Jug 15.00--20.00
2283　7" Plate 1.00----3.00
2283　8" Plate 2.00----4.00

NEEDLE ETCHING NO. 80
"SPARTAN" DESIGN
Made in Amber, Green, Orchid Bowl w/Crystal Ft.

5297　Goblet 5.00----8.00

5297　High Sherbet 4.00----6.00
5297　Low Sherbet 2.00----4.00
5297　Parfait 5.00----8.00
5297　Claret 5.00----8.00
5297　Wine 5.00----8.00
5297　Cocktail 5.00----8.00
5297　Cordial 5.00----8.00
5200　Oyster Cocktail 4.00----6.00
869　Finger Bowl 2.00----4.00
2283　6" Plate 2.00----3.00
5297½—Grape Fruit 2.00----4.00
945½—Grape Fruit Liner 2.00----4.00
5200　12 oz. Ftd. Tumbler . . 3.00----5.00
5200　9 oz. Ftd. Tumbler 3.00----4.00
5200　5 oz. Ftd. Tumbler . . . 3.00----4.00
5200　2½ oz. Ftd. Tumbler . . 3.00----4.00
5000　7 Ftd. Jug 20.00--30.00
2283　7" Plate 2.00----3.00
2283　8" Plate 2.00----4.00
869　Table Tumbler 2.00----4.00
869　12 oz. Tumbler 2.00----4.00
869　5 oz. Tumbler 2.00----4.00
869　2 oz. Tumbler 2.00----4.00

NEEDLE ETCHING NO. 82
"CORDELIA" PATTERN
Made in Green and Orchid

877　10 oz. Goblet 4.00----7.00
877　6 oz. High Sherbet . . . 4.00----7.00
877　6 oz. Low Sherbet . . . 2.00----4.00
877　5½ oz. Parfait 3.00----4.00
877　3½ oz. Cocktail 4.00----7.00
877　2¾ oz. Wine 4.00----7.00
877　4 oz. Claret 4.00----7.00
877　¾ oz. Cordial 4.00----7.00
877　4½ oz. Oyster Cocktail . . 3.00----5.00
869　Finger Bowl 2.00----4.00
2283　6" Finger Bowl Plate . . 1.00----2.00
877　Grape Fruit 2.00----4.00
877　Grape Fruit Liner (945½) 2.00----4.00
877　12 oz. Ftd. Tumbler . . 2.00----4.00
877　9 oz. Ftd. Tumbler . . . 2.00----4.00
877　5 oz. Ftd. Tumbler . . . 2.00----4.00
877　2½ oz. Ftd. Tumbler . . 2.00----4.00
5100　7 Ftd. Jug 20.00--30.00
2283　7" Plate 2.00----3.00
2283　8" Plate 2.00----3.00

NEEDLE ETCHING NO. 83
"EILENE" PATTERN
*Made in Green, Rose (Dawn) and Azure Bowl
with Crystal Foot. Also made in Solid Crystal*

5282　Goblet 5.00----8.00
5282　High Sherbet 5.00----8.00
5282　Low Sherbet 2.00----4.00
4282　Parfait 3.00----4.00
5282　Claret 5.00----8.00
5282　Wine 5.00----8.00
5282　Cocktail 5.00----8.00
5282　Cordial 5.00----8.00
4295　Oyster Cocktail 4.00----6.00
869　Finger Bowl 2.00----4.00
5282½—Grape Fruit 2.00----4.00
945½—Grape Fruit Liner 2.00----4.00
5298　5" Comport 4.00----6.00
5298　6" Nappy 4.00----6.00
4295　12 oz. Ftd. Tumbler . . 3.00----5.00

4295	9 oz. Ftd. Tumbler	3.00----4.00
4295	5 oz. Ftd. Tumbler	3.00----5.00
4295	2½ oz. Ftd. Tumbler	3.00----5.00
4095	Ftd. Jug (Sol. Color)	20.00--35.00
2283	6" Plate	1.00----2.00
2283	7" Plate (Plain)	2.00----3.00
2283	8" Plate (Plain)	2.00----3.00
4095	13 oz. Ftd. Tumbler	3.00----5.00
4095	10 oz. Ftd. Tumbler	3.00----4.00

NEEDLE ETCHING NO. 84
"CAMDEN" DESIGN
Made in Amber and Green Bowl w/Crystal Foot

5298	Goblet	5.00----8.00
5298	High Sherbet	5.00----8.00
5298	Low Sherbet	3.00----4.00
5298	Parfait	3.00----4.00
5298	Claret	5.00----8.00
5298	Wine	5.00----8.00
5298	Cocktail	5.00----8.00
5298	Cordial	5.00----8.00
5298	Oyster Cocktail	4.00----6.00
869	Finger Bowl	2.00----4.00
2283	6" Plate	1.00----2.00
5282½	—Grape Fruit	2.00----4.00
945½	—Grape Fruit Liner	2.00----4.00
5298	12 oz. Ftd. Tumbler	3.00----5.00
5298	9" Ftd. Tumbler	3.00----5.00
5298	5 oz. Ftd. Tumbler	3.00----4.00
5298	2½ oz. Ftd. Tumbler	3.00----5.00
5298	5" Comport	4.00----6.00
5298	6" Ftd. Nappy	4.00----6.00
5000	7 Ftd. Jug	25.00--35.00
2283	7" Plate	1.00----2.00
2283	8" Plate	2.00----3.00

NEEDLE ETCHING NO. 85
"AVALON" DESIGN
Made in Rose and Azure Bowl with Crystal Foot

5293	Goblet	5.00----8.00
5293	High Sherbet	5.00----8.00
5293	Low Sherbet	3.00----4.00
5293	Parfait	3.00----4.00
5293	Claret	5.00----8.00
5293	Wine	5.00----8.00
5293	Cocktail	5.00----8.00
5293	Cordial	5.00----8.00
5200	Oyster Cocktail	4.00----6.00
869	Finger Bowl	2.00----4.00
2283	6" Plate	1.00----2.00
5282½	—Grape Fruit	2.00----4.00
945½	—Grape Fruit Liner	2.00----4.00
5200	12 oz. Ftd. Tumbler	3.00----5.00
5200	9 oz. Ftd. Tumbler	3.00----4.00
5200	5 oz. Ftd. Tumbler	3.00----4.00
5200	2½ oz. Ftd. Tumbler	3.00----4.00
5000	7 Ftd. Jug	20.00--35.00
2283	7" Plate	1.00----2.00
2283	8" Plate	2.00----3.00

DEEP PLATE ETCHING NO. 253
"PERSIAN" DESIGN

863	9 oz. Goblet	2.00----3.00
863	7 oz. Goblet	2.00----3.00
863	5½ oz. Saucer Champagne	2.00----3.00
863	Fruit	1.00----2.00
899	Parfait	2.00----3.00
863	3 oz. Wine	2.00----3.00
863	3½ oz. Cocktail	2.00----3.00
863	1 oz. Cordial	2.00----3.00
1769	Finger Bowl	1.00----2.00
1769	F. Bowl Plate (1736-6")	1.00----2.00
945½	—Grape Fruit	2.00----3.00
945½	—Grape Fruit Liner	2.00----3.00
880	4½" Bon Bon	2.00----3.00
803	5" Comport	2.00----3.00
803	6" Comport	2.00----3.00
803	5" Ftd. Nappy	2.00----3.00
803	6" Ftd. Nappy	2.00----3.00
803	7" Ftd. Nappy	3.00----4.00
820	Table Tumbler	1.00----2.00
4061	Ftd. Ice Tea, Handled	3.00----4.00
701	5" Tumbler Plate	1.00----2.00
701	14 oz. Tumbler	1.00----2.00
701	8 oz. Tumbler	1.00----2.00
889	5 oz. Tumbler	1.00----2.00
303	7 Jug	10.00--15.00
2214	Sugar & Cover	3.00----4.00
2214	Cream & Cover	3.00----4.00
1465	5 oz. Oil, Cut Neck	12.00--15.00
2219	¼ lb. Candy Jar & Cover	6.00----8.00
2219	½ lb. Candy Jar & Cover	8.00----10.00
2219	1 lb. Candy Jar & Cover	10.00--12.00
2238	8¼" Salad Plate	1.00----2.00
2241	Cologne & Stopper	6.00----8.00
2242	Cologne & Stopper	6.00----8.00
2243	Cologne & Stopper	6.00----8.00

DEEP PLATE ETCHING NO. 255
"MODERN VINTAGE" PATTERN

766	9 oz. Goblet	2.00----3.00
766	5 oz. Saucer Champagne	2.00----3.00
766	Fruit	1.00----2.00
837	Oyster Cocktail	2.00----3.00
766½	—Parfait	2.00----3.00
766	2¾ oz. Wine	2.00----3.00
766	¾ oz. Cordial	2.00----3.00
766	3 oz. Cocktail	2.00----3.00
766	Finger Bowl	2.00----3.00
766	F. Bowl Plate (1736-6")	1.00----2.00
945½	—Grape Fruit	2.00----3.00
945½	—Grape Fruit Liner	2.00----3.00
858	Sweetmeat	2.00----3.00
880	4½" Bon Bon	2.00----3.00
803	5" Comport	2.00----3.00
803	6" Comport	2.00----4.00
803	5", 6", 7" Ftd. Nappy	3.00----4.00
896	Bowl & Cover	6.00----8.00
820	Table Tumbler	1.00----2.00
766	Ftd. Ice Tea, Handled	2.00----4.00
4011	12 oz. Tumbler, Handled	2.00----3.00
701	5" Tumbler Plate	1.00----2.00
701	14 oz. Tumbler	1.00----2.00
4011½	—Table Tumbler	1.00----2.00
4011	12, 8, 5 oz. Tumbler	1.00----2.00
300	7 Jug	12.00--15.00
303	7 Jug	12.00--15.00
318	7 Jug	12.00--15.00
317½	—Jug & Cover	15.00--20.00
1478	Sugar	2.00----3.00
1478	Cream	2.00----3.00
2214	Sugar & Cover	3.00----4.00
2214	Cream & Cover	3.00----4.00
2083	Salad Dressing Bottle	8.00----10.00
1465	7 oz. Oil, Cut Neck	12.00--15.00
1465	5 oz. Oil, Cut Neck	12.00--15.00

2022	Shaker, F. Glass Top . .	2.00----3.00
1968	Marmalade & Cover	2.00----4.00
1831	Mustard & Cover . . .	2.00----4.00
1697	Carafe	8.00--10.00
1697	Carafe Tumbler (4023-6 oz)	3.00----5.00
2194	8 oz. Syrup, Nickel Top	10.00--12.00
2194	12 oz. Syrup, Nickel Top	10.00--12.00
2138	Mayonnaise Bowl	2.00----3.00
2138	Mayonnaise Plate . . .	2.00----3.00
2138	Mayonnaise Ladle . . .	1.00----2.00
2219	¼, ½, 1 lb. Candy Jar & Cover	8.00--12.00
1848	9'' Sandwich Plate	3.00----4.00
1897	7'' Plate, Optic	1.00----2.00

DEEP PLATE ETCHING NO. 256
"FLORID" PATTERN

858	9 oz. Goblet	2.00----3.00
858	5½ oz. Saucer Champagne	2.00----3.00
858	Fruit	1.00----2.00
858	3 Sherbet (Low Oy. C'tail)	2.00----3.00
805	Parfait	2.00----3.00
858	2¾ oz. Wine	2.00----3.00
858	2 oz. Sherry	2.00----3.00
858	3½ oz. Cocktail	2.00----3.00
858	Finger Bowl	2.00----3.00
858	F. Bowl Plate (1736-6'')	1.00----2.00
945½	—Grape Fruit	2.00----3.00
945½	—Grape Fruit Liner	2.00----3.00
4057	Grape Fruit Liner (Tumbler Shape)	1.00----2.00
858	Sweetmeat	2.00----3.00
880	4½'' Bon Bon	2.00----3.00
803	5'' Comport	2.00----3.00
803	6'' Comport	2.00----3.00
803	5'' Ftd. Nappy	2.00----3.00
803	6'' Ftd. Nappy	2.00----3.00
803	7'' Ftd. Nappy	3.00----4.00
1227	4½'' Nappy	1.00----2.00
1227	8'' Nappy	3.00----4.00
896	Candy Bowl & Cover . .	6.00----8.00
2099	Sandwich Bowl & Cover	10.00--12.00
820	Table Tumbler	1.00----2.00
833	8 oz. Tumbler	1.00----2.00
833	8 oz. Tumbler, ½ Sham, Pty	1.00----2.00
766	Ftd. Ice Tea, Handled . .	2.00----4.00
4011	12 oz. Tumbler, Handled	3.00----4.00
701	5'' Tumbler Plate . . .	1.00----2.00
701	14 oz. Tumbler	1.00----2.00
858	Table, 14, 12, 8, 5 oz. Tumb.	1.00----2.00
300	7 Jug	12.00--15.00
318	7 Jug	12.00--15.00
303	7 Jug	12.00--15.00
1236	6 Jug	12.00--15.00
317½	—Jug & Cover	15.00--20.00
1478	Sugar	2.00----3.00
1478	Cream	2.00----3.00
2083	Salad Dressing Bottle . .	10.00--12.00
1465	7 oz. Oil, Cut Neck	15.00--18.00
1465	5 oz. Oil, Cut Neck	12.00--15.00
2022	Shaker, F. Glass Top . .	3.00----4.00
2223	Shaker, F. Glass Top . .	3.00----4.00
1968	Marmalade & Cover	3.00----4.00
1831	Mustard & Cover	3.00----4.00
1697	Carafe	8.00--10.00
1697	Carafe Tumbler (4023-6 oz)	3.00----5.00
2194	8 oz. Syrup, Nickel Top	15.00--20.00
2194	12 oz. Syrup, Nickel Top	15.00--20.00
2138	Mayonnaise Bowl	2.00----4.00

2138	Mayonnaise Plate	2.00----3.00
2138	Mayonnaise Ladle	1.00----2.00
2219	¼, ½, 1 lb. Candy Jar & Cover	8.00--12.00
1897	7'' Salad Plate	1.00----2.00
1848	9'' Sandwich Plate . . .	2.00----3.00
1719	10½'' Sandwich Plate . .	2.00----4.00
2238	8¼'', 11'' Salad Plate . .	2.00----4.00

DEEP PLATE ETCHING NO. 257
"VICTORY" PATTERN

945½	—Grape Fruit	2.00----3.00
825	Saucer Champagne	2.00----3.00
825	Jelly & Cover	4.00----6.00
803	5'' Ftd. Nappy & Cover. .	4.00----6.00
803	5'' Ftd. Comport & Cover	4.00----6.00
2250	¼, ½, 1 lb. Candy Jar & Cov.	8.00--12.00
766	9 oz. Goblet	2.00----3.00
755	7 oz. Goblet	2.00----3.00
766	5 oz. Saucer Champagne .	2.00----3.00
766	Fruit	1.00----2.00
766	Sherbet	1.00----2.00
837	Oyster Cocktail	2.00----3.00
766½	—Parfait	2.00----3.00
766	4½ oz. Claret	2.00----3.00
766	2¾ oz. Wine	2.00----3.00
766	3 oz. Cocktail	2.00----3.00
766	Almond	2.00----3.00
766	Finger Bowl	1.00----2.00
766	Finger Bowl Plate (1736-6-)	1.00----2.00
766	Grape Fruit	2.00----3.00
766	Grape Fruit Liner . . .	2.00----3.00
4057	G. Fruit Liner (Tumb. Shape)	1.00----2.00
858	Sweetmeat	2.00----3.00
880	4½'' Bon Bon	2.00----3.00
803	5'', 6'' Comport	3.00----4.00
803	5'', 6'', 7'' Ftd. Nappy . .	3.00----4.00
820	Table Tumbler	1.00----2.00
766	Ftd. Ice Tea, Handled . .	2.00----3.00
4011	12 oz. Tumbler, Handled	2.00----3.00
701	5'' Tumbler Plate . . .	1.00----2.00
701	14 oz. Tumbler	1.00----2.00
4011½	—Table Tumbler	1.00----2.00
4011	12, 8, 5 oz. Tumbler . .	1.00----2.00
300	7 Jug	12.00--15.00
318	7 Jug	12.00--15.00
303	7 Jug	12.00--15.00
2100	7 Jug	14.00--16.00
1480	Sugar	2.00----3.00
1480	Cream	2.00----3.00
1465	7 oz. Oil, Cut Neck	12.00--15.00
1465	5 oz. Oil, Cut Neck	12.00--15.00
2083	Salad Dressing Bottle . .	8.00--10.00
1968	Marmalade & Cover	6.00----8.00
1831	Mustard & Cover	6.00----8.00
1697	Carafe	8.00--10.00
1697	Carafe Tumbler (4023-6 oz)	2.00----4.00
2194	8 oz. Syrup, Nickel Top	15.00--18.00
2194	12 oz. Syrup, Nickel Top	15.00--20.00
2138	Mayonnaise Bowl	2.00----3.00
2138	Mayonnaise Plate	2.00----3.00
2138	Mayonnaise Ladle	1.00----2.00
1848	9'' Sandwich Plate	2.00----4.00
2238	8¼'' Salad Plate	2.00----3.00
2238	11'' Salad Plate	2.00----4.00
2219	¼, ½, 1 lb. Candy Jar & Cov.	8.00--12.00

CANDLESTICKS

1490	8" Candle Etched C-2	12.00--15.00
1218	8" Candle Etched A	12.00--15.00
1964	9" Candle Etched	12.00--15.00
1963	9" Candle Etched	12.00--15.00
1204	8½" Candle Etched D	12.00--15.00
1639	8" Candle Etched D	12.00--15.00
1856	8" Candle Etched	12.00--15.00
1965	8" Candle Etched	12.00--15.00

BLOWN CRYSTAL GLASS BOUQUET HOLDERS

1798	9" Dp. Etched Daisy & Fern Design	8.00--12.00
763	9" Dp. Etched Daisy & Fern Design	8.00--12.00
764	9" Dp. Et. Daffodil Design	8.00--12.00
762	8" Dp. Et. Oriental Design	8.00--12.00
1799	1-2 7¼" Dp. Et. Poppy Design	12.00--15.00
1634	1-2 8" Dp. Et. Landscape w/Floral Border	10.00--15.00
1694	8" Dp. Et. Marine Scene w/Art Nauvoe Panal	10.00--15.00
1796	9" Cut & Engraved No. 5	8.00--12.00
1797	1-2 7" Cutting 116	6.00--10.00
1797	1-2 7" Dp. Et. Persian Design	8.00--10.00
4056	5½" A Dp. Et. Wild Flower Design	6.00----8.00
4056	5" B Dp. Et. Oriental Design	6.00----8.00
4056	6½" C Dp. Et. Wild Flower Design	6.00----8.00
4056	7½" D Dp. Et. Crysanthemum Design	8.00--10.00
4055	7½" D Dp. Et. Daffodil Design	8.00--10.00
4055	6½" C Dp. Et. Orange Blossom Design	4.00----6.00
4055	6" B Dp. Et. Persian Design	4.00----6.00
4055	5½" A Dp. Et. Louis XVI Style	4.00----6.00
1966	8" Blown Flower Bowl w/6" Wire Screen Silver Plated	3.00----5.00
761	10" Dp. Et. Greek Figure	10.00--15.00
483	Flower Set (w/Silver Plated Mesh) Cut 116 Mission Cutting Plate Cut Mat Star	12.00--15.00
1848	Flower Bowl (w/Silver Plated Mesh) Dp. Et. Art Nauvoe	6.00----8.00
1848	6" Pressed Flower Bowl w/Wire Screen Silver Plated	2.00----4.00

DEEP PLATE ETCHING NO. 264 "WOODLAND" PATTERN

660	Goblet	2.00----3.00
660	Saucer Champagne	2.00----3.00
660	Fruit	2.00----3.00
660	Wine	2.00----3.00
660	Cordial	2.00----3.00
660	Cocktail	2.00----3.00
660	Parfait	2.00----3.00
837	Oyster Cocktail	2.00----3.00
766	Finger Bowl	1.00----2.00
1736	6" Plate	1.00----2.00
945½	—Grape Fruit	2.00----3.00

945½	—Grape Fruit Liner	2.00----3.00
766	Sweetmeat	2.00----3.00
825	Jelly	2.00----3.00
825	Jelly & Cover	3.00----4.00
803	5" Comport	2.00----3.00
803	6" Comport	2.00----3.00
803	5" Nappy	1.00----2.00
803	6" Nappy	1.00----2.00
803	7" Nappy	2.00----4.00
4076	10 oz. Table Tumbler	1.00----2.00
889	14 oz. Tumbler	1.00----2.00
4011½	—Tumbler	1.00----2.00
4011	12 Tumbler	1.00----2.00
4011	12 oz. Tumbler, Handled	2.00----3.00
4011	5 oz. Tumbler	1.00----2.00
4011	3 oz. Tumbler	2.00----3.00
701	5" Tumbler Plate	1.00----2.00
4095	13, 10, 5 oz. Ftd. Tumbler	2.00----3.00
4095	2½ oz. Ftd. Tumbler (Toothpick)	4.00----6.00
300	7 Jug	12.00--15.00
303	7 Jug	12.00--15.00
1743	7 Jug & Cover	15.00--20.00
1743	4 Grape Juice Jug & Cover	15.00--20.00
1851	Sugar	2.00----3.00
1851	Cream	2.00----3.00
1465	7 oz. Oil, Cut Neck	12.00--15.00
1465	5 oz. Oil, Cut Neck	12.00--15.00
2083	Salad Dressing Bottle	10.00--12.00
2022	Shaker, F. G. T.	3.00----4.00
4089	Marmalade & Cover	8.00--10.00
1831	Mustard & Cover	6.00----8.00
1697	Carafe	8.00--10.00
4023	6 oz. Carafe Tumbler	3.00----4.00
2194	8 oz. Syrup, Nickel Top	15.00--18.00
2138	Mayonnaise Bowl	2.00----4.00
2138	Mayonnaise Plate	1.00----2.00
2138	Mayonnaise Ladle	1.00----2.00
840	5" Sherbet Plate	1.00----2.00
1897	7" Salad Plate	1.00----2.00
2238	8¼" Salad Plate	2.00----3.00
2238	11" Plate	3.00----4.00
2250	¼, ½, 1 lb. Candy Jar & Cov	8.00--12.00
300	Qt. Decanter, Cut Neck	20.00--25.00

DEEP PLATE ETCHING NO. 265 "ORIENT" PATTERN

661	9 oz. Goblet	2.00----3.00
661	Saucer Champagne	2.00----3.00
661	Claret	2.00----3.00
661	Fruit	2.00----3.00
661	Wine	2.00----4.00
661	Cocktail	2.00----4.00
661	Parfait	2.00----3.00
837	Oyster Cocktail	2.00----3.00
1769	Finger Bowl	1.00----2.00
1736	6" Plate	1.00----2.00
945½	—Grape Fruit	2.00----3.00
945½	—Grape Fruit Liner	2.00----3.00
880	Bon Bon	2.00----3.00
825	Jelly	2.00----3.00
825	Jelly & Cover	3.00----4.00
803	5" Comport	2.00----3.00
803	6" Comport	3.00----4.00
803	5" Nappy	1.00----2.00
803	5" Nappy & Cover	3.00----5.00
803	6" Nappy	1.00----2.00
803	7" Nappy	2.00----3.00
4085	Table Tumbler	1.00----2.00
4085	13 oz. Tumbler	1.00----2.00

4058	13 oz. Tumbler, Handled	2.00----3.00
889	5 oz. Tumbler	1.00----2.00
840	5" Plate	1.00----2.00
1852	6 Jug	12.00--15.00
318	7 Jug	12.00--15.00
317	Jug, Cut Neck	12.00--15.00
317½	Jug & Cover	15.00--20.00
2133	Sugar	2.00----3.00
2133	Cream	2.00----3.00
1465	7 oz. Oil, Cut Neck	12.00--15.00
1465	5 oz. Oil, Cut Neck	12.00--15.00
2083	Salad Dressing Bottle	8.00--12.00
4087	Marmalade & Cover	8.00--10.00
2022	Shaker, F. G. T.	3.00----4.00
2022	Shaker, Pearl Top	4.00----5.00
1697	Carafe	6.00----8.00
4023	6 oz. Carafe Tumbler	2.00----3.00
2238	8¼" Salad Plate	1.00----2.00
2238	11" Salad Plate	3.00----4.00
300	Qt. Decanter, Cut Neck	18.00--20.00

BLOWN OPTIC CRYSTAL CENTER SET

1939	Center Set	
	Large 7¾" High	10.00--15.00
	Small 4½" High	3.00----4.00

COLOGNES WITH DRIP STOPPERS

2243	Cologne Eng. B	6.00----8.00
2243	Cologne Eng. A	6.00----8.00
2243	Cologne Etch. 253	6.00----8.00
2243	Cologne Etch. 263	6.00----8.00
2242	Cologne Eng. 14	6.00----8.00
2242	Cologne Eng. C	6.00----8.00
2242	Cologne Etch. 253	6.00----8.00
2242	Cologne Etch. 262	6.00----8.00
2241	Cologne Eng. D	6.00----8.00
2241	Cologne Eng. E	6.00----8.00
2241	Cologne Etch. 253	6.00----8.00
2241	Cologne Etch. 261	6.00----8.00

DEEP PLATE ETCHING NO. 266 "WASHINGTON" PATTERN

300	7 Tankard	15.00--20.00
303	7 Jug	15.00--20.00
318	7 Jug	15.00--20.00
318	3½ Jug	9.00--12.00
2270	Jug	15.00--20.00
2270	Jug & Cover (Cover not etched)	20.00--30.00
1851	Sugar	4.00----6.00
1851	Cream	4.00----6.00
1465	7 oz. Oil, Cut Neck	15.00--20.00
1465	5 oz. Oil, Cut Neck	15.00--18.00
2083	Salad Dressing Bottle	15.00--20.00
2235	Shaker, F. G. T.	3.00----4.00
2235	Shaker, Pearl Top	4.00----5.00
4087	Marmalade & Cover	8.00--12.00
1831	Mustard & Cover	7.00----9.00
1697	Carafe	6.00----8.00
4023	6 oz. Carafe Tumbler	2.00----4.00
1697	Carafe Set—2 Piece	10.00--12.00
2194	8 oz. Syrup, Nickel Top	18.00--22.00
2138	Mayonnaise Bowl	5.00----7.00
2138	Mayonnaise Plate	2.00----3.00
2138	Mayonnaise Ladle	1.00----2.00
2138	Mayonnaise Set—3 Piece	8.00--12.00
2283	5" Sherbet Plate	1.00----2.00

2283	7" Salad Plate	2.00----3.00
2283	8" Salad Plate	2.00----3.00
2283	11" Plate	4.00----5.00
2283	9" Plate	2.00----4.00
2250	¼, ½ lb. Candy Jar & Cover	10.00--15.00
300	Qt. Decanter, Cut Neck	15.00--20.00
2275	9½" Candlestick	8.00--12.00
2267	9" Console Bowl	8.00--10.00
660	Goblet	6.00----8.00
660	Saucer Champagne	4.00----6.00
660	Fruit	6.00----8.00
660	Claret	6.00----8.00
660	Wine	6.00----8.00
660	Cordial	6.00----8.00
660	Cocktail	6.00----8.00
660	Parfait	6.00----8.00
837	Oyster Cocktail	5.00----7.00
481	Custard	4.00----6.00
766	Finger Bowl	2.00----3.00
2283	6" Plate	1.00----2.00
766	Mayonnaise Set—3 Piece	6.00----9.00
945½	Grape Fruit	3.00----5.00
945½	Grape Fruit Liner	1.00----2.00
766	Sweetmeat	3.00----4.00
825	Jelly	6.00----8.00
825	Jelly & Cover	8.00--10.00
5078	5" Compote	7.00----9.00
5078	6" Compote	8.00--10.00
5078	5" Nappy	4.00----6.00
5078	6" Nappy	5.00----7.00
5078	7" Nappy	5.00----7.00
5078	8" Nappy	6.00----8.00
5078	5" Compote & Cover	9.00--12.00
5078	6" Compote & Cover	10.00--14.00
5078	5" Nappy & Cover	5.00----7.00
5078	6" Nappy & Cover	6.00----8.00
5078	7" Nappy & Cover	6.00----8.00
5078	8" Nappy & Cover	7.00----9.00
4076	9 oz. Table Tumbler	4.00----6.00
889	13 oz. Tumbler	4.00----6.00
889	8 oz. Tumbler	4.00----6.00
889	5 oz. Tumbler	3.00----5.00
887	2½ oz. Tumbler	3.00----5.00
869	12 oz. Tumbler, Hdld. (837)	5.00----7.00
4095	13, 10, 5, 2½ oz. Ftd. Tumbler	5.00----9.00

DEEP PLATE ETCHING NO. 267 "VIRGINIA" PATTERN

2270	Jug & Cover (Cover not etched)	20.00--30.00
2270	Jug	15.00--20.00
4095	7 Footed Jug	20.00--30.00
303	7 Jug	15.00--20.00
318	7 Jug	15.00--20.00
1852	6 Jug	15.00--20.00
303	3 Jug	9.00--12.00
2133	Sugar	4.00----6.00
2133	Cream	4.00----6.00
1465	7 oz. Oil, Cut Neck	15.00--20.00
1465	5 oz. Oil, Cut Neck	15.00--18.00
2083	Salad Dressing Bottle	15.00--20.00
4089	Marmalade & Cover	8.00--12.00
1831	Mustard & Cover	7.00----9.00
2235	Shaker, F. G. T.	3.00----4.00
2235	Shaker, Pearl Top	4.00----5.00
2138	Mayonnaise Bowl	5.00----7.00
2138	Mayonnaise Plate	2.00----3.00
2138	Mayonnaise Ladle	1.00----2.00

2138	Mayonnaise Set—3 Piece Pl.	8.00--12.00
1697	Carafe	7.00----9.00
4023	6 oz. Carafe Tumbler	2.00----3.00
1697	Carafe Set—2 Piece	9.00--12.00
2283	5" Sherbet Plate	1.00----2.00
2283	7" Plate	2.00----3.00
2283	8" Salad Plate	2.00----3.00
2283	11" Salad Plate	4.00----6.00
2283	9" Sandwich Plate	3.00----5.00
2250	¼, ½ lb. Candy Jar & Cover	10.00--15.00
300	Qt. Decanter, Cut Neck	15.00--20.00
4055	D Vase	9.00--12.00
2241	Cologne	8.00--10.00
2194	8 oz. Syrup, Nickel Top	18.00--22.00
2275	9½" Candlestick	8.00--12.00
2267	9" Console Bowl	8.00--10.00
661	9 oz. Goblet	6.00----8.00
661	Saucer Champagne	5.00----7.00
661	Fruit	6.00----8.00
661	Claret	6.00----8.00
661	Wine	6.00----8.00
661	Cordial	6.00----8.00
661	Cocktail	6.00----8.00
661	Parfait	6.00----8.00
837	Oyster Cocktail	5.00----7.00
1769	Finger Bowl	2.00----3.00
2283	6" Plate	1.00----2.00
1769	Mayonnaise Set—3 Pieces	8.00--10.00
945½	—Grape Fruit	3.00----5.00
945½	—Grape Fruit Liner	1.00----2.00
880	Sweetmeat	3.00----5.00
825	Jelly	6.00----8.00
825	Jelly & Cover	10.00--15.00
5078	5" Compote	7.00----9.00
5078	6" Compote	8.00--10.00
5078	5" Nappy	4.00----6.00
5078	6" Nappy	5.00----7.00
5078	7" Nappy	5.00----7.00
5078	8" Nappy	6.00----8.00
5078	5" Compote & Cover	10.00--15.00
5078	6" Compote & Cover	10.00--15.00
5078	5" Nappy & Cover	9.00--12.00
5078	6" Nappy & Cover	10.00--15.00
5078	7" Nappy & Cover	14.00--18.00
5078	8" Nappy & Cover	15.00--20.00
4085	Table Tumbler	2.00----4.00
4085	13 oz. Tumbler	2.00----4.00
4085	13 oz. Tumbler, Handled	3.00----5.00
4085	6 oz. Tumbler	2.00----4.00
4085	2½ oz. Tumbler	2.00----4.00
4095	13, 10, 5, 2½ oz. Footed Tumbler	5.00----7.00
869	12 oz. Hdld. Tumbler (837)	3.00----5.00

DEEP PLATE ETCHING NO. 268
"MELROSE" PATTERN

661	Goblet	6.00----8.00
661	Saucer Champagne	5.00----7.00
661	Fruit	6.00----8.00
661	Claret	6.00----8.00
661	Wine	6.00----8.00
661	Cocktail	6.00----8.00
661	Cordial	6.00----8.00
661	Parfait	6.00----8.00
837	Oyster Cocktail	5.00----7.00
1769	Finger Bowl	2.00----3.00
2283	6" Plate	1.00----2.00
825	Jelly	6.00----8.00
825	Jelly & Cover	10.00--15.00

945½	—Grape Fruit	3.00----5.00
945½	—Grape Fruit Liner	1.00----2.00
5039	Oyster Cocktail Liner—not etched	1.00----2.00
5039	Oyster Cocktail	4.00----6.00
803	5" Compote	7.00----9.00
803	6" Compote	8.00--10.00
803	5" Nappy	4.00----6.00
803	6" Nappy	5.00----7.00
803	7" Nappy	5.00----7.00
4085	13 oz. Hdld. Tumbler	3.00----5.00
4085	13 oz, Table, 6, 2½ oz. Tumbler	2.00----4.00
4095	13, 10, 5, 2½ oz. Ftd. Tumbler	5.00----7.00
1852	6 Jug	15.00--20.00
303	7 Jug	15.00--20.00
4095	7 Jug	20.00--25.00
4095	4 Jug	15.00--20.00
1480	Sugar	4.00----6.00
1480	Cream	4.00----6.00
1465	5 oz. Oil, Cut Neck	15.00--20.00
4087	Marmalade & Cover	10.00--12.00
2235	Shaker, F. G. Top	3.00----4.00
2235	Shaker, Pearl Top	4.00----5.00
2138	Mayonnaise Bowl	5.00----7.00
2138	Mayonnaise Plate	2.00----3.00
2138	Mayonnaise Ladle	1.00----2.00
1697	Carafe	6.00----8.00
4023	6 oz. Tumbler	2.00----3.00
2283	7" Plate	2.00----3.00
2283	8" Plate	2.00----3.00
2283	11" Plate	4.00----6.00
2283	11" Plate, Cut Mat Star	4.00----6.00
300	Qt. Decanter, Cut Neck	15.00--20.00
2287	Lunch Tray, Fleur-de-Lis	8.00--10.00

DEEP PLATE ETCHING NO. 269
"ROGENE" PATTERN

5082	Goblet	6.00----8.00
5082	Saucer Champagne	5.00----8.00
5082	Fruit	2.00----3.00
5082	Parfait	5.00----8.00
5082	Claret	5.00----8.00
5082	Wine	5.00----8.00
5082	Cordial	5.00----8.00
5082	Cocktail	5.00----8.00
837	Oyster Cocktail	3.00----5.00
2283	5" Sherbet Plate	1.00----2.00
766	Finger Bowl	2.00----3.00
2283	6" Plate	1.00----2.00
766	Mayonnaise Set—3 Piece	8.00--12.00
825	Jelly	6.00----8.00
825	Jelly & Cover	10.00--15.00
945½	—Grape Fruit	2.00----3.00
945½	—Grape Fruit Liner	2.00----3.00
5078	5" Compote	5.00----8.00
5078	6" Compote	6.00----9.00
5078	5" Nappy	4.00----6.00
5078	6" Nappy	5.00----7.00
5078	7" Nappy	8.00--10.00
4095	13 oz. Ftd. Tumbler	4.00----6.00
4095	10 oz. Ftd. Tumbler	3.00----5.00
4095	5 oz. Ftd. Tumbler	3.00----5.00
4095	2½ oz. Ftd. Tumbler	3.00----5.00
4095	Nut	2.00----3.00
869	12 oz. Hdld. Tumbler (837)	3.00----5.00
701	5" Tumbler Plate	1.00----2.00
4076	9 oz. Table Tumbler	2.00----3.00

889	13 oz. Tumbler	2.00----4.00
889	8 oz. Tumbler	2.00----3.00
889	5 oz. Tumbler	2.00----3.00
887	2½ oz. Tumbler	2.00----3.00
1852	6 Jug	20.00--25.00
318	7 Jug	20.00--25.00
4095	7 Jug, Footed	25.00--30.00
4095	4 Jug, Footed	10.00--15.00
2270	7 Jug	20.00--25.00
2270	7 Jug & Cover	30.00--35.00
1851	Sugar	4.00----6.00
1851	Cream	4.00----6.00
1465	5 oz. Oil, Cut Neck	18.00--22.00
1968	Marmalade & Cover	10.00--14.00
2235	Shaker, F. G. Top	4.00----5.00
2235	Shaker, Pearl Top	4.00----6.00
2138	Mayonnaise Bowl	3.00----5.00
2138	Mayonnaise Plate	2.00----3.00
2138	Mayonnaise Ladle	1.00----2.00
2138	Mayonnaise Set—3 Piece	8.00--10.00
1697	Carafe	8.00--10.00
4023	6 oz. Tumbler	2.00----3.00
2283	7" Plate	1.00----2.00
2283	8" Plate	2.00----3.00
2283	11" Plate	3.00----4.00
2283	11" Plate, Cut Mat Star	4.00----6.00
300	Qt. Decanter, Cut Neck	15.00--20.00
4095	8½" Vase, Rolled Edge	8.00--12.00

CANDLESTICKS DEEP ETCHED

2245	6" Candle	4.00----6.00
2268	6" Candle	6.00----8.00
2244	6" Candle	6.00----8.00
2269	6" Candle	6.00----8.00
2275	9½" Candle	8.00--10.00
1490	15" Candle	10.00--15.00

PLATE ETCHING NO. 270½
"MYSTIC" DESIGN
Made in Solid Green—Spiral Optic

5082	Goblet	9.00--12.00
5082	High Sherbet	8.00--10.00
5082	Low Sherbet	6.00----8.00
5082	Parfait	8.00--10.00
5082	Wine	9.00--12.00
5082	Cocktail	9.00--12.00
4095	Oyster Cocktail	8.00--10.00
4095	4½" Finger Bowl	4.00----6.00
2283	6" Plate	2.00----3.00
4095	13 oz. Ftd. Tumbler	8.00--10.00
4095	10 oz. Ftd. Tumbler	6.00----8.00
4095	5 oz. Ftd. Tumbler	6.00----8.00
4095	2½ oz. Ftd. Tumbler	8.00--10.00
4095	7 Ftd. Jug	25.00--45.00
2283	7" Plate	2.00----3.00
2283	8" Plate	2.00----4.00
2283	13" Plate	10.00--15.00

Crystal Only

660	Goblet	5.00----8.00
660	Saucer Champagne	4.00----6.00
660	Fruit	2.00----4.00
660	Parfait	4.00----6.00
660	Claret	5.00----8.00
660	Wine	5.00----8.00
660	Cordial	5.00----8.00
660	Cocktail	5.00----8.00
837	Oyster Cocktail	3.00----5.00
4095	4 Ftd. Jug	20.00--25.00

4095	8½" Vase Rolled Edge	10.00--15.00
4095	Finger Bowl	3.00----4.00

PLATE ETCHING NO. 272
"DELPHIAN" PATTERN
BLUE STEM AND FOOT

5082	Goblet	9.00--12.00
5082	Saucer, Champagne	8.00--10.00
5082	Fruit	6.00----8.00
5082	Parfait	8.00--10.00
5082	Cocktail	9.00--12.00
5082	Wine	9.00--12.00
5082	Cordial	9.00--12.00
4095	Oyster Cocktail	8.00--10.00
4095	Finger Bowl (4½" Nappy)	4.00----6.00
2283	6" Plate	2.00----3.00
4095	5" Nappy	4.00----6.00
4095	6" Nappy	6.00----8.00
4095	7" Nappy	9.00--12.00
4095½	Candy Jar & Cover	15.00--25.00
4095	5" Nappy & Cover	10.00--15.00
4095	6" Nappy & Cover	12.00--18.00
4095	7" Nappy & Cover	15.00--20.00
4095	13 oz. Tumbler	8.00--10.00
4095	10 oz. Tumbler	7.00----9.00
4095	5 oz. Tumbler	7.00----9.00
4095	2½ oz. Tumbler	8.00--10.00
4095	7 Jug	35.00--50.00
2283	7" Plate	2.00----3.00
2283	8" Plate	3.00----4.00
4095½	8" Vase	20.00--25.00

COIN GOLD BAND NO. 51, "DUCHESS"
Crystal Bowl—Blue Stem and Foot

5082	Goblet	9.00--12.00
5082	Saucer Champagne, High Sherbet	8.00--10.00
5082	Low Sherbet	6.00----8.00
5082	Cocktail	9.00--12.00
5082	Wine	9.00--12.00
5082	Parfait	8.00--10.00
4095	Oyster Cocktail	8.00--10.00
4095	2½ oz. Ftd. Tumbler	9.00--12.00
4095	5 oz. Ftd. Tumbler	7.00----9.00
4095	10 oz. Ftd. Tumbler	7.00----9.00
4095	13 oz. Ftd. Tumbler	8.00--10.00
4095	7 Ftd. Jug	35.00--50.00
4095	4½" Ftd. Nappy	6.00----8.00
2283	6" Plate	2.00----3.00
2283	7" Plate	3.00----4.00
2283	8" Plate	3.00----4.00

PLATE ETCHING NO. 273
"ROYAL" PATTERN
Made in Crystal, Amber, Green and Blue.

2297	12" Deep Bowl "A"	12.00--18.00
2315	10½" Ftd. Bowl "A"	18.00--22.00
2324	13" Ftd. Bowl	25.00--35.00
2324	10" Ftd. Bowl	20.00--30.00
2324	Small Urn	15.00--25.00
2324	12" Candles	15.00--20.00
2324	9" Candles	12.00--18.00
*2324	4" Candles	6.00--10.00
2324	2" Candles	5.00----7.00
2329	13" Centerpiece	20.00--25.00
*2329	11" Centerpiece	15.00--25.00

2371	13" Oval Centerpiece	20.00--25.00
2292	8" Vase, Flared	15.00--20.00
2250	½ lb. Candy Jar & Cover	15.00--20.00
*2331	3 Candy Box & Cover	20.00--30.00
2378	Ice Bucket N. P. Handle	15.00--20.00
2378	Ice Bucket N.P. Hdl., Drainer & Tongs	18.00--25.00
*2276	Vanity Set	20.00--25.00
2322	Tall Cologne	10.00--15.00
2323	Squat Cologne	9.00--12.00
869	Goblet	10.00--14.00
869	High Sherbet	9.00--12.00
869	Low Sherbet	3.00----5.00
869	Parfaits	9.00--12.00
869	Cocktails	10.00--14.00
869	Wines	10.00--14.00
869	Cordials	10.00--14.00
869	Oyster Cocktail	8.00--10.00
869	Finger Bowl	3.00----5.00
2283	6" Plates	1.00----3.00
945½	—Grape Fruit	9.00--12.00
945½	—Grape Fruit Liner	9.00--12.00
869	12 oz. Hdld. Tumbler	10.00--15.00
869	12 oz. Tumbler	6.00--10.00
869	Table Tumbler	5.00----8.00
869	8 Tumbler	5.00----8.00
869	5 Tumbler	5.00----8.00
869	2 Tumbler	5.00----8.00
1236	6 Jug	50.00--85.00
5100	Ftd. Shaker, F.G.T.	9.00--10.00
5100	12 oz. Ftd. Tumbler	7.00--10.00
5100	9 oz. Ftd. Tumbler	6.00----9.00
5100	5 oz. Ftd. Tumbler	6.00----9.00
5100	2½ oz. Ftd. Tumbler	7.00--10.00
5100	7 Ftd. Jug	75.00--125.00
2350	6" Bread & Butter Plate	1.00----3.00
2350	7" Salad Plate	2.00----4.00
2350	8" Salad Plate	3.00----5.00
2350	9" Dinner Plate	5.00----8.00
2350	10" Dinner Plate	6.00----9.00
2350	13" Chop Plate	9.00--12.00
2350	15" Chop Plate	10.00--15.00
2350	5" Fruit	2.00----3.00
2350	6" Cereal	3.00----4.00
2350	7" Soup	3.00----5.00
2350	Cup	4.00----6.00
2350	Saucer	1.00----2.00
2350½	—Footed Cup	4.00----6.00
2350	After Dinner Cup	3.00----5.00
2350	A. D. Saucer	1.00----3.00
2350	Bouillon	3.00----5.00
2350	Cream Soup	4.00----6.00
2350	Cream Soup Plate(2332-7")	2.00----4.00
2350	9" Oval Baker	12.00--16.00
2350	10½" Baker, Oval Baker	15.00--18.00
2350	8" Nappy	8.00--12.00
2350	9" Nappy	10.00--15.00
2350	10" Salad Bowl	15.00--18.00
2350	10½" Oval Platter	10.00--12.00
2350	12" Oval Platter	10.00--15.00
2350	15" Oval Platter	15.00--20.00
2350	Sauce Boat	15.00--20.00
2350	Sauce Boat Plate	3.00----5.00
2350	8" Comport	8.00--12.00
2350	Pickle	3.00----5.00
2350	Celery	5.00----7.00
2350	Butter & Cover	50.00--75.00
2350½	—Cream	7.00--10.00
2350½	—Sugar	7.00--10.00
2350½	—Sugar & Cover	30.00--40.00
2315	Sugar	8.00--10.00

2315½	—Cream	7.00--10.00
2315	Grape Fruit—Mayonnaise	10.00--14.00
1861½	—Jelly	8.00--10.00
*2267	7" Low Ft. Bowl	8.00--12.00
*2327	7" Comport	9.00--15.00
2276	Cov. Cheese & Plate, Amber & Green	35.00--50.00
2287	11" Hdld. Lunch Tray	9.00--14.00
2283	7" Plates	2.00----4.00
2283	8" Plates	3.00----5.00
2283	9" Plates	4.00----6.00
2283	10" Plates	5.00----8.00
2290	7" Plates	2.00----4.00
2290	8" Plates	3.00----5.00
2321	8" Plates	3.00----5.00
5000	12 oz. Ftd. Tumbler	7.00--10.00
5000	9 oz. Ftd. Tumbler	6.00----9.00
5000	5 oz. Ftd. Tumbler	6.00----9.00
5000	2½ oz. Ftd. Tumbler	7.00--10.00
5000	7 Ftd. Jug	75.00--125.00
2350½	—Ftd. Bouillon	3.00----5.00
2350½	—Ftd. Cream Soup	4.00----6.00
2350	Egg Cup—Not made in blue	6.00----9.00
2350	Small Ash Tray	7.00--10.00
2316	8" Soup Plate	4.00----6.00
2290	13" Plate	9.00--12.00
869	Saucer Champagne	9.00--12.00
869	Fruit	2.00----4.00

**Pieces made in Ebony in 1925 & 1926*

DECORATION NO. 49 "CORONADA"
BLUE GLASS—ETCHING NO. 273
White and Yellow Gold Decoration

2324	2" Candle	6.00----9.00
2324	4" Candle	8.00--12.00
2324	9" Candle	12.00--18.00
2324	10" Console Bowl	20.00--30.00
2329	11" Centerpiece	20.00--25.00
2338	Puff Box & Cover	10.00--15.00
2276	Vanity Set	15.00--25.00
2322	Cologne	10.00--15.00
2323	Cologne	10.00--14.00
2250	½ lb. Candy Jar & Cover	20.00--25.00
2331	3 Candy Box & Cover	20.00--25.00
2315	Grape Fruit	12.00--15.00
2315	Sugar	8.00--12.00
2315	Cream	8.00--12.00
2327	7" Compote	10.00--15.00
2287	Lunch Tray	10.00--15.00
2297	12" Dp. Bowl "A"	20.00--25.00
2297	10¼" Shallow Bowl "A"	18.00--22.00
2315	10½" Console Bowl "A"	20.00--30.00
2283	7" Plate	2.00----4.00
2283	8" Plate	3.00----5.00
2283	10" Plate	8.00--10.00
2290	13" Plate	10.00--14.00
2316	8" Soup Plate	6.00----8.00

"SEVILLE" PATTERN
PLATE ETCHING NO. 274
Made in Crystal, Amber and Green

2350	6" Bread & Butter Plate	2.00----3.00
2350	7" Salad Plate	2.00----4.00
2350	8" Salad Plate	3.00----5.00
2350	9" Dinner Plate	4.00----6.00
2350	10" Dinner Plate	5.00----8.00
2350	13" Chop Plate	8.00--12.00

2350	15" Round Plate	10.00--15.00
2350	5" Fruit	2.00----3.00
2350	6" Cereal	3.00----4.00
2350	7" Soup	3.00----5.00
2350	Cup	4.00----6.00
2350	Saucer	1.00----2.00
2350½—Footed Cup		4.00----6.00
2350	After Dinner Cup	3.00----5.00
2350	A. D. Saucer	1.00----3.00
2350	Bouillon	3.00----5.00
2350	Cream Soup	4.00----6.00
2350	Cream Soup Plate (2332)	2.00----4.00
2350	9" Oval Baker	12.00--16.00
2350	10½" Oval Baker	15.00--18.00
2350	10½" Oval Platter	10.00--14.00
2350	12" Oval Platter	12.00--15.00
2350	15" Oval Platter	15.00--20.00
2350	8" Nappy	8.00--12.00
2350	9" Nappy	10.00--15.00
2350	10" Salad Bowl	15.00--18.00
2350	Sauce Boat	15.00--20.00
2350	Sauce Boat Plate	3.00----5.00
2350	8" Comport	8.00--12.00
2350	Pickle	3.00----5.00
2350	Celery	4.00----6.00
2350	Butter & Cover	50.00--75.00
2350½—Sugar		7.00--10.00
2350½—Sugar & Cover		35.00--45.00
2350½—Cream		7.00--10.00
2315	Sugar	7.00----9.00
2315½—Cream		7.00----9.00
2315	Grape Fruit—Mayonnaise	10.00--12.50
2267	7" Low Foot Bowl	8.00--10.00
2327	7" Comport	9.00--12.00
2368	Cheese	4.00----6.00
2368	Cracker Plate	8.00--12.00
2368	Cheese & Cracker	12.00--18.00
2287	11" Hdld. Lunch Tray	9.00--12.00
2297	12" Dp. Bowl Flared "A"	12.00--15.00
2315	10½" Ftd. Bowl Flared	15.00--20.00
2324	10" Ftd. Bowl	20.00--30.00
2324	Small Urn	15.00--20.00
2324	2" Candle	4.00----6.00
2324	4" Candle	6.00----9.00
2324	9" Candle	10.00--15.00
2329	11" Centerpiece	15.00--18.00
2329	13" Centerpiece	15.00--20.00
2371	13" Oval Centerpiece	20.00--25.00
2292	8" Vase	15.00--20.00
2250	½ lb. Candy Jar & Cover	18.00--22.00
2331	3 Candy Box & Cover	20.00--25.00
2378	Ice Bucket N.P. Handle	15.00--20.00
2378	Ice Bucket N.P. Hdl., Drainer & Tongs	18.00--22.00
870	Goblet	10.00--14.00
870	Saucer Champagne (High Sherbet)	9.00--12.00
870	Fruit (Low Sherbet)	3.00----5.00
870	Parfait	9.00--12.00
870	Cocktail	10.00--14.00
870	Wine	10.00--14.00
870	Cordial	10.00--14.00
870	Oyster Cocktail	7.00--10.00
869	Finger Bowl	4.00----6.00
2283	6" Plates	1.00----2.00
945½—Grape Fruit		5.00----8.00
945½—Grape Fruit Liner		5.00----8.00
5100	Footed Shaker	8.00--12.00
5084	12 oz. Ftd. Tumbler	6.00----9.00
5084	9 oz. Ftd. Tumbler	5.00----8.00
5084	5 oz. Ftd. Tumbler	5.00----8.00

5084	2 oz. Ftd. Tumbler	6.00----9.00
5084	7 Footed Jug	50.00--85.00
2350½—Footed Cream Soup		4.00----6.00
2350½—Footed Bouillon		3.00----5.00
2350	Ash Tray	8.00--10.00
2350	Egg Cup	6.00----9.00

DECORATION NO. 58 "AMHERST"
ETCHING NO. 274
Green Glass—White Gold

2324	4" Candle	7.00--10.00
2324	9" Candle	12.00--15.00
2324	10" Bowl	20.00--25.00
2297	10" Shallow Bowl A	18.00--22.00
2297	12" Deep Bowl A	15.00--20.00
2315	10½" Deep Bowl A	18.00--22.00
2329	11" Center Piece	20.00--25.00
2327	7" Compote	9.00--15.00
2315	Mayonnaise (Grape Fruit)	10.00--14.00
2315	Sugar	6.00--10.00
2315	Cream	6.00--10.00
2276	Vanity Set	20.00--25.00
2250	½ lb. Candy Jar & Cover	15.00--20.00
2331	3 Candy Box & Cover	15.00--20.00
2287	Lunch Tray	10.00--12.50
2283	7" Plate	2.00----4.00
2283	8" Plate	3.00----5.00
2283	10" Plate	8.00--10.00
2283	13" Plate	10.00--15.00

PLATE ETCHING NO. 275
"VESPER" PATTERN
Made in Amber, Green and Blue

2315	Grape Fruit—Mayonnaise	10.00--14.00
2267	7" Low Ft. Bowl	8.00--12.00
2327	7" Comport	10.00--15.00
2368	Cheese	5.00----8.00
2368	Cracker Plate	8.00--12.00
2368	Cheese & Cracker Plate	14.00--20.00
2287	11" Hdld. Lunch Tray	12.00--16.00
2297	12" Dp. Bowl Flared	15.00--20.00
2315	10½" Ftd. Bowl Flared	15.00--20.00
2324	10" Ftd. Bowl	20.00--35.00
2324	Small Urn	20.00--30.00
2324	2" Candle	6.00----8.00
2324	4" Candle	7.00----9.00
2324	9" Candle	15.00--20.00
2329	11" Centerpiece	15.00--20.00
2329	13" Centerpiece	20.00--25.00
2371	Oval Centerpiece	20.00--25.00
2292	8" Vase	18.00--22.00
2250	½ lb. Candy Jar & Cover	20.00--25.00
2331	3 Candy Box & Cover	20.00--30.00
2378	Ice Bucket N.P. Handle	15.00--20.00
2378	Ice Bucket N. P. Hdl., Drainer & Tongs	18.00--25.00
2276	Vanity Set	20.00--25.00
5093	Goblet	12.00--15.00
5093	High Sherbet	9.00--12.00
5093	Low Sherbet	5.00----8.00
5093	Parfait	9.00--12.00
5093	Cocktail	12.00--15.00
5093	Wine	12.00--15.00
5093	Cordial	12.00--15.00
5100	Oyster Cocktail	9.00--12.00
869	Finger Bowl	4.00----6.00
2283	6" Plates	2.00----3.00
5082½—Grape Fruit		8.00--12.00

945½—Grape Fruit Liner 8.00--12.00
5100 Footed Shaker 8.00--12.00
5100 12 oz. Ftd. Tumbler . . . 8.00--12.00
5100 9 oz. Ftd. Tumbler 6.00--10.00
5100 5 oz. Ftd. Tumbler 6.00--10.00
5100 2 oz. Ftd. Tumbler 8.00--12.00
5100 7 Ftd. Jug 85.00--135.00
2350 6" Bread & Butter Plate 2.00----3.00
2350 7" Salad Plate 3.00----4.00
2350 8" Salad Plate 4.00----6.00
2350 9" Dinner Plate 6.00----8.00
2350 10" Dinner Plate 7.00--10.00
2350 13" Chop Plate 10.00--15.00
2350 15" Round Plate . . . 15.00--20.00
2350 5" Fruit 3.00----4.00
2350 6" Cereal 4.00----6.00
2350 7" Soup 5.00----8.00
2350 Coffee Cup 5.00----8.00
2350 Saucer 2.00----3.00
2350½—Ftd. Tea Cup 5.00----8.00
2350 After Dinner Cup 4.00----7.00
2350 A. D. Saucer 2.00----3.00
2350 Bouillon 4.00----6.00
2350 Cream Soup 5.00----8.00
2350 Cream Soup Plate (2332) 7' 3.00----5.00
2350 9" Oval Baker 12.00--18.00
2350 10½" Oval Baker . . . 15.00--20.00
2350 10½" Oval Platter . . . 10.00--14.00
2350 12" Oval Platter 12.00--18.00
2350 15" Oval Platter 20.00--25.00
2350 8" Nappy 12.00--15.00
2350 9" Nappy 14.00--18.00
2350 10" Salad Bowl 15.00--20.00
2350 Sauce Boat 15.00--20.00
2350 Sauce Boat Plate . . . 5.00----8.00
2350 8" Comport 10.00--16.00
2350 Pickle 4.00----6.00
2350 Celery 6.00----9.00
2350 Butter & Cover 60.00--85.00
2350½—Sugar 8.00--12.00
2350½—Sugar & Cover 35.00--45.00
2350½—Cream 8.00--12.00
2315 Sugar 8.00--12.00
2315½—Cream 8.00--12.00
2321 8" Plate 4.00----6.00

Not made in blue

5000 12 oz. Ftd. Tumbler . . 7.00--10.00
5000 9 oz. Ftd. Tumbler . . . 6.00----8.00
5000 5 oz. Ftd. Tumbler . . 6.00----9.00
5000 2½ oz. Ftd. Tumbler . 7.00--10.00
5000 7 Ftd. Jug 85.00--125.00
2350 Small Ash Tray 6.00--10.00
5000 4½ oz. Oyster Cocktail . . 8.00--10.00
2350½—Ftd. Cream Soup . . . 4.00----6.00
2350½—Ftd. Bouillon 3.00----5.00
2350 Egg Cup 7.00--10.00

PLATE ETCHING NO. 276
"BEVERLY" PATTERN
Made in Crystal, Amber, Green, Orchid and Azure.

2350 6" Bread & Butter Plate 1.00----3.00
2350 7" Salad Plate 2.00----3.00
2350 8" Salad Plate 3.00----4.00
2350 9" Dinner Plate 5.00----8.00
2350 10" Dinner Plate 6.00----9.00
2350 13" Chop Plate 10.00--14.00
2350 5" Fruit 3.00----4.00
2350 6" Cereal 4.00----6.00
2350 7" Soup 4.00----7.00

2350 Cup 5.00----8.00
2350 Saucer 1.00----3.00
2350½—Footed Cup 5.00----8.00
2350 After Dinner Cup 4.00----7.00
2350 A. D. Saucer 1.00----3.00
2350 Bouillon 3.00----5.00
2350 Cream Soup 4.00----6.00
2350 Cream Soup Plate (2332) 2.00----4.00
2350 9" Oval Baker 12.00--18.00
2350 10½" Oval Baker . . . 16.00--20.00
2350 8" Nappy 8.00--12.00
2350 9" Nappy 12.00--16.00
2350 10" Salad Bowl 15.00--20.00
2350 10½" Oval Platter . . . 10.00--14.00
2350 12" Oval Platter 12.00--15.00
2350 15" Oval Platter 15.00--20.00
2350 Pickle 3.00----6.00
2350 Celery 6.00----9.00
2350 Sauce Boat 15.00--20.00
2350 Sauce Boat Plate . . . 5.00----8.00
2350½—Cream 7.00--10.00
2350½—Sugar 7.00--10.00
2350½—Sugar & Cover 30.00--40.00
2350 8" Low Comport 8.00--12.00
2327 7" Comport 9.00--14.00
2315 Grape Fruit—Mayonnaise 9.00--12.00
2287 11" Lunch Tray 10.00--15.00
2297 12" Deep Bowl, A 12.00--18.00
2324 10" Footed Bowl 20.00--25.00
2324 4" Candlestick 6.00----9.00
2324 6" Candlestick 7.00--10.00
2324 9" Candlestick 12.00--18.00
2371 Oval Centerpiece . . . 15.00--22.00
2329 11" Centerpiece 14.00--18.00
2329 13" Centerpiece 16.00--22.00
2292 8" Vase 15.00--20.00
2331 3" Candy Box & Cover . . 15.00--25.00
2378 Ice Bucket—N.P. Handle 14.00--20.00
2378 Ice Bucket—N.P. Hdl., Drainer
      & Tongs 18.00--22.00
2368 Cheese & Cracker Plate . . 14.00--18.00
2350 Small Ash Tray 6.00----9.00
2368 Ftd. Cheese 4.00----7.00
2368 Cracker Plate 8.00--11.00
2350½—Ftd. Bouillon 3.00----6.00
2350½—Ftd. Cream Soup . . . 4.00----7.00
5000 Footed Shaker 6.00--10.00
2350 Egg Cup 5.00----8.00

PLATE ETCHING NO. 276
BEVERLY DESIGN STEMWARE
Made in Solid Crystal
Crystal Base with Green Bowl
Crystal Base with Amber Bowl

5097 9 oz. Goblet 10.00--14.00
5097 5½ oz. High Sherbet . . 8.00--12.00
5097 5½ oz. Low Sherbet . . 6.00----8.00
5097 5½ oz. Parfait 8.00--12.00
5097 4 oz. Claret 10.00--14.00
5097 2½ oz. Wine 10.00--14.00
5097 3 oz. Cocktail 10.00--14.00
5097 ¾ oz. Cordial 10.00--14.00
5000 4½ oz. Oyster Cocktail . . 6.00----9.00
5097½—Grape Fruit 6.00--10.00
945½—Grape Fruit Liner 6.00--10.00
869 Finger Bowl 4.00----6.00
2283 6" F. B. Plate, R/O 2.00----3.00
5000 12 oz. Ftd. Tumbler . . 7.00--10.00
5000 9 oz. Ftd. Tumbler 5.00----8.00
5000 5 oz. Ftd. Tumbler 5.00----8.00

5000	2½ oz. Ftd. Tumbler	7.00--10.00
5000	7 Footed Jug	75.00--100.00

Made in Crystal, Amber and Green

5297	Goblet	10.00--14.00
5297	High Sherbert (Saucer Champ.)	8.00--12.00
5297	Low Sherbet (Fruit)	6.00----8.00
5297	Parfait	8.00--12.00
5297	Claret	10.00--14.00
5297	Wine	10.00--14.00
5297	Cocktail	10.00--14.00
5297	Cordial	10.00--14.00
5297½—	Grape Fruit	6.00--10.00
5200	Footed Shaker	6.00--10.00
5200	Oyster Cocktail	6.00----8.00
5200	12 oz. Ftd. Tumbler	7.00--10.00
5200	9 oz. Ftd. Tumbler	5.00----8.00
5200	5 oz. Ftd. Tumbler	5.00----8.00
5200	2 oz. Ftd. Tumbler	7.00--10.00
5200	Jug Footed	75.00--100.00

PLATE ETCHING NO. 277 "VERNON" DESIGN

**Made in Crystal, Amber, Green, Azure and Orchid.*

2375	6" Plate	2.00----4.00
2375	7" Plate	3.00----5.00
2375	8" Plate	5.00----7.00
2375	9" Plate	7.00----9.00
2375	10" Plate	8.00--12.00
2375	13" Plate	15.00--20.00
2375	5" Fruit	3.00----5.00
2375	6" Cereal	4.00----6.00
2375	7" Soup	6.00----8.00
2375½—	Footed Cup	7.00--10.00
2375	Saucer	3.00----5.00
2375	After Dinner Cup	6.00----9.00
2375	After Dinner Saucer	3.00----5.00
2375	Ftd. Bouillon	5.00----8.00
2375	Ftd. Cream Soup	7.00--10.00
2375	Cream Soup Plate	3.00----4.00
2375	9" Baker	15.00--25.00
2375	12" Platter	15.00--25.00
2375	15" Platter	20.00--30.00
2375	Sauce Boat	20.00--25.00
2375	Sauce Boat Plate	6.00----8.00
2375	8½" Relish	7.00--10.00
2375	11½" Celery	9.00--12.00
2375½—	Ftd. Sugar & Cover	35.00--50.00
2375½—	Ftd. Sugar	10.00--15.00
2375½—	Ftd. Cream	10.00--15.00
2375	Mayonnaise	12.00--15.00
2375	Mayonnaise Plate	6.00----9.00
2375	Ftd. Oil	25.00--35.00
2375	Hdld. Lunch Tray	20.00--25.00
2375	Whip Cream	6.00----9.00
2375	Sweetmeat	6.00----9.00
2375	Bon Bon	6.00----9.00
2375	Lemon Dish	6.00----9.00
2375	Ice Bucket, N.P. Hdl.	20.00--35.00
2368	Ftd. Cheese	6.00----9.00
2368	Cracker Plate	9.00--12.00
2368	Cheese & Cracker	18.00--22.00
2375	7" Comport	15.00--20.00
2400	8" Comport	15.00--25.00
2331	3 Candy Box & Cover	25.00--35.00
2350	Small Ash Tray	10.00--15.00
2375	12" Bowl	20.00--30.00
2375	3" Candle	8.00--12.00
2375½—	13" Oval Centerpieces	20.00--35.00

2375½—	Candle	10.00--12.00
2394	12" Bowl	20.00--30.00
2394	2" Candle	6.00--10.00
2415	Combination Bowl	20.00--35.00
877	10 oz. Goblet	15.00--20.00
877	6 oz. High Sherbet	10.00--16.00
877	6 oz. Low Sherbet	8.00--12.00
877	5½ Parfait	10.00--15.00
877	3½ oz. Cocktail	15.00--20.00
877	2¾ oz. Wine	15.00--20.00
877	4 oz. Claret	15.00--20.00
877	¾ oz. Cordial	15.00--20.00
877	4½ oz. Oyster Cocktail	10.00--15.00
869	Finger Bowl	5.00----8.00
2283	6" Finger Bowl Plate	2.00----3.00
5100	Ftd. Shaker, Glass Top	15.00--17.00
877	Grape Fruit	10.00--15.00
945½—	Grape Fruit Liner (945½)	10.00--15.00
877	12 oz. Ftd. Tumbler	10.00--15.00
877	9 oz. Ftd. Tumbler	8.00--12.00
877	5 oz. Ftd. Tumbler	8.00--12.00
877	2½ oz. Ftd. Tumbler	8.00--12.00
5100	7 Ftd. Jug	100.00--150.00
2378	Ice Bucket, N.P. Hdl.	20.00--30.00
2378	Ice Bucket, N.P. Hld., Drainer & Tongs	20.00--35.00
2375	Ftd. Shaker	15.00--20.00

PLATE ETCHING NO. 278 "VERSAILLES" DESIGN

Rose, Topaz, Azure and Green

2375	6" Plate	2.00----4.00
2375	7" Plate	3.00----5.00
2375	8" Plate	5.00----7.00
2375	9" Plate	7.00----9.00
2375	10" Plate	8.00--12.00
2375	13" Plate	16.00--20.00
2375	5" Fruit	4.00----6.00
2375	6" Cereal	5.00----8.00
2375	7" Soup	6.00----9.00
2394	3" Candle	7.00--10.00
2375½—	Footed Cup	8.00--11.00
2375	Saucer	3.00----5.00
2375	After Dinner Cup	7.00----9.00
2375	After Dinner Saucer	2.00----4.00
2375	Footed Bouillon	6.00----9.00
2375	Cream Soup	8.00--12.00
2375	Cream Soup Plate	3.00----5.00
2375	9" Baker	20.00--25.00
2375	12" Platter	20.00--25.00
2375	15" Platter	25.00--30.00
2375	Sauce Boat	20.00--25.00
2375	Sauce Boat Plate	6.00--10.00
2375	8½" Relish	9.00--12.00
2375	11½" Celery	10.00--14.00
2375½—	Ftd. Sugar & Cover	35.00--50.00
2375½—	Ftd. Sugar	10.00--15.00
2375½—	Ftd. Cream	10.00--15.00
2375½—	Tea Sugar	8.00--12.00
2375½—	Tea Cream	8.00--12.00
2375	Mayonnaise	12.00--15.00
2375	Mayonnaise Plate	6.00----9.00
2375	Handled Lunch Tray	20.00--25.00
2375	Whip Cream	6.00--10.00
2375	Sweetmeat	6.00--10.00
2375	Bon Bon	6.00--10.00
2375	Lemon Dish	6.00--10.00

**Solid Crystal will be 25% lower.*

2375	10'' Cake Plate	10.00--14.00
2375	Large Dessert	15.00--20.00
2375	Ice Bucket	20.00--35.00
2375	Salad Dressing Bottle	20.00--35.00
2375	Footed Oil	25.00--35.00
2375	Footed Shaker	15.00--20.00
2375	Cheese & Cracker	20.00--25.00
2368	Cheese & Cracker	20.00--25.00
2451	Ice Dish	15.00--20.00
2451	Ice Dish Plate	4.00----6.00
2331	3 Candy Box & Cover	25.00--35.00
2394	Mint	5.00----7.00
2394	6'' Bowl	7.00--10.00
2375	7'' Comport	15.00--20.00
2400	6'' Comport	14.00--18.00
2350	Small Ash Tray	10.00--15.00
2394	12'' Bowl ''A''	20.00--28.00
2394	2'' Candlestick	7.00--10.00
2375	12'' Centerpiece	20.00--30.00
2375½—Candlestick		8.00--12.00
2375	12'' Bowl	25.00--30.00
2375	3'' Candlestick	8.00--10.00
2395	10'' Bowl	25.00--30.00
2395½—5'' Candlestick		12.00--18.00
4100	8'' Vase, Reg. Opt.	20.00--30.00
2395	3'' Candle—Not made in Tz.	8.00--10.00
2375	11'' Centerpiece—Not made in Tz.	20.00--25.00
2375½—13'' Oval C. Piece—Not made in Tz.		25.00--35.00
2378	Ice Bucket—N.P. Handle— Not made in Tz.	20.00--35.00
2378	Whip Cream Pail—N.P. Hdl.	20.00--35.00
2378	Sugar Pail—N.P. Handle	20.00--35.00
2368	Ftd. Cheese	8.00--10.00
2368	Cracker Plate	12.00--15.00
2400	8'' Comport—Not made in Tz.	20.00--25.00
2385	8½'' Ftd. Fan Vase—Not made in Tz.	20.00--25.00
2429	Service Tray	10.00--15.00
2429	Service & Lemon Tray	10.00--15.00
2375	10'' Grill Plate Not made in Az-Gr-Ro.	8.00--12.00

STEMWARE
Made in Crystal Base w/Rose Bowl—Crystal Base w/Azure Bowl—Crystal Base w/Green Bowl

5098	9 oz. Goblet	18.00--22.00
5098	6 oz. High Sherbet	15.00--18.00
5098	6 oz. Low Sherbet	8.00--12.00
5098	6 oz. Parfait	14.00--18.00
5098	4 oz. Claret	18.00--22.00
5098	2½ oz. Wine	18.00--22.00
5098	3 oz. Cocktail	18.00--22.00
5098	¾ oz. Cordial	18.00--22.00
5098	5 oz. Oyster Cocktail	12.00--15.00
869	Finger Bowl	6.00----8.00
2283	6'' F. Bowl Plate, Reg. Opt.	2.00----3.00
5082½—Grape Fruit		12.00--15.00
945½—Grape Fruit Liner		12.00--15.00
5098	12 oz. Ftd. Tumbler	12.00--15.00
5098	9 oz. Ftd. Tumbler	8.00--12.00
5098	5 oz. Ftd. Tumbler	8.00--12.00
5098	2½ oz. Ftd. Tumbler	8.00--12.00
5098	5'' Comport	15.00--20.00
5000	7 Ftd. Jug	120.00--150.00

Following made in Crystal Base w/Topaz Bowl

5099	9 oz. Goblet	15.00--20.00
5099	6 oz. High Sherbet	12.00--15.00
5099	6 oz. Low Sherbet	6.00----9.00
5099	5½ oz. Parfait	12.00--15.00
5099	4 oz. Claret	15.00--20.00
5099	2½ oz. Wine	15.00--20.00
5099	3 oz. Cocktail	15.00--20.00
5099	¾ oz. Cordial	15.00--20.00
5099	4½ oz. Oyster Cocktail	9.00--12.00
5082½—Grape Fruit		12.00--15.00
5099	12 oz. Footed Tumbler	10.00--14.00
5099	9 oz. Ftd. Tumbler	9.00--12.00
5099	5 oz. Ftd. Tumbler	9.00--12.00
5099	2½ oz. Ftd. Tumbler	9.00--12.00
5099	6'' Comport	15.00--18.00

PLATE ETCHING NO. 278
"VERSAILLES" DESIGN
Made in Rose, Azure and Green

5298	Goblet	18.00--22.00
5298	High Sherbet	15.00--18.00
5298	Low Sherbet	8.00--12.00
5298	Parfait	14.00--18.00
5298	Claret	18.00--22.00
5298	Wine	18.00--22.00
5298	Cocktail	18.00--22.00
5298	Cordial	18.00--22.00
5298	Oyster Cocktail	12.00--15.00
5282½—Grape Fruit		12.00--15.00
2375	Footed Shaker	12.00--18.00
5298	12 oz. Ftd. Tumbler	12.00--15.00
5298	9 oz. Ftd. Tumbler	10.00--12.00
5298	5 oz. Ftd. Tumbler	9.00--12.00
5298	2½ oz. Ftd. Tumbler	9.00--12.00
2375	Canape Plate	6.00----9.00
5298	5'' Comport	15.00--20.00
5298	6'' Nappy, Ftd.	10.00--15.00
2375	7'' Comport	15.00--20.00
2400	6'' Comport	14.00--18.00
2400	8'' Comport	15.00--20.00
2350	Small Ash Tray	10.00--15.00
2331	3 Candy Box & Cover	25.00--35.00

Made in Topaz

5299	Goblet	15.00--20.00
5299	High Sherbet	12.00--15.00
5299	Low Sherbet	6.00----9.00
5299	Parfait	12.00--15.00
5299	Claret	15.00--20.00
5299	Wine	15.00--20.00
5299	Cocktail	15.00--20.00
5299	Cordial	15.00--20.00
5299	Oyster Cocktail	9.00--12.00
5299	12 oz. Ftd. Tumbler*	10.00--14.00
5299	9 oz. Ftd. Tumbler	9.00--12.00
5299	5 oz. Ftd. Tumbler	9.00--12.00
5299	2½ oz. Ftd. Tumbler	9.00--12.00
5299	6'' Comport	15.00--18.00
2350	Large Ash Tray	12.00--18.00
2394	½ lb. Candy Jar & Cover	25.00--35.00

PLATE ETCHING NO. 279
JUNE DESIGN
Made in Crystal, Rose, Topaz and Azure
*Items marked * not made in Crystal*

2375	6'' Plate	2.00----4.00
2375	7'' Plate	3.00----5.00
2375	8'' Plate	5.00----7.00
2375	9'' Plate	8.00--10.00
2375	10'' Plate	9.00--12.00

2375	13" Plate	16.00--20.00
2375	10" Grill Plate	7.00--10.00
2375	5" Fruit	4.00----6.00
2375	6" Cereal	5.00----8.00
2375	7" Soup	6.00----9.00
2375½—Ftd. Cup		8.00--12.00
2375	Saucer	3.00----5.00
2375	After Dinner Cup	7.00--10.00
2375	After Dinner Saucer	3.00----4.00
2375	Ftd. Bouillon	6.00----9.00
2375	Ftd. Cream Soup	8.00--12.00
2375	Cream Soup Plate	3.00----5.00
2375	9" Baker	20.00--25.00
2375	12" Platter	20.00--25.00
2375	15" Platter	25.00--30.00
2375	Sauce Boat	20.00--25.00
2375	Sauce Boat Plate	6.00--10.00
2375	8½" Relish	8.00--12.00
2375	11½" Celery	9.00--14.00
2375½—Ftd. Sugar & Cover		35.00--50.00
2375½—Ftd. Sugar		10.00--15.00
2375½—Ftd. Cream		10.00--15.00
2375½—Tea Sugar		8.00--12.00
2375½—Tea Cream		8.00--12.00
*2375	Mayonnaise	12.00--15.00
2375	Mayonnaise Plate	6.00----9.00
2375	Handled Lunch Tray	15.00--25.00
2375	Whip Cream	6.00--10.00
2375	Sweetmeat	6.00--10.00
2375	Bon Bon	5.00--10.00
2375	Lemon Dish	5.00--10.00
2375	10" Cake Plate	10.00--15.00
2375	Large Desert	14.00--20.00
2375	Ice Bucket, N.P. Handle	20.00--35.00
2378	Whip Cream Pail	20.00--35.00
2378	Sugar Pail	20.00--35.00
2375	Ftd. Oil	25.00--35.00
2375	Ftd. Shaker	12.00--20.00
2375	Ftd. Cheese	6.00--10.00
2375	Cracker Plate	10.00--15.00
2375	Cheese & Cracker	20.00--25.00
2368	Cheese & Cracker	20.00--25.00
2429	Service Tray	10.00--15.00
2429	Service & Lemon Tray	12.00--18.00
2350	Small Ash Tray	10.00--15.00
*2375	7" Comport	15.00--20.00
2400	6" Comport	14.00--18.00
*2400	8" Comport	20.00--25.00
*2385	8½" Ftd. Fan Vase	22.00--28.00
*4100	8" Vase	22.00--30.00
*2331	3 Candy Box & Cover	25.00--40.00
*2394	Mint	4.00----8.00
2394	12" Bowl	20.00--30.00
2394	2" Candle	6.00--10.00
2375	12" Centerpiece	20.00--30.00
2375½—13" Oval Centerpiece		25.00--35.00
2375½—Candle		7.00--12.00
2375	12" Bowl	20.00--30.00
2375	3" Candle	8.00--12.00
2395	10" Bowl	20.00--30.00
2395½—5" Candlestick		12.00--18.00
5098	Goblet	16.00--22.00
5098	High Sherbet	14.00--18.00
5098	Low Sherbet	8.00--12.00
5098	Parfait	14.00--18.00
5098	Claret	16.00--22.00
5098	Wine	16.00--22.00
5098	Cocktail	16.00--22.00
5098	Cordial	16.00--22.00
5098	Oyster Cocktail	10.00--15.00
5098	12 oz. Ftd. Tumbler	10.00--15.00
5098	9 oz. Ftd. Tumbler	8.00--12.00
5098	5 oz. Ftd. Tumbler	8.00--12.00
5098	2½ oz. Ftd. Tumbler	8.00--12.00
2375	Canape Plate	8.00--10.00
5098	5" Comport	15.00--20.00
5098	6" Ftd. Nappy	8.00--12.00
5082½—Grape Fruit		10.00--15.00
2375	11" Centerpiece	20.00--25.00
2385	5½" Ftd. Fan Vase	20.00--25.00
2378	Ice Bucket	20.00--35.00
2368	Cracker Plate	12.00--15.00
2451	Ice Dish Plate	4.00----6.00
2451	T. J. Liner (Not Etched)	2.00----4.00
2451	C.M. Liner (Not Etched)	2.00----4.00
2451	F. C. Liner (Not Etched)	2.00----4.00
2451	Ice Dish	15.00--20.00
2375	Salad Dressing Bottle	20.00--35.00
2394	6" Bowl	6.00--10.00
2394	½ lb. Candy Jar & Cover	20.00--35.00
2375	7" Round Nappy	9.00--12.00
2368	Ftd. Cheese	8.00--10.00
2350	Large Ash Tray	10.00--15.00
2083	Salad Dressing Bottle	25.00--30.00
2439	Decanter	50.00--75.00

Rose, Topaz, Azure Bowl w/Crystal Base.

5298	Goblet	18.00--22.00
5298	High Sherbet	16.00--18.00
5298	Low Sherbet	9.00--12.00
5298	Parfait	15.00--18.00
5298	Claret	18.00--22.00
5298	Wine	18.00--22.00
5298	Cocktail	18.00--22.00
5298	Cordial	18.00--22.00
5298	Oyster Cocktail	12.00--15.00
869	Finger Bowl	6.00----8.00
2283	6" Plate, Reg. Optic	2.00----4.00
5282½—Grape Fruit		10.00--15.00
945½—Grape Fruit Liner		10.00--15.00
5298	12 oz. Ftd. Tumbler	12.00--15.00
5298	9 oz. Ftd. Tumbler	10.00--12.00
5298	5 oz. Ftd. Tumbler	10.00--12.00
5298	2½ oz. Ftd. Tumbler	10.00--12.00
5298	5" Comport	15.00--20.00
5298	6" Ftd. Nappy	8.00--12.00
5000	7 Ftd. Jug	125.00--150.00

PLATE ETCHING NO. 280
TROJAN DESIGN
Made in Rose & Topaz

2375	6" Plate	2.00----3.00
2375	7" Plate	3.00----4.00
2375	8" Plate	4.00----6.00
2375	9" Plate	7.00----9.00
2375	10" Plate	8.00--10.00
2375	13" Plate	15.00--18.00
2375	10" Grill Plate	7.00----9.00
2375	5" Fruit	3.00----5.00
2375	6" Cereal	4.00----6.00
2375	7" Soup	6.00----8.00
2375½—Ftd. Cup		7.00----9.00
2375	Saucer	2.00----3.00
2375	After Dinner Cup	6.00----8.00
2375	After Dinner Saucer	2.00----3.00
2375	Ftd. Bouillon	5.00----8.00
2375	Ftd. Cream Soup	6.00----9.00
2375	Cream Soup Plate	2.00----3.00
2375	9" Baker	15.00--20.00
2375	12" Platter	15.00--20.00

2375	15" Platter	20.00--25.00
2375	Sauce Boat	18.00--22.00
2375	Sauce Boat Plate	5.00----8.00
2375	8½" Relish	7.00--10.00
2375	11½" Celery	8.00--12.00
2350	3 Compartment Relish	8.00--12.00
2375½—Ftd. Sugar & Cover		35.00--40.00
2375½—Ftd. Sugar		10.00--12.00
2375½—Ftd. Cream		10.00--12.00
2375½—Tea Sugar		8.00--10.00
2375½—Tea Cream		8.00--10.00
2375	Mayonnaise	8.00--12.00
2375	Mayonnaise Plate	4.00----6.00
2375	Ftd. Oil	20.00--25.00
2375	Hdld. Lunch Tray	15.00--20.00
2375	Whip Cream	5.00----8.00
2375	Sweetmeat	5.00----8.00
2375	Bon Bon	4.00----7.00
2375	Lemon Dish	4.00----7.00
2375	10" Cake Plate	9.00--12.00
2375	Large Desert	12.00--16.00
2375	Ice Bucket	20.00--25.00
2378	Whip Cream Pail	20.00--25.00
2378	Sugar Pail	20.00--25.00
5299	Goblet	15.00--18.00
5299	High Sherbet	10.00--15.00
5299	Low Sherbet	6.00--10.00
5299	Parfait	10.00--15.00
5299	Claret	15.00--18.00
5299	Wine	15.00--18.00
5299	Cocktail	15.00--18.00
5299	Cordial	15.00--18.00
5299	Oyster Cocktail	6.00--10.00
869	Finger Bowl	3.00----5.00
2283	6" Plate, Reg. Optic	2.00----3.00
5282½—Grape Fruit		9.00--12.00
945½—Grape Fruit Liner		9.00--12.00
5299	12 oz. Ftd. Tumbler	8.00--12.00
5299	9 oz. Ftd. Tumbler	6.00--10.00
5299	5 oz. Ftd. Tumbler	6.00--10.00
5299	2½ oz. Ftd. Tumbler	6.00--10.00
2375	Canape Plate	5.00----8.00
5299	6" Comport	12.00--16.00
5000	7 Ftd. Jug	100.00--150.00
2375	Ftd. Shaker	12.00--15.00
2400	6" Comport	12.00--15.00
2350	Small Ash Tray	8.00--12.00
2350	Large Ash Tray	10.00--15.00
2368	Ftd. Cheese	5.00----8.00
2368	Cracker Plate	12.00--15.00
2368	Cheese & Cracker	18.00--22.00
2375	Ftd. Cheese	5.00----8.00
2375	Cracker Plate	12.00--15.00
2375	Cheese & Cracker	18.00--22.00
2429	Service Tray	8.00--12.00
2429	Service & Lemon Tray	10.00--15.00
2394	½ lb. Candy Jar & Cover	20.00--30.00
2394	6" Bowl	5.00----8.00
2394	Mint	3.00----5.00
2394	12" Bowl	20.00--25.00
2394	2" Candlestick	7.00--10.00
2375	12" Centerpiece	20.00--25.00
2375½—Candlestick		7.00----9.00
2375	12" Bowl	18.00--22.00
2375	3" Candlestick	7.00--10.00
2395	10" Bowl	15.00--20.00
2395½—5" Candlestick		8.00--10.00
4105	8" Vase, Reg. Optic	20.00--25.00

2417	8" Vase, Reg. Optic	20.00--25.00
2415	Combination Bowl	20.00--30.00
2451	Ice Dish	8.00--10.00
2451	Ice Dish Plate	3.00----5.00
2451	T. J. Liner (Not Etched)	2.00----4.00
2451	C. M. Liner (Not Etched)	2.00----4.00
2451	F. C. Liner (Not Etched)	2.00----4.00
2375	Ftd. Shaker	12.00--15.00
2375	7" Round Nappy	10.00--15.00

STEMWARE
Made in Crystal Base w/Rose Bowl
Crystal Base w/Topaz Bowl

5082½—Grape Fruit		9.00--12.00
5099	9 oz. Goblet	15.00--18.00
5099	6 oz. High Sherbet	10.00--15.00
5099	6 oz. Low Sherbet	6.00--10.00
5099	5½ oz. Parfait	10.00--15.00
5099	4 oz. Claret	15.00--18.00
5099	2½ oz. Wine	15.00--18.00
5099	3 oz. Cocktail	15.00--18.00
5099	¾ oz. Cordial	15.00--18.00
5099	4½ oz. Oyster Cocktail	6.00--10.00
5099	12 oz. Ftd. Tumbler	8.00--12.00
5099	9 oz. Ftd. Tumbler	6.00--10.00
5099	5 oz. Ftd. Tumbler	6.00--10.00
5099	2½ oz. Ftd. Tumbler	6.00--10.00
5099	6" Comport	12.00--16.00
5000	7 Ftd. Jug	100.00--150.00

PLATE ETCHING NO. 281
"VERONA" DESIGN
Made in Crystal, Green & Rose.

890	Goblet	9.00--12.00
890	High Sherbet	8.00--10.00
890	Low Sherbet	5.00----7.00
890	Parfait	8.00--10.00
890	Claret	9.00--12.00
890	Wine	9.00--12.00
890	Cocktail	9.00--12.00
890	Cordial	9.00--12.00
890	Oyster Cocktail	6.00----9.00
877	Grape Fruit	6.00--10.00
945½—Grape Fruit Liner		6.00--10.00
890	Finger Bowl	3.00----5.00
2283	6" Plate, Reg. Optic	1.00----2.00
890	12 oz. Ftd. Tumbler	6.00----9.00
890	9 oz. Ftd. Tumbler	6.00----8.00
890	5 oz. Ftd. Tumbler	6.00----8.00
890	2½ oz. Ftd. Tumbler	6.00----8.00
890	7 Ftd. Jug	50.00--85.00
2375	6" Plate	1.00----2.00
2375	7" Plate	2.00----4.00
2375	8" Plate	4.00----6.00
2375	13" Plate	10.00--15.00
2375½—Ftd. Cup		4.00----6.00
2375	Saucer	1.00----2.00
2375½—Ftd. Sugar & Cover		20.00--30.00
2375½—Ftd. Sugar		6.00--10.00
2375½—Ftd. Cream		6.00--10.00
2400	8" Comport	10.00--15.00
2394	12" Bowl	12.00--18.00
2394	2" Candle	4.00----7.00

DECORATION NO. 502 "FIRENZE" DESIGN
Etching No. 281 w/Gold Edge
Made in Topaz—Not Illustrated

2394	12" Bowl	15.00--20.00

2394	2" Candlestick	5.00----8.00
2395	10" Bowl	15.00--18.00
2395½—5" Candlestick		6.00----9.00
2375	Lemon Dish	4.00----6.00
2375	Bon Bon	4.00----6.00
2375	10" Cake Plate	10.00--15.00
2375	Ftd. Cheese	5.00----8.00
2375	Cracker Plate	9.00--12.00
2375	Cheese & Cracker	15.00--20.00
2375	Ice Bucket	20.00--25.00
2375	Handled Lunch Tray	15.00--20.00
2400	6" Comport	10.00--15.00
2427	Cigarette Box & Cover	20.00--30.00
2417	8" Vase	22.00--28.00
4105	8" Vase	25.00--30.00

PLATE ETCHING NO. 287
"GRAPE" PATTERN
Made in Green, Orchid and Blue

2297	12" Deep Bowl "A"	20.00--30.00
2297	Shallow Bowl, A, 10½"	20.00--25.00
2297	Deep Bowl, C	20.00--30.00
2297	Deep Bowl, E	20.00--30.00
2339	Bowl, D, 7½"	18.00--22.00
2371	Oval Centerpiece	25.00--30.00
2329	11" Centerpiece	15.00--25.00
2329	13" Centerpiece	20.00--30.00
2372	2" Candlestick	6.00----9.00
2324	4" Candlestick	7.00--10.00
2362	3" Candlestick	7.00--10.00
2362	12" Low Bowl	15.00--25.00
2362	11" Ftd. Comport	20.00--30.00
2327	7" Comport	10.00--15.00
4100	6" Vase	10.00--20.00
4100	8" Vase	15.00--25.00
4103	3" Vase	6.00--10.00
4103	4" Vase	9.00--12.00
4103	5" Vase	9.00--15.00
4103	6" Vase	10.00--16.00
2369	7" Vase	20.00--25.00
2369	9" Vase	25.00--30.00
2292	8" Vase	15.00--25.00
2331	3 Candy Box	20.00--30.00
2342	Lunch Tray (2370)	12.00--18.00
2287	11" Hdld. Lunch Tray	15.00--20.00
2378	Ice Bucket—N.P. Handle	20.00--25.00
2378	Ice Bucket—N.P. Hdl., drainer & Tongs	20.00--30.00
2375	Whip Cream—Green only	6.00----8.00
2375	Sweetmeat—Green only	6.00----8.00
2375	Bon Bon—Green only	6.00----8.00
2375	Lemon Dish—Green only	6.00----8.00

PLATE ETCHED CIGARETTE HOLDERS
Made in solid Cry., Am., Gr., Bl. and Eb.

2354	Cigarette Etched Dog	10.00--20.00
2354	Cigarette Etched Horse	10.00--20.00
2354	Cigarette Etched Cupid	10.00--20.00
2354	Cigarette Etched Deer	10.00--20.00

PLATE ETCHING NO. 288
"CUPID" PATTERN
**Top prices are for Ebony*
Made in Green, Blue and Ebony

2297	Deep Bowl, A	20.00--35.00
2324	4" Candlestick	8.00--12.00

2329	11" Centerpiece	20.00--30.00
2329	13" Centerpiece	20.00--35.00
2276	Vanity Set	15.00--25.00
2359½—Puff & Cover		10.00--15.00
2322	Cologne	8.00--12.00
2298	Candle	8.00--12.00
2298	Clock	20.00--40.00
2298	Clock Set	40.00--65.00
	Set includes clock & pair of candles	

PLATE ETCHING NO. 289
"PARADISE" PATTERN
Green and Orchid

2297	Shallow Bowl "A"	20.00--25.00
2297	Deep Bowl "A"	18.00--22.00
2315	Ftd. Bowl "C"	20.00--25.00
2342	12" Bowl	20.00--25.00
2362	12" Bowl	20.00--25.00
2329	11" Centerpiece	15.00--20.00
2371	13" Centerpiece	20.00--25.00
2324	4" Candlestick	6.00----9.00
2362	3" Candlestick	6.00----9.00
2372	2" Candle Block	3.00----5.00
2327	7" Comport	10.00--15.00
2350	8" Comport	15.00--18.00
2362	11" Comport	20.00--25.00
2331	3 Candy Box & Cover	20.00--25.00
2380	Confection & Cover	20.00--25.00
2342	12" Lunch Tray	15.00--18.00
2378	Ice Bucket, N.P. Handle	20.00--25.00
2378	Ice Bucket, N.P. Hld. Drainer & Tongs	20.00--30.00
2378	Ice Bucket, N.P. Hld., S.F. Drainer & Tongs	20.00--30.00
4100	6" Vase	15.00--20.00
4100	8" Vase	20.00--25.00
4103	3" Vase	8.00--12.00
4103	5" Vase	10.00--15.00
2369	7" Vase	20.00--25.00
2369	9" Vase	25.00--30.00

PLATE ETCHING NO. 290
"OAK LEAF" DESIGN
Made in Crystal, Green and Rose
Items also made in Ebony marked †
*Items not made in Crystal marked **

†2395	10" Bowl	20.00--35.00
†2395	3" Candlestick	8.00--12.00
2394	12" Bowl	18.00--25.00
2394	2" Candlestick	6.00----9.00
2342	12" Bowl	18.00--25.00
2375	12" Centerpiece	20.00--25.00
2375	3" Candlestick	8.00--10.00
2375½—Oval Centerpiece		20.00--30.00
2375½—Candlestick		8.00--10.00
2398	11" Bowl	20.00--25.00
2350	8" Comport	10.00--15.00
2400	8" Comport	15.00--18.00
2315	12" Salver	15.00--20.00
2394	Mint	4.00----6.00
2331	3 Candy Box & Cover	20.00--25.00
*2380	Confection & Cover	20.00--25.00
*2395	Oval Confection & Cover	25.00--30.00
*2413	Urn & Cover	20.00--25.00
2342	Handled Lunch Tray	15.00--18.00
2378	Ice Bucket, N.P. Hdle.	20.00--25.00
2378	Whip Cream Pail	20.00--25.00

2378	Sugar Pail	20.00--25.00
2368	Ftd. Cheese	6.00----8.00
2368	Cracker Plate	10.00--12.00
2368	Cheese & Cracker	18.00--20.00
2375	Whip Cream	4.00----6.00
2375	Sweetmeat	4.00----6.00
2375	Bon Bon	3.00----5.00
2375	Lemon Dish	3.00----5.00
2375	10'' Cake Plate	10.00--15.00
2375	Large Desert	8.00--10.00
2283	7'' Plate	3.00----5.00
2283	8'' Plate	4.00----6.00
2315	Mayonnaise	7.00----9.00
2315	13'' Lettuce Plate	10.00--15.00
2332	7'' Mayonnaise Plate	3.00----5.00
†2391	Sm. Cigarette Box & Cover	9.00--12.00
†2391	Lg. Cigarette Box & Cover	12.00--15.00
4105	6'' Vase, Reg. Optic	12.00--18.00
4105	8'' Vase, Reg. Optic	20.00--25.00
4103	3'' Vase, Reg. Optic	8.00--12.00
2369	7'' Vase, Reg. Optic	20.00--22.00
2369	9'' Vase, Reg. Optic	20.00--25.00
†2385	8½'' Ftd. Fan Vase	20.00--25.00
†2373	Sm. Window Vase & Cover	10.00--20.00
†2373	Lg. Window Vase & Cover	15.00--25.00
2292	8'' Vase	15.00--20.00
2387	8'' Vase	20.00--25.00
*2415	Combination Bowl	20.00--30.00

2380	Confection & Cover	25.00--30.00
2342	Hld. Lunch Tray	15.00--20.00
2378	Ice Bucket—G.F. Handle	22.00--27.00
2378	Whip Cream Pail—G.F. Hdl	22.00--27.00
2378	Sugar Pail—G.F. Handle	22.00--27.00
2375	Whip Cream 2 Hld.	5.00----7.00
2375	Sweetmeat 2 Hld.	5.00----7.00
2375	Lemon Dish 2 Hld.	4.00----6.00
2375	Bon Bon 2 Hld.	4.00----6.00
2283	7'' Plate	4.00----6.00
2283	8'' Plate	5.00----7.00
2315	13'' Plate	15.00--20.00
2315	Mayonnaise	8.00--10.00
2332	7'' Mayonnaise Plate	3.00----6.00
2391	Sm. Cig. Box & Cover	12.00--15.00
2391	Lge. Cig. Box & Cover	15.00--18.00
4105	6'' Vase	12.00--18.00
4105	8'' Vase	20.00--25.00
2385	8½'' Ftd. Fan Vase	20.00--25.00
2373	Sm. Wind. Vase & Cover	15.00--20.00
2373	Lge. Wind. Vase & Cover	20.00--25.00
2387	8'' Vase	20.00--25.00
877	Goblet	15.00--18.00
877	High Sherbet	10.00--14.00
877	Low Sherbet	5.00----7.00
877	Parfait	6.00----9.00
877	Claret	15.00--18.00
877	Wine	15.00--18.00
877	Cocktail	15.00--18.00
877	Cordial	15.00--18.00
877	Oys. Cocktail	6.00----9.00
869	Finger Bowl	5.00----7.00
2283	6'' Plate	3.00----5.00
877	Grape Fruit	4.00----6.00
877	Grape Fruit Liner	2.00----4.00
877	12 oz. Ftd. Tumbler	10.00--15.00
877	9 oz. Ftd. Tumbler	8.00--10.00
877	5 oz. Ftd. Tumbler	8.00--10.00
877	2½ oz. Ftd. Tumbler	10.00--15.00
5000	7 Ftd. Jug	100.00--125.00

BROCADE ETCHING NO. 290
"Oak Leaf" Pattern
Made in Crystal and Green

877½—Goblet		10.00--15.00
877	High Sherbet	8.00--12.00
877	Low Sherbet	4.00----6.00
877	Parfait	5.00----7.00
877	Claret	10.00--15.00
877	Cocktail	10.00--15.00
877	Wine	10.00--15.00
877	Cordial	10.00--15.00
877	Oys. Cocktail	5.00----7.00
869	Finger Bowl	4.00----6.00
2283	6'' Plate	2.00----4.00
877	Grape Fruit	2.00----4.00
877	Grape Fruit Liner	1.00----2.00
877	12 oz. Ftd. Tumbler	10.00--12.00
877	9 oz. Ftd. Tumbler	7.00----9.00
877	5 oz. Ftd. Tumbler	7.00----9.00
877	2½ oz. Ftd. Tumbler	10.00--12.00
5000	7 Ftd. Jug	75.00--100.00

DECORATION NO. 72
"OAK WOOD" PATTERN
With Brocade Etching No. 290
Iridescent and Gold Edge
Made in Orchid & Azure—Not Illustrated

2342	12'' Bowl	20.00--25.00
2394	12'' Bowl	20.00--25.00
2394	2'' Candle	6.00--10.00
2398	11'' Bowl	25.00--30.00
2375	11'' Centerpiece	25.00--30.00
2375	3'' Candle	6.00--10.00
2375½—Oval Centerpiece		25.00--30.00
2375½—Candle		6.00--10.00
2400	8'' Comport	15.00--20.00
2315	Salver	15.00--20.00
2331	3 Candy Box & Cover	25.00--30.00

PLATE ETCHING NO. 305
"FERN" DESIGN
Made in Crystal, Amber, Green and Rose

5098	Goblet	8.00--12.00
5098	High Sherbet	5.00----9.00
5098	Low Sherbet	3.00----5.00
5098	Parfait	4.00----7.00
5098	Claret	8.00--12.00
5098	Wine	8.00--12.00
5098	Cocktail	8.00--12.00
5098	Cordial	8.00--12.00
5098	Oyster Cocktail	6.00----9.00
869	Finger Bowl	3.00----5.00
2283	6'' Plate, Reg. Optic	2.00----3.00
5082½—Grape Fruit		3.00----5.00
945½—Grape Fruit Liner		3.00----5.00
5098	12 oz. Ftd. Tumbler	6.00----9.00
5098	9 oz. Ftd. Tumbler	5.00----8.00
5098	5 oz. Ftd. Tumbler	5.00----8.00
5098	2½ oz. Ftd. Tumbler	6.00----9.00
5000	7 Ftd. Jug	60.00--85.00
2419	8'' Square Plate	3.00----5.00
2419	7'' Square Plate	2.00----4.00
2419	6'' Square Plate	2.00----3.00
2350½—Footed Cup		3.00----5.00
2419	Saucer	2.00----3.00
2350	After Dinner Cup	3.00----5.00
2419	After Dinner Saucer	2.00----3.00

2297	12" Bowl	15.00--20.00
2324	4" Candlestick	5.00----8.00
2395	10" Bowl	15.00--20.00
2395½—5" Candlestick		6.00----9.00
2375	Lemon Dish	3.00----5.00
2375	Bon Bon	3.00----5.00
2375	10" Cake Plate	9.00--12.00
2400	6" Comport	8.00--12.00
4105	8" Vase, Reg. Optic	12.00--18.00

Crystal Bases

5298	Goblet	8.00--12.00
5298	High Sherbet	5.00----9.00
5298	Low Sherbet	3.00----5.00
5298	Parfait	4.00----7.00
5298	Claret	8.00--12.00
5298	Wine	8.00--12.00
5298	Cocktail	8.00--12.00
5298	Cordial	8.00--12.00
5298	Oyster Cocktail	6.00----9.00
5282½—Grape Fruit		3.00----5.00
5298	12 oz. Ftd. Tumbler	6.00----9.00
5298	9 oz. Ftd. Tumbler	5.00----8.00
5298	5 oz. Ftd. Tumbler	5.00----8.00
5298	2½ oz. Ftd. Tumbler	6.00----9.00

Square Base

4120	Goblet	8.00--12.00
4120	High Sherbet	5.00----9.00
4120	7 oz. Low Sherbet	3.00----5.00
4120	5 oz. Low Sherbet	3.00----4.00
4120	3½ oz. Cocktail	8.00--10.00
4120	2 oz. Whiskey	8.00--10.00
4120	16 oz. Tumbler	8.00--12.00
4120	13 oz. Tumbler	7.00--11.00
4120	10 oz. Tumbler	6.00--10.00
4120	5 oz. Tumbler	5.00----8.00
4121	Finger Bowl	3.00----5.00

Crystal Bowl w/Square Ebony Base

4020	Goblet	7.00--10.00
4020	High Sherbet	5.00----8.00
4020	7 oz. Low Sherbet	3.00----5.00
4020	5 oz. Low Sherbet	2.00----4.00
4020	3½ oz. Cocktail	5.00----8.00
4020	2 oz. Whiskey	5.00----8.00
4020	16 oz. Tumbler	8.00--10.00
4020	13 oz. Tumbler	6.00----8.00
4020	10 oz. Tumbler	5.00----7.00
4020	5 oz. Tumbler	5.00----7.00
4021	Finger Bowl	2.00----4.00
4020½—4 oz. Cocktail		5.00----8.00
4020	Ftd. Jug	40.00--50.00
4020	Ftd. Sugar	5.00----7.00
4020	Ftd. Cream	5.00----7.00
2419	9" Plate	4.00----5.00
4020	Sugar	5.00----7.00
4020	Cream	5.00----7.00
4120	Sugar	5.00----7.00
4120	Cream	5.00----7.00
4120	Ftd. Jug	40.00--50.00

DECORATION NO. 501
"FERN" DESIGN
ETCHING NO. 305 WITH GOLD EDGE
Made in Ebony—Not Illustrated

2297	12" Bowl	25.00--30.00
2324	4" Candlestick	10.00--12.00
2395	10" Bowl	20.00--30.00
2395½—5" Candlestick		10.00--12.00

2415	Combination Bowl	25.00--35.00
2375	Lemon Dish	7.00----8.00
2375	Bon Bon	7.00----8.00
2375	10" Cake Plate	12.00--15.00
2400	6" Comport	12.00--18.00
2427	Cigarette Box & Cover	20.00--25.00
2373	Large Window Vase	22.00--28.00
2385	8½" Fan Vase	25.00--30.00
2409	7½" Vase	20.00--25.00
4105	8" Vase	20.00--25.00

PLATE ETCHING NO. 306
"QUEEN ANNE" DESIGN STEMWARE
Made in Crystal, Amber base w/Crystal bowl

4020	Goblet	6.00----9.00
4020	High Sherbet	4.00----6.00
4020	7 oz. Low Sherbet	3.00----4.00
4020	5 oz. Low Sherbet	2.00----4.00
4020½—4 oz. Cocktail		5.00----8.00
4020	3½ oz. Cocktail	5.00----8.00
4020	2 oz. Whiskey	5.00----8.00
4020	16 oz. Ftd. Tumbler	6.00----9.00
4020	13 oz. Ftd. Tumbler	5.00----8.00
4020	10 oz. Ftd. Tumbler	5.00----7.00
4020	5 oz. Ftd. Tumbler	4.00----6.00
4021	Finger Bowl	2.00----3.00
4020	Ftd. Jug	35.00--45.00
4020	Ftd. Sugar	5.00----7.00
4020	Ftd. Cream	5.00----7.00
4020	Ftd. Shaker	5.00----8.00
2419	8" Square Plate	3.00----5.00
2419	7" Square Plate	2.00----4.00
2419	6" Square Plate	1.00----3.00
2350	6" Plate	1.00----3.00
2350	7" Plate	2.00----4.00
2350	9" Plate	3.00----6.00
2350½—Ftd. Cup		2.00----4.00
2350	Saucer	1.00----2.00
2419	Saucer	1.00----2.00
2350	After Dinner Cup	2.00----4.00
2350	After Dinner Saucer	1.00----2.00
2419	After Dinner Saucer	1.00----2.00
2350	Cream Soup	3.00----4.00
4120	Goblet	6.00----9.00
4120	High Sherbet	5.00----8.00
4120	7 oz. Low Sherbet	3.00----5.00
4120	5 oz. Low Sherbet	3.00----4.00
4120	3½ oz. Cocktail	5.00----8.00
4120	2 oz. Whiskey	5.00----8.00
4120	16 oz. Tumbler	6.00----8.00
4120	13 oz. Tumbler	5.00----7.00
4120	10 oz. Tumbler	4.00----6.00
4120	5 oz. Tumbler	5.00----7.00
4121	Finger Bowl	2.00----4.00
4121	Sugar	5.00----7.00
4121	Cream	5.00----7.00
4121	Ftd. Jug	35.00--45.00

PLATE ETCHING NO. 307
"FOUNTAIN" DESIGN—SQUARE BASE
Made in Crystal, Green base w/Crystal Bowl

4020	Goblet	6.00----8.00
4020	High Sherbet	4.00----6.00
4020	7 oz. Low Sherbet	2.00----4.00
4020	5 oz. Low Sherbet	2.00----4.00
4020	3½ oz. Cocktail	6.00----8.00
4020	2 oz. Whiskey	6.00----8.00

4020	16 oz. Tumbler	6.00----8.00
4020	13 oz. Tumbler	4.00----6.00
4020	10 oz. Tumbler	4.00----6.00
4020	5 oz. Tumbler	6.00----8.00
4021	Finger Bowl	2.00----4.00
2419	8" Square Plate	3.00----5.00
2419	7" Square Plate	3.00----4.00
2419	6" Square Plate	2.00----3.00
2350	6" Plate	2.00----3.00
2350	7" Plate	2.00----3.00
2350	9" Plate	4.00----6.00
2350½—Ftd. Cup		2.00----3.00
2350	Saucer	1.00----2.00
2419	Saucer	1.00----2.00
2350	After Dinner Cup	2.00----3.00
2350	After Dinner Saucer	1.00----2.00
2419	After Dinner Saucer	1.00----2.00
2350	Cream Soup	2.00----4.00
4120	Goblet	6.00----9.00
4120	High Sherbet	5.00----7.00
4120	7 oz. Low Sherbet	3.00----5.00
4120	5 oz. Low Sherbet	3.00----4.00
4120	3½ oz. Cocktail	5.00----8.00
4120	2 oz. Whiskey	5.00----8.00
4120	16 oz. Tumbler	5.00----9.00
4120	13 oz. Tumbler	4.00----6.00
4120	10 oz. Tumbler	4.00----6.00
4120	5 oz. Tumbler	4.00----6.00
4121	Finger Bowl	2.00----3.00
4120	Cream	4.00----6.00
4120	Sugar	4.00----6.00
4120	Jug	35.00--45.00

CUTTING NO. 167
"FAIRFAX" PATTERN

863	9 oz. Goblet	2.00----3.00
863	Saucer Champagne	2.00----3.00
863	Fruit	1.00----2.00
863	3 oz. Wine	2.00----3.00
863	3½ oz. Cocktail	2.00----3.00
661	Parfait	2.00----3.00
837	Oyster Cocktail	2.00----3.00
880	Ftd. Salt Dip	3.00----4.00
1769	Finger Bowl	1.00----2.00
1736	6" Plate	1.00----2.00
880	Bon Bon	2.00----3.00
825	Jelly	2.00----3.00
825	Jelly & Cover	3.00----5.00
803	5" Comport	2.00----3.00
803	5" Comport & Cover	3.00----5.00
803	6" Comport	2.00----3.00
803	5" Nappy	1.00----2.00
803	5" Nappy & Cover	2.00----4.00
803	6" Nappy	1.00----2.00
803	7" Nappy	2.00----3.00
820	Table Tumbler	1.00----2.00
701	14 oz. Tumbler	1.00----2.00
701	12 oz. Tumbler	1.00----2.00
701	5" Tumbler Plate	1.00----2.00
4011½—Table Tumbler		1.00----2.00
4011	12 oz. Tumbler	1.00----2.00
4011	12 oz. Tumbler, Hdld.	2.00----3.00
303	7 Jug	12.00--15.00
2082	7 Jug	10.00--15.00
2040	3 Jug	10.00--12.00
2230	7 Jug & Cover	15.00--20.00
1712½—Cream		2.00----3.00
1712	Sugar	2.00----3.00
1712	Sugar & Cover	3.00----4.00

300½—Small Oil		12.00--15.00
2236	Shaker, F.G.T.	2.00----3.00
2263	Individual Salt	3.00----4.00
1968	Marmalade & Cover	3.00----4.00
1697	Carafe	8.00--10.00
4023	6 oz. Carafe Tumbler	2.00----3.00
2194	8 oz. Syrup, Nickel Top	10.00--15.00
2194	12 oz. Syrup, Nickel Top	12.00--18.00
2138	Mayonnaise Bowl	4.00----6.00
2138	Mayonnaise Plate	2.00----3.00
2138	Mayonnaise Ladle	1.00----2.00
840	5" Sherbet Plate	1.00----2.00
2238	8¼" Salad Plate	2.00----3.00
4069	9" Vase	9.00--12.00
2219	¼, ½, 1 lb. Candy Jar & Cov.	10.00--15.00

CUTTING NO. 168
"LOUISA" PATTERN

661	Goblet	2.00----3.00
661	Saucer Champagne	2.00----3.00
661	Fruit	1.00----2.00
661	Wine	2.00----3.00
661	Cocktail	2.00----3.00
661	Parfait	2.00----3.00
1769	Finger Bowl	1.00----2.00
1736	6" Plate	1.00----2.00
880	Bon Bon	2.00----3.00
825	Jelly	2.00----3.00
825	Jelly & Cover	3.00----4.00
945½—Grape Fruit		1.00----2.00
945½—Grape Fruit Liner		1.00----2.00
803	5" Comport	1.00----2.00
803	5" Comport & Cover	2.00----3.00
803	6" Comport	1.00----2.00
803	5" Nappy	1.00----2.00
803	5" Nappy & Cover	2.00----3.00
803	6" Nappy	1.00----2.00
803	7" Nappy	2.00----3.00
4085	Table Tumbler	1.00----2.00
4085	13 oz. Tumbler	1.00----2.00
4011	12 oz. Tumbler, Handled	2.00----3.00
840	5" Plate	1.00----2.00
303	7 Jug	12.00--15.00
1852	6 Jug	12.00--15.00
317	Jug, Cut Neck	12.00--15.00
317½—Jug & Cover		15.00--20.00
1480	Sugar	2.00----3.00
1480	Cream	2.00----3.00
1465	5 oz. Oil, Cut Neck	12.00--15.00
1465	7 oz. Oil, Cut Neck	15.00--18.00
2235	Shaker, F.G.T.	2.00----3.00
2235	Shaker, Pearl Top	2.00----3.00
2263	Individual Salt	3.00----4.00
4087	Marmalade & Cover	3.00----4.00
1697	Carafe	8.00--10.00
4023	6 oz. Carafe Tumbler	2.00----4.00
2194	8 oz. Syrup, Nickel Top	10.00--15.00
2194	12 oz. Syrup, Nickel Top	15.00--18.00
2138	Mayonnaise Bowl	4.00----6.00
2138	Mayonnaise Plate	2.00----3.00
2138	Mayonnaise Ladle	1.00----2.00
2250	¼, ½, 1 lb. Candy Jar & Cov.	10.00--15.00
2238	8¼" Salad Plate	2.00----3.00
2238	11" Salad Plate	3.00----4.00
2241	Cologne & Stopper	6.00----8.00
2209	9" Vase	8.00--12.00

CUTTING NO. 169 "TRELLIS" PATTERN

660	Goblet	2.00----4.00

660	Saucer Champagne	2.00----3.00
660	Fruit	2.00----3.00
660	Parfait	2.00----3.00
660	Cocktail	2.00----4.00
660	Wine	2.00----4.00
660	Cordial	2.00----4.00
837	Oyster Cocktail	2.00----3.00
766	Finger Bowl	2.00----3.00
2283	6" Plate	1.00----2.00
766	Mayonnaise Set—3 Piece	6.00----9.00
766	Sweetmeat	3.00----5.00
5078	5" Compote	4.00----6.00
5078	6" Compote	4.00----6.00
5078	5" Nappy	1.00----2.00
5078	6" Nappy	1.00----2.00
5078	7" Nappy	2.00----3.00
5078	8" Nappy	3.00----5.00
4076	9 oz. Tumbler	1.00----2.00
889	13 oz. Tumbler	2.00----3.00
889	8 oz. Tumbler	1.00----2.00
889	5 oz. Tumbler	1.00----2.00
887	2½ oz. Tumbler	2.00----4.00
4011	12 oz. Tumbler, Hdld.	3.00----4.00
4095	13 oz. Tumbler, Ftd.	2.00----3.00
4095	10 oz. Tumbler, Ftd.	2.00----3.00
4095	5 oz. Tumbler, Ftd.	2.00----3.00
724	7 Jug	10.00--15.00
303	7 Jug	10.00--15.00
2270	Jug	10.00--15.00
2270	Jug & Cover (Cov. not cut)	15.00--18.00
1851	Sugar	2.00----4.00
1851	Cream	2.00----4.00
1465	5 oz. Oil, C. N..Polsh. Stop.	15.00--20.00
2235	Shaker, F. G. Top	2.00----4.00
2235	Shaker, Pearl Top	2.00----4.00
1968	Marmalade & Cover	4.00----6.00
1831	Mustard & Cover	3.00----5.00
1697	Carafe	8.00--12.00
4023	6 oz. Carafe Tumbler	2.00----4.00
1697	Carafe Ste—2 Piece	10.00--15.00
2194	8 oz. Syrup	15.00--20.00
2283	5" Plate	1.00----2.00
2237	7" Plate	2.00----3.00
2337	8" Plate	2.00----3.00
1848	9" Plate, Cut Mat Star	3.00----4.00
2250	¼ lb. Candy Jar & Cover	6.00----9.00
2276	Vanity Set	12.00--15.00
810	Finger Bowl	2.00----3.00
945½	—Grape Fruit	2.00----3.00
945½	—Grape Fruit Liner	2.00----3.00
5078	5" Compote & Cover	8.00--10.00
825	Jelly	4.00----6.00
825	Jelly & Cover	10.00--12.00
2250	½ lb. Candy Jar & Cover	8.00--12.00
2250	1 lb. Candy Jar & Cover	10.00--15.00
300	Qt. Decanter, Cut Neck	15.00--20.00
1787	3 Jug	10.00--12.00

CUTTING NO. 170 "CYNTHIA" PATTERN

661	Parfait	2.00----3.00
837	Oyster Cocktail	1.00----2.00
1769	Finger Bowl	1.00----2.00
2283	6" Plate	1.00----2.00
1769	Mayonnaise Set—3 Piece	4.00----6.00
945½	—Grape Fruit	2.00----3.00
945½	—Grape Fruit Liner	2.00----3.00
880	Sweetmeat	2.00----3.00
825	Jelly	2.00----3.00
825	Jelly & Cover	3.00----4.00

5078	5" Compote	4.00----6.00
5078	6" Compote	4.00----6.00
5078	5" Nappy	1.00----2.00
5078	6" Nappy	1.00----2.00
5078	5" Compote & Cover	6.00----9.00
5078	6" Compote & Cover	7.00--10.00
5078	5" Nappy & Cover	6.00----9.00
5078	6" Nappy & Cover	7.00--10.00
4085	Table Tumbler	1.00----2.00
4085	13 oz. Tumbler	2.00----3.00
4085	13 oz. Tumbler, Hdl.	3.00----5.00
4085	6 oz. Tumbler	1.00----2.00
4085	2½ oz. Tumbler	2.00----3.00
4095	2½, 5, 10, 13 oz. Ftd. Tumb	3.00----4.00
4011	12 oz. Handled Tumbler	2.00----4.00
2270	Jug & Cover (Cov. not cut)	15.00--20.00
2270	Jug, no Cover	12.00--15.00
1852	6 Jug	10.00--12.00
724	7 Tankard	12.00--15.00
2133	Sugar	3.00----5.00
2133	Cream	3.00----5.00
1465	5 oz. Oil, Cut Neck	15.00--18.00
4087	Marmalade & Cover	6.00----8.00
2235	Shaker, F. G. Top	2.00----3.00
2235	Shaker, Pearl Top	2.00----3.00
1697	Carafe	8.00--12.00
4023	6 oz. Carafe Tumbler	2.00----3.00
1697	Carafe Set—2 Piece	10.00--15.00
2337	7" Plate	1.00----2.00
2337	8" Salad Plate	1.00----2.00
1848	9" Sandwich Plate	2.00----3.00
2250	¼, ½, 1 lb. Candy Jar & Cov.	9.00--15.00
300	Qt. Decanter, Cut Neck	15.00--20.00
661	Cocktail	2.00----4.00
661	Wine	2.00----4.00
661	Cordial	2.00----4.00
661	9 oz. Goblet	2.00----4.00
661	Saucer Champagne	2.00----4.00
661	Fruit	1.00----2.00

CUTTING No. 175 "AIRDALE" PATTERN

880	10 oz. Goblet	2.00----3.00
880	5½ oz. Saucer, Champagne	2.00----3.00
880	Fruit	1.00----2.00
880	2¾ oz. Wine	2.00----3.00
880	Cocktail	2.00----3.00
880	Almond	2.00----3.00
822	Parfait	2.00----3.00
837	Oyster Cocktail	2.00----3.00
1769	Finger Bowl	1.00----2.00
2283	6" Plate	1.00----2.00
880	Sweetmeat	2.00----3.00
945½	—Grape Fruit	2.00----3.00
495½	—Grape Fruit Liner	2.00----3.00
5039	Liner—tumbler Shape, N.C.	1.00----2.00
803	5" Compote	2.00----3.00
803	5" Nappy	1.00----2.00
803	6" Nappy	1.00----2.00
820	Tumbler	1.00----2.00
701	13 oz. Tumbler	1.00----2.00
889	5 oz. Tumbler	1.00----2.00
887	2½ oz. Tumbler	1.00----2.00
4011	12 oz. Hdld. Tumbler	2.00----3.00
701	5" Tumbler Plate	.50----1.00
2082	7 Jug	8.00--12.00
2040	3 Jug	8.00--10.00
303	7 Jug	10.00--15.00
1712	Sugar	2.00----3.00
1712½	—Cream	2.00----3.00
2235	Shaker, F.G.T.	2.00----3.00

2283	7" Plate	1.00----2.00
2283	11" Plate	2.00----4.00
2263	Salt Dip	2.00----4.00
1697	Carafe	6.00----8.00
4023	6 oz. Tumbler	2.00----3.00
2290	8¼" Plate	1.00----2.00
2194	12 oz. Syrup	12.00--15.00
2219	¼ lb. Candy Jar & Cover	6.00----9.00
2219	½ lb. Candy Jar & Cover	6.00----9.00
2250	¼ lb. Candy Jar & Cover	4.00----6.00
2250	½ lb. Candy Jar & Cover	4.00----6.00
2241	Cologne	6.00----8.00
2287	Lunch Tray, "Fleur-de-Lis"	5.00----8.00

CUTTING No. 176 "KENMORE" PATTERN
Made with Blue foot optic

5082	Goblet	5.00----7.00
5082	Saucer Champagne	3.00----5.00
5082	Fruit	2.00----3.00
5082	Parfait	3.00----5.00
5082	Wine	5.00----7.00
5082	Cocktail	5.00----7.00
1769	Finger Bowl	2.00----3.00
1769	Finger Bowl Plate (1499-6")	1.00----2.00
820	Table Tumbler	2.00----3.00
4011	12 oz. Tumbler, Hdld.	3.00----4.00
701	13 oz. Tumbler	2.00----3.00
889	5 oz. Tumbler	2.00----3.00
887	2½ oz. Tumbler	2.00----3.00
2082	7 Jug	9.00--12.00
303	7 Jug	10.00--15.00
2315	Sugar	3.00----4.00
2315	Cream	3.00----4.00
2315	Mayonnaise	4.00----6.00
2315	Mayonnaise Plate (2332-7")	2.00----3.00
2287	Lunch Tray	6.00----9.00
2337	7 Plate	1.50----2.00
2337	8 Plate	2.00----3.00
2283	13 Plate	4.00----5.00
5082	High Sherbet	2.00----4.00
5082	Low Sherbet	2.00----3.00
4095	13 Tumbler	1.00----3.00
4095	10 Tumbler	1.00----2.00
4095	5 Tumbler	1.00----2.00
4095	Oyster Cocktail	1.00----3.00
4095	Candy Jar & Cover	10.00--14.00
4095	7 Jug	15.00--20.00
4095	Finger Bowl (4½ Nappy)	2.00----3.00
2283	6" Plate, Blue	1.00----2.00
2283	8" Plate, Blue	2.00----3.00
2287	"Fleur-de-Lis" Lunch Tray Cut 175 Diameter 11½"	5.00----8.00
2287	"Fleur-de-Lis" Lunch Tray Cut B Diameter 11½"	5.00----8.00
2218	7 piece Relish Set, Diameter of Tray 13"	9.00--12.00
2283	No. 7 Salad Plate Cut 175 Crys-Gr-Am-Canary	1.00----3.00
1693½—3½" Coaster		1.00----2.00
2283	No. 7 Salad Plate, Cut 178 Crys-Gr-Am-Canary	1.00----3.00
2272	4" Coaster Cut 172	1.00----2.00
2316	Soup Plate, Diameter 10", Height 1½"	2.00----4.00
2321	Mah Jongg Set Diameter of Plate 8½" Capacity of Sherbet 5½ oz, Height of Sherbet 3½" Crys-Gr-Am-Canary-Eb	4.00----6.00

2283	No. 7 Salad Plate, Cut 177 Crys-Gr-Am-Canary	1.00----3.00

ENGRAVED No. 25 "ROSEDALE" PATTERN

802	Goblet	2.00----4.00
802½—Saucer Champagne		2.00----4.00
802½—Fruit		1.00----2.00
802	3½ oz. Wine	2.00----4.00
661	Parfait	2.00----4.00
803	7" Deep Nappy	4.00----6.00
4085	Tumbler	1.00----2.00
4085	13 oz. Ice Tea	1.00----3.00
4085	13 oz. Hdld. Ice Tea	2.00----4.00
1852	6 Jug	10.00--14.00
4069	9" Vase	8.00--10.00
2219	½ lb. Candy Jar & Cover	10.00--15.00
2276	Vanity Set	12.00--15.00

MISCELLANEOUS CUT WARE

2276	Covered Cheese Cut C	3.00----5.00
2276	Cheese Plate Cut C	8.00--10.00
2276	Vanity Set Cut 15	12.00--15.00
2331	Candy Box & Cover Cut D	8.00--12.00
2273	Vanity Set Cut 18	12.00--15.00
1432	Sugar Cut E	3.00----5.00
1432	Cream Cut E	3.00----5.00
5085	8" Bud Vase Cut 31	3.00----5.00
5085	8" Bud Vase Cut 32	6.00----8.00
785	10" Bud Vase Cut 30	4.00----6.00
5087	8" Bud Vase Cut 83	3.00----6.00
762	8" Vase Cut 181	4.00----6.00
2263	Ind. Salt Eng. 26	3.00----4.00
880	Ftd. Salt Eng. 26	3.00----5.00
2272	Coaster Cut 172	1.00----2.00
1590	3½" Coaster Cut 171	1.00----3.00
803	7" Nappy	6.00----8.00
2276	Vanity Set Eng. A.	12.00--15.00
2219	½ lb. Candy Jar & Cover	10.00--15.00
1852	6 Jug	10.00--12.00
2315	Bowl B Shape Cut D	12.00--15.00
4055	D Vase Cut 182	8.00--10.00
2072	8" Vase, Cut 182	8.00--12.00
4095½—8" Vase, Cut 182		8.00--12.00
4069	9" Vase, Cut 181	6.00----8.00

CUTTING No. 180 "LYNN" PATTERN

5083	Goblet	2.00----4.00
5083	Saucer Champagne	2.00----4.00
5083	Parfait	2.00----3.00
5083	Fruit	1.00----3.00
5083	Wine	2.00----4.00
5083	Cocktail	2.00----4.00
1769	Finger Bowl	1.00----2.00
1769	Finger Bowl Plate (2283-6")	1.00----2.00
820	Table Tumbler	1.00----2.00
4011	12 oz. Tumbler, Hdld.	3.00----4.00
701	13 oz. Tumbler	1.00----3.00
889	5 oz. Tumbler	1.00----2.00
2040	3 Jug	12.00--15.00
2082	7 Jug	8.00--12.00
2315	Sugar	2.00----4.00
2315	Cream	2.00----4.00
2315	Mayonnaise	4.00----6.00
2315	Mayonnaise Plate (2332-7")	1.00----3.00
2332	Grape Fruit	3.00----4.00
2332	Grape Fruit Plate	1.00----2.00

2321	Sherbet	1.00----3.00
2321	Plate	1.00----3.00
2327	7" Compote	4.00----6.00
2222	Grape Fruit	2.00---3.00
2222	Grape Fruit Plate	1.00----2.00
2222	7" Plate	2.00----4.00
2222	8" Plate	3.00----4.00
2222	10" Plate	6.00----8.00

CUTTING No. 184 "ARBOR" PATTERN
Made in Amber, Green and Blue

869	Goblet	8.00--10.00
869	High Sherbet	6.00----8.00
869	Low Sherbet	3.00----4.00
869	Parfait	3.00----5.00
869	Cocktail	8.00----10.00
869	Wine	8.00----10.00
869	Oyster Cocktail	6.00----8.00
869	Finger Bowl	3.00----4.00
2283	6" Plates	2.00----4.00
5100	2½, 5, 9, 12 oz. Ftd. Tumb.	4.00----8.00
5100	7 Ftd. Jug	40.00--60.00
2283	7" Plates	3.00----5.00
2283	8" Plates	4.00----6.00
2283	13" Plates	8.00--12.00
2287	11" Hdld. Lunch Tray	12.00--15.00
2327	7" Comport	8.00--10.00
2292	8" Vase	10.00--14.00
4100	8" Vase	10.00--12.00
2315	Sugar	6.00--10.00
2315	Cream	6.00--10.00
2329	13" Centerpiece	20.00--25.00
2329	11" Centerpiece	15.00--20.00
2324	4" Candle	6.00----9.00
2324	9" Candles	9.00--12.00
2324	10" Ftd. Bowl	15.00--18.00
2324	Small Urn	10.00--15.00
2297	12" Deep Bowl A	15.00--18.00
2297	10" Shallow Bowl A	10.00--15.00
2250	½ lb. Candy Jar & Cover	8.00--12.00
2331	3 Candy Box & Cover	10.00--14.00
2276	Vanity Set	12.00--15.00

CUTTING No. 185 "ARVIDA" PATTERN
Made in Amber, Green, Blue, and Orchid

2297	12" Deep Bowl, A	15.00--20.00
2315	Ftd. Bowl, A	18.00--22.00
2329	11" Centerpiece	15.00--20.00
2329	13" Centerpiece	20.00--25.00
2371	Oval Centerpiece	20.00--25.00
2372	2" Candle Block	5.00----8.00
2324	4" Candle	6.00----9.00
4100	6", 8", 10", 12" Vase	10.00--25.00
4103	3" Vase	8.00--10.00
4103	4" Vase	8.00--12.00
4103	5" Vase	10.00--15.00
4103	6" Vase	12.00--15.00
2369	7" Vase	18.00--20.00
2369	9" Vase	20.00--30.00
2327	7" Comport	10.00--15.00
2362	11½" Comport	12.00--18.00
2287	Handled Lunch Tray	12.00--16.00
2368	Cheese & Plate	15.00--20.00
2350	13" Plate	15.00--20.00
2331	3 Candy Box & Cover	12.00--18.00
2378	Ice Bucket—N.P. Handle	15.00--20.00
2378	Ice Bkt.—N.P. Hdl. Drainer & Tongs	18.00--25.00

CUTTING No. 186 "THELMA" PATTERN
Made in Amber, Green, Rose (Dawn) & Orchid

2362	12½" Bowl	15.00--20.00
2362	3" Candle	5.00----8.00
2297	12" Dp. Bowl "A"	15.00--20.00
2342	12½" Dp. Bowl "A"	15.00--20.00
2329	11" Centerpiece	15.00--18.00
2329	13" Centerpiece	20.00--30.00
2324	4" Candle	6.00----9.00
2331	3 C. Box & Cover	12.00--15.00
2368	Cheese	3.00----5.00
2368	11½" Cracker Plate	8.00--10.00
2368	Cheese & Plate	10.00--15.00
2327	7" Comport	8.00--10.00
2378	Ice Bucket, N.P. Hdl.	15.00--20.00
2378	Sugar Pail & N.P. Hdl.	15.00--20.00
2378	Whip Cream Pail & N.P. Hdl.	15.00--20.00
2287	11" Hld. Lunch Tray	12.00--16.00
2342	12" Hld. Lunch Tray	14.00--18.00
4100	6" Vase Opt.	9.00--12.00
4100	8" Vase Opt.	10.00--14.00
4103	4", 5", 6" Vase Opt.	8.00--12.00
2369	7" Vase Opt.	12.00--15.00
2369	9" Vase Opt.	15.00--20.00

CUTTING No. 188 "BERRY" PATTERN
Made in Green and Rose (Dawn)

5298	Goblet	10.00--12.00
5298	High Sherbet	8.00--10.00
5298	Low Sherbet	3.00----5.00
5298	Parfait	5.00----8.00
5298	Wine	10.00--12.00
5298	Cocktail	10.00--12.00
5282½	—Grape Fruit	3.00----5.00
945½	—Grape Fruit Liner	3.00----5.00
869	Finger Bowl	3.00----4.00
2283	6" Plate	2.00----3.00
5298	Oyster Cocktail	5.00----8.00
5298	2½, 5, 9, 12, oz. Ftd. Tumb.	5.00----8.00
5000	Ftd. Jug	60.00--85.00
2350½	—Ftd. Sugar	6.00--10.00
2350½	—Ftd. Cream	6.00--10.00
2400	8" Comport	10.00--15.00
2315	Mayonnaise	8.00--10.00
2332	7" Plate	3.00----5.00
2315	13" Plate	12.00--15.00
2368	Ftd. Cheese	5.00----8.00
2368	Cracker Plate	8.00--12.00
2394	Mint	6.00----8.00
2342	12" Bowl	20.00--25.00
2329	11" Centerpiece	15.00--20.00
2329	13" Centerpiece	20.00--25.00
2324	4" Candle	6.00----9.00
2394	12" Bowl	20.00--25.00
2394	2" Candle	5.00----8.00
2373	Sm. Wind. Vase & Cover	9.00--12.00
2373	Lge. Wind. Vase & Cover	12.00--15.00
4100	8" Vase	15.00--20.00
4103	6" Vase	15.00--20.00
4105	6" Vase	15.00--20.00
4105	8" Vase	16.00--22.00
2369	7" Vase	18.00--22.00
2369	9" Vase	20.00--25.00
2342	Hld. Lunch Tray	12.00--15.00
2378	Ice Bucket	15.00--20.00
2378	Whip Cream Pail	15.00--20.00
2378	Sugar Pail	15.00--20.00
2331	3 C. Box & Cover	12.00--18.00

2283	7'' Plate	3.00----5.00
2283	8'' Plate	4.00----6.00

CUTTING No. 192 "KINGSLEY" DESIGN
Made in Crystal, Rose and Azure

2297	12'' Deep Bowl A	15.00--25.00
2342	12'' Bowl A	15.00--25.00
2329	11'' Centerpiece	15.00--20.00
2329	14'' Centerpiece Not made in Azure	20.00--30.00
2324	4'' Candlestick	6.00--10.00
2375	3'' Candlestick	5.00----9.00
2400	8'' Comport	12.00--16.00
2400	6'' Comport	10.00--14.00
2331	3 Candy Box and Cover	12.00--20.00
2368	Ftd. Cheese	5.00----8.00
2368	Cracker Plate	8.00--12.00
2368	Cheese and Cracker	10.00--20.00
2315	Mayonnaise	6.00--10.00
2332	7'' Mayonnaise Plate	3.00----4.00
2342	Handled Lunch Tray	15.00--18.00
2378	Ice Bucket N.P. Hdle.	15.00--25.00
2373	Sm. Window Vase & Cover	10.00--15.00
2373	Lg. Window Vase & Cover	12.00--18.00
2292	8'' Vase	10.00--20.00
2369	7'' Vase	15.00--20.00
2369	9'' Vase	15.00--25.00
4105	8'' Vase	15.00--20.00

CUTTING No. 194 "ORLEANS" DESIGN
Made in Topaz and Azure

2394	12'' Bowl	20.00--30.00
2394	2'' Candlestick	8.00--10.00
2375	12'' Bowl	20.00--30.00
2375	3'' Candlestick	8.00--10.00
2395	10'' Bowl	20.00--25.00
2395½—5'' Candlestick		9.00--12.00
2375	Handled Lunch Tray	12.00--16.00
2394	½ lb. Candy Jar & Cover	15.00--20.00
2395	Oval Confection & Cover	18.00--25.00
2400	6'' Comport	8.00--12.00
2368	Ftd. Cheese	5.00----8.00
2368	Cracker Plate	8.00--12.00
2368	Cheese & Cracker	15.00--20.00
2375	Ice Bucket N.P. Hdle.	20.00--30.00
2375	Sweetmeat	6.00--10.00
2375	Bon Bon	6.00--10.00
2375	Lemon Dish	6.00--10.00
2375	10'' Cake Plate	10.00--15.00
2375	Large Desert	8.00--12.00
2417	8'' Vase, Reg. Optic	15.00--25.00
4105	8'' Vase, Reg. Optic	15.00--25.00

CUTTING No. 195 "MILLEFLEUR" DESIGN
Square Base—Made in Crystal
Ebony Base—Crystal Bowl

4020	Goblet	6.00----8.00
4020	High Sherbet	4.00----6.00
4020	7 oz. Low Sherbet	3.00----4.00
4020	5 oz. Low Sherbet	2.00----4.00
4020	3½ oz. Cocktail	6.00----8.00
4020	2 oz. Whiskey	6.00----8.00
4020	5, 10, 13, 16 oz. Tumbler	5.00----7.00
4021	Finger Bowl	3.00----4.00
2419	6'', 7'', 8'' Square Plate	3.00----6.00
2350	6'', 7'', 9'' Plate	3.00----6.00

2350½—Ftd. Cup		3.00----5.00
2350	Saucer	2.00----3.00
2419	Saucer	2.00----3.00
2350	After Dinner Cup	3.00----4.00
2350	After Dinner Saucer	2.00----3.00
2419	After Dinner Saucer	2.00----3.00
2350	Cream Soup	3.00----5.00
4120	Goblet	8.00--10.00
4120	High Sherbet	5.00----7.00
4120	7 oz. Low Sherbet	3.00----5.00
4120	5 oz. Low Sherbet	3.00----4.00
4120	3½ oz. Cocktail	8.00--10.00
4120	2 oz. Whiskey	8.00--10.00
4120	5, 10, 13, 16 oz. Tumbler	6.00----9.00
4121	Finger Bowl	3.00----4.00
4020½—4 oz. Cocktail		8.00--10.00
4020	Footed Jug	25.00--35.00
4020	Footed Sugar	4.00----6.00
4020	Footed Cream	4.00----6.00

CUTTING No. 196 "LATTICE" DESIGN

Made in Crystal
Not in Fostoria Book

877	Goblet	6.00----9.00
877	High Sherbet	5.00----7.00
877	Low Sherbet	2.00----4.00
877	Parfait	6.00----9.00
877	Claret	6.00----9.00
877	Wine	6.00----9.00
877	Cocktail	6.00----9.00
877	Cordial	6.00----9.00
877	Oyster Cocktail	5.00----7.00
869	Finger Bowl	2.00----4.00
2283	6'' Plate, Reg. Optic	2.00----3.00
877	2½, 5, 9, 12 oz. Ftd. Tumb.	3.00----6.00
2283	7'' Plate	2.00----3.00
2283	8'' Plate	3.00----4.00
2394	12'' Bowl	10.00--15.00
2394	2'' Candlestick	3.00----5.00

CUTTING No. 197 "CHATTERIS" DESIGN
ROCK CRYSTAL—Made in Crystal

877	Goblet	6.00----9.00
877	High Sherbet	5.00----7.00
877	Low Sherbet	2.00----4.00
877	Parfait	6.00----9.00
877	Claret	6.00----9.00
877	Wine	6.00----9.00
877	Cocktail	6.00----9.00
877	Cordial	6.00----9.00
877	Oyster Cocktail	5.00----7.00
869	Finger Bowl	2.00----4.00
2283	6'' Plate, Reg. Optic	2.00----3.00
877	2½, 5, 9, 12 oz. Ftd. Tumb.	3.00----6.00
2283	7'' Plate	2.00----3.00
2283	8'' Plate	3.00----4.00
2350½—Ftd. Sugar		3.00----5.00
2350½—Ftd. Cream		3.00----5.00
2394	12'' Bowl	10.00--15.00
2394	2'' Candlestick	3.00----5.00
2329	11'' Centerpiece	10.00--15.00
2324	4'' Candlestick	3.00----5.00
2400	6'' Comport	8.00--12.00
2375	Footed Cheese	3.00----5.00
2375	Cracker Plate	6.00----9.00
2375	Cheese & Cracker	10.00--14.00
2315	Mayonnaise	4.00----6.00

2332	7" Mayonnaise Plate	2.00----3.00
2375	Handled Lunch Tray	8.00--10.00
2378	Ice Bucket, N.P. Handle	10.00--15.00
2369	7" Vase	9.00--12.00
2417	8" Vase	8.00--10.00
4105	8" Vase	9.00--12.00

CUTTING No. 198 "WARWICK" DESIGN
ROCK CRYSTAL

890	Goblet	6.00----9.00
890	High Sherbet	5.00----7.00
890	Low Sherbet	3.00----4.00
890	Parfait	6.00----9.00
890	Claret	6.00----9.00
890	Wine	6.00----9.00
890	Cocktail	6.00----9.00
890	Cordial	6.00----9.00
890	Oyster Cocktail	5.00----7.00
890	Finger Bowl	2.00----3.00
2283	6" Plate, Reg. Optic	2.00----3.00
890	2½, 5, 9, 12 oz. Ftd. Tumb.	3.00----6.00
2283	7" Plate	2.00----4.00
2283	8" Plate	3.00----4.00
2283	13" Plate	9.00--12.00
2350	10" Plate	8.00--10.00
2419	6", 7", 8" Square Plate	2.00----4.00
2350½	Ftd. Sugar	3.00----6.00
2350½	Ftd. Cream	3.00----6.00
2394	12" Bowl	12.00--15.00
2394	2" Candlestick	3.00----4.00
2400	6" Comport	8.00--10.00
2400	8" Comport	8.00--12.00
2350½	Cream Soup	3.00----5.00
2350	Cream Soup Plate	2.00----3.00
2375	Handled Lunch Tray	8.00--10.00
2375	Ice Bucket	10.00--15.00
2417	8" Vase	8.00--10.00
4105	8" Vase	9.00--12.00
2430	11" Bowl	12.00--15.00
2430	8" Vase	8.00--10.00
2430	½ lb. Candy Jar & Cover	10.00--14.00
2430	5½" Mint	5.00----7.00
2430	7" Jelly	6.00----9.00

MISCELLANEOUS CUT WARE
Made in Gr-Rose-Azure

2375	Sweetmeat Cut A	6.00----8.00
2385	8½" Fan Vase Cut B	15.00--20.00
2375	Bon Bon Cut C	6.00----9.00
2391	Small Cigarette Cut A	8.00--12.00
2391	Large Cigarette Cut C	10.00--15.00
2385	8½" Fan Vase Cut A	15.00--20.00
2375	Lemon Dish Cut B	6.00----9.00
2385	8½" Fan Vase Cut C	15.00--20.00

CUTTING No. 199
"DELPHINE" DESIGN
ROCK CRYSTAL
Not in Fostoria Book

5098	Goblet	6.00----9.00
5098	High Sherbet	5.00----7.00
5098	Low Sherbet	3.00----5.00
5098	Parfait	6.00----9.00
5098	Claret	6.00----9.00
5098	Wine	6.00----9.00
5098	Cocktail	6.00----9.00

5098	Cordial	6.00----9.00
5098	Oyster Cocktail	5.00----7.00
5098	2½, 5, 9, 12 oz. Ftd. Tumb.	3.00----6.00
2283	8" Plate, Reg. Opt.	3.00----5.00

GOBLETS
Gold Decorations

766	9 oz. Goblet, Coin Gold Band No. 9 "Newport"	3.00----5.00
661	9 oz. Goblet, Encrusted Gold No. 29 "Empress"	3.00----5.00
766	9 oz. Goblet, Encrusted Gold No. 31 "Laurel"	3.00----5.00
766	9 oz. Goblet Encrusted Gold No. 32 "Regent"	3.00----5.00
661	9 oz. Goblet, Coin Gold Band No. 40 "Nome"	3.00----5.00
661	9 oz. Goblet, Coin Gold Band No. 42 "Miami"	4.00----6.00
5082	9 oz. Goblet, Coin Gold Band No. 43 "Princess"	4.00----6.00
660	9 oz. Goblet, Etched No. 264, Coin Gold Decoration	4.00----6.00

2290	8¼" Deep Salad Plate Decoration No. 25	6.00----8.00
2269	6" Candle	4.00----6.00
2267	7" Console Bowl, Encrusted, Gold No. 36 "Poinsetta"	10.00--12.00
2276	Vanity Set, Rose Tint Encrusted Gold No. 37 "Vase & Scroll"	8.00--10.00
2276	Vanity Set Amber Encrusted Gold No. 39 "Royal"	8.00--10.00

ENCRUSTED GOLD No. 44 "RIVERA"
Furnished in Amber, Green and Canary

2297	10¼" Shallow Bowl (A)	10.00--20.00
2241	Cologne	8.00--15.00
2219	¼ lb. Candy Jar	10.00--16.00
2297	10½" Deep Bowl (C)	10.00--20.00
2321	Mah Jongg Set	10.00--18.00
2250	½ lb. Candy Jar	10.00--15.00
2286	5" Pin Tray, Ebony	3.00----5.00
2286	10½" Comb & Brush Tray, Eb	8.00--12.00

MAYFAIR PATTERN
No. 2419 DINNERWARE
Made in Crystal, Amber, Green, Rose & Topaz

2419	6" Br. & But. Plate Also made in Az-Eb-Wis	1.00----3.00
2419	7" Salad Plate Also made in Az-Eb-Wis	2.00----4.00
2419	8" Luncheon Plate Also made in Az-Eb-Wis	2.00----5.00
2419	9" Dinner Plate Also made in Eb-Wis	3.00----6.00
2419	5" Fruit	2.00----3.00
2419	6" Cereal	2.00----4.00
2419	7" Soup	3.00----4.00
2419	Footed Cup	2.00----4.00
2419	Saucer (Also made in Eb.)	1.00----3.00
2419	After Dinner Cup	2.00----3.00
2419	After Dinner Saucer Also made in Ebony	1.00----3.00

2419	Cream Soup	2.00----4.00
2419	10" Baker	8.00--12.00
2419	12" Platter	7.00--10.00
2419	15" Platter	9.00--12.00
2419	Sauce Bowl & Stand	12.00--15.00
2419	8½" Pickle	3.00----5.00
2419	11" Celery	4.00----6.00
2419	8½" Relish	3.00----6.00
2419	Sugar	4.00----6.00
2419	Cream	4.00----6.00
2419½	Footed Sugar	5.00----7.00
2419½	Footed Cream	5.00----7.00
*2419	Tea Sugar	4.00----6.00
	Also made in Eb-Wis	
*2419	Tea Cream	4.00----6.00
	Also made in Eb-Wis	
2419	Shaker (also made in Eb.)	4.00----6.00
2419	Syrup & Cover	10.00--16.00
2419	Syrup Saucer	2.00----4.00
*2419	Ash Tray	6.00----9.00
	Also made in Eb-Wis-Ruby	
2419	6 oz. Oil, G/S	15.00--18.00
2419	4 Part Relish	5.00--10.00
	Also made in Ebony, Ruby	
2419	5 Part Relish	8.00--12.00
2419	Condiment Tray	4.00----6.00
2419	Handled Lunch Tray	6.00--10.00
	Also made in Ebony	
2419	6" Comport	6.00--10.00
	Also made in Ebony	
2419	Jelly, 2 Handles	3.00----5.00
	Also made in Ebony	
2419	Mayonnaise, 2 Handles	3.00----4.00
2419	Bon Bon, 2 Handles	3.00----5.00
	Also made in Wisteria	
2419	Lemon Dish, 2 Handles	3.00----4.00
	Also made in Wisteria	
2419	Cake Plate, 2 Hdl.	5.00----8.00
	Also made in Eb-Wis	

Made in Empire Green, Burgundy and Regal Blue

No. 2433 LINE
Made in Solid Crystal, also Am-Gr-Eb Foot—Crystal Bowl—Made in Rose, Topaz, Azure Bowl —Crystal Foot

2433	6" Low Comport	6.00----9.00
2433	6" Tall Comport	8.00--12.00
2433	3" Candlestick	5.00----7.00
2433	12" Bowl A	15.00--20.00

BOWLS CANDLESTICKS & VASE

2433	7½" Bowl D	15.00--20.00
2430	9½" Candlestick	10.00--15.00
	Ro-Az-Gr-Am-Eb-Crys-Tz.	
2430	8" Vase, Ro-Az-Gr-Am-Eb-Crys-Tz.	8.00--12.00

TABLEWARE

2236	Shaker, Ro-Gr-Am-Tz.	2.00----4.00
4101	6½ oz. Sherbet, Ro-Az-Gr-Am-Tz.	2.00----3.00
4101	13 oz. Ice Tea, Ro-Az-Gr-Am-Tz.	3.00----5.00
2083	Salad Dressing Bottle, Ro-Az-Gr-Am-Crys-Tz.	12.00--16.00
4020	Cream, Crys.	2.00----4.00

4220	Cream, Ro-Tz.	3.00----5.00
4120	Cream, Gr-Am-Eb.	3.00----6.00
4020	Sugar, Crystal	2.00----4.00
4220	Sugar, Ro-Tz.	3.00----5.00
4120	Sugar, Gr-Am-Eb.	3.00----6.00
2439	Decanter, Ro-Az-Gr-Am-Crys-Tz.	12.00--18.00
2436	9" Lustre, Ro-Gr-Am-Crys-Eb-Tz., Made with Tear Drops or U.D. Prisms	25.00--35.00
5088	8½" Bud Vase, Eb-Crys.	4.00----6.00
5188	8½" Bud Vase, Gr-Am-Eb.	6.00----8.00
2428	6" Vase, Ro-Gr-Am-Eb-Tz.	4.00----7.00
4101	5½" Vase, Ro-Gr-Am-Tz-Wis.	4.00----6.00
2428	13" Vase, Ro-Gr-Am-Eb-Tz-Wis.	12.00--15.00
2428	9" Vase, Ro-Gr-Am-Eb-Tz-Wis.	9.00--12.00

LAFAYETTE PATTERN
No. 2440 DINNERWARE
Made in Crystal, Topaz & Wisteria

2440	6", 7", 8", 9", 10" Plate	1.00----6.00
2440	5" Fruit	1.00----3.00
2440	6" Cereal	2.00----4.00
2440	Cup	2.00----5.00
	Also made in RB-Bur-Emp.	
2440	Saucer	1.00----3.00
	Also made in RB-Bur-Emp.	
2440	After Dinner Cup	2.00----5.00
2440	After Dinner Saucer	1.00----2.00
2440	Crm. Soup (Not made in Tz)	2.00----5.00
2440	10" Oval Baker	6.00--10.00
2440	8" Round Nappy	6.00----9.00
2440	12" Platter	6.00----9.00
2440	11½" Celery	6.00----8.00
	Also made in Ro-Gr-Am.	
2440	8½" Pickle	3.00----5.00
	Also made in Ro-Gr-Am.	
2440	6½" Olive	2.00----4.00
	Also made in Ro-Gr-Am.	
2440	Individual Almond	2.00----3.00
	Also made in Ro-Gr-Am.	
2440	Footed Sugar	3.00----8.00
	Also made in Ro-Gr-Am-RB-Bur-Emp.	
2440	Footed Cream	3.00----8.00
	Also made in Ro-Gr-Am-RB-Bur-Emp.	
2440	13" Torte Plate,	10.00--20.00
	Also made in Ro-Gr-Am-RB-Bur-Emp.	
2440	4½" Hld. Sweetmeat	2.00----5.00
	Ro-Gr-Am-Crys-RB-Bur-Emp-Tz-Wis.	
2440	5" Hld. Bon Bon	2.00----5.00
	Ro-Gr-Am-Crys-RB-Bur-Emp-Tz-Wis.	
2440	5" Hld. Lemon	2.00----5.00
	Ro-Gr-Am-Crys-RB-Bur-Emp-Tz-Wis.	
2440	10½" Oval Cake Plate	6.00--10.00
	Ro-Gr-Am-Crys-RB-Bur-Emp-Tz.	
2440	8½" Oval Tray	4.00----8.00
	Ro-Gr-Am-Crys-Tz-Wis-RB-Bur-Emp.	
2440	6½" Oval Sauce Dish	2.00----6.00
	Ro-Gr-Am-Crys-Tz-Wis-RB-Bur-Emp.	
2440	6½" 2 Part Mayonnaise	3.00----7.00
	Ro-Gr-Am-Crys-Tz-Wis-RB-Bur-Emp.	
2440	2 Part Hld. Relish	3.00----6.00
	Ro-Gr-Am-Crys-Tz-Wis-RB-Bur-Emp.	
2440	3 Part Hld. Relish	5.00----9.00
	Ro-Gr-Am-Crys-Tz-Wis-RB-Bur-Emp.	

2440 7" Bowl "D" 7.00--10.00
Also made in Ro-Gr-Am.
2440 10" Bowl "B" 8.00--12.00
Also made in Ro-Gr-Am.
2440 12" Salad Bowl 9.00--14.00
Also made in Ro-Gr-Am.
2440 7" Vase 5.00----8.00
Also made in Ro-Gr-Am. — Not made in Wis.

HERMITAGE PATTERN, No. 2449 LINE
Made in Azure, Green, Amber, Crystal, Topaz and Wisteria

2449 9 oz. Goblet 5.00----9.00
2449 5½ oz. High Sherbet . . 4.00----8.00
2449 7 oz. Low Sherbet . . . 2.00----5.00
2449 5 oz. Fruit Cocktail 2.00----4.00
2449 4 oz. Cocktail 4.00----8.00
2449 4 oz. Claret 4.00----8.00
Not made in Az-Wis.
2449 2, 5, 9, 12 oz. Ftd. Tumb. 4.00----8.00
Not made in Az-Wis.
2449 9 oz. Ftd. Beer Mug 4.00----8.00
Made in Crys. only
2449 12 oz. Ftd. Beer Mug . . 3.00----5.00
Made in Crys. only
2449½—2, 5, 9, 13 oz. Tumbler 3.00----7.00
2449½—6 oz. Old Fash. Cocktail 3.00----6.00
2449½—Finger Bowl 2.00----3.00
2449 Coaster 2.00----3.00
2449½—6", 7", 8", 9" Plates . . 2.00----5.00
2449 8" Luncheon Plate . . . 2.00----4.00
2449 12" Sandwich Plate 6.00--10.00
Not made in Az-Wis.
2449 Crescent Salad Plate . . 3.00----5.00
2449½—Crescent Salad Plate . . 3.00----4.00
Made in Crys. only
2449½—6½" Coupe Salad 3.00----4.00
2449½—7½" Coupe Salad 3.00----5.00
2449½—5" Fruit 3.00----4.00
2449½—6" Cereal 3.00----4.00
2449½—7" Soup 2.00----4.00
Not made in Gr-Wis.
2449 Footed Cup 2.00----5.00
2449 Saucer 1.00----3.00
2449 8" Pickle 3.00----5.00
2449 11" Celery 4.00----6.00
2449 Ftd. Sugar 2.00----5.00
2449 Ftd. Cream 2.00----5.00
2449 Shaker 3.00----5.00
2449 3 Part Relish 4.00----6.00
Not made in Azure
2449 2 Part Relish 3.00----5.00
Not made in Azure
2449½—7" Nappy 2.00----4.00
Not made in Gr-Wis.
2449 6" Comport 4.00----7.00
2449 Mayonnaise 3.00----4.00
Not made in Az-Wis.
2449 7" Mayonnaise Plate . . 1.00----3.00
Not made in Az-Wis.
2449 Individual Salt 2.00----3.00
Not made in Az-Wis.
2449 Condiment Tray 3.00----5.00
Not made in Az-Wis.
2449 3 oz. Oil 8.00--12.00
Not made in Az-Wis.
2449 Mustard & Cover 5.00----8.00
Not made in Az-Wis.

2449 Mustard Spoon 1.00----2.00
Made in Crystal only
2449 Ice Dish 2.00----4.00
2449 7" Ice Dish Plate 2.00----3.00
2449 Grape Fruit 2.00----4.00
Not made in Az-Wis.
2449 Grape Fruit Liner 1.00----2.00
Made in Crystal only
2449 Pint Cereal Pitcher 6.00----9.00
2449 3 Pint Ftd. Jug 15.00--18.00
2449 Hall Boy Jug 8.00--12.00
Not made in Azure
2449 Qt. Ice Jug (Lipped) . . 12.00--15.00
Not made in Azure
2449 Bar Bottle & Stopper . . 10.00--15.00
Made in Crystal only
2449 Decanter & Stopper 10.00--20.00
2449 Ice Tub 6.00--10.00
2449 Ash Tray Set 4.00----8.00
Not made in Wisteria
2449 Ash Tray (Also made in Eb.) 2.00----3.00
Not made in Wisteria
2449 11" Salver 8.00--12.00
2449 10" Bowl, Flared 7.00----9.00
Not made in Az-Wis.
2449 10" Bowl, Shallow 7.00----9.00
2449 8" Deep Bowl 8.00--10.00
2449 6" Candlestick 5.00----9.00
2449 6" Vase 5.00----8.00
Not made in Az-Wis.

No. 2470 LINE

2470 Sugar & Cream Tray . . 2.00----4.00
Ro-Gr-Am-Crys-Tz.
2470 9" Service Dish 6.00---8.00
Ro-Gr-Am-Crys-Tz.
2470 9¾" Round Tray 7.00--10.00
Ro-Gr-Am-Eb-Tz.
2470 3 Part Round Relish . . 5.00----8.00
Ro-Gr-Am-Crys-Tz.
2470 4 Part Oval Relish 6.00---8.00
Ro-Gr-Am-Crys-Tz.
2470 10" Cake Plate 5.00----8.00
Ro-Gr-Am-Crys-Tz.
2470 Lemon Dish, 2 Hdles. . . 2.00----4.00
Ro-Gr-Am-Crys-Tz.
2470 Bon Bon, 2 Hdles. 2.00----4.00
Ro-Gr-Am-Crys-Tz.
2470 Sweetmeat, 2 Hdles. . . 2.00----4.00
Ro-Gr-Am-Crys-Tz.
2470 6" Tall Comport—Solid 5.00----7.00
Crystal—Gr-Am-Wis. Base w/Crystal
Bowl—Crystal Base w/Ro-Tz-Bowl
2470 6" Low Comport—Solid 3.00----5.00
Crystal—Gr-Am-Wis. Base w/Crystal
Bowl—Crystal Base w/Ro-Tz-Bowl
2470 12" Bowl—Solid Crystal . 10.00--15.00
Gr-Am-Wis. Base w/Crystal Bowl
Crystal Base w/RO-Tz-Bowl
2470 5½" Candlestick—Solid 6.00----9.00
Crystal—Gr-Am-Wis. Base w/Crystal
Bowl—Crystal Base w/Ro-Tz-Bowl
2470½—10½" Bowl 10.00--20.00
Ro-Gr-Am-Crys-Tz-Wis-Ruby
2470½—5½" Candlestick 5.00--10.00
Ro-Gr-Am-Crys-Tz-Wis-Ruby
2470½—7" Bowl 4.00----8.00
Ro-Gr-Am-Crys-Tz-Wis.

2470	8″, 10″ Vase	10.00--15.00
	RB-Bur-Emp-Ruby	
2470	11½″ Vase	12.00--18.00
	Solid Crystal—Colored Bowl	

BOWLS & CANDLESTICKS

4024	6″ Candlestick	5.00----9.00
4024	10½″ Footed Bowl	10.00--15.00
	Height 4-1/8″	
2533	Duo Candlestick	9.00--15.00
	Height 6¼″ Spread 6½″	
	to make 2533 2 light	
	Candelabra with 16 U.D.P.	
	use No. 2527 Bobache	
2533	9″ Handled Bowl	12.00--18.00
	Height 4-5/8″	
2472	Duo Candlestick	9.00--15.00
	use with 2470½, 10½″ bowl	
	Height 4-7/8″ Spread 8″	
2482	Trindle Candlestick	10.00--18.00
	use with 2470½ 10½″ Bowl	
	Height 6¾″ Spread 8¼″	
2447	Duo Candlestick	5.00--10.00
	Height 5″ Spread 6½″	

BAROQUE PATTERN No. 2496 LINE
Made in Crystal, Gold Tint and Azure
Except as Noted
STEMWARE

2496	9 oz. Goblet	7.00--10.00
2496	5 oz. Sherbet	4.00----6.00
2496	12 oz. Footed Tumbler	5.00----8.00
2496	9 oz. Footed Tumbler	5.00----8.00
2496½	5, 9, 14 oz. Tumbler	4.00----8.00
2496½	7 oz. Old Fash. Cocktail	5.00 ---8.00
2496	Footed Cocktail	5.00----8.00
2496	3 Pint Jug	20.00--35.00
	(Not Made in AZ-GT)	
2496	Ice Jug, 3 Pint	20.00--35.00

DINNERWARE

2496	Footed Cup	3.00----5.00
2496	Saucer	2.00----3.00
2496	6″, 7″, 8″, 9″ Plate	2.00----8.00
2496	5″ Fruit	2.00----3.00
2496	Cream Soup	3.00----5.00
2496	Cream Soup Plate	2.00----3.00
2496	12″ Oval Platter	12.00--15.00
2496	9½″ Vegetable Dish	10.00--15.00
2496	11″ Oval Tray	8.00--12.00
2496	Shaker, F.G.T.	4.00----6.00
2496½	Individual Shaker, F.G.T.	4.00----6.00
2496	8″ Pickle	4.00----6.00
2496	11″ Celery	6.00----9.00
2496	Footed Sugar	5.00----8.00
2496	Footed Cream	5.00----8.00
2496	Individual Sugar	5.00----8.00
2496	Individual Cream	5.00----8.00
1496	3½ oz. Oil, Crys. Stopper	15.00--20.00
2496	Mustard & Cover & Spoon	8.00--12.00
2496	Mustard & Cover	7.00--10.00
2496	Mustard Spoon	1.00----2.00
2496½	Mayonnaise & Plate & Ldl.	10.00--15.00
2496½	Mayonnaise	6.00----9.00
2496	Mayonnaise Plate	2.00----4.00
2496	Mayonnaise Ladle	1.00----2.00
2496½	6½″ Sugar & Cream Tray	4.00----6.00
2496	3 pc. Ind. Sugar & Cm. Set	18.00--22.00
	Consisting of—	
	2496 Individual Sugar	
	2496 Individual Cream	
	2496½—6½″ Sugar & Cream Tray	
2496	4 pc. Condiment Set	20.00--25.00
	Consisting of—	
	2496½—Sugar & Cream Tray	
	2496 Mustard & Cover & Spoon	
	2496 Shaker, F.G.T.	

BUFFET and RELISH DISHES

2496	14″ Torte Plate	15.00--20.00
2496	2-Part Relish	5.00----8.00
2496	3-Part Relish	8.00--10.00
2496	4-Part Relish	8.00--12.00
2496	Cheese & Cracker	12.00--18.00
2496	Footed Cheese	4.00----6.00
2496	Cracker Plate	8.00--12.00
2496	10½″ Salad Bowl	10.00--14.00
2496	3 pc. Salad Set	25.00--35.00
	Consisting of—	
	2496 10½″ Salad Bowl	
	2496 14″ Torte Plate	
	2496 Salad Fork & Spoon (Wd.)	

NOVELTY ITEMS

2496	Ice Bucket (Metal Handle)	15.00--20.00
2496	Ice Tongs (Metal)	2.00----3.00
2496	Ftd. Punch Bowl, 1½ Gal.	30.00--45.00
2496	6 oz. Punch Cup	2.00----4.00
2496	Handled Nappy, Regular	3.00----5.00
2496	Handled Nappy, Flared	3.00----5.00
2496	Handled Nappy, Square	3.00----5.00
2496	Handled Nappy, 3-Corner	3.00----5.00
2496	3-Toed Bon Bon	3.00----5.00
2496	3-Toed Tid Bit, Flat	3.00----5.00
2496	3-Toed Nut Bowl, Cupped	3.00----5.00
2496	Jelly	4.00----7.00
2496	Jelly & Cover	10.00--18.00
2496	Preserve & Cover	12.00--20.00
2496	5½″ Comport	12.00--16.00
2496½	6½″ Tall Comport	15.00--18.00
2496	Handled Mint	3.00----5.00
2496	Sweetmeat	4.00----6.00
2496	8″ Oblong Tray	3.00----5.00
2496	6½″ Oblong Sauce Dish	6.00----9.00
2496	6½″ 2-part Mayonnaise	4.00----7.00
2496	10″ Cake Plate (2 Handles)	8.00--10.00
2496	8½″ Serving Dish (2 Hdls)	7.00----9.00
2496	3-Part Candy Box & Cover	15.00--25.00
2496	Cigarette Box & Cover	6.00----9.00
2496	Oblong Ash Tray	1.00----2.00
2496	5-pc. Smoker Set	12.00--20.00
	Consisting of—	
	2496 Cigarette Box & Cover	
	2496 Oblong Ash Tray	

BOWLS and CANDLESTICKS

2496	10″ Floating Garden	6.00--10.00
2496	10½″ Handled Bowl	15.00--20.00
2496	12″ Bowl, Flared	10.00--14.00
2496	11″ Bowl, Rolled Edge	10.00--15.00
2496	7″ Bowl, Cupped	8.00--12.00
2484	10″ Hld. Bowl	12.00--20.00
	(Also Made in Gr-Am-Tz.)	

2496	4" Candlestick	4.00----7.00
2496	5½" Candlestick	4.00----6.00
2496	Duo Candlestick	6.00----9.00
2496	Trindle Candlestick	8.00--12.00
	(Also made in Gr-Am-Bur-Emp-Tz-Ruby)	
2484	Lustre, U.D.P.	15.00--25.00
2484	2-Lt. Candelabra, U.D.P.	25.00--40.00
	(Also made in Topaz)	
2484	3-Lt. Candelabra, U.D.P.	35.00--50.00

VASES

2484	7" Vase	6.00----9.00
2496	8" Vase	8.00--12.00
2496	3½" Rose Bowl	4.00----7.00

ROSETTE DESIGN No. 2501 LINE
Made in Crystal Intaglio

2501	7" Plate	4.00----6.00
2501	8" Plate	5.00----8.00
2501	13" Torte Plate	9.00--12.00
2501	Oval Cake Plate	9.00--12.00
2501	Cigarette Box & Cover	6.00----9.00
2501	Ind. Ash Tray	1.00----2.00
2501	Lge. Ash Tray	2.00----3.00
2496	14" Torte Plate	10.00--14.00
2496	7" Plate	4.00----6.00
2496	Oblong Ash Tray	1.00----2.00
2510½	Individual Ash Tray	1.00----2.00
2510	Sugar & Cream Tray	3.00----5.00

SUN-RAY PATTERN No. 2510 LINE
Made in Crystal, except as noted

STEMWARE

2510	Goblet	5.00----8.00
	(Also made in Az-Gr-Am-Tz)	
2510	Low Sherbet	2.00----4.00
	(Also made in Az-Gr-Am-Tz)	
2510	3½ oz. Fruit Cocktail	2.00----4.00
2510	4½ oz. Claret	5.00----7.00
2510	4 oz. Ftd. Cocktail	3.00----5.00
2510	13 oz. Ftd. Tumbler	4.00----6.00
2510	Ftd. Table Tumbler	5.00----8.00
	(Also made in Az-Gr-Am-Tz)	
2510	5 oz. Ftd. Tumbler	3.00----5.00
2510½	5, 9, 13 oz. Tumbler	2.00----4.00
2510½	6 oz. O. F. Cocktail	2.00----4.00
2510½	2 oz. Whiskey	2.00----4.00
2510	2 Qt. Jug	12.00--18.00
2510	Ice Jug	12.00--18.00
2510	Pint Cereal Pitcher	8.00--12.00
2510	Coaster	2.00----3.00

DINNERWARE

2510	Cup	2.00----3.00
2510	Saucer	1.00----2.00
2510	6", 7", 8", 9" Plate	2.00----4.00
2510	5" Fruit	2.00----3.00
2510	Frozen Dessert	2.00----4.00
	(Also made in Az-Gr-Am-Tz)	
2510	Onion Soup & Cover	9.00--12.00
2510	Cream Soup	2.00----4.00
2510	Cream Soup Plate	1.00----2.00
2510	Shaker, F.G.T.	2.00----3.00
2510½	Individual Shaker, F.G.T.	2.00----3.00

2510	Salt Dip	2.00----3.00
*2510	Pickle, Handled	3.00----6.00
2510	Celery, Handled	3.00----5.00
2510	Footed Sugar	3.00----5.00
2510	Footed Cream	3.00----5.00
2510	Individual Sugar	2.00----4.00
2510	Individual Cream	2.00----4.00
2510	Sugar & Cream Tray	2.00----4.00
2510	3 oz. Oil & Stopper	10.00--15.00
2510	Mustard & Cover & Spoon	8.00--12.00
2510	Mayonnaise	3.00----5.00
2510	Mayonnaise Plate	1.00----3.00
2510	Mayonnaise Ladle (2375)	1.00----2.00
2510	Mayo. & Plate & Ladle	8.00--10.00
2510	9½" Flared Nappy	6.00----9.00
2510	3 pc. Sugar & Cream Set	10.00--15.00
	Consisting of—	
	2510 Ind. Sugar	
	2510 Ind. Cream	
	2510 Sugar & Cream Tray	
2510	Cheese & Cov. or But. & Cov.	10.00--15.00
2510	Cheese or Butter Cov. only	8.00--10.00
2510	Cheese or Butter Tray	3.00----5.00
*2510	Ice Bucket, No Handle	10.00--15.00
2510	15" Torte Plate & Comport	15.00--22.00

BUFFET and RELISH DISHES

*2510	11" Torte Plate	6.00--10.00
2510	15" Torte Plate	10.00--15.00
*2510	12" Sandwich Plate	10.00--15.00
*2510	16" Flat Plate	12.00--18.00
*2510	2-Part Relish	5.00--10.00
*2510	3-Part Relish	5.00--10.00
*2510	4-Part Relish	8.00--12.00
2510	8½" Condiment Tray	6.00----9.00
2510	5 pc. Condiment Set	40.00--60.00
2510	12" Salad Bowl	10.00--15.00
2510	Salad Fork & Spoon (wood)	1.00----2.00
2510	3 pc. Salad Set	20.00--30.00
	Consisting of—	
	2510 12" Salad Bowl	
	2510 16" Flat Plate	
	2510 Salad Fork & Spoon (wood)	

NOVELTY ITEMS

*2510	Ice Bucket, Chrom. Hdle.	12.00--18.00
2510	Ice Tongs, Chrom.	1.00----2.00
*2510	Hld. Nappy, Reg.	4.00----7.00
*2510	Hld. Nappy, Fld.	4.00----7.00
*2510	Hld. Nappy, Sq.	4.00----7.00
*2510	Hld. Nappy, 3 Cor.	4.00----7.00
*2510	3 Toed Bon Bon	4.00----7.00
*2510	Bon Bon, Hld.	4.00----7.00
*2510	Oval Tray, Hld.	4.00----7.00
*2510	Divided Sweetmeat, Hld.	5.00----8.00
*2510	Ftd. Individual Almond	3.00----5.00
2510	Jelly & Cover	8.00--12.00
2510	Jelly	5.00----8.00
2510	Comport	5.00----7.00
2510	Candy Jar & Cover	9.00--12.00
2510	18 oz. Decanter & Stopper	15.00--20.00
2510	10½" Oblong Tray	4.00----6.00
2510	10" Square Tray	5.00----8.00
2510	Cigarette & Cover	6.00----9.00
2510	Square Ash Tray	2.00----3.00

Made in Ruby

2510½—Individual Ash Tray . . 2.00----3.00
2510 5 pc. Smoker Set 12.00--18.00
    Consisting of—
        2510 Cigarette & Cover
        2510 Square Ash Tray
2510½—5 pc. Smoker Set 12.00--18.00
    Consisting of—
        2510 Cigarette & Cover
        2510½—Ind. Ash Tray
2510 No. 3 Smoker Set 15.00--20.00
    Consisting of—
        2510 Sugar & Cream Tray
        2510 Cigarette & Cover
        2510 Square Ash Tray
2510 8 pc. Decanter Set 25.00--35.00
    Consisting of—
        2510 Decanter & Stopper
        2510½—2 oz. Whiskey
        2510 10½'' Oblong Tray

BOWLS AND CANDLESTICKS

2510 13'' Bowl, R.E. 10.00--15.00
2510 Hld. Bowl 10.00--15.00
2510 2 Light Candelabra, U.D.P. 25.00--35.00
2510 Duo Candlestick 9.00--12.00
2510 5½'' Candlestick 6.00----9.00
2510 3'' Candlestick 5.00----8.00

VASES

2510 3½'' Rose Bowl 2.00----4.00
2510 5'' Rose Bowl 4.00----6.00
2510 6'' Vase, Crimped . . . 6.00----8.00
2510 7'' Vase 7.00--10.00
2510 9'' Square Ftd. Vase . . 10.00--15.00
2510 Sweetpea Vase 6.00----9.00
2510½—Oblg. Decanter & Stop.
      26 oz. 15.00--20.00
2510½—Oblong Cigarette Box . . 6.00----9.00

GLACIER DESIGN
2510 LINE WITH RIBS IN SILVER MIST
STEMWARE

2510 9 oz. Goblet 5.00----8.00
2510 5 oz. Low Sherbet . . . 2.00----4.00
2510 3 oz. Fruit Cocktail . . . 2.00----4.00
2510 4½ oz. Claret 3.00----5.00
2510 4 oz. Ftd. Cocktail . . . 3.00----5.00
2510 13 oz. Ftd. Tumbler . . 4.00----6.00
2510 Ftd. Table Tumbler . . . 5.00----8.00
2510 5 oz. Ftd. Tumbler . . . 3.00----5.00
2510½—5, 9, 13 oz. Tumbler . . 2.00----4.00
2510½—6 oz. O. F. Cocktail . . 2.00----4.00
2510½—2 oz. Whiskey 2.00----4.00
2510 2 Qt. Jug 12.00--18.00
2510 Ice Jug 12.00--18.00

DINNERWARE

2510 Cup 2.00----3.00
2510 Saucer 1.00----2.00
2510 6'', 7'', 8'', 9'' Plate . . . 2.00----4.00
2510 5'' Fruit 1.00----3.00
2510 Frozen Dessert 2.00----4.00
2510 Onion Soup & Cover . . 9.00--12.00
2510 Cream Soup 2.00----4.00
2510 Cream Soup Plate . . . 1.00----2.00
2510 Shaker, F.G.T. 2.00----3.00
2510½—Individual Shaker, F.G.T. 2.00----3.00

2510 Salt Dip 2.00----4.00
2510 Pickle, Handled 3.00----5.00
2510 Celery, Handled 3.00----5.00
2510 Footed Sugar 3.00----5.00
2510 Footed Cream 3.00----5.00
2510 Individual Sugar 2.00----4.00
2510 Individual Cream 2.00----4.00
2510 6½'' Sugar & Cream Tray 2.00----4.00
2510 3 oz. Oil & Stopper 10.00--15.00
2510 Mustard & Cover & Spoon 8.00--12.00
2510 Mayonnaise & Plate & Ldl. 8.00--10.00
2510 Mayonnaise 3.00----5.00
2510 Mayonnaise Plate 1.00----3.00
2510 Mayo. Ladle (2375-Crys.) 1.00----2.00
2510 3 pc. Sugar & Cream Set 10.00--15.00
    Consisting of—
        2510 Ind. Sugar
        2510 Ind. Cream
        2510 Sugar & Cream Tray
2510 Cheese or Butter Tray . . 3.00----5.00

VASES

2510 3½'' Rose Bowl 2.00----4.00
2510 5'' Rose Bowl 4.00----6.00
2510 6'' Vase 6.00----8.00
2510 7'' Vase 7.00--10.00
2510 9'' Sq. Ftd. Vase 10.00--15.00
2510 Sweetpea Vase 6.00----9.00

BUFFET AND RELISH DISHES

2510 11'' Torte Plate 6.00----9.00
2510 15'' Torte Plate 10.00--15.00
2510 12'' Sandwich Plate 10.00--12.00
2510 16'' Flat Plate 12.00--16.00
2510 2, 3, & 4 Part Relishes . . 5.00--10.00
2510 12'' Salad Bowl 10.00--15.00
2510 3 Piece Salad Set 20.00--30.00
    Consisting of—
        2510 12'' Salad Bowl
        2510 16'' Flat Plate
        2510 Salad Fork & Spoon (wood)

NOVELTY ITEMS

2510 Ice Bucket, Chrom. Hdle. 12.00--16.00
2510 Ice Tongs, Chrom. 1.00----2.00
2510 Handled Nappy, Reg. . . 4.00----6.00
2510 Handled Nappy, Flared . . 4.00----6.00
2510 Handled Nappy, Square . 4.00----6.00
2510 Handled Nappy, 3-Cor. . . 4.00----6.00
2510 Bon Bon, Handled 4.00----6.00
2510 Oval Tray, Handled 4.00----6.00
2510 Divided Sweetmeat, Hdld. 4.00----6.00
2510 Jelly & Cover 8.00--12.00
2510 Jelly 5.00----8.00
2510 Comport 5.00----7.00
2510 Candy Jar & Cover 9.00--12.00
2510 10½'' Oblong Tray 4.00----6.00
2510 10'' Square Tray 5.00----8.00
2510 18 oz. Decanter & Stopper 15.00--20.00
2510 Cigarette & Cover 6.00----9.00
2510 Square Ash Tray 2.00----3.00
2510 Individual Ash Tray 2.00----3.00
2510 5 pc. Smoker Set 12.00--18.00
    Consisting of—
        2510 Cigarette & Cover
        2510 Square Ash Tray
2510½—5 pc. Smoker Set 12.00--18.00
    Consisting of—
        2510 Cigarette & Cover
        2510½—Ind. Ash Tray

2510	No. 3 Smoker Set . . .	15.00--20.00
	Consisting of—	
	2510 Sugar & Cream Tray	
	2510 Cigarette & Cover	
	2510 Square Ash Tray	
2510½—Oblg. Cigarette Box & Cov		6.00----9.00

BOWLS AND CANDLESTICKS

2510	13" Bowl, R.E.	10.00--15.00
2510	Hld. Bowl	10.00--15.00
2510	Duo Candlestick	9.00--12.00
2510	2 Lt. Candelabra . . .	25.00--35.00
2510	5½" Candlestick	6.00----9.00
2510	3" Candlestick	5.00----8.00

FROSTED STEM No. 6011 LINE

6011	10 oz. Goblet	4.00----6.00
6011	5½ oz. Saucer Champ. . .	4.00----6.00
6011	5½ oz. Low Sherbet . .	3.00----4.00
6011	4½ oz. Rhine Wine	4.00----6.00
6011	3 oz. Cocktail	4.00----6.00
6011	4½ oz. Claret	4.00----6.00
6011	3 oz. Wine	4.00----6.00
6011	2 oz. Sherry	4.00----6.00
6011	1 oz. Cordial	4.00----6.00
6011	1 oz. Brandy	4.00----6.00
6011	4 oz. Oyster Cocktail . .	4.00----6.00
6011	2, 5, 10, 13 oz. Ftd. Tumb.	4.00----6.00

SILVER MIST

Made in Crystal Glass with a Soft Smooth Finish

STEMWARE

4024½—11 oz. Goblet		5.00----8.00
4024	10 oz. Goblet	4.00----7.00
4024	6 oz. Saucer Champagne	3.00----5.00
4024	5½ oz. Sherbet	2.00----3.00
4024	4 oz. Cocktail	5.00----8.00
4024	3½ oz. Rhine Wine	5.00----8.00
4024	3½ oz. Claret	5.00----8.00
4024	2 oz. Sherry	5.00----8.00
4024	1 oz. Cordial	5.00----8.00
4024	4 oz. Oyster Cocktail . .	5.00----7.00
4024	5, 8, 12 oz. Ftd. Tumbler	4.00----6.00
4024	2 oz. Footed Whiskey . .	4.00----6.00
701	10, 12 oz. Tumb., Sham. Pl.	2.00----3.00
1184	7 oz. O.F. Cocktail, Sham.,	
	Plain	1.00----2.00
887	1¾ oz. Whiskey, Optic . .	1.00----2.00

PLATES
Made with Silver Mist Rim Only

2510	6" Plate	1.00----2.00
2510	7" Plate	1.00----3.00
2510	8" Plate	2.00----4.00

MISCELLANEOUS TABLEWARE

2419	5 Part Relish	8.00--10.00
2419	4 Part Relish	6.00----8.00
2440	8½" Oval Tray	4.00----6.00
2440	6½" Oval Sauce Dish . .	3.00----5.00
2440	6½" 2 Pt. Mayonnaise . .	4.00----6.00
2440	2 Part Handled Relish . .	3.00----5.00
2440	3 Part Handled Relish . .	4.00----6.00
2497	Seafood Cocktail	8.00--12.00
2497½—Sugar		5.00----8.00

2497½—Cream		5.00----8.00
2513	Mayonnaise and Ladle . .	7.00--10.00
2513	Mayonnaise	6.00----9.00
2513	Mayonnaise Ladle, Plain	1.00----2.00
2513	2 Part Relish	4.00----6.00
2513	3 Part Relish	5.00----8.00
2513	4" Handled Mint	3.00----5.00
2513	5" Handled Preserve . .	3.00----5.00
2517	Bon Bon	3.00----5.00
2517	Sweetmeat	3.00----5.00
2517	Lemon	3.00----5.00
2518	Jug	15.00--20.00
2518	10 oz. Tumbler	2.00----3.00
2518	3 oz. Ftd. Cocktail . . .	2.00----4.00
2519	Puff & Cover	8.00--10.00
2519	Cologne & Stopper	9.00--12.00
2521	Bird	10.00--15.00
2531	Penguin	30.00--40.00
2531	Pelican	30.00--40.00
2531	Seal	35.00--45.00
2531	Polar Bear	35.00--45.00
2538	11" Nappy	10.00--14.00
2538	6" Nappy	2.00----3.00
2538	4½" Nappy	2.00----3.00
2538	9 Piece Salad Set . . .	20.00--30.00
	Consisting of—	
	2538 11" Nappy	
	2538 6" Nappy	
2538	9 Piece Berry Set	20.00--30.00
	Consisting of—	
	2538 11" Nappy	
	2538 4½" Nappy	
4099	Candy Jar & Cover	10.00--15.00

SMOKING ACCESSORIES

2391	Large Cigarette Box & Cov.	6.00----9.00
2419	Ash Tray	2.00----3.00
2520	Ash Tray	2.00----3.00
2457	Ash Tray	3.00----4.00
2534	Ash Tray	4.00----6.00
5092	Cigarette	5.00----7.00

LIQUOR ITEMS

2494	Decanter	15.00--20.00
2494	Cordial Bottle	10.00--15.00
2494	Bitters Bottle	8.00--12.00
2429	Cordial Tray	10.00--14.00
2518	Decanter	15.00--20.00
2518	Cocktail Shaker, Gold Top	20.00--25.00
2518½—Cocktail Shaker, Gd. Top		20.00--25.00
2518	3 oz. Ftd. Cocktail . . .	1.00----3.00
2518	5 oz. Wine	1.00----2.00
2518	2 oz. Whiskey	1.00----3.00
2525	Cocktail Shaker, Gold Top	20.00--25.00
2525½—Cocktail Shaker, Gd. Top		20.00--25.00
2502	Decanter & Stopper	15.00--20.00
2502	Whiskey	1.00----2.00
2503	Wine Jug	12.00--16.00
2492	Fish Canape	8.00--12.00
4115½—4 oz. Ftd. Cocktail . .		2.00----4.00
4024	Sherry	5.00----8.00
4024	Cordial	5.00----8.00
887	1¾ oz. Whiskey, Optic . .	1.00----2.00

BOWLS AND CANDLESTICKS

2472	Duo Candlestick	8.00--10.00
2484	2 Lt. Candlestick, only . .	12.00--18.00
2484	2 Lt. Candle & Drips . .	15.00--20.00

2484½ 3½'' Candle Drips 2.00----4.00
2484 10'' Handled Bowl 12.00--16.00
2496 Trindle Candlestick 10.00--12.00
2496 Duo Candlestick 10.00--12.00
2536 9'' Handled Bowl 8.00--10.00
2535 5½'' Candlestick 6.00----9.00
4024 10'' Ftd. Bowl 12.00--18.00
4024 6'' Candlestick 7.00----9.00

VASES

2404 6'' Vase 8.00--12.00
2428 9'' Vase 7.00--10.00
2428 13'' Vase 8.00--12.00
2489 5½'' Vase 8.00--10.00
2522 8'' Vase 6.00----9.00
2523 6½'' Vase 6.00----9.00
4103 4'' Vase 3.00----5.00
4110 7½'' Vase 6.00----8.00
4129 2½'' Bubble Ball 2.00----4.00
4116 4'', 5'', 6'', 7'', 8'', 9'' Bubble
         Ball 5.00--15.00
5088 8'' Bud Vase 8.00--12.00
5091 6½'' Bud Vase 6.00----8.00

SPOOL PATTERN No. 2550 LINE

2550 Sweetmeat 2.00----4.00
2550 Mayonnaise & Plate & Ldl. 5.00----8.00
2550 Mayonnaise 3.00----4.00
2550 Mayonnaise Plate   . . . 2.00----4.00
2550 Mayonnaise Ladle   . . . 1.00----2.00
2550 6'' Low Comport   . . . 3.00----5.00
2550 6½'' Nappy 2.00----3.00
2550 14'' Buffet Plate 8.00--12.00
2550 Cigarette & Cover   . . . 5.00----8.00
2550½ Oblg. Cigarette Box & Cov. 5.00----8.00
2550 Round Ash Tray 1.00----2.00
2550½ Ind. Ash Tray 1.00----2.00
2550½ Medium Ash Tray 1.00----2.00
2550½ 5½'' Large Ash Tray . . 2.00----3.00
2550½ 3 pc. Ash Tray Set, S. C. 5.00----7.00
         Consisting of:
         2550½ Large Ash Tray, Crys.
         2550½ Medium Ash Tray, Crys.
         2550½ Ind. Ash Tray, Crys.
2550½ 3 pc. Ash Tray St. AZ-Crys. 5.00----7.00
         Consisting of:
         2550½ Large Ash Tray, Azure
         2550½ Med. Ash Tray, Crys.
         2550½ Ind. Ash Tray, Azure
2550½ 3 pc. Ash Ty. St. Az-Crys.-
         Consisting of: GT 5.00----7.00
         2550½ Lg. Ash Tray, Azure
         2550½ Med. Ash Tray, Crys.
         2550½ Ind. Ash Tray, G. T.
2550 8'' Bowl, Straight   . . . 4.00----6.00
2550 9½'' Bowl, Flared   . . . 6.00----8.00
2550 11'' Oval Bowl 6.00----9.00
2550 Centerpiece 7.00--10.00
2550 3'' Candlestick 3.00----5.00
2550½ Candlestick 3.00----5.00
2550 6'' Vase, Flared 5.00----8.00
2550 6'' Vase, Straight 5.00----8.00
2550 13'' Plate 7.00--10.00
2550 Qt. Decanter & Stopper . 10.00--15.00
2518 1½ oz. Whiskey 2.00----4.00
2550½ 5½'' Vase, Straight   . . 4.00----6.00
2550½ 5'' Vase, Flared 4.00----6.00

CORONET PATTERN No. 2560 LINE
Made in Crystal Only

BOWLS & CANDLESTICKS

2560 13'' Fruit Bowl 8.00--12.00
2560 12'' Bowl, Flared 8.00--10.00
2560 11½'' Bowl, Crimped . . 8.00--12.00
2560 8½'' Bowl, Cupped 7.00--10.00
2560 Handled Bowl 10.00--15.00
2560 4½'' Candlestick 6.00----9.00
2560½ 4'' Candlestick 6.00--9.00
2560 Duo Candlestick 8.00--12.00

BUFFET DISHES

2560 Cheese & Cracker 8.00--12.00
2560 Ftd. Cheese 3.00----5.00
2560 Cracker Plate 5.00----7.00
2560 6¾'' Olive 2.00----4.00
2560 8¾'' Pickle 2.00----4.00
2560 11'' Celery 3.00----5.00

NAPPIES, HANDLED & UNHANDLED

2560 Whip Cream 2.00----4.00
2560 Sweetmeat 2.00----4.00
2560 Lemon 2.00----4.00
2560 Bon Bon 2.00----4.00
2560 3 Toed Bon Bon 2.00----4.00
2560 3 Toed Tid Bit, Flat   . . 2.00----4.00
2560 3 Toed Nut Bowl, Cupped 2.00----4.00

MAYONNAISE SETS

2560 Mayonnaise & Plate & Ldl. 6.00----9.00
2560 Ftd. Mayonnaise 3.00----5.00
2560 Mayonnaise Plate 2.00----3.00
2560 2-Part Mayonnaise 4.00----6.00
2560 2-Part Mayo. w/2 Ladles 5.00----8.00

MISCELLANEOUS

2560 Ftd. Shaker, & F. Top . . 2.00----4.00
2560 3 oz. Ftd. Oil & Stop. . . 9.00--12.00
2560 6'' Comport 4.00----6.00
2560 Ice Bucket, Chrom. Hdld. 8.00--12.00
2560 Ice Tongs, Chrom (2510) 1.00----2.00

DINNERWARE

2560 5'' Fruit 1.00----2.00
2560 6'' Cereal 2.00----3.00
2560 Ftd. Cup 2.00----4.00
2560 Saucer 1.00----2.00

PLATES

2560 6'' Plate 50----1.00
2560 7'' Plate 1.00----1.50
2560 8'' Plate 2.00----3.00
2560 9'' Plate 2.00----4.00
2560 14'' Torte Plate 8.00--12.00

RELISH DISHES

2560 2-Part Relish 2.00----4.00
2560 3-Part Relish 4.00----6.00
2560 4-Part Relish 4.00----6.00
2560 5-Part Relish 5.00----8.00

HANDLED TRAYS

2560 Handled Cake Plate 4.00----6.00
2560 Handled Serving Dish   . . 4.00----6.00
2560 Handled Muffin Tray   . . 4.00----6.00

2560	11½" Handled Lunch Tray	5.00----8.00

SALAD SETS

2560	10" Salad Bowl	8.00--10.00
2560	2-Part Salad Bowl	8.00--12.00
2560	Salad Fork & Spoon (Wood)	2.00----3.00
2560	3 pc. Salad Set	18.00--22.00

Consisting of:
2560 10" Salad Bowl
2560 13" Torte Plate
2560 Salad Fork & Spoon (wood)

SUGARS & CREAMS

2560	Ftd. Sugar	3.00----5.00
2560	Ftd. Cream	3.00----5.00
2560	Ind. Sugar	3.00----5.00
2560	Ind. Cream	3.00----5.00
2560	7½" Sugar & Cream Tray	3.00----5.00
2560	Ind. Sugar & Cm. & Tray	3.00----5.00

VASES

2560	3¾" Pansy Vase	2.00----4.00
2560	6" Handled Vase	5.00----8.00

COLONY PATTERN No. 2412 LINE
Made in Crystal
**Matching Only 1978*

*	2412	9 oz. Goblet	4.00----6.00
*	2412	5 oz. Sherbet	3.00----4.00
	2412	3½ oz. Cocktail	4.00----6.00
*	2412	3¼ oz. Wine	4.00----6.00
	2412	4 oz. Oyster Cocktail	3.00----5.00
*	2412	12 oz. Ftd. Tumbler	4.00----6.00
	2412	12 oz. Tumbler	2.00----4.00
	2412	9 oz. Tumbler	2.00----4.00
*	2412	5 oz. Ftd. Tumbler	4.00----6.00

BOWLS AND CANDLESTICKS

2412	8" Bowl, Cupped	5.00----8.00
2412	8¼" Bowl, Flared	5.00----8.00
2412	9" Bowl, Rolled Edge	5.00----8.00
2412	9" Lily Pond	5.00----8.00
2412	10" Fruit Bowl	5.00----8.00
2412	10" Lily Pond	6.00----9.00
2412	10½" Fruit Bowl	6.00----9.00
2412	Low Ft. Bowl	10.00--12.00
2412	11" Bowl, Flared	6.00----9.00
2412	11" Ftd. Oval Bowl	8.00--12.00
2412	13" Lily Pond	9.00--12.00
2412	14" Fruit Bowl	12.00--15.00
2412	3" Candlestick	3.00----5.00
2412	7" Candlestick	4.00----6.00
2412	Duo Candlestick	6.00----9.00
2412	13" Centerpiece	10.00--15.00
2412	7½" Lustre, 8 U.D. Prisms	20.00--25.00

DINNERWARE & OTHER ACCESSORIES

2412	Bon Bon	2.00----4.00
2412	Ftd. Bon Bon	2.00----4.00
2412	3-Toed Bon Bon	2.00----4.00
2412	9¾" Salad Bowl	5.00----8.00
2412	Salad Fork & Spoon (Wood)	1.00----2.00
2412	9¾" 4 pc Salad Set	15.00--20.00

Consisting of:
2412 9¾" Salad Bowl
2412 13" Torte Plate
2412 Salad Fork & Spoon (wood)

2412	Oblong Butter & Cover	8.00--12.00
2412	10" Handled Cake Plate	6.00----9.00
2412	Candy Box & Cover	8.00--10.00
2412	9-5/8" Celery	3.00----5.00
2412	Cheese & Cracker	8.00--12.00
2412	Ftd. Cheese	3.00----4.00
2412	12½" Cracker Plate	5.00----8.00
2412	6-3/8" Low Comport & Cov.	6.00----8.00
2412	4" Low Comport	4.00----6.00
2412	Ftd. Cup	2.00----4.00
2412	Saucer	1.00----2.00
2412	Ice Bowl	4.00----6.00
2412	5½" Ice Cream	2.00----3.00
2412	Jelly & Cover	5.00----8.00
2412	1 pt. Cereal Pitcher	10.00--15.00
2412	3 pt. Ice Jug	15.00--20.00
2412	2 qt. Ice Jug	15.00--20.00
2412	Lemon	2.00----3.00
2412	Mayonnaise	2.00----4.00
2412	Mayonnaise & Plate & Ldl.	6.00----8.00
2412	Mayonnaise Plate	1.00----2.00
2412	Mayonnaise Ladle (2630)	1.00----2.00
2412	4½" Round Nappy	2.00----3.00
2412	5" Round Nappy	2.00----3.00
2412	4 oz. Oil & Stopper	10.00--15.00
2412	6¼" Olive	2.00----4.00
2412	8" Pickle	2.00----4.00
2412	6", 7", 8", 9" Plate	1.00----4.00
2412	12½" Platter	6.00----9.00
2412	13" Torte Plate	9.00--12.00
2412½	11" Ftd. Bowl	10.00--15.00
2412	High Ft. Bowl	12.00--18.00
2412	Bobache, Wired	2.00----3.00
2412	3 pc Ind. Sugar & Cm. & Ty.	10.00--14.00
2412	Individual Sugar	3.00----5.00
2412	Individual Cream	3.00----5.00
2412	6¾" Sugar & Cream Tray	2.00----4.00
2412	Sweetmeat	2.00----4.00
2412	Handled Lunch Tray	8.00--10.00
2412	Handled Muffin Tray	4.00----6.00
2412	10½" Snack Tray	4.00----6.00
2412	Vegetable Dish	4.00----6.00
2412	2-Part Vegetable Dish	4.00----6.00
2412	Whip Cream	2.00----3.00
2412	15" Torte Plate	10.00--15.00
2412	18" Torte Plate	15.00--20.00
2412	Punch Bowl	15.00--25.00
2412	Punch Cup	2.00----3.00
2412	Punch Bowl Ldl. (Plastic)	.50----1.00
2412	2-Part Relish	2.00----4.00
2412	3-Part Relish	3.00----5.00
2412	12" Salver	10.00--15.00
2412	8½" Handled Serving Dish	4.00----6.00
2412	Shaker & Chrome Top "B"	2.00----4.00
2412	Ind. Shaker & C.T. "C"	2.00----4.00
2412	Ind. Shaker Tray	1.00----2.00
2412	3 pc. Ind. Shaker Set	6.00----9.00
2412	Cream Soup	3.00----4.00
2412	Ftd. Sugar	3.00----5.00
2412	Ftd. Cream	3.00----5.00
2412	Ftd. Almond	2.00----3.00
2412	Hld. Serving Dish Tray	6.00---8.00
2412	10½" Celery	4.00----6.00

SMOKING ACCESSORIES

2412½	3pc. Rd. Ash Tray Set	5.00---8.00

Consisting of:
2412½ 3" Rd. Ash Tray
2412½ 4½" Rd. Ash Tray
2412½ 6" Rd. Ash Tray

2412 3 pc Ash Tray Set 5.00----7.00
    Consisting of:
      2412 3'' Ind. Ash Tray
      2412 3½'' Small Ash Tray
      2412 4½'' Lge. Ash Tray
2412 3'' Ind. Ash Tray . . . 1.00----2.00
2412 3½'' Small Ash Tray . . 1.00----2.00
2412 4½'' Lge. Ash Tray . . . 2.00----3.00
2412½—3'' Rd. Ash Tray . . . 1.00----2.00
2412½—4½'' Rd. Ash Tray . . 1.00----2.00
2412½—6'' Rd. Ash Tray . . . 2.00----3.00

VASES

2412 6'' Rose Bowl 8.00--12.00
2412 Cornucopia Vase . . . 7.00--10.00
2412 6'' Ftd. Bud Vase, Flared 2.00----4.00
2412 7'' Ftd. Vase, Cupped . . 5.00----8.00
2412 7½'' Vase, Flared 5.00----8.00
2412 Ftd. Urn 10.00--15.00
2412 Ftd. Urn & Cover 15.00--20.00
2412 12'' Vase 8.00--10.00
2412 14'' Vase 8.00--12.00
2412 3-Toed Nut Bowl 2.00----4.00
2412 3-Toed Tricorne 2.00----4.00
2412 Oblg. Cig. Box & Cover . . 6.00----8.00
2412 2-Lt. Candelabra, 8 B Prisms
    (2412 Bobache) 20.00--30.00
2412 7'' Ftd. Tid Bit 6.00----8.00
2412 3-Toed Tid Bit 3.00----4.00
2412 No. 4 Lustre (10 UDP) 9¾'' 25.00--35.00
1103 14½'' Lustre (10UDP) . . 45.00--60.00

FLAME PATTERN
No. 2545 LINE

BOWLS, CANDLESTICKS & CANDELABRA

2545 ½ lb. Oval Candy Bx. & Cov. 7.00--10.00
2545 12'' Hdld. Lunch Tray . . 9.00--12.00
2545 Sauce Boat 5.00----8.00
2545 Sauce Boat Plate 2.00----3.00
2545 12½'' ''Flame'' Oval Bowl 6.00--12.00
2545 2'' ''Flame'' Candlestick 2.00----5.00
2545 4½'' ''Flame'' Candlestick 6.00----9.00
2545 ''Flame'' Lustre, 8 U.D.P. 20.00--25.00
2545 2 Lt. ''Flame'' Candelabra, L-2''
    Prisms (2545 Bobache) 20.00--30.00
2545 ''Flame'' Duo Candlestick 10.00--15.00
2545 10'' Vase 8.00--12.00
2056 3'' Candlestick 3.00----5.00
2546 Quadrangle Candlestick . 15.00--20.00
    Ht. 4¾'' Spread Bowl 7¼''
2546 4½'' Quadrangle Bowl . . 3.00----5.00
    Ht. 2¾''—4½'' Sq.
2510 3'' Candlestick 3.00----5.00
2535 9'' Bowl Flared 3-5/8'' high 8.00--12.00
4113 6'' Candlestick 4.00----6.00
2535 7'' Bowl, Cupped 4-1/8'' hg. 8.00--10.00
*2535 5½'' Candlestick 5.00--10.00
*2536 9'' Hdld. Bowl 3¼'' high 8.00--15.00
2527 2 Lt. Candelabra 16 U.D.P.
    using 2527 Bobache
    Ht. 8½'' Spread 7½'' 20.00--30.00
2527 9'' Ftd. Bowl 4¼'' 8.00--10.00

Ruby-Emp-Gr-RB-Bur.

RALEIGH PATTERN No. 2574 LINE
Made in Crystal

SUGARS & CREAMS

2574 Ftd. Sugar 2.00----4.00
2574 Ftd. Cream 2.00----4.00
2574 Ind. Sugar 2.00----4.00
2574 Ind. Cream 2.00----4.00
2574 6¾'' Sugar & Cream Tray 2.00----3.00
2574 3 pc. Ind. Sugar & Cr. & Ty. 6.00--10.00

PLATES

2574 6'' Plate 50----1.00
2574 7'' Plate 75----1.25
2574 8'' Plate 1.00----2.00
2574 9'' Plate 2.00----3.00
2574 14'' Torte Plate 8.00--10.00

NAPPIES, HANDLED

2574 Lemon 2.00----4.00
2574 Sweetmeat 2.00----4.00
2574 Whip Cream 2.00----4.00
2574 Bon Bon 2.00----4.00

MISCELLANEOUS

2574 5'' Comport 6.00----8.00
2574 4¼ oz. Oil, Ground Stop. 10.00--14.00
2574 Shaker & F. Top. 2.00----4.00
2574 Ice Tub 5.00----7.00
2574 Ice Tongs, Chrom. (2510) 1.00----2.00

MAYONNAISE SET

2574 Mayo. & Plate & Ladle . . 6.00----8.00
2574 Mayonnaise 3.00----5.00
2574 Mayonnaise Plate 1.00----2.00
2574 Mayonnaise Ladle (2375) 1.00----2.00

DINNERWARE

2574 Footed Cup 2.00----3.00
2574 Saucer 1.00----2.00

BUFFET & RELISH DISHES

2574 6'' Olive 2.00----3.00
2574 8'' Pickle 2.00----4.00
2574 10½'' Celery 3.00----5.00
2574 3-Part Relish 4.00----6.00

BOWLS & CANDLESTICKS

2574 12'' Bowl, Flared 8.00--12.00
2574 13'' Fruit Bowl 8.00--12.00
2574 9½'' Handled Bowl 8.00--12.00
2574 4'' Candlestick 3.00----4.00
2574 Duo Candlestick 5.00----8.00

HANDLED TRAYS

2574 10'' Cake Plate 7.00----9.00
2574 8½'' Serving Dish 5.00----7.00
2574 Handled Muffin Tray . . 5.00----7.00

LIQUOR STEMS *(In colors)*

1184 7 oz. O. F. Cocktail 1.00----2.00
    Sham. Height 3-3/8''

1184	7 oz. O. F. Cocktail . . . . Narrow Optic, 3-3/8" High	1.00----2.00
*2518	3 oz. Ftd. Cocktail 3-3/8" Hg. for use w/2518 Cocktail Shaker	2.00----4.00
* 889	5 oz. Whiskey Sour Plain 3½" High	1.00----3.00
1185	5 oz. Whiskey Sour Sham. 3-7/8" High	1.00----2.00
1185	8 oz. O. F. Cocktail . . . . Sham. 3½" High	1.00----2.00
*6012	3 oz. Cocktail 4-5/8" . . for use w/2518 Cocktail Shaker	5.00----8.00
*2518	Cocktail Shaker Metal Top Capacity 38 oz., Height 12¾"	30.00--50.00
*2518½	Cocktail Shaker Metal Tp. Capacity 28 oz., 7-3/8" High	25.00--35.00
2524	Cocktail Mixer Cap'ty' 21 oz. 6½" High	8.00--10.00
4115	3 oz. Ftd. Cocktail 3-1/8" Hg	2.00----4.00
*4115½	4 oz. Ftd. Cocktail 3¾" Hg. for use w/2525 Cocktail Shaker	3.00----5.00
*6011	3 oz. Cocktail 4-5/8" High for use w/2525 Cocktail Shaker	5.00----8.00
2528	Cocktail Tray Length 11¾" Width 10¾"	8.00--12.00
*2525	Cocktail Shaker Metal Top Capacity 42 oz., 12½" High	25.00--45.00
*2525½	Cocktail Shaker Metal Tp. Capacity 30 oz., 7½" High	20.00--25.00

REFRESHMENT SETS
Am-Azure-Regal Blue

4140	7 pc. Ice Tea Set . . . . Consisting of: 60 oz. Jug, Height 7½" 6-12 oz. Tumbler, Height 5"	35.00--45.00
4140	7 pc. Water Set . . . . . . Consisting of: 60 oz. Jug, Height 7½" 6-10 oz. Tumbler, Height 4½"	35.00--45.00
4140	10 oz. Tumbler, Ht. 4½"	2.00----4.00
4142	10 oz. Tumbler, Ht. 4" . .	2.00----4.00
4141	7 Pc. Ice Tea Set . . . . Consisting of: 59 oz. Jug, Ht. 7" 6-12 oz. Tumbler, Ht. 4¾"	35.00--45.00
4141	7 pc. Water Set . . . . . . Consisting of: 59 oz. Jug, Ht. 7" 6-10 oz. Tumbler, Ht. 3-3/8"	35.00--45.00
4141	10 oz. Tumbler, Ht. 3-3/8"	2.00----4.00
4142	7 pc. Ice Tea Set . . . . Consisting of: 58 oz. Jug, Ht. 7¼" 6-12 oz. or 10 oz. Tumbler	35.00--45.00

GRAPE-LEAF PATTERN
No. 2513 LINE *(Crystal)*

2513	Mayonnaise & Plate & Ladle	5.00----8.00
2513	Mayonnaise	3.00----5.00
2513	Mayonnaise Plate	2.00----3.00
2513	Mayonnaise Ladle (2375)	.50----1.00
2513	7" Salad Plate	2.00----3.00
2513	4" Hld. Mint	2.00----4.00
2513	5" Hld. Preserve	2.00----4.00
2513	2-Part Relish	3.00----5.00
2513	3-Part Relish	4.00----6.00

Ruby-Emp. Gr-RB-Bur.

2513	Candy Jar & Cover	8.00--10.00
2513	Ind. Almond—RB-Bur-Emp.	2.00----4.00

BLOWN STEMWARE
No. 5056 AMERICAN LADY
Regal Blue, Emp. Green, Burgundy Bowl
Discontinued 1973

5056	10 oz. Goblet, Ht. 6-1/8"	4.00----6.00
5056	5½ oz. Sherbet, Ht. 4-1/8"	2.00----4.00
5056	2½ oz. Wine, Ht. 4-1/8"	4.00----6.00
5056	3½ oz. Cocktail, Ht. 4" . .	4.00----6.00
5056	12 oz. Ftd. Tumbler, Ht. 5½"	4.00----6.00

MISCELLANEOUS

2276	Vanity Set, Ht. 7½" over all Diameter of Box 4½", Ht. of Box 1¼"	9.00--15.00
2517	5¼" Hdld. Sweetmeat . .	2.00----4.00
2400	6" Comport, Ht. 4½" . .	5.00----9.00
2517	6" Hdld. Lemon	2.00----3.00
2564	Horse Book End, Length 5¼", Ht. 7¾" . . . . *(This piece has been made in Crystal and colors by other companies up to 1970)*	25.00--30.00
2538	11" Nappy	6.00--10.00
2538	4½", 6" Nappy	2.00----4.00
2497½	Seafood Cocktail	8.00--12.00
2545	12" Hdld. Lunch Tray . .	10.00--15.00
2491	Tea Warmer, Ht. 3¼" . .	6.00--10.00
2491	Wax Pot and Candle Included with Tea Warmer . .	1.00----2.00

SONATA PATTERN No. 2364 LINE
Made in Crystal

BOWLS & CANDLESTICK

2364	12" Lily Pond	8.00--10.00
2364	12" Bowl, Flared	8.00--10.00
2364	13" Fruit Bowl	8.00--10.00
6023	Duo Candlestick	6.00----9.00

CANDY CONTAINER

2364	Candy Box & Cover	4.00----6.00

MAYONNAISE & SALAD SETS

2364	Mayonnaise & Plate & Ladle	3.00----5.00
2364	Mayonnaise	2.00----3.00
2364	Mayonnaise Plate	1.00----2.00
2364	Mayonnaise Ladle	.50----1.00
2364	9" Salad Bowl	4.00----6.00
2364	10½" Salad Bowl	8.00--10.00
2364	2-Part Mayo. & 2 Ladles	4.00----6.00
2364	2-Part Mayonnaise	3.00----5.00
2364	5" Fruit	1.00----2.00
2364	6" Baked Apple	2.00----3.00
2364	8" Rim Soup	2.00----3.00
2364	8" Comport	5.00----7.00
2400	6" Comport	4.00----6.00
2364	Individual Almond	1.00----2.00
2364	Handled Lunch Tray . .	6.00----8.00
2364	Crescent Plate	2.00----3.00
2364	11" Sandwich Plate	4.00----6.00
2364	14" Torte Plate	6.00----8.00
2364	16" Torte Plate	8.00--12.00
2364	Salad Fork & Spoon (wood)	1.00----2.00

2364	Oval Sauce Dish	1.00----2.00
2364	Cheese & Cracker	8.00--10.00
2364	Ftd. Cheese	2.00----3.00
2364	11" Cracker Plate	5.00----7.00
2364	8" Pickle	2.00----3.00
2364	11" Celery	2.00----4.00
2364	2-Part Relish	2.00----3.00
2364	3-Part Relish	3.00----4.00
2364	Lg. Shaker & Chrome Top "B"	1.00----2.00
2364	Shaker & Chrome Top "C"	1.00----2.00
2364	Shaker & "E" Top	2.00----3.00

SMOKING ACCESSORIES

2364	Cigarette Holder	1.00----2.00
2364	Ind. Ash Tray	1.00----2.00

KENT PATTERN No. 2424 LINE
Made in Crystal

BOWLS & CANDLESTICKS

2424	11½" Fruit Bowl	8.00--12.00
2424	8" Bowl, Regular	8.00--12.00
2424	9½" Bowl, Flared	8.00--12.00
2424	Duo Candlestick	5.00----7.00
2424	3½" Candlestick	2.00----4.00

CANDY CONTAINERS

2424	Sweetmeat	2.00----4.00
2424	Candy Jar & Cover	5.00----7.00
2424	5½" Low Comport	3.00----4.00
2424	5½" Low Comport & Cover	5.00----7.00

MAYONNAISE SETS

2424	Mayonnaise & Plate & Ladle	6.00----8.00
2424	Mayonnaise	3.00----5.00
2424	Mayonnaise Plate	2.00----3.00
2424	Mayonnaise Ladle (2375)	1.00----2.00

MISCELLANEOUS

2424	Individual Salt	2.00----3.00
2424	Almond	2.00----3.00

PLATE

2424	12" Plate	8.00--12.00

SMOKING ACCESSORIES

2424	2-Part Cigarette Box & Cov.	5.00----7.00
2424	Ash Tray	1.00----2.00

VASES

2424	5½" Ftd. Urn, Reg.	6.00----9.00
2424	5" Ftd. Urn, Flared	6.00----9.00
2424	7½" Ftd. Urn, Regular	7.00--10.00
2424	6½" Ftd. Urn, Flared	7.00--10.00

MYRIAD PATTERN No. 2592 LINE
Made in Crystal

BOWLS & CANDLESTICKS

2592	11" Fruit Bowl	8.00--10.00
2592	8½" Bowl	6.00----8.00
2592	10½" Lily Pond	6.00----9.00
2592	4" Candlestick	2.00----4.00

CANDY CONTAINER

2592	Candy Box & Cover	8.00--10.00

VASE

2592	9" Vase, Flared	6.00----9.00

SALVER

2592	12" Salver	7.00--10.00

SMOKING ACCESSORIES

2592	Oblg. Cigarette Box & Cov.	8.00--10.00
2592	4" Oblong Ash Tray	2.00----3.00
2592	Ind. Ash Tray	1.00----2.00

MISCELLANEOUS

2594	Trindle Candlestick Ht. 8", Spread 6½"	10.00--12.00
4147	7 oz. Jam Pot & Cover Ht. including cover 3¾", top Diameter 3", Capacity 7 oz.	3.00----4.00
4147	3 pc. Jam Set Jam Pot & Cover 7½" Oblong Tray	8.00--10.00
2616	Oval Candy Box & Cover Ht. 3¼", Wd. 2¾"	8.00--10.00
2593	Ind. Salt, Ht. 1¾" Wd. 2-1/8"	3.00----4.00
2595	4¼" Sleigh, Ht. 1¾" Wd. 2-1/8"	10.00--15.00
2595	6" Sleigh, Ht. 3-3/8" Wd. 4-3/8"	15.00--20.00
6030	5" Comport Blown Bowl	6.00----8.00
2615	Owl Book End, Ht. 7½"	20.00--30.00
2601	Lyre Book End, Ht. 7" Wd. 5½"	20.00--25.00
2589½	Colt, Ht. 2¼", Lgh. 2¾"	18.00--22.00
2589	Colt, Ht. 3-7/8", Lgh. 2½"	20.00--25.00
2531	Pelican, Ht. 3-7/8" Length 4½"	30.00--40.00
2589	Deer, Ht. 4", Lgh. 2"	20.00--25.00
2531	Seal, Ht. 3-7/8", Lgh. 3¾"	30.00--40.00
2589½	Deer, Ht. 2-3/8" Length 2"	18.00--22.00
2585	Eagle Book End, Ht. 7½" Width 5"	20.00--30.00
2531	Polar Bear, Ht. 4-5/8" Length 4"	30.00--40.00
2564	Horse Book End, Ht. 5¼" Length 7-3/8"	25.00--30.00
2580	Elephant Book End, Ht. 6½", Length 7¼"	40.00--50.00
2531	Penguin, Ht. 4-5/8"	30.00--40.00

WISTAR PATTERN No. 2620 LINE
Made in Crystal

2620	9 oz. Goblet	6.00----9.00
2620	6 oz. High Sherbet	3.00----4.00
2620	12 oz. Tumbler	5.00----8.00
2620	5 oz. Tumbler	3.00----5.00

2620	7" Plate	2.00----4.00
2620	Ftd. Sugar	4.00----6.00
2620	Ftd. Cream	4.00----6.00
2620	9½" Celery	3.00----4.00
2620	Mayonnaise & Plate & Ladle	8.00--12.00
2620	Mayonnaise	6.00----8.00
2620	Mayonnaise Plate	2.00----4.00
2620	3-Toed Bon Bon	3.00----5.00
2620	3-Toed Nut Bowl	3.00----5.00
2620	3-Toed Tricorne	3.00----5.00
2620	Hld. Nappy, Reg.	3.00----5.00
2620	Hld. Nappy, Flared	3.00----5.00
2620	Hld. Nappy, Square	3.00----5.00
2620	Hld. Nappy, 3-Cor.	3.00----5.00
2620	10" Salad Bowl	9.00--12.00
2620	14" Torte Plate	10.00--15.00
2620	12" Lily Pond	9.00--12.00
2620	13" Fruit Bowl	10.00--14.00
2620	4" Candlestick	6.00----9.00

MONROE DESIGN
NEEDLE ETCHING No. 86
Made in Solid Crystal—Regular Optic

6000	10 oz. Goblet	2.00----4.00
6000	6 oz. Saucer Champagne	2.00----4.00
6000	6 oz. Low Sherbet	1.00----3.00
6000	3½ oz. Cocktail	2.00----4.00
6000	3 oz. Wine	2.00----4.00
6000	4 oz. Oyster Cocktail	2.00----4.00
6000	13 oz. Ftd. Tumbler	2.00----4.00
4076	9 oz. Tumbler	1.00----2.00
889	5 oz. Tumbler	1.00----2.00
887	2½ oz. Tumbler	1.00----2.00
2283	7" Plate	1.00----3.00
6000	5 oz. Ftd. Tumbler	2.00----3.00

CASTLE DESIGN
NEEDLE ETCHING No. 87
Made in Solid Crystal

6007	10 oz. Goblet	3.00----5.00
6007	5½ oz. Saucer Champagne	3.00----5.00
6007	5½ oz. Low Sherbet	2.00----4.00
6007	3½ oz. Cocktail	3.00----5.00
6007	4 oz. Claret	3.00----5.00
6007	3 oz. Wine	3.00----5.00
6007	1 oz. Cordial	3.00----5.00
6007	4½ oz. Oyster Cocktail	3.00----5.00
6007	2, 5, 9, 12 oz. Ftd. Tumb.	2.00----4.00
869	Finger Bowl	1.00----3.00
2283	6" Plate, Reg. Opt.	1.00----3.00
2283	7" Plate, Reg. Opt.	2.00----3.00
2283	8" Plate, Reg. Opt.	2.00----4.00

CAMEO DESIGN
DOUBLE NEEDLE ETCHING No. 88
Made in Crystal

6009	9 oz. Goblet	3.00----5.00
6009	5½ oz. Saucer Champagne	3.00----5.00
6009	5½ oz. Low Sherbet	2.00----4.00
6009	3¾ oz. Claret	3.00----5.00
6009	4¾ oz. Oyster Cocktail	3.00----5.00
6009	5, 9, 12 oz. Ftd. Tumbler	2.00----4.00
869	Finger Bowl	1.00----3.00
701	10, 12 oz. Tumbl, Sham., Pl.	1.00----2.00
1184	7 oz. O. F. Cocktail, Sham. Plain	1.00----2.00
887	1¾ oz. Whiskey, Sham., Pl.	1.00----2.00
6009	3½ oz. Cocktail	3.00----5.00
6009	1 oz. Cordial	3.00----5.00
4122	1½ oz. Whiskey, Sham. Pl.	1.00----3.00

ELSINORE DESIGN
DOUBLE NEEDLE ETCHING No. 89
Made in Crystal

4024	10 oz. Goblet	2.00----4.00
4024	6 oz. Saucer Champagne	2.00----4.00
4024	5½ oz. Sherbet	2.00----3.00
4024	1 oz. Cordial	2.00----4.00
4024	4 oz. Oyster Cocktail	2.00----4.00
4024	5, 8, 12 oz. Ftd. Tumbler	2.00----4.00
4024	5" Comport	4.00----6.00
869	Finger Bowl	1.00----2.00
701	10 oz. Tumb., Sham., Pl.	1.00----2.00
1184	7 oz. O. F. Cocktail, Sham., Plain	1.00----2.00
887	1¾ oz. Whiskey, Sham., Pl.	1.00----2.00
4122	1½ oz. Whiskey, Sham., Pl.	1.00----2.00
4024	2 oz. Ftd. Whiskey	2.00----4.00
4024½—11 oz. Goblet		2.00----4.00
4024	3½ oz. Claret	2.00----4.00
4024	2 oz. Sherry	2.00----4.00
4024	3½ oz. Rhine Wine	2.00----4.00

PAGODA DESIGN
NEEDLE ETCHING No. 90
Made in Solid Crystal—Optic

660	9 oz. Goblet	2.00----4.00
660	5 oz. Saucer Champagne	2.00----4.00
660	5 oz. Low Sherbet	1.00----3.00
660	3 oz. Cocktail	2.00----4.00
660	4 oz. Claret	2.00----4.00
660	2¾ oz. Wine	2.00----4.00
660	¾ oz. Cordial	2.00----4.00
4095	Oyster Cocktail	2.00----4.00
4095	5, 10, 13 oz. Ftd. Tumbler	2.00----4.00
869	Finger Bowl	1.00----2.00
2337	6" Plate	1.00----2.00
2337	7" Plate	1.00----3.00
2337	8" Plate	2.00----4.00

BALLET DESIGN
NEEDLE ETCHING No. 91
Made in Solid Crystal—Optic

661	9 oz. Goblet	2.00----4.00
661	5½ oz. Saucer Champagne	2.00----4.00
661	5½ oz. Low Sherbet	1.00----3.00
661	3 oz. Cocktail	2.00----4.00
661½—4 oz. Claret		2.00----4.00
661	2¾ oz. Wine	2.00----4.00
661	¾ oz. Cordial	2.00----4.00
4095	Oyster Cocktail	2.00----4.00
4095	5, 10, 13 oz. Ftd. Tumbler	2.00----4.00
1769	Finger Bowl	1.00----2.00
2337	6" Plate	1.00----2.00
2337	7" Plate	1.00----3.00
2337	8" Plate	2.00----4.00

BARONET DESIGN
NEEDLE ETCHING No. 92
Made in Solid Crystal—Optic

870	9 oz. Goblet	3.00----5.00
870	6 oz. Saucer Champagne	3.00----4.00
870	6 oz. Low Sherbet	2.00----4.00

870	3 oz. Cocktail	3.00----5.00
870	4½ oz. Claret	3.00----5.00
870	2¾ oz. Wine	3.00----5.00
870	¾ oz. Cordial	3.00----5.00
5084	Oyster Cocktail	3.00----5.00
5084	5, 9, 12 oz. Ftd. Tumbler	2.00----4.00
869	Finger Bowl	1.00----2.00
2337	6" Plate, Optic	1.00----2.00
2337	7" Plate, Optic	1.00----3.00
2337	8" Plate, Optic	2.00----4.00

SPENCERIAN DESIGN
Tracing No. 94 *(Made in Crystal)*

6023	9 oz. Goblet	2.00----4.00
6023	6 oz. Saucer Champagne	2.00----4.00
6023	6 oz. Low Sherbet	1.00----3.00
6023	3¾ oz. Cocktail	2.00----4.00
6023	4 oz. Claret-Wine	2.00----4.00
6023	1 oz. Cordial	2.00----4.00
6023	4 oz. Oyster Cocktail	2.00----4.00
6023	5, 9, 12 oz. Ftd. Tumbler	2.00----4.00
766	Finger Bowl	1.00----2.00
2337	7" Plate	1.00----2.00

ARIEL DESIGN—Tracing No. 93
and
RINGLET DESIGN—Tracing No. 95
Made in Crystal

892	11 oz. Goblet	2.00----4.00
892	7 oz. Saucer Champagne	2.00----4.00
892	6½ oz. Low Sherbet	1.00----3.00
892	4 oz. Cocktail	2.00----4.00
892	4 oz. Claret	2.00----4.00
892	3 oz. Wine	2.00----4.00
892	4½ oz. Oyster Cocktail	2.00----4.00
892	12 oz. Ftd. Tumbler	2.00----4.00
892	5 oz. Ftd. Tumbler	1.00----3.00
1769	Finger Bowl	1.00----2.00
2337	7" Plate	1.00----2.00

ACANTHUS DESIGN
PLATE ETCHING No. 282
STEMWARE
Made in
Crystal Base with Green Bowl (5298)
Crystal Base with Amber Bowl (5298)

5098	Goblet	8.00--12.00
5098	High Sherbet	8.00--10.00
5098	Low Sherbet	8.00--10.00
5098	Parfait	8.00--12.00
5098	Claret	8.00--12.00
5098	Wine	8.00--12.00
5098	Cocktail	8.00--12.00
5098	Cordial	8.00--12.00
5098	Oyster Cocktail	8.00--10.00
869	Finger Bowl	2.00----4.00
2283	6" Plate, Reg. Opt.	2.00----3.00
5082½	Grape Fruit	4.00----6.00
945½	Grape Fruit Liner	4.00----6.00
5098	2½, 5, 9, 12 oz. Ftd. Tumb	6.00----9.00
5098	6" Comport	7.00--12.00
5000	7 Ftd. Jug	75.00--100.00
4095	Individual Almond, R/O	4.00----6.00

DINNERWARE
Made in Green & Amber

4375	6", 7", 8", 9", 10" Plate	2.00----9.00

2375	13" Chop Plate	8.00--10.00
2375	10" Grill Plate	5.00----8.00
2375	5" Fruit	3.00----4.00
2375	6" Cereal	4.00----5.00
2375	7" Soup	4.00----6.00
2375½	Ftd. Cup	3.00----5.00
2375	Saucer	2.00----3.00
2375	After Dinner Cup	3.00----5.00
2375	After Dinner Saucer	2.00----3.00
2375	Bouillon	3.00----5.00
2375	Cream Soup	4.00----6.00
2375	Cream Soup Plate	2.00----3.00
2375	9" Baker	12.00--16.00
2375	12" Platter	9.00--12.00
2375	15" Platter	10.00--15.00
2375	Sauce Boat	15.00--18.00
2375	Sauce Boat Plate	4.00----6.00
2375	8½" Relish	5.00----8.00
2375	8½" Pickle	5.00----8.00
2375	11½" Celery	6.00----9.00
2375½	Sugar & Cover	15.00--20.00
2375½	Footed Sugar	5.00----8.00
2375½	Footed Cream	5.00----8.00
2375½	Tea Sugar	5.00----7.00
2375½	Tea Cream	5.00----7.00
2375	Mayonnaise	6.00----9.00
2375	Mayonnaise Plate	2.00----3.00
2375	Footed Oil	20.00--25.00
2083	Salad Dressing Bottle	18.00--22.00
2375	Footed Shaker	6.00----9.00
2350	Small Ash Tray	7.00--10.00
2375	Handled Lunch Tray	12.00--15.00
2375	Sweetmeat	4.00----6.00
2375	Bon Bon	3.00----5.00
2375	Lemon Dish	3.00----5.00
2375	10" Cake Plate	8.00--12.00
2375	Large Dessert	7.00--10.00
2375	Ice Bucket	20.00--25.00
2375	Footed Cheese	4.00----6.00
2375	Cracker Plate	8.00--10.00
2394	6" Bowl	4.00----6.00
2394	12" Bowl "A"	18.00--22.00
2394	2" Candlestick	5.00----8.00
2430	11" Bowl	15.00--20.00
2430	9½" Candlestick	8.00--10.00
2430	8" Vase	8.00--12.00
2430	½ lb. Candy Jar & Cover	15.00--20.00
2430	5½" Mint	3.00----4.00
2430	7" Jelly	4.00----6.00
2375	12" Centerpiece	15.00--20.00
2375½	Candlestick	6.00----8.00
2375	12" Bowl	16.00--20.00
2375	3" Candlestick	5.00----8.00
2395	10" Bowl	15.00--20.00
2395½	5" Candlestick	6.00----9.00
2417	8" Vase, Reg. Opt.	9.00--12.00
4105	8" Vase, Reg. Opt.	12.00--15.00

KASHMIR DESIGN
PLATE ETCHING No. 283—STEMWARE
Made in Green Base with Crystal Bowl (4120)

4020	11 oz. Goblet	8.00--10.00
4020	7 oz. High Sherbet	6.00----8.00
4020	7 oz. Low Sherbet	3.00----4.00
4020	5 oz. Low Sherbet	2.00----4.00
4020½	4 oz. Cocktail	5.00----8.00
4020	3 oz. Cocktail	5.00----8.00
4020	2 oz. Whiskey	5.00----8.00
4020	5, 10, 13, 16 oz. Ftd. Tumb	7.00----9.00
4021	Finger Bowl	3.00----4.00

4020	Footed Jug	35.00--45.00
4020	3½ oz. Cocktail	5.00----8.00
4120	Goblet	8.00--10.00
4120	High Sherbet	6.00----8.00
4120	7 oz. Low Sherbet	3.00----4.00
4120	5 oz. Low Sherbet	2.00----4.00
4120	3½ oz. Cocktail	5.00----8.00
4120	2 oz. Whiskey	5.00----8.00
4120	5, 10, 13, 16 oz. Tumbler	5.00----7.00
4121	Finger Bowl	3.00----4.00

DINNERWARE
Made in Green

2419	6" Bread & Butter Plate	2.00----3.00
2419	7" Salad Plate	2.00----4.00
2419	8" Luncheon Plate	3.00----5.00
2350½—Footed Cup		4.00----5.00
2419	Saucer	2.00----3.00
2350	After Dinner Cup	4.00----5.00
2419	After Dinner Saucer	1.00----2.00

STEMWARE
Made in Crystal Base with Topaz Bowl
Crystal Base with Azure Bowl

5099	9 oz. Goblet	10.00--12.00
5099	6 oz. High Sherbet	8.00--10.00
5099	6 oz. Low Sherbet	3.00----5.00
5099	5½ oz. Parfait	8.00--10.00
5099	4 oz. Claret	10.00--12.00
5099	2½ oz. Wine	10.00--12.00
5099	3 oz. Cocktail	10.00--12.00
5099	¾ oz. Cordial	10.00--12.00
5099	4½ oz. Oyster Cocktail	8.00--10.00
869	Finger Bowl	2.00----4.00
2283	6" F.B. Plate, R/O	2.00----3.00
5082½—Grape Fruit		3.00----4.00
945½—Grape Fruit Liner		3.00----4.00
5099	2½, 5, 9, 12 oz. Ftd. Tumb.	8.00--10.00
5000	7 Ftd. Jug	50.00--75.00
5099	6" Comport	8.00--12.00

DINNERWARE
Made in Topaz and Azure

2375	6", 7", 8", 9", 10" Plate	2.00----9.00
2375	13" Chop Plate	8.00--12.00
2375	5" Fruit	3.00----4.00
2375	6" Cereal	4.00----6.00
2375	7" Soup	4.00----6.00
2375½—Footed Cup		3.00----5.00
2375	Saucer	2.00----3.00
2375	After Dinner Cup	3.00----5.00
2375	After Dinner Saucer	2.00----3.00
2375	Bouillon	3.00----4.00
2375	Cream Soup	3.00----4.00
2375	Cream Soup Plate	2.00----3.00
2375	9" Baker	12.00--16.00
2375	12" Platter	8.00--12.00
2375	15" Platter	10.00--15.00
2375	Sauce Boat	15.00--20.00
2375	Sauce Boat Plate	5.00----8.00
2375	8½" Relish	5.00----8.00
2375	8½" Pickle	5.00----8.00
2375	11½" Celery	6.00----9.00
2375½—Footed Sugar		5.00----7.00
2375½—Footed Cream		5.00----7.00
2375½—Tea Sugar		5.00----7.00
2375½—Tea Cream		5.00----7.00
2375	Mayonnaise	6.00----9.00

2375	Mayonnaise Plate	2.00----3.00
2375	Footed Oil	18.00--24.00
2375	Footed Shaker	6.00----9.00
2375	Handled Lunch Tray	12.00--15.00
2375	Sweetmeat	4.00----6.00
2375	Bon Bon	3.00----5.00
2375	Lemon Dish	3.00----5.00
2375	10" Cake Plate	10.00--12.00
2375	Large Dessert	8.00--10.00
2375	Ice Bucket	18.00--22.00
2375	Footed Cheese	4.00----7.00
2375	Cracker Plate	8.00--12.00
2394	6" Bowl	4.00----6.00
2394	12" Bowl "A"	20.00--25.00
2394	2" Candlestick	5.00----8.00
2430	11" Bowl	12.00--15.00
2430	9½" Candlestick	10.00--12.00
2430	8" Vase	9.00--12.00
2430	½ lb. Candy Jar & Cover	15.00--20.00
2430	5½" Mint	4.00----6.00
2430	7" Jelly	6.00----8.00
2375	12" Centerpiece	15.00--18.00
2375½—Candlestick		6.00----9.00
2375	12" Bowl	16.00--20.00
2375	3" Candlestick	5.00----8.00
2395	10" Bowl	15.00--20.00
2395½—5" Candlestick		6.00----9.00
2417	8" Vase	9.00--12.00
4105	8" Vase	12.00--15.00
2350	Small Ash Tray	1.00----3.00
5299	6" Comport	10.00--14.00

NEW GARLAND DESIGN
PLATE ETCHING No. 284—STEMWARE
Made in Amber Base with Crystal Bowl (4120)
Crystal Base with Rose Bowl (4120)
Crystal Base with Topaz Bowl (4220)

4020	Goblet	8.00--12.00
4020	High Sherbet	5.00----8.00
4020	7 oz. Low Sherbet	3.00----5.00
4020	5 oz. Low Sherbet	2.00----4.00
4020½—4 oz. Cocktail		8.00--12.00
4020	3½ oz. Cocktail	8.00--12.00
4020	2 oz. Whiskey	8.00--12.00
4020	5, 10, 13, 16 oz. Ftd. Tumb	4.00----8.00
4021	Finger Bowl	2.00----4.00
4020	Footed Jug	50.00--75.00

Made in Rose Bowl—Crystal
Foot—Regular Optic

6202	Goblet	8.00--12.00
6202	High Sherbet	5.00----8.00
6202	Low Sherbet	3.00----5.00
6202	Claret	8.00--12.00
6202	Wine	8.00--12.00
6202	Cordial, Oyster Cocktail	7.00--10.00
6202	2, 5, 10, 13 oz. Ftd. Tumb.	4.00----8.00
6202	Finger Bowl	2.00----4.00
5000	7 Ftd. Jug	40.00--60.00
4220	Sugar (also made w/Tz. Bowl)	5.00----7.00
4220	Cream " " " "	5.00----7.00
6002	Goblet	8.00--12.00
6002	High Sherbet	5.00---8.00
6002	Low Sherbet	3.00----5.00
6002	Claret	8.00--12.00
6002	Wine	8.00--12.00
6002	Cordial	8.00--12.00
6002	Oyster Cocktail	7.00--10.00

6002	2, 5, 10, 13 oz. Ftd. Tumb.	4.00----7.00
6002	Finger Bowl	2.00----4.00

DINNERWARE
Made in Amber, Rose and Topaz

2419	6", 7", 8", 9" Plate	2.00----9.00
2419	5" Fruit	3.00----4.00
2419	6" Cereal	4.00---6.00
2419	7" Soup	4.00---6.00
2419	Footed Cup	3.00----5.00
2419	Saucer	2.00----3.00
2419	After Dinner Cup	3.00----5.00
2419	After Dinner Saucer	2.00----3.00
2419	Cream Soup	4.00---6.00
2419	10" Baker	12.00--16.00
2419	12" Platter	8.00--12.00
2419	15" Platter	10.00--15.00
2419	Sauce Bowl & Stand	15.00--20.00
2419	8½" Pickle	5.00----8.00
2419	11" Celery	6.00----9.00
2419	8½" Relish	5.00----8.00
2419	4-Part Relish	6.00----9.00
2419	Shaker	6.00----9.00
2419½—Footed Sugar		8.00--10.00
2419½—Footed Cream		8.00--10.00
2419	Sugar	5.00----8.00
2419	Cream	5.00----8.00
2419	Tea Sugar	4.00---6.00
2419	Tea Cream	4.00---6.00
2419	Jelly, 2 Handles	3.00----5.00
2419	Mayonnaise, 2 Handles	3.00----5.00
2419	Lemon Dish, 2 Handles	3.00----5.00
2419	Bon Bon, 2 Handles	3.00----5.00
2419	10" Cake Plate, 2 Handles	8.00--12.00
2451	Ice Dish	10.00--12.00
2375	Salad Dressing Bottle	15.00--20.00
2375	Footed Oil	18.00--24.00
2375	Ice Bucket	15.00--20.00
4020	Footed Sugar	8.00--10.00
4020	Footed Cream	8.00--10.00
4020	Individual Almond	2.00----4.00
2400	6" Comport	10.00--12.00
2430	½ lb. Candy Jar & Cover	15.00--18.00
2430	8" Vase	8.00--12.00
2430	11" Bowl	10.00--15.00
2394	12" Bowl "A"	18.00--22.00
2394	7½" Bowl "D"	15.00--18.00
2394	2" Candlestick	5.00----7.00
2441	12" Bowl	15.00--20.00
2375	3" Candlestick	5.00----8.00
2433	12" Bowl, A	20.00--25.00
2433	7½" Bowl, D	20.00--25.00
2433	3" Candlestick	5.00----8.00
2433	6" Tall Comport	8.00--12.00
2433	6" Low Comport	7.00--10.00
2439	Decanter	20.00--25.00
2430	9½" Candlestick	10.00--15.00
2430	7" Jelly	8.00--10.00
4020	Footed Decanter	25.00--35.00
4020	Footed Shaker	6.00----9.00

MINUET DESIGN—PLATE ETCHING No. 285
STEMWARE
Green Base with Crystal Bowl (4120)

4020	Goblet	7.00--10.00
4020	High Sherbet	6.00----8.00
4020	7 oz. Low Sherbet	3.00----5.00
4020	5 oz. Low Sherbet	3.00----5.00

4020½—4 oz. Cocktail		5.00----7.00
4020	3½ oz. Cocktail	5.00----7.00
4020	2 oz. Whiskey	5.00----7.00
4020	5, 10, 13, 16 oz. Ftd. Tumb.	6.00----9.00
4021	Finger Bowl	3.00----4.00
4020	Footed Jug	30.00--50.00
4020	Ftd. Decanter (Also made in Tz.	25.00--35.00
4020	Ftd. Shaker (also made in Tz.)	4.00----6.00
4020	Ftd. Sugar (also made in Tz.)	4.00----6.00
4020	Ftd. Cream (also made in Tz.)	4.00----6.00
4120	Goblet	7.00--10.00
4120	High Sherbet	6.00----8.00
4120	7 oz. Low Sherbet	3.00----5.00
4120	5 oz. Low Sherbet	3.00----5.00
4120	3½ oz. Cocktail	5.00----7.00
4120	2 oz. Whiskey	5.00----7.00
4120	5, 10, 13, 16 oz. Tumbler	6.00----9.00
4121	Finger Bowl	3.00----4.00
4120	Footed Jug	30.00--50.00
4120	Sugar	4.00----6.00
4120	Cream	4.00----6.00

Crystal Base with Topaz Bowl (6202)

6002	Goblet	8.00--12.00
6002	High Sherbet	8.00--10.00
6002	Low Sherbet	4.00----6.00
6002	Claret	8.00--12.00
6002	Wine	8.00--12.00
6002	Cordial	8.00--12.00
6002	Oyster Cocktail	7.00--10.00
6002	2, 5, 10, 13 oz. Ftd. Tumb.	6.00--10.00
6002	Finger Bowl	3.00----4.00
5000	7 Ftd. Jug	40.00--60.00

DINNERWARE
Made in Green and Topaz

2419	6", 7", 8", 9" Plate	2.00----6.00
2419	5" Fruit	3.00----4.00
2419	6" Cereal	3.00----5.00
2419	7" Soup	4.00---6.00
2419	Footed Cup	5.00----7.00
2419	Saucer	2.00----3.00
2419	After Dinner Cup	4.00---6.00
2419	After Dinner Saucer	2.00----3.00
2419	Cream Soup	4.00---6.00
2419	10" Baker	10.00--15.00
2419	12" Platter	10.00--15.00
2419	15" Platter	12.00--16.00
2419	Sauce Bowl and Stand	10.00--15.00
2419	8½" Pickle	5.00----7.00
2419	11" Celery	6.00----8.00
2419	8½" Relish	5.00----7.00
2419	4 Part Relish	7.00----9.00
2419	Sugar	7.00----9.00
2419	Cream	7.00----9.00
2419	Tea Sugar	4.00---6.00
2419	Tea Cream	4.00---6.00
2419	Jelly, 2 Handles	5.00----7.00
2419	Mayonnaise, 2 Handles	5.00----7.00
2419	Lemon Dish, 2 Handles	5.00----7.00
2419	Bon Bon, 2 Handles	5.00----7.00
2419	Cake Plate, 2 Handles	8.00--12.00
2451	Ice Dish	10.00--15.00
2083	Salad Dressing Bottle	15.00--20.00
2375	Footed Oil	18.00--22.00
2439	Decanter	20.00--30.00
2375	Ice Bucket	15.00--20.00
2400	6" Comport	8.00--12.00

2430	5½" Mint	4.00----6.00
2430	7" Jelly	4.00----6.00
2430	½ lb. Candy Jar & Cover	10.00--15.00
2430	8" Vase	8.00--12.00
2430	11" Bowl	12.00--16.00
2430	9½" Candlestick	8.00--12.00
2394	12" Bowl "A"	15.00--20.00
2394	7½" Bowl "D"	15.00--20.00
2394	2" Candlestick	4.00----6.00
2441	12" Bowl	15.00--20.00
2375	3" Candlestick	4.00----6.00
2433	12" Bowl "A"	20.00--30.00
2433	7½" Bowl "D"	20.00--25.00
2433	3" Candlestick	4.00----6.00
2433	6" Tall Comport	8.00--12.00
2433	6" Low Comport	7.00--10.00

MANOR DESIGN
PLATE ETCHING No. 286
STEMWARE
Solid Crystal—Crystal Base with Green Bowl
Crystal Base with Topaz Bowl
Wisteria Base with Crystal Bowl

6003	10 oz. Goblet	9.00--12.00
6003	6 oz. High Sherbet	6.00----9.00
6003	6 oz. Low Sherbet	3.00----5.00
6003	3½ oz. Cocktail	9.00--12.00
6003	4½ oz. Claret	9.00--12.00
6003	1¼ oz. Cordial	9.00--12.00
6003	4½ oz. Oyster Cocktail	8.00--10.00
6003	2½, 5, 9, 12 oz. Ftd. Tumb.	6.00----9.00
4021	Finger Bowl	2.00----4.00
4020	Footed Jug	30.00--50.00

Made in Solid Crystal

6007	10 oz. Goblet	9.00--12.00
6007	5½ oz. High Sherbet	8.00--10.00
6007	5½ oz. Low Sherbet	6.00----9.00
6007	3½ oz. Cocktail	9.00--12.00
6007	4 oz. Claret	9.00--12.00
6007	3 oz. Wine	9.00--12.00
6007	1 oz. Cordial	9.00--12.00
6007	4½ oz. Oyster Cocktail	8.00--10.00
6007	2, 5, 9, 12 oz. Ftd. Tumb.	7.00--10.00

DINNERWARE
Made in Crystal, Green and Topaz

2419	8½" Pickle	6.00----8.00
2419	11" Celery	7.00----9.00
2419	8½" Relish	6.00----8.00
2419	Sugar	6.00----9.00
2419	Cream	6.00----9.00
2419	Tea Sugar	6.00----8.00
2419	Tea Cream	6.00----8.00
2419	Jelly	6.00----8.00
2419	Mayonnaise	6.00----8.00
2419	Lemon Dish	6.00----8.00
2419	Bon Bon	6.00----8.00
2419	Cake Plate	8.00--12.00
2419	Handled Lunch Tray	12.00--15.00
2419	4 Part Relish	8.00--10.00
2419	Syrup	15.00--18.00
2419	Syrup & Cover	15.00--20.00
2419	Syrup Saucer	2.00----3.00
2419	Ash Tray	5.00----8.00
2419	Comport	9.00--12.00
2430	½ lb. Candy Jar & Cover	12.00--18.00

2451	Ice Dish	10.00--15.00
2451	5 oz. T.J. Liner (Not Et.)	2.00----4.00
2451	4 oz. C.M. Liner (Not Et.)	2.00----4.00
2443	6" Ice Tub	10.00--15.00
2443	10" Oval Bowl	14.00--18.00
2443	3" Candlestick	5.00----9.00
2394	12" Bowl "A"	15.00--25.00
2394	2" Candlestick	4.00----6.00
2433	12" Bowl "A"	20.00--30.00
2433	3" Candlestick	6.00----9.00
2433	6" Tall Comport	8.00--12.00
2433	6" Low Comport	7.00--10.00
4106	7" Vase	15.00--20.00
4107	9" Vase	15.00--20.00
4108	5", 6", 7" Vase	15.00--20.00
4020	Footed Decanter	25.00--35.00
4020	Footed Shaker	4.00----6.00
2419	Shaker	4.00----5.00
4020	Individual Almond	2.00----3.00
2419	6", 7", 8", 9" Plate	2.00----8.00
2419	5" Fruit	3.00----4.00
2419	6" Cereal	4.00----5.00
2419	7" Soup	4.00----6.00
2419	Footed Cup	5.00----7.00
2419	Saucer	2.00----3.00
2419	After Dinner Cup	4.00----6.00
2419	After Dinner Saucer	2.00----3.00
2419	Cream Soup	4.00----6.00
2419	10" Baker	10.00--15.00
2419	12" Platter	10.00--14.00
2419	15" Platter	15.00--18.00
2419	Sauce Bowl & Stand	10.00--15.00
2419½	Footed Sugar	5.00----8.00
2419½	Footed Cream	5.00----8.00
2451	Ice Dish Plate	2.00----3.00
2451	Fruit Cocktail Liner (Not Etched)	1.00----2.00

WILDFLOWER DESIGN
PLATE ETCHING No. 308
Made in Amber and Green

2419	Jelly	5.00----7.00
2419	Mayonnaise	5.00----7.00
2419	Lemon Dish	5.00----7.00
2419	Bon Bon	5.00----7.00
2419	Cake Plate	10.00--12.00
2419	Handled Lunch Tray	12.00--15.00
2419	4 Part Relish	8.00--10.00
2364	16" Plate	15.00--20.00
2375	Cheese & Cracker	16.00--20.00
4020	Footed Sugar	5.00----8.00
4020	Footed Cream	5.00----8.00
4020	Footed Decanter	20.00--30.00
4020	2 oz. Whiskey	5.00----7.00
2400	6" Comport	8.00--12.00
2430	½ lb. Candy Jar & Cover	10.00--15.00
2447	Duo Candlestick	8.00--12.00
2433	12" Bowl "A"	20.00--30.00
2433	3" Candlestick	6.00----9.00
2433	6" Tall Comport	8.00--12.00
2433	6" Low Comport	7.00--10.00
2443	6" Ice Tub	10.00--15.00
2443	10" Oval Bowl	15.00--18.00
2443	4" Candlestick	6.00--10.00
2419	Syrup	15.00--18.00
2419	Syrup & Cov. (Cov. Not Et)	15.00--20.00
2419	Syrup Saucer	2.00----3.00
4106	7" Vase	15.00--20.00
4107	9", 12", 15" Vase	20.00--25.00
4108	5", 6", 7" Vase	15.00--20.00

LEGION DESIGN
PLATE ETCHING No. 309
Made in Solid Crystal

6000	10 oz. Goblet	6.00----9.00
6000	6 oz. High Sherbet	5.00----8.00
6000	6 oz. Low Sherbet	3.00----5.00
6000	3½ oz. Cocktail	6.00----9.00
6000	3 oz. Wine	6.00----9.00
6000	4 oz. Oyster Cocktail	5.00----7.00
6000	13 oz. Footed Tumbler	6.00----8.00
6000	5 oz. Footed Tumbler	6.00----8.00
889	13 oz. Tumbler	4.00----6.00
4076	9 oz. Tumbler	4.00----6.00
889	5 oz. Tumbler	4.00----6.00
887	2½ oz. Tumbler	4.00----6.00
2375	6", 7", 8", 9" Plate	2.00----6.00
2375½—Footed Cup		3.00----5.00
2375	Saucer	2.00----3.00
2375½—Footed Sugar		4.00----6.00
2375½—Footed Cream		4.00----6.00

Made in Crystal, Rose and Topaz

2470	12" Bowl	15.00--25.00
2470	5½" Candlestick	8.00--15.00
2470	6" Tall Comport	10.00--15.00
2470	6" Low Comport	8.00--12.00
2470	Sugar & Cream Tray	5.00----8.00
2470	9" Service Dish	10.00--12.00
2470	3 Part Round Relish	8.00--10.00
2470	4 Part Oval Relish	10.00--12.00
2470	10" Cake Plate	10.00--12.00
2470	Bon Bon	3.00----5.00
2470	Lemon Dish	3.00----5.00
2470	Sweetmeat	3.00----5.00
2440	12" Salad Bowl	15.00--20.00
2440	10½" Bowl "B"	15.00--20.00
2440	13" Torte Plate	15.00--20.00
2440	7" Vase	12.00--16.00
2454	8" Vase	15.00--25.00
2456	½ lb. Candy Jar & Cover	15.00--25.00
2419	6" Comport	8.00--12.00
2424	8" Bowl	10.00--12.00
2375	3" Candlestick	5.00----8.00

FUCHSIA DESIGN
PLATE ETCHING No. 310
Solid Crystal—Wisteria Base with Crystal Bowl

6004	9 oz. Goblet	9.00--12.00
6004	5½ oz. High Sherbet	8.00--10.00
6004	5½ oz. Low Sherbet	6.00----8.00
6004	5½ oz. Parfait	9.00--12.00
6004	3 oz. Cocktail	9.00--12.00
6004	4 oz. Claret	9.00--12.00
6004	2½ oz. Wine	9.00--12.00
6004	¾ oz. Cordial	9.00--12.00
6004	4½ oz. Oyster Cocktail	8.00--10.00
6004	2½, 5, 9, 12 oz. Ftd. Tumb.	6.00--10.00
869	Finger Bowl	2.00----3.00
833	2, 5, 8, 12 oz. Tumbler	4.00----7.00
2440	6", 7", 8", 9" Plate	5.00----8.00
2440	Cup	4.00----6.00
2440	Saucer	2.00----3.00
2440	Footed Sugar	5.00----8.00
2440	Footed Cream	5.00----8.00
2440	10½" Bowl "B"	10.00--15.00
2375	3" Candlestick	5.00----8.00
2395	10" Bowl	15.00--20.00
2395½—5" Candlestick		8.00--10.00

2470½—10½" Bowl		12.00--18.00
2470½—5½" Candlestick		8.00--10.00
*2470	12" Bowl	15.00--20.00
*2470	5½" Candlestick	8.00--12.00
*2470	6" Tall Comport	10.00--15.00
*2470	6" Low Comport	7.00--10.00
2470	10" Cake Plate	8.00--12.00
2470	Lemon Dish	3.00----5.00
2470	Bon Bon	3.00----5.00
2470	Sweetmeat	3.00----5.00

FLORENTINE DESIGN
PLATE ETCHING No. 311
Made in Solid Crystal
Topaz Base with Crystal Bowl

6005	9 oz. Goblet	9.00--12.00
6005	5½ oz. High Sherbet	8.00--10.00
6005	7 oz. Low Sherbet	6.00----8.00
6005	6 oz. Parfait	9.00--12.00
6005	4 oz. Cocktail	9.00--12.00
6005	5 oz. Claret	9.00--12.00
6005	3 oz. Wine	9.00--12.00
6005	1 oz. Cordial	9.00--12.00
6005	6 oz. Oyster Cocktail	8.00--10.00
6005	2½, 5, 9, 12 oz. Ftd. Tumb.	6.00--10.00
2440	13" Torte Plate	10.00--15.00

Made in Crystal only

Not made in Topaz

869	Finger Bowl	2.00----4.00
4005	2½, 5, 9, 12 oz. Tumbler	3.00----5.00

Made in Crystal and Topaz

2440	6", 7", 8", 9" Plate	5.00----8.00
2440	Cup	4.00----5.00
2440	Saucer	2.00----3.00
2440	Footed Sugar	5.00----8.00
2440	Footed Cream	5.00----8.00
2470	12" Bowl	15.00--18.00
2470	5½" Candlestick	8.00--10.00
2470½—10½" Bowl		10.00--15.00
2470½—5½" Candlestick		6.00----9.00
2470	6" Tall Comport	10.00--15.00
2470	6" Low Comport	7.00--10.00
2470	Sugar & Cream Tray	5.00----7.00
2470	3 Part Round Relish	6.00----9.00
2470	10" Cake Palte	8.00--10.00
2470	Lemon Dish	3.00----5.00
2470	Bon Bon	3.00----5.00
2470	Sweetmeat	3.00----5.00
2470	9" Service Dish	10.00--12.00
2470	4 Part Oval Relish	8.00--12.00

MAYDAY DESIGN
PLATE ETCHING
No. 312

(1931–1932)

Green Base with Crystal Bowl

Not in Fostoria Book

6005	Goblet	9.00--12.00

Made in Wisteria

6005	High Sherbet	8.00--10.00
6005	Low Sherbet	6.00----8.00
6005	Parfait	9.00--12.00
6005	Cocktail	9.00--12.00
6005	Claret	9.00--12.00
6005	Wine	9.00--12.00
6005	Cordial	9.00--12.00
6005	Oyster Cocktail	8.00--10.00
6005	2½, 5, 9, 12 oz. Ftd. Tumb.	6.00--10.00

Made in Solid Crystal Only

869	Finger Bowl	2.00----3.00
2440	6", 7", 8", 9" Plate	2.00----6.00
2440	Cup	3.00----5.00
2440	Saucer	2.00----3.00
2440	Sugar	4.00----6.00
2440	Cream	4.00----6.00
2400	6" Comport	6.00----8.00
2440	10½" Bowl, "B"	8.00--10.00
2375	3" Candlestick	4.00----6.00

MORNING GLORY DESIGN
PLATE ETCHING No. 313
Made in Solid Crystal
Amber Base with Crystal Bowl

6007	10 oz. Goblet	9.00--12.00
6007	5½ oz. High Sherbet	8.00--10.00
6007	5½ oz. Low Sherbet	6.00----8.00
6007	3½ oz. Cocktail	9.00--12.00
6007	4 oz. Claret	9.00--12.00
6007	3 oz. Wine	9.00--12.00
6007	1 oz. Cordial	9.00--12.00
6007	4½ oz. Oyster Cocktail	8.00--10.00
6007	2, 5, 9, 12 oz. Ftd. Tumbler	4.00----7.00
2470	6" Low Comport	9.00--12.00
2470	12" Bowl	15.00--20.00
2470	5½" Candlestick	8.00--10.00

Made in Solid Crystal Only

869	Finger Bowl	2.00----4.00
2270	Jug	25.00--35.00
2440	6", 7", 8", 9", 10" Plate	2.00----8.00
2440	5" Fruit	2.00----3.00
2440	6" Cereal	3.00----4.00
2440	Cup	3.00----5.00
2440	Saucer	2.00----3.00
2440	After Dinner Cup	2.00----4.00
2440	After Dinner Saucer	1.00----2.00
2440	Cream Soup	3.00----5.00
2440	10" Baker	10.00--15.00
2440	12" Platter	9.00--11.00
2440	Footed Sugar	4.00----6.00
2440	Footed Cream	4.00----6.00
2440	6½" Olive	3.00----5.00
2440	8½" Pickle	4.00----6.00
2440	11½" Celery	5.00----7.00
2440	13" Torte Plate	10.00--15.00
2440	7" Vase	8.00--10.00
2451	Ice Dish	9.00--12.00
2451	Ice Dish Plate	3.00----5.00
2419	4 Part Relish	4.00----6.00
2470	3 Part Relish	4.00----6.00
2470	Lemon Dish	2.00----4.00
2470	Sweetmeat	2.00----4.00
2470	Bon Bon	2.00----4.00
2470	10" Cake Plate	8.00--10.00
2470	Sugar & Cream Tray	3.00----4.00
2470½—10" Bowl		10.00--14.00

2470½—5½" Candlestick		5.00----8.00
2467	7½" Vase	8.00--12.00

CHATEAU DESIGN
PLATE ETCHING No. 315
Solid Crystal

6008	10 oz. Goblet	7.00--10.00
6008	5½ oz High Sherbet	6.00----8.00
6008	5½ oz. Low Sherbet	3.00----5.00
6008	3¼ oz. Cocktail	7.00--10.00
6008	4 oz. Wine	7.00--10.00
6008	5 oz. Oyster Cocktail	7.00--10.00
6008	1 oz. Cordial	7.00--10.00
6008	5, 9, 12 oz. Ftd. Tumbler	5.00----8.00
1769	Finger Bowl	2.00----4.00
2440	6", 7", 8", 9" Plate	2.00----7.00
2440	Cup	3.00----5.00
2440	Saucer	2.00----3.00
2440	Cream Soup	4.00----6.00
2440	Footed Sugar	4.00----6.00
2440	Footed Cream	4.00----6.00
2440	6½" Olive	3.00----5.00
2440	8½" Pickle	4.00----6.00
2440	11½" Celery	5.00----7.00
2440	13" Torte Plate	10.00--15.00
2470	Sweetmeat	2.00----4.00
2470	Lemon	2.00----4.00
2470	Bon Bon	2.00----4.00
2470	Cake Plate	8.00--10.00
2451	Ice Dish	8.00--10.00
2451	Ice Dish Plate	3.00----5.00
2470	6" Low Comport	6.00----8.00
2419	4 Part Relish	6.00----8.00
2472	Duo Candlestick	8.00--10.00
2482	Trindle Candlestick	10.00--12.00
2481	Oblong Bowl	10.00--12.00
2481	5" Candlestick	6.00----8.00
2470½—10½" Bowl		10.00--15.00
2470½—5½" Candlestick		6.00----8.00
2467	7½" Vase	8.00--10.00

MIDNIGHT ROSE DESIGN
PLATE ETCHING No. 316
Made in Solid Crystal

6009	9 oz. Goblet	7.00--10.00
6009	5½ oz. High Sherbet	6.00----8.00
6009	5½ oz. Low Sherbet	3.00----5.00
6009	3¾ oz. Cocktail	7.00--10.00
6009	3¾ oz. Claret-Wine	7.00--10.00
6009	1 oz. Cordial	7.00--10.00
6009	4¾ oz. Oyster Cocktail	6.00----9.00
6009	5, 9, 12 oz. Ftd. Tumbler	5.00----8.00
869	Finger Bowl	2.00----4.00
795	5½ oz. Hol. Stem Champ.	5.00----8.00
846	2 oz. Sherry	6.00----9.00
1184	7 oz. O. F. Cocktail, Sham, Plain	3.00----5.00
906	Brandy Inhaler	8.00--10.00
887	1¾ oz. Whiskey, Sham, Plain	2.00----4.00
2440	6", 7", 8", 9" Plate	2.00----7.00
2440	Cup	3.00----5.00
2440	Saucer	2.00----3.00
2440	Footed Sugar	4.00----6.00
2440	Footed Cream	4.00----6.00
2440	6½" Olive	3.00----5.00
2440	8½" Pickle	4.00----6.00
2440	11½" Celery	5.00----7.00
2440	13" Torte Plate	10.00--15.00
2375	Cake Plate	8.00--12.00

2419	4 Part Relish	6.00----8.00
2419	5 Part Relish	6.00----8.00
2462	5 Part Relish	6.00----8.00
2470	4 Part Relish	6.00----8.00
2440	4½'' Handled Sweetmeat	3.00----5.00
2440	5'' Handled Bon Bon	3.00----5.00
2440	5'' Handled Lemon	3.00----5.00
2440	10½'' Oval Cake Plate	8.00--10.00
2440	8½'' Oval Tray	6.00----8.00
2440	6½'' Oval Sauce Dish	6.00----8.00
2440	6½'' 2 Part Mayonnaise	6.00----8.00
2440	2 Part Handled Relish	6.00----8.00
2440	3 Part Handled Relish	6.00----8.00
2462	Metal Handled Relish	8.00--12.00
2470	Sugar & Cream Tray	3.00----5.00
4099	Candy Jar & Cover	10.00--14.00
2464	Ice Jug	20.00--30.00
2464	10 oz. Tumbler	3.00----5.00
2470½—10½'' Bowl		10.00--15.00
2470½—5½'' Candlestick		6.00----8.00
2470½—7'' Bowl		8.00--10.00
2481	11'' Oblong Bowl	10.00--15.00
2481	5'' Candlestick	6.00----8.00
2482	Trindle Candlestick	10.00--12.00
2472	Duo Candlestick	8.00--10.00
2467	7½'' Vase	8.00--10.00
2470	10'' Vase	10.00--12.00
2485	5'' Crescent Vase	8.00--10.00
2486	6'' Square Vase	10.00--15.00
2485	7'' Crescent Vase	10.00--12.00
2486	9'' Square Vase	15.00--18.00
4110	7½'' Vase	10.00--12.00
4111	6½'' Vase	8.00--10.00
4112	8½'' Vase	10.00--12.00

SHERATON DESIGN
PLATE ETCHING No. 317
Made in Crystal

6010	9 oz. Goblet	7.00----9.00
6010	5½ oz. High Sherbet	5.00----8.00
6010	5½ oz. Low Sherbet	3.00----5.00
6010	4 oz. Cocktail	7.00----9.00
6010	4½ oz. Claret-Wine	7.00----9.00
6010	1 oz. Cordial	7.00----9.00
6010	5½ oz. Oyster Cocktail	6.00----8.00
6010	5, 9, 12 oz. Ftd. Tumbler	2.00----6.00
869	Finger Bowl	2.00----4.00
2283	5'' Plate, R/O	2.00----3.00
2337	7'', 8'' Plate, R/O	3.00----5.00

SPRINGTIME DESIGN
PLATE ETCHING No. 318
6012 STEMWARE
Made in Solid Crystal

6012	10 oz. Goblet	7.00--10.00
6012	5½ oz. Saucer Champagne	5.00----8.00
6012	5½ oz. Low Sherbet	3.00----5.00
6012	4½ oz. Rhine Wine	7.00--10.00
6012	3 oz. Cocktail	7.00--10.00
6012	4½ oz. Claret	7.00--10.00
6012	3 oz. Wine	7.00--10.00
6012	2 oz. Sherry	7.00--10.00
6012	2 oz. Creme de Menthe	7.00--10.00
6012	1 oz. Cordial	7.00--10.00
6012	1 oz. Brandy	7.00--10.00
6012	4 oz. Ftd. Cocktail, Oyster	6.00----9.00
6012	5, 10, 13 oz. Ftd. Tumbler	3.00----8.00
6011	Ftd. Jug	20.00--30.00

DINNERWARE
Made in Crystal

2440	4½'' Handled Sweetmeat	3.00----5.00
2440	5'' Handled Bon Bon	3.00----5.00
2440	5'' Handled Lemon	3.00----5.00
2440	8½'' Oval Tray	8.00--10.00
2440	6½'' Sauce Dish	4.00----6.00
2440	6½'' 2 Part Mayonnaise	4.00----7.00
2440	2 Part Handled Relish	4.00----6.00
2440	3 Part Handled Relish	6.00----8.00
2419	5 Part Relish	8.00--10.00

SPRINGTIME DESIGN
PLATE ETCHING No. 318
Made in Crystal and Topaz

891	9 oz. Goblet	9.00--12.00
891	6½ oz. High Sherbet	5.00----8.00
891	6½ oz. Low Sherbet	3.00----5.00
891	4 oz. Cocktail	9.00--12.00
891	4 oz. Claret-Wine	9.00--12.00
891	1 oz. Cordial	9.00--12.00
891	5 oz. Oyster Cocktail	8.00--10.00
891	5, 9, 12 oz. Ftd. Tumbler	5.00----8.00
869	Finger Bowl	2.00----4.00
2440	6'', 7'', 8'', 9'' Plate	2.00----8.00
2440	5'' Fruit	2.00----4.00
2440	6'' Cereal	3.00----5.00
2440	Cup	3.00----5.00
2440	Saucer	2.00----3.00
2440	Cream Soup	4.00----6.00
2440	Footed Sugar	5.00----8.00
2440	Footed Cream	5.00----8.00
2440	6½'' Olive	5.00----7.00
2440	8½'' Pickle	5.00----8.00
2440	11½ Celery	6.00----9.00
2440	13'' Torte Plate	10.00--12.00
2470	Lemon	3.00----5.00
2470	Sweetmeat	3.00----5.00
2470	Cake Plate	8.00--10.00
2470	4 Part Oval Relish	8.00--12.00
2419	4 Part Relish	8.00--10.00
2400	6'' Comport	7.00----9.00
2482	Trindle Candlestick	10.00--15.00
2481	11'' Oblong Bowl	12.00--18.00
2481	5'' Candlestick	5.00----8.00
2470½—10½'' Bowl		12.00--18.00
2470½—5½'' Candlestick		5.00----8.00
2470½—7'' Bowl		8.00--12.00
2470	10'' Vase	12.00--14.00
4111	6½'' Vase	10.00--12.00
4112	8½'' Vase	12.00--14.00

FLEMISH DESIGN
PLATE ETCHING No. 319
Made in Crystal

2440	4½'' Handled Sweetmeat	3.00----5.00
2440	5'' Handled Bon Bon	3.00----5.00
2440	5'' Handled Lemon	3.00----5.00
2440	10½'' Oval Cake Plate	10.00--12.00
2440	8½'' Oval Tray	8.00--10.00
2440	6½'' Oval Sauce Dish	6.00----9.00
2440	6½'' 2 Part Mayonnaise	6.00----9.00
2440	2 Part Handled Relish	5.00----8.00
2440	3 Part Handled Relish	6.00----9.00
2440	Footed Sugar	5.00----7.00
2440	Footed Cream	5.00----7.00
2470	Sugar & Cream Tray	3.00----5.00
4099	Candy Jar & Cover	10.00--14.00

FRUIT DESIGN
PLATE ETCHING No. 320
Made in Crystal

2440	4½'' Handled Sweetmeat	3.00----5.00
2440	5'' Handled Bon Bon	3.00----5.00
2440	5'' Handled Lemon	3.00----5.00
2440	10½'' Oval Cake Plate	10.00--12.00
2440	8½'' Oval Tray	8.00--10.00
2440	6½'' Oval Sauce Dish	6.00----9.00
2440	6½'' 2 Part Mayonnaise	6.00----9.00
2440	2 Part Handled Relish	6.00----9.00
2440	3 Part Handled Relish	6.00----9.00
2440	Footed Sugar	5.00----7.00
2440	Footed Cream	5.00----7.00
2470	Sugar & Cream Tray	3.00----5.00
2449½—Crescent Salad Plate		3.00----5.00
2419	5 Part Relish	8.00--10.00
4099	Candy Jar & Cover	10.00--14.00
2337	8'' Plate	3.00----5.00
2440	13'' Torte Plate	10.00--15.00

REPEAL GLASSWARE CRYSTAL

4098	12 oz. Hollow Stem Beer Ht. 4¾'', Crest A	5.00----8.00
4098	12 oz. Hollow Stem Beer Ht. 4¾'' Crest B	5.00----8.00
4098	12 oz. Hollow Stem Beer Ht. 4¾'' Crest C	5.00----8.00
4098	12 oz. Hollow Stem Beer Ht. 4¾'' Crest D	5.00----8.00
4098	12 oz. Hollow Stem Beer Ht. 4¾'' Crest E	5.00----8.00
4098	12 oz. Hollow Stem Beer Ht. 4¾'' Crest F	5.00----8.00

RYE DESIGN
PLATE ETCHING no. 321
Made in Crystal

319	29 oz. Bar Bottle & Stop.	10.00--15.00
322	26 oz. Bar Bottle & Stop.	10.00--15.00
1928	24 oz. Pinch Bottle & Stop.	10.00--15.00
2052	29 oz. Pinch Bottle & Stop.	10.00--15.00
1918	24 oz. Decanter & Stopper	15.00--20.00
1918	24 oz. Decanter & Stopper Handled	20.00--25.00

NECTAR DESIGN
PLATE ETCHING No. 322
Made in Solid Crystal

6011	10 oz. Goblet.	5.00----8.00
6011	5½ oz. Saucer Champagne	4.00----6.00
6011	5½ oz. Low Sherbet	2.00----4.00
6011	3 oz. Cocktail	5.00----8.00
6011	4½ oz. Rhine Wine	5.00----8.00
6011	4½ oz. Claret	5.00----8.00
6011	3 oz. Wine	5.00----8.00
6011	2 oz. Sherry	5.00----8.00
6011	2 oz. Creme de Menthe	5.00----8.00
6011	1 oz. Cordial	5.00--—8.00
6011	1 oz. Brandy	5.00----8.00
6011	4 oz. Oyster Cocktail	5.00----7.00
6011	2, 5, 10, 13 oz. Ftd. Tumb.	3.00----5.00
6011	Footed Jug	20.00--25.00
6011	Footed Decanter	15.00--20.00
795	5½ oz. Hol. Stem Champagne	4.00----6.00

863	5 oz. Hol. Stem Champ. C/F	4.00----6.00
906	Brandy Inhaler	6.00----9.00
701	10, 12 oz. Tumb., Sham, Pl.	2.00----4.00
1184	7 oz. O. F. Cocktail, Sham, Plain	1.00----3.00
4122	1½ oz. Shiskey, Sham., Pl.	1.00---3.00
1769	Finger Bowl	2.00----3.00
2235	Shaker, F.G.T.	3.00----4.00
4024	5'' Comport	4.00----6.00
2337	6'', 7'', 8'', 11'' Plate	2.00----8.00
2350½—Footed Cup		3.00----4.00
2350	Saucer	2.00----3.00
2350	After Dinner Cup	2.00----3.00
2350	After Dinner Saucer	1.00----2.00
2350½—Footed Sugar		3.00----5.00
2350½—Footed Cream		3.00----5.00
2449	Dessert Dish	2.00----3.00
2503	Wine Jug	12.00--15.00
2440	13'' Torte Plate	10.00--15.00
2511	Cheese & Cracker	10.00--12.00
4024	10'' Footed Bowl	10.00--15.00
4024	6'' Candlestick	4.00----6.00

RAMBLER DESIGN
PLATE ETCHING No. 323
Made in Crystal

6012	10 oz. Goblet	5.00----8.00
6012	5½ oz. Saucer Champagne	4.00----6.00
6012	5½ oz. Low Sherbet	2.00----4.00
6012	4½ oz. Rhine Wine	5.00----8.00
6012	3 oz. Cocktail	5.00----8.00
6012	4½ oz. Claret	5.00----8.00
6012	3 oz. Wine	5.00----8.00
6012	2 oz. Sherry	5.00----8.00
6012	2 oz. Creme de Menthe	5.00----8.00
6012	1 oz. Cordial	5.00----8.00
6012	1 oz. Brandy	5.00----8.00
6012	4 oz. Ftd. Cocktail (Oyster	5.00----8.00
6012	5, 10, 13 oz. Ftd. Tumbler	3.00----5.00
795	Hollow Stem Champagne	3.00----5.00
701	12 oz. Tumbler, Sham	2.00----3.00
701	10 oz. Tumbler, Sham	2.00----3.00
1184	O. F. Cocktail, Sham	2.00----3.00
4122	1½ oz. Whiskey, Sham	2.00----3.00
1769	Finger Bowl	2.00----3.00
6011	Footed Jug	20.00--25.00
6011	Footed Decanter	15.00--20.00
2525	Decanter	15.00--20.00
2525	Cooktail Shaker, Gold Top	18.00--25.00
2524	Cocktail Mixer	10.00--15.00
2235	Shaker, F.G.T.	2.00----4.00
2337	6'', 7'', 8'' Plate	2.00----7.00
2350½—Footed Cup		3.00----4.00
2350	Saucer	2.00----3.00
2350½—Footed Sugar		4.00----6.00
2350½—Footed Cream		4.00----6.00
2440	4½'' Handled Sweetmeat	2.00---4.00
2440	5'' Handled Bon Bon	2.00---4.00
2440	5'' Handled Lemon	2.00---4.00
2440	8½'' Oval Tray	4.00----6.00
2440	6½'' Sauce Dish	3.00----5.00
2440	2 Part Oval Mayonnaise	2.00----4.00
2440	2, 3 Part Handled Relish	3.00----6.00
2440	13'' Torte Plate	10.00--15.00
2514	5 Part Square Relish	9.00--12.00
2419	4, 5 Part Relish	8.00--10.00
4117	Bubble Candy Jar & Cover	7.00----9.00
2484	10'' Handled Bowl	10.00--15.00
2496	Trindle Candlestick	8.00--10.00

2470½—10½" Bowl	10.00--15.00
2470½—5½" Candlestick	5.00----7.00
2472	Duo Candlestick	7.00----9.00
2482	Trindle Candlestick	9.00--12.00
2470	11½" Vase	10.00--14.00

DAISY DESIGN
PLATE ETCHING No. 324
Made in Solid Crystal

6013	10 oz. Goblet	6.00----9.00
6013	9 oz. Low Goblet	5.00----8.00
6013	6 oz. Saucer Champagne	4.00----6.00
6013	5 oz. Low Sherbet	3.00----5.00
6013	3½ oz. Cocktail	6.00----9.00
6013	4 oz. Claret	6.00----9.00
6013	3 oz. Wine	6.00----9.00
6013	1 oz. Cordial	6.00----9.00
6013	4 oz. Oyster Cocktail	6.00----9.00
6013	5, 13 oz. Ftd. Tumbler	3.00----5.00
6013	5" Comport	6.00----8.00
766	Finger Bowl, N. O.	2.00----4.00
701	12 oz. Tumb. N. O., Sham.	2.00----4.00
701	10 oz. Tumb., N. O., Sham	2.00----4.00
1184	7 oz. O. F. Cocktail, N. O.	2.00----3.00
5000	Footed Jug	20.00--30.00
2337	6", 7", 8" Plate	1.00----4.00
2350½—Footed Cup	3.00----4.00
2350	Saucer	2.00----3.00
2350½—Footed Sugar	4.00----6.00
2350½—Footed Cream	4.00----6.00
2419	4 Part Relish	4.00----6.00
2514	5 Part Relish	6.00----8.00
2440	2, 3 Part Relish	3.00----5.00
2440	2 Part Oval Mayonnaise	3.00----5.00
2440	6½" Oval Sauce Dish	3.00----5.00
2440	8½" Oval Tray	4.00----6.00
2440	10½" Oval Cake Plate	8.00--10.00
2440	13" Torte Plate	10.00--14.00
2364	16" Plate	12.00--16.00
2528	Cocktail Tray	10.00--15.00
2375	Mayonnaise, Plate, & Ladle	9.00--12.00
2375	Mayonnaise	5.00----7.00
2375	Mayonnaise Plate	3.00----5.00
2375	Mayonnaise Ladle, Plain	1.00----2.00
2535	Cheese & Cracker	10.00--15.00
2470	8" Vase	6.00----9.00
2470	10" Vase	8.00--10.00
760	12" Vase	8.00--12.00
5090	8" Bud Vase	3.00----4.00
5092	8" Bud Vase	3.00----4.00
2536	9" Handled Bowl	10.00--15.00
2535	5½" Candlestick	5.00----7.00
2533	9" Handled Bowl	10.00--15.00
2533	Duo Candlestick	8.00--10.00

CORSAGE DESIGN
PLATE ETCHING No. 325
Made in Solid Crystal

6014	9 oz. Goblet	6.00----9.00
6014	5½ oz. Saucer Champagne	4.00----6.00
6014	5½ oz. Low Sherbet	2.00----4.00
6014	3½ oz. Cocktail	6.00----9.00
6014	4 oz. Claret	6.00----9.00
6014	3 oz. Wine	6.00----9.00
6014	1 oz. Cordial	6.00----9.00
6014	4 oz. Oyster Cocktail	6.00----8.00
6014	5, 9, 12 oz. Ftd. Tumbler	3.00----5.00
869	Finger Bowl	2.00----4.00
4119	4" Footed Nappy	2.00----4.00
5000	Footed Jug	30.00--40.00
2337	6", 7", 8" Plate	2.00----8.00
2440	Cup	3.00----5.00
2440	Saucer	2.00----3.00
2440	Sugar	5.00----7.00
2440	Cream	5.00----7.00
2440	Pickle	3.00----5.00
2440	Celery	5.00----7.00
2440	2, 3 Part Relish	4.00----7.00
2496	2, 3, 4 Part Relish	4.00--10.00
2440	2 Part Mayonnaise	4.00----6.00
2440	6½" Oval Sauce Dish	3.00----5.00
2440	8½" Oval Tray	4.00----6.00
2440	10½" Cake Plate	8.00--10.00
2440	13" Torte Plate	10.00--12.00
2364	16" Plate	12.00--15.00
2419	4, 5 Part Relish	8.00--10.00
5092	8" Bud Vase	3.00----5.00
2470	10" Vase	8.00--10.00
2484	10" Handled Bowl	10.00--15.00
2496	12" Bowl, Fld.	10.00--15.00
2496	Duo Candlestick	8.00--10.00
2496	Trindle Candlestick	8.00--12.00
2496	5½" Candlestick	6.00----9.00
2536	9" Handled Bowl	8.00--12.00
2535	5½" Candlestick	5.00----7.00
2527	9" Ftd. Bowl	15.00--20.00
2527	2 Lt. Candelabra, U.D.P.	15.00--25.00
2496	3 Pc. Ind. Sugar & Cream & Tray	10.00--15.00
2496	3-Toed Tid Bit	3.00----5.00
2496	Ice Bucket, Metal Hdl.	15.00--18.00
2666	1 Qt. Pitcher	15.00--18.00
2496½—Mayonnaise, Plate & Ladle	9.00--12.00
2496	Handled Nappy, Flared	3.00----5.00
2496	Handled Nappy, 3-Cor.	3.00----5.00
2496	3-Part Candy Box & Cover	10.00--15.00
2496	Cheese & Cracker	10.00--15.00
2496	5½" Comport	8.00--12.00
2545	12½" Oval Bowl	10.00--15.00
2496	10" Handled Cake Plate	8.00--10.00
2496	3-Toed Bon Bon	3.00----5.00
2545	Duo Candlestick	10.00--12.00
2337	9" Plate, Plain	2.00----4.00

ARCADY DESIGN
PLATE ETCHING No. 326
Made in Crystal

6014	9 oz. Goblet	6.00----9.00
6014	5½ oz. Saucer Champagne	4.00----6.00
6014	5½ oz. Low Sherbet	3.00----5.00
6014	3½ oz. Cocktail	6.00----9.00
6014	4 oz. Claret	6.00----9.00
6014	3 oz. Wine	6.00----9.00
6014	1 oz. Cordial	6.00----9.00
6014	4 oz. Oyster Cocktail	6.00----8.00
6014	5, 9, 12 oz. Ftd. Tumbler	3.00----5.00
2440	Finger Bowl	2.00----3.00
5000	Ftd. Jug	25.00--35.00
2440	6", 7", 8", 9" Plate	2.00----8.00
2440	Cup	3.00----5.00
2440	Saucer	2.00----4.00
2440	Sugar	4.00----6.00
2440	Cream	4.00----6.00
2375	Ftd. Shaker	2.00----4.00
2440	6½" Pickle	2.00----4.00
2440	11½" Celery	3.00----5.00

2440	Cake Plate	6.00----9.00
2400	6" Comport	7.00--10.00
2375	Ice Bucket	10.00--15.00
2375	Mayonnaise	2.00----3.00
2375	Mayonnaise Plate	1.00----2.00
2375	Mayonnaise, Plate & Ladle	4.00----6.00
2419	5 Part Relish	6.00----9.00
2496	2, 3, 4 Part Relish	3.00----8.00
2496	Sweetmeat	3.00----4.00
2496	6½" Oblong Sauce Dish	2.00----4.00
2496	8½" Oblong Tray	2.00----4.00
2496	2 Part Mayonnaise	3.00----5.00
2496	14" Torte Plate	10.00--15.00
2496	10½" Handled Bowl	10.00--15.00
2496	12" Bowl, Flared	12.00--18.00
2496	Duo Candlestick	8.00--10.00
2496	Trindle Candlestick	10.00--12.00
2496	5½" Candlestick	4.00----6.00
2470½—10½" Bowl		10.00--15.00
2472	Duo Candlestick	8.00--10.00
2482	Trindle Candlestick	8.00--12.00
2470	10" Vase	10.00--12.00
4121	5" Vase	3.00----5.00
4128	5" Vase	3.00----5.00

4121	5" Vase	6.00----9.00
4128	5" Vase	6.00----9.00
2496	3 Pc. Ind. Sugar & Cream & Tray	18.00--22.00
2496½—6½" Sugar & Cream Tray		4.00----6.00
2496	3-Toed Tid Bit	7.00----9.00
2496	Ice Bucket, Metal Handle	15.00--20.00
2666	1 Qt. Pitcher	15.00--20.00
2496½—Mayonnaise, Plate & Ladle		9.00--12.00
2496	Handled Nappy, Flared	3.00----5.00
2496	Handled Nappy, 3-Cor.	3.00----5.00
2496	8" Pickle	3.00----5.00
2496	3-Part Candy Box & Cov.	10.00--15.00
2496	Cheese & Cracker	10.00--15.00
2496	5½" Comport	6.00----8.00
2545	12½" "Flame" Oval Bowl	10.00--15.00
2496	10" Handled Cake Plate	8.00--10.00
2496	4" Candlestick	5.00----7.00
2364	16" Torte Plate	15.00--20.00
2364	Shaker & Chrome Top "C"	3.00----5.00
2496	3-Toed Bon Bon	3.00----5.00
2545	"Flame" Duo Candlestick	10.00--12.00
2660	8" Flip Vase	8.00--10.00
2496	10" Floating Garden	10.00--12.00
2083	Salad Dressing Bottle & Stopper	12.00--15.00
2545	"Flame" Lustre using 8 U.D.P., 7½"	15.00--20.00

NAVARRE DESIGN
PLATE ETCHING No. 327
Made in Crystal

6016	10 oz. Goblet	7.00--10.00
6016	6 oz. Saucer Champagne	6.00----9.00
6016	6 oz. Low Sherbet	3.00----5.00
6016	3½ oz. Cocktail	7.00--10.00
6016	4½ oz. Claret	7.00--10.00
6016	3¼ oz. Wine	7.00--10.00
6016	¾ oz. Cordial	7.00--10.00
6016	4 oz. Oyster Cocktail	7.00----9.00
6016	5, 10, 13 oz. Ftd. Tumbler	4.00----7.00
869	Finger Bowl	2.00----4.00
5000	Ftd. Jug	35.00--45.00
2440	6", 7", 8", 9" Plate	2.00----8.00
2440	Cup	3.00----5.00
2440	Saucer	2.00----4.00
2440	Sugar	5.00----8.00
2440	Cream	5.00----8.00
2375	Ftd. Shaker	5.00----8.00
2440	6½" Pickle	3.00----5.00
2440	11½" Celery	5.00----7.00
2440	Cake Plate	8.00--10.00
2400	6" Comport	6.00----9.00
2375	Ice Bucket	15.00--20.00
2375	Mayonnaise	4.00----6.00
2375	Mayonnaise Plate	2.00----4.00
2375	Mayonnaise, Plate & Ladle	10.00--12.00
2419	5 Part Relish	8.00--12.00
2496	2, 3, 4 Part Relish	6.00--10.00
2496	Sweetmeat	4.00----6.00
2496	6½" Oblg. Sauce Dish	3.00----5.00
2496	8½" Oblong Tray	4.00----6.00
2496	2 Part Mayonnaise	5.00----7.00
2496	14" Torte Plate	10.00--14.00
2496	10½" Bowl, Handled	12.00--15.00
2496	12" Bowl, Flared	8.00--12.00
2496	Duo Candlestick	8.00--10.00
2496	Trindle Candlestick	8.00--12.00
2496	5½" Candlestick	6.00----9.00
2470½—10½" Bowl		10.00--15.00
2472	Duo Candlestick	10.00--14.00
2482	Trindle Candlestick	12.00--16.00
2470	10" Vase	10.00--15.00

Being made in 1978; this price listing from 1978 sales catalog:

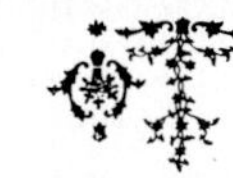

NAVARRE DESIGN
PLATE ETCHING

COLOR KEY:
NA 01—Crystal
NA 02—Blue Bowl with Crystal Base
NA 03—Pink Bowl with Crystal Base

Retail Price Ea.

002	10 oz.	Goblet	Crystal 13.95
			Pink or Blue
008	6 oz.	High Dessert/Champagne	Crystal 13.95
			Pink or Blue
011	6 oz.	Low Dessert/Champagne	Crystal 13.95
025	4 1/2 oz.	Claret	Crystal 13.95
			Pink or Blue
027	6 1/2 oz.	Large Claret	Crystal 13.95
			Pink or Blue
029	3/4 oz.	Cordial	Crystal 13.95
031	15 oz.	Brandy Inhaler	Crystal 15.95
035	16 oz.	Wine Goblet	Crystal 14.95
047		Bell	Crystal 13.95
			Pink or Blue
063	13 oz.	Luncheon Goblet/Ice Tea	Crystal 13.95
			Pink or Blue
084	5 oz.	Continental Champagne	Crystal 13.95
088	5 oz.	Footed Juice	Crystal 13.95
549	7 in.	Plate	Crystal 13.50
550	8 in.	Plate	Crystal 15.95

MEADOW ROSE DESIGN
PLATE ETCHING No. 328
Made in Crystal and Azure

6016	10 oz. Goblet	10.00--14.00
6016	6 oz. Saucer Champagne	8.00--10.00
6016	6 oz. Low Sherbet	6.00----8.00
6016	3½ oz. Cocktail	10.00--14.00
6016	4½ oz. Claret	10.00--14.00
6016	3¼ oz. Wine	10.00--14.00
6016	¾ oz. Cordial	10.00--14.00
6016	4 oz. Oyster Cocktail	9.00--12.00
6016	5, 10, 13 oz. Ftd. Tumbler	5.00----8.00
869	Finger Bowl	4.00----6.00
5000	7 Ftd. Jug	40.00--60.00
2496	6'', 7'', 8'', 9'' Plate	3.00----9.00
2337	7'' Plate (Crystal only)	2.00----3.00
2496	Ftd. Cup	5.00----7.00
2496	Saucer	2.00----3.00
2496	Footed Sugar	5.00----8.00
2496	Footed Cream	5.00----8.00
2496	Individual Sugar	4.00----6.00
2496	Individual Cream	4.00----6.00
2375	Footed Shaker	4.00----6.00
2496	8'' Pickle	5.00----8.00
2496	11'' Celery	7.00----9.00
2496	Handled Nappy, Flared	3.00----5.00
2496	Handled Nappy, 3-Cor.	3.00----5.00
2496	3-Toed Bon Bon	3.00----5.00
2496	3-Toed Tid Bit, Flat	3.00----5.00
2375	11'' Handled Lunch Tray	10.00--14.00
2496	10'' Cake Plate, 2 Handles	10.00--14.00
2496	8½'' Serving Dish, 2 Hdls.	8.00--12.00
2496	Jelly & Cover	10.00--14.00
2496	5½'' Comport	9.00--12.00
2496	3-Part Candy Box & Cov.	15.00--20.00
2496	Ice Bucket, Chrom. Hdl.	15.00--20.00
2496½	Mayonnaise	7.00----9.00
2496	Mayonnaise Plate	2.00----3.00
2496½	Mayonnaise, Plate & Ladle	9.00--12.00
2375	Mayonnaise	7.00----9.00
2375	Mayonnaise Plate	2.00----3.00
2375	Mayonnaise, Plate & Ladle	9.00--12.00
2419	5 Part Relish (Crystal Only)	10.00--12.00
2496	3 Part Relish	8.00--12.00
2440	3 Part Relish (Crystal Only)	3.00----5.00
2496	2 Part Relish	3.00----6.00
2496	Sweetmeat	4.00----6.00
2496	6½'' Oblg. Sauce Dish	4.00----6.00
2496	8'' Oblong Tray	3.00----5.00
2496	6½'' 2 Part Mayonnaise	5.00----7.00
2496	Cheese & Cracker	12.00--18.00
2083	S. D. Bottle & Stopper (Crystal Only)	12.00--18.00
2496	14'' Torte Plate	12.00--18.00
2364	16'' Plate	15.00--20.00
2496	10½'' Handled Bowl	12.00--18.00
2496	12'' Bowl, Flared	12.00--18.00
2496	10'' Floating Garden	12.00--18.00
2496	Duo Candlestick	10.00--12.00
2496	Trindle Candlestick	12.00--14.00
2496	5½'' Candlestick	8.00--10.00
2496	4'' Candlestick	7.00----9.00
2510	2-Lt. Candelabra, U.D.P. (Crystal Only)	20.00--25.00
2545	12½'' "Flame" Oval Bowl	15.00--18.00
2545	"Flame" Duo Candlestick	10.00--12.00
2545	2-Lt. "Flame" Candelabra, B Prisms	20.00--25.00
2470	10'' Vase	10.00--14.00
4128	5'' Vase	8.00--10.00

2666	1 Qt. Pitcher	15.00--20.00
2496½	6½'' Sugar & Cream Tray	3.00----5.00
2364	Shaker & Chrome Top "C"	2.00----4.00
2496	3 pc. Ind. Sugar & Cream & Tray	10.00--15.00

Being made in 1978; this price listing from 1978 sales catalog:

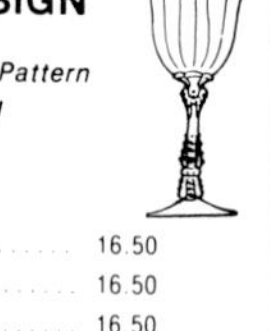

MEADOW ROSE DESIGN
Plate Etching
Stemware Shapes - See Wilma Pattern
Page 22 of Color Catalog

ME 02/002	10 oz	Goblet	16.50
ME 02/008	6 oz	High Dessert/Champagne	16.50
ME 02/011	6 oz	Low Dessert/Champagne	16.50
ME 02/025	4 1/2 oz	Claret	16.50
ME 02/060	13 oz	Luncheon Goblet/Ice Tea	16.50
ME 02/088	5 oz	Footed Juice	16.50

LIDO DESIGN
PLATE ETCHING No. 329
Made in Solid Crystal
**Stemware Made in Crystal Base w/Azure Bowl*
**Miscellaneous Pieces Made in Solid Azure*

*6017	9 oz. Goblet	9.00--12.00
*6017	6 oz. Saucer Champagne	7.00----9.00
*6017	6 oz. Low Sherbet	3.00----5.00
*6017	3½ oz. Cocktail	9.00--12.00
*6017	4 oz. Claret	9.00--12.00
*6017	3 oz. Wine	9.00--12.00
*6017	¾ oz. Cordial	9.00--12.00
*6017	4 oz. Oyster Cocktail	8.00--10.00
*6017	5, 9, 12, 14 oz. Ftd. Tumb.	5.00----8.00
4132	4, 5, 7, 9, 12, 14 oz. Tumbler, Sham.	3.00----5.00
4132	7½ oz. O. F. Cocktail	2.00----3.00
4132	1½ oz. Whiskey, Sham	2.00----3.00
* 766	Finger Bowl	2.00----4.00
6011	Footed Jug	30.00--40.00
*2496	6'', 7'', 8'', 9'' Plate	5.00----8.00
2337	7'' Plate	2.00----3.00
*2496	Footed Cup	5.00----7.00
*2496	Saucer	2.00----3.00
*2496	Footed Sugar	4.00----6.00
*2496	Footed Cream	4.00----6.00
*2496	Individual Sugar	3.00----5.00
*2496	Individual Cream	3.00----5.00
2496½	6½'' Sugar & Cream Tray	2.00----4.00
*2496	Shaker, & F. Top	3.00----5.00
2496	8'' Pickle	4.00----6.00
2496	11'' Celery	5.00----7.00
2496	10'' Cake Plate, 2 Hdls.	8.00--10.00
2496	8½'' Serving Dish, 2 Hdls.	6.00----9.00
2496	Jelly and Cover	10.00--12.00
2496	5½'' Comport	6.00----9.00
2496	6½'' Tall Comport	9.00--12.00
*2496	Ice Bucket, Chrom. Hdl.	10.00--18.00
2496½	Mayonnaise, Plate & Ladle	12.00--18.00
2496	3½ oz. Oil—Crystal Stopper	12.00--18.00
2419	5 Part Relish	8.00--10.00
*2496	3 Part Relish	8.00--10.00
2496	2 Part Relish	3.00----5.00

2496	Sweetmeat	3.00----5.00
2496	6½" Oblong Sauce Dish	3.00----5.00
2496	8" Oblong Tray	3.00----5.00
2496	6½" 2 Part Mayonnaise	3.00----5.00
*2496	3 Toed Bon Bon	4.00----6.00
2496	3 Toed Tid Bit, Flat	3.00----5.00
2496	3 Toed Nut Bowl, Cupped	3.00----5.00
2496	Hdld. Nappy, Reg., Fl., Sq.	3.00----5.00
2496	Hdld. Nappy, 3-Cor.	3.00----5.00
2496	Cheese & Cracker	10.00--14.00
*2496	3 Part Candy Bx. & Cov.	15.00--20.00
2496	14" Torte Plate	10.00--14.00
2496	10½" Handled Bowl	10.00--15.00
*2496	12" Bowl, Flared	15.00--18.00
*2496	Duo Candlestick	8.00--12.00
*2496	4" Candlestick	5.00----7.00
*2496	5½" Candlestick	7.00----9.00
2545	12½" "Flame" Oval Bowl	10.00--15.00
2545	"Flame" Duo Candlestick	8.00--10.00
*2545	2-Lt. "Flame" Candlestick	
	L-2" Prisms	20.00--30.00
*2545	Lustre, 8 U.D.P.	15.00--25.00
*2470	10" Vase	10.00--12.00
*4128	5" Vase	7.00----9.00

LENOX DESIGN
PLATE ETCHING No. 330
Made in Crystal

6017	9 oz. Goblet	3.00----5.00
6017	6 oz. Saucer Champagne	2.00----4.00
6017	6 oz. Low Sherbet	1.00----2.00
6017	3½ oz. Cocktail	3.00----5.00
6017	4 oz. Claret	3.00----5.00
6017	3 oz. Wine	3.00----5.00
6017	¾ oz. Cordial	3.00----5.00
6017	4 oz. Oyster Cocktail	2.00----4.00
6017	5, 9, 12, 14 oz. Ftd. Tumb.	2.00----4.00
4132	5, 7, 9, 12, 14 oz. Tumbler	
	Sham	1.00----3.00
4132	4 oz. Whiskey Sour, Sham	1.00----2.00
4132	7½ oz. O.F. Cocktail, Sham	1.00----2.00
4132	1½ oz. Whiskey, Sham	1.00----2.00
766	Finger Bowl	1.00----2.00
6011	Footed Jug	20.00--30.00
2337	6", 7", 8" Plate	1.00----3.00
2350½—	Footed Sugar	2.00----4.00
2350½—	Footed Cream	2.00----4.00

SHIRLEY DESIGN
PLATE ETCHING No. 331
Made in Crystal

6017	9 oz. Goblet	6.00----9.00
6017	6 oz. Saucer Champagne	4.00----6.00
6017	6 oz. Low Sherbet	3.00----5.00
6017	3½ oz. Cocktail	6.00----9.00
6017	4 oz. Claret	6.00----9.00
6017	3 oz. Wine	6.00----9.00
6017	¾ oz. Cordial	6.00----9.00
6017	4 oz. Oyster Cocktail	6.00----8.00
6017	9, 12, 14 oz. Ftd. Tumbler	2.00----7.00
6017	5 oz. Ftd. Tumbler	2.00----3.00
766	Finger Bowl	2.00----3.00
6011	Footed Jug	35.00--45.00
2337	6", 7", 8", 9" Plate	2.00----7.00

Stemware Made in Crystal Base w/Azure Bowl
Miscellaneous Pieces Made in Solid Azure

2350½—	Footed Cup	3.00----4.00
2350	Saucer	2.00----3.00
2496	Footed Sugar	4.00----6.00
2496	Footed Cream	4.00----6.00
2496	Individual Sugar	3.00----5.00
2496	Individual Cream	3.00----5.00
2496	Shaker, & F. Top	2.00----4.00
2496	8" Pickle	3.00----4.00
2496	11" Celery	3.00----5.00
2496	Cream Soup	2.00----4.00
2496	5½" Fruit	2.00----3.00
2496	12" Oval Platter	8.00--12.00
2496	9½" Vegetable Dish	7.00--10.00
2496	10" Cake Plate, 2 Hdls.	7.00--10.00
2496	5½" Comport	5.00----7.00
2496	Ice Bucket, Chrom. Hdl.	8.00--10.00
2496½—	Mayonnaise, Plate & Ladle	8.00--10.00
2496	3 Part Relish	6.00----9.00
2496	2 Part Relish	3.00----5.00
2496	Sweetmeat	2.00----4.00
2496	6½" Oblong Sauce Dish	4.00----6.00
2496	6½" 2 Part Mayonnaise	4.00----6.00
2496	3 Toed Bon Bon	3.00----5.00
2496	3 Toed Tid Bit, Flat	2.00----4.00
2496	3 Toed Nut Bowl, Cupped	3.00----5.00
2496	Handled Nappy, Regular	2.00----3.00
2496	Handled Nappy, Flared	2.00----3.00
2496	Handled Nappy, Square	2.00----3.00
2496	Handled Nappy, 3-Cor.	2.00----3.00
2496	Cheese & Cracker	9.00--12.00
2496	3 Part Candy Bx. & Cov.	10.00--14.00
1496	14" Torte Plate	10.00--12.00
2496	10½" Handled Bowl	10.00--15.00
2496	12" Bowl, Flared	10.00--15.00
2496	Duo Candlestick	8.00--10.00
2496	4, 5½" Candlestick	6.00----9.00
2545	12½" "Flame" Oval Bowl	8.00--12.00
2545	"Flame" Duo Candlestick	10.00--12.00
2545	2-Lt. "Flame" Candelabra	
	L-2" Prisms	15.00--20.00
2545	"Flame" Lustre, 8 U.D.P.	15.00--20.00
2545	4½" "Flame" Candlestick	6.00----8.00
2545	10" Vase	8.00--10.00

MAYFLOWER DESIGN
PLATE ETCHING No. 332
Made in Crystal

6020	9 oz. Goblet	6.00----9.00
6020	6 oz. Saucer Champagne	4.00----6.00
6020	6 oz. Low Sherbet	3.00----5.00
6020	5½ oz. Parfait	6.00----9.00
6020	3½ oz. Cocktail	6.00----9.00
6020	4½ oz. Claret	6.00----9.00
6020	3½ oz. Wine	6.00----9.00
6020	1 oz. Cordial	6.00----9.00
6020	4 oz. Oyster Cocktail	6.00----8.00
6020	5, 9, 12 oz. Ftd. Tumbler	2.00----7.00
869	Finger Bowl	2.00----4.00
4140	Jug	25.00--35.00
2560	6", 7", 8", 9" Plate	2.00----7.00
2560	5" Fruit	2.00----3.00
2560	6" Cereal	2.00----4.00
2560	Cup	2.00----4.00
2560	Saucer	2.00----3.00
2560	Ftd. Sugar	4.00----6.00
2560	Ftd. Cream	4.00----6.00
2560	Individual Sugar	3.00----5.00
2560	Individual Cream	3.00----5.00
2560	7½" Sugar & Cream Tray	2.00----4.00

2560	Ftd. Shaker, & F. Top	2.00----4.00
2560	3 oz. Ftd. Oil & Stopper	10.00--12.00
2560	Mayonnaise, Plate & Ladle	8.00--10.00
2560	2 Part Mayonnaise	3.00----5.00
2560	2 Pt. Mayonnaise w/2 Ladles	4.00----6.00
2560	14" Torte Plate	10.00--12.00
2560	6¾" Olive	2.00----4.00
2560	8¾" Pickle	2.00----4.00
2560	11" Celery	4.00----6.00
2560	2, 3, 4, 5 Part Relish	5.00--12.00
2560	Cheese & Cracker	9.00--12.00
2560	Ice Bucket, Chrom. Hdld.	10.00--15.00
2560	Ice Tongs (2510) Chrom.	1.00----2.00
2560	Whip Cream	2.00----4.00
2560	Sweetmeat	2.00----4.00
2560	Lemon	2.00----4.00
2560	Bon Bon	2.00----4.00
2560	3-Toed Bon Bon	3.00----5.00
2560	3-Toed Tid Bit, Flat	3.00----5.00
2560	3-Toed Nut Bowl, Cupped	3.00----5.00
2560	6" Comport	4.00----6.00
2560	Cake Plate	7.00----9.00
2560	Serving Dish	6.00----8.00
2560	Handled Muffin Tray	6.00----8.00
2586	Sani-Cut Syrup	10.00--15.00
2430	5½" Mint	2.00----4.00
2430	Candy Jar & Cover	8.00--10.00
2276	Vanity Set	8.00--10.00
2560	10" Salad Bowl	9.00--11.00
2560	11½" Bowl, Crimped	10.00--12.00
2560	12" Bowl, Flared	10.00--12.00
2560	13" Fruit Bowl	10.00--12.00
2560	Handled Bowl	10.00--14.00
2560	4½" Candlestick	3.00----4.00
2560	Duo Candlestick	4.00----6.00
2430	11" Bowl	10.00--12.00
2430	2" Candlestick	2.00----4.00
2545	12½" Oval Bowl	10.00--15.00
2545	4½" Candlestick	6.00----8.00
2545	Duo Candlestick	10.00--12.00
2545	2-Lt. Candelabra, L-2" Pms.	15.00--20.00
2545	Lustre, 8 U.D. Prisms	15.00--20.00
2496	Handled Bowl	10.00--14.00
2496	Duo Candlestick	8.00--10.00
2560½	4" Candlestick	6.00----8.00
2430	3¾", 8" Vase	4.00----8.00
2545	10" Vase	8.00--12.00
2560	6" Handled Vase	6.00----9.00
5100	10" Vase	8.00--10.00

*WILLOWMERE DESIGN
PLATE ETCHING No. 333
Made in Crystal

6024	10 oz. Goblet	7.00--10.00
6024	6 oz. Saucer Champagne	5.00----8.00
6024	6 oz. Low Sherbet	2.00----4.00
6024	3½ oz. Cocktail	7.00--10.00
6024	4½ oz. Claret	7.00--10.00
6024	3½ oz. Wine	7.00--10.00
6024	1 oz. Cordial	7.00--10.00
6024	4 oz. Oyster cocktail	7.00----9.00
6024	5, 9, 12 oz. Ftd. Tumbler	2.00----8.00
869	Finger Bowl, Optic	2.00----4.00
5000	Ftd. Jug, Optic	35.00--45.00
2560	6", 7", 8", 9" Plate	2.00----8.00
2560	Ftd. Cup	3.00----5.00

**Matching Service discontinued in 1975.*

2560	Saucer	2.00----3.00
2560	Ftd. Sugar	5.00----8.00
2560	Ftd. Cream	5.00----8.00
2560	Individual Sugar	4.00----6.00
2560	Individual Cream	4.00----6.00
2560	7½" Sugar & Cream Tray	2.00----4.00
2560	5" Fruit	2.00----3.00
2560	6" Cereal	3.00----4.00
2560	Ftd. Shaker, F. G. T.	3.00----4.00
2560	6¾" Olive	3.00----5.00
2560	8¾" Pickle	4.00----6.00
2560	11" Celery	5.00----7.00
2560	3 oz. Ftd. Oil & Stopper	12.00--16.00
2560	Mayonnaise, Plate & Ladle	9.00--12.00
2560	Mayonnaise	5.00----8.00
2560	Mayonnaise Plate	2.00----4.00
2560	Mayonnaise Ladle	1.00----2.00
2560	2-Part Mayonnaise	4.00----6.00
2560	2-Pt. Mayonnaise w/2 Ladles	5.00----7.00
2560	2, 3, 4, 5-Part Relish	5.00--12.00
2560	2-Part Salad Bowl	10.00--14.00
2560	10" Salad Bowl	10.00--14.00
2560	14" Torte Plate	10.00--15.00
2560	Handled Lunch Tray	8.00--12.00
2560	11½" Hdld. Cake Plate	8.00--10.00
2560	Hdld. Serving Dish	7.00----9.00
2560	Hdld. Muffin Tray	6.00----9.00
2586	Sani Cut Server	15.00--20.00
2560	Whip Cream	3.00----5.00
2560	Sweetmeat	3.00----5.00
2560	Lemon	3.00----5.00
2560	Bon Bon	3.00----5.00
2560	3-Toed Bon Bon	4.00----6.00
2560	3-Toed Tid Bit	4.00----6.00
2560	3-Toed Nut Bowl	4.00----6.00
2560	Cheese & Cracker	10.00--15.00
2560	Cheese	3.00----5.00
2560	Cracker Plate	8.00--10.00
2560	Ice Bucket, Chrom. Hdle.	10.00--15.00
2560	Ice Tongs, Chrom.	1.00----2.00
2560	6" Comport	7.00--10.00
2276	Vanity Set	8.00--12.00
2560	11½" Bowl, Crimped	10.00--15.00
2560	12" Bowl, Flared	10.00--15.00
2560	13" Fruit Bowl	10.00--15.00
2560	Handled Bowl	12.00--17.00
2560	4½" Candlestick	6.00----8.00
2560½	4" Candlestick	3.00----5.00
2560	Duo Candlestick	8.00--10.00
2567	7½" Vase	10.00--15.00
2568	9" Vase	10.00--15.00
2470	10" Vase	8.00--12.00
2560	6" Handled Vase	5.00----7.00
5100	10" Vase	8.00--10.00
2560	10" 4 Pc. Salad Set	20.00--30.00

Consisting of:
2560 10" Salad Bowl
2560 14" Torte Plate
2560 Salad Fork & Spoon (wood)

2560	11" Handled Bowl	10.00--15.00
2666	1 Qt. Pitcher	10.00--15.00
2364	Shaker & Chome Top "C"	3.00----4.00

COLONIAL MIRROR DESIGN
PLATE ETCHING No. 334
Made in Crystal (1939-1945)

6023	9 oz. Goblet	4.00----6.00

6023	6 oz. Saucer Champagne	3.00----5.00
6023	6 oz. Low Sherbet	2.00----4.00
6023	3¾ oz. Cocktail	4.00----6.00
6023	4 oz. Claret-Wine	4.00----6.00
6023	1 oz. Cordial	4.00----6.00
6023	4 oz. Oyster Cocktail	4.00----6.00
6023	5, 9, 12 oz. Ftd. Tumbler	2.00----5.00
766	Finger Bowl	2.00----4.00
6011	Ftd. Jug	20.00--30.00
2574	6", 7", 8", 9" Plate	1.00----5.00
2574	Ftd. Cup	2.00----3.00
2574	Saucer	1.00----2.00
2574	Ftd. Sugar	3.00----5.00
2574	Ftd. Cream	3.00----5.00
2574	Individual Sugar	2.00----4.00
2574	Individual Cream	2.00----4.00
6023	5" Comport	4.00----6.00
2574	5" Comport	3.00----5.00
2574	Shaker, F. G. T.	3.00----4.00
2574	4½ oz. Oil, Ground Stopper	8.00--12.00
2574	6" Olive	2.00----4.00
2574	8" Pickle	3.00----4.00
2574	10½" Celery	4.00----6.00
2574	Mayonnaise	3.00----5.00
2574	Mayonnaise Plate	2.00----3.00
2574	Mayonnaise, Plate & Ladle	6.00----8.00
2574	3-Part Relish	5.00----8.00
2574	10" Cake Plate	6.00----8.00
2574	8½" Serving Dish	6.00----8.00
2574	Handled Muffin Tray	6.00----8.00
2574	Lemon	2.00----4.00
2574	Sweetmeat	2.00----4.00
2574	Whip Cream	2.00----4.00
2574	Bon Bon	2.00----4.00
2574	14" Torte Plate	10.00--15.00
2574	Ice Tub	10.00--14.00
2574	12" Bowl, Flared	10.00--15.00
2574	13" Fruit Bowl	10.00--15.00
6023	Ftd. Bowl	10.00--15.00
2324	6" Candlestick	4.00----6.00
2574	Handled Bowl	10.00--15.00
2574	4" Candlestick	3.00----5.00

WILLOW DESIGN
PLATE ETCHING No. 335
Erratum: Willow Design was discontinued in 1952 instead of 1945 as Fostoria Book states.
Made in Crystal

6023	9 oz. Goblet	5.00----8.00
6023	6 oz. Saucer Champagne	4.00----6.00
6023	6 oz. Low Sherbet	2.00----4.00
6023	3¾ oz. Cocktail	5.00----8.00
6023	4 oz. Claret-Wine	5.00----8.00
6023	1 oz. Cordial	5.00----8.00
6023	4 oz. Oyster Cocktail	5.00----8.00
6023	5, 9, 12 oz. Ftd. Tumbler	3.00----5.00
766	Finger Bowl	2.00----4.00
6011	Ftd. Jug	25.00--35.00
2574	6", 7", 8" Plate	1.00----4.00
2574	Ftd. Sugar	3.00----5.00
2574	Ftd. Cream	3.00----5.00
2574	Individual Sugar	2.00----4.00
2574	Individual Cream	2.00----4.00
2574	5" Comport	4.00----6.00
6023	Ftd. Bowl	12.00--18.00
2324	6" Candlestick	4.00----6.00
2574	Handled Bowl	10.00--15.00
2574	4" Candlestick	3.00----5.00
2574	Shaker, & F. Top	3.00----4.00

2574	4¼ oz. Oil, Ground Stop.	10.00--15.00
2574	6" Olive	2.00----4.00
2574	8" Pickle	3.00----5.00
2574	10½" Celery	4.00----6.00
2574	Mayonnaise	3.00----5.00
2574	Mayonnaise Plate	2.00----3.00
2574	Mayonnaise, Plate & Ladle	5.00----8.00
2574	3 Part Relish	5.00----8.00
2574	10" Cake Plate	6.00----8.00
2574	8½" Serving Dish	8.00--10.00
2574	Handled Muffin Tray	6.00----8.00
2574	Lemon	2.00----4.00
2574	Sweetmeat	2.00----4.00
2574	Whip Cream	2.00----4.00
2574	Bon Bon	2.00----4.00
2574	14" Torte Plate	10.00--15.00
2574	Ice Tub	10.00--14.00
2574	12" Bowl, Flared	10.00--15.00
2574	13" Fruit Bowl	10.00--15.00
2574	9" Plate	3.00----5.00
2574	Footed Cup	2.00----4.00
2574	Saucer	1.00----2.00
6023	5" Comport	4.00----6.00

PLYMOUTH DESIGN
PLATE ETCHING No. 336
Made in Crystal

6025	10 oz. Goblet	5.00----8.00
6025	6 oz. Sherbet	4.00----6.00
6025	3½ oz. Cocktail	5.00----8.00
6025	4 oz. Claret-Wine	5.00----8.00
6025	1 oz. Cordial	5.00----8.00
6025	4 oz. Oyster Cocktail	5.00----7.00
6025	5, 12 oz. Ftd. Tumbler	3.00----5.00
1769	Finger Bowl, Plain	2.00----4.00
6011	Footed Jug	25.00--35.00
2574	6", 7", 8", 9" Plate	2.00----6.00
2574	Footed Cup	2.00----3.00
2574	Saucer	1.00----2.00
2574	Footed Sugar	3.00----5.00
2574	Footed Cream	3.00----5.00
2574	Individual Sugar	2.00----4.00
2574	Individual Cream	2.00----4.00
6023	5" Comport	4.00----6.00
2574	5" Comport	3.00----5.00
2574	Shaker, & F. Top	3.00----4.00
2574	4¼ oz. Oil, Ground Stop.	10.00--15.00
2574	6" Olive	2.00----4.00
2574	8" Pickle	2.00----5.00
2574	10½" Celery	4.00----6.00
2574	Mayonnaise	3.00----5.00
2574	Mayonnaise Plate	2.00----3.00
2574	Mayonnaise, Plate & Ladle	6.00----8.00
2574	3 Part Relish	5.00----8.00
2574	10" Cake Plate	6.00----8.00
2574	8½" Serving Dish	6.00----8.00
2574	Handled Muffin Tray	6.00----8.00
2574	Lemon	2.00----4.00
2574	Sweetmeat	2.00----4.00
2574	Whip Cream	2.00----4.00
2574	Bon Bon	2.00----4.00
2574	14" Torte Plate	10.00--15.00
2574	Ice Tub	10.00--14.00
2574	12" Bowl, Flared	10.00--15.00
2574	13" Fruit Bowl	10.00--15.00
6023	Footed Bowl	12.00--18.00
2324	6" Candlestick	4.00----6.00
2574	Handled Bowl	10.00--15.00
2574	4" Candlestick	3.00----5.00

SAMPLER DESIGN
PLATE ETCHING No. 337
Made in Crystal

6025	10 oz. Goblet	5.00----8.00
6025	6 oz. Sherbet	3.00----5.00
6025	3½ oz. Cocktail	5.00----8.00
6025	4 oz. Claret-Wine	5.00----8.00
6025	1 oz. Cordial	5.00----8.00
6025	4 oz. Oyster Cocktail	5.00----7.00
6025	5, 12 oz. Ftd. Tumbler	3.00----5.00
1769	Finger Bowl, Plain	2.00----4.00
6011	Ftd. Jug	25.00--35.00
2574	6", 7", 8", 9" Plate	2.00----6.00
2574	Ftd. Cup	2.00----3.00
2574	Saucer	1.00----2.00
2574	Ftd. Sugar	3.00----5.00
2574	Ftd. Cream	3.00----5.00
2574	Individual Sugar	2.00----4.00
2574	Individual Cream	2.00----4.00
6023	5" Comport	4.00----6.00
2574	5" Comport	3.00----5.00
2574	Shaker, & F. Top	3.00----4.00
2574	4¼ oz. Oil, Ground Stop.	10.00--15.00
2574	6" Olive	2.00----4.00
2574	8" Pickle	3.00----4.00
2574	10½" Celery	4.00----6.00
2574	Mayonnaise	3.00----5.00
2574	Mayonnaise Plate	2.00----3.00
2574	Mayonnaise, Plate & Ladle	6.00----8.00
2574	3 Part Relish	6.00----8.00
2574	10" Cake Plate	6.00----8.00
2574	8½" Serving Dish	6.00----8.00
2574	Handled Muffin Tray	6.00----8.00
2574	Lemon	2.00----4.00
2574	Sweetmeat	2.00----4.00
2574	Whip Cream	2.00----4.00
2574	Bon Bon	2.00----4.00
2574	14" Torte Plate	10.00--15.00
2574	Ice Tub	10.00--14.00
2574	12" Bowl, Flared	10.00--15.00
2574	13" Fruit Bowl	10.00--15.00
6023	Footed Bowl	12.00--18.00
2324	6" Candlestick	4.00----6.00
2574	Handled Bowl	10.00--15.00
2574	4" Candlestick	3.00----5.00

*CHINTZ DESIGN
PLATE ETCHING No. 338
Made in Crystal

6026	9 oz. Goblet	7.00--10.00
6026	9 oz. Low Goblet	6.00----8.00
6026	6 oz. Saucer Champagne	6.00----8.00
6026	6 oz. Low Sherbet	3.00----5.00
6026	4 oz. Cocktail	7.00--10.00
6026	4½ oz. Claret-Wine	7.00--10.00
6026	1 oz. Cordial	7.00--10.00
6026	4 oz. Ftd. Cocktail	7.00--10.00
6026	5, 13 oz. Ftd. Tumbler	5.00----8.00
869	Finger Bowl	2.00----4.00
5000	Ftd. Jug	35.00--45.00
2496	6", 7", 8", 9" Plate	2.00----6.00
2496	Ftd. Cup	3.00----5.00
2496	Saucer	2.00----3.00
2496	Ftd. Sugar	5.00----8.00
2496	Ftd. Cream	5.00----8.00
2496	Individual Sugar	4.00----6.00
2496	Individual Cream	4.00----6.00
2496	S. & C. Tray	2.00----4.00

2496	Shaker, & F. Top	3.00----5.00
2496	5" Fruit	2.00----3.00
2496	Cream Soup	3.00----5.00
2496	Cream Soup Plate	2.00----3.00
2496	12" Oval Platter	10.00--15.00
2496	9½" Vegetable Dish	8.00--12.00
2496	Pickle	3.00----4.00
2496	Celery	4.00----6.00
2496	3½ oz. Oil	12.00--16.00
2083	S. D. Bottle	10.00--15.00
2496½	—Mayonnaise	5.00----8.00
2496	Mayonnaise Plate	2.00----4.00
2496	Mayonnaise, Plate & Ladle	8.00--12.00
2586	Sani-Cut Syrup	15.00--20.00
2364	16" Plate	12.00--18.00
2496	14" Torte Plate	10.00--15.00
2496	Footed Cheese	3.00----5.00
2496	Cracker Plate	8.00--10.00
2496	Cheese & Cracker	10.00--15.00
2496	2, 3 Part Relish	6.00--10.00
2419	5 Part Relish	9.00--12.00
2496	Ice Bucket, Chrom. Hdl.	10.00--15.00
2496	Hdld. Nappy, Flared	2.00----4.00
2496	Hdld. Nappy, 3-Cor.	2.00----4.00
2496	3-Toed Bon Bon	3.00----4.00
2496	3-Toed Tid Bit	3.00----4.00
2496	Jelly	6.00----9.00
2496	Jelly & Cover	12.00--16.00
2496	5½" Comport	6.00----8.00
2496	8" Oblong Tray	4.00----6.00
2496	Oblong Sauce Dish	5.00----7.00
2496	2 Part Mayonnaise	5.00----7.00
2375	Handled Lunch Tray	9.00--12.00
2496	Cake Plate	8.00--10.00
2496	Serving Dish	8.00--10.00
2496	3 Part Candy Bx. & Cov.	12.00--16.00
2496	10½" Handled Bowl	10.00--15.00
2496	12" Bowl, Flared	10.00--15.00
2484	10" Handled Bowl	10.00--15.00
2496	4", 5½" Candlestick	3.00----6.00
2496	Duo Candlestick	6.00----8.00
2496	Trindle Candlestick	9.00--12.00
6023	Ftd. Bowl	15.00--20.00
6023	Duo Candlestick	6.00----8.00
4128	5" Vase	4.00----6.00
4143	6", 7½" Ftd. Vase	5.00--10.00
2496	Hld. Serving Dish Tray	10.00--12.00
2470	10" Ftd. Vase	10.00--15.00
2660	8" Flip Vase	10.00--12.00
2364	Shaker & Chrome Top "C"	3.00----4.00
2666	1 Qt. Pitcher	10.00--15.00

ROSEMARY DESIGN
PLATE ETCHING No. 339
Made in Crystal

892	11 oz. Goblet	4.00----6.00
892	7 oz. Saucer Champagne	3.00----5.00
892	6½ oz. Low Sherbet	2.00----4.00
892	4 oz. Cocktail	4.00----6.00
892	4 oz. Claret	4.00----6.00
892	3 oz. Wine	4.00----6.00
892	1 oz. Cordial	4.00----6.00
892	4½ oz. Oyster Cocktail	4.00----6.00
892	5, 12 oz. Ftd. Tumbler	3.00----5.00
1769	Finger Bowl	2.00----4.00
6011	Ftd. Jug	20.00--30.00

Matching service discontinued in 1977.

2337	6", 7", 8" Plate	1.00----4.00
2364	14" Torte Plate	10.00--12.00
2364	10½" Salad Bowl	10.00--12.00
2364	13" Fruit Bowl	10.00--12.00
2364	12" Bowl, Flared	10.00--12.00
6023	9" Ftd. Bowl	15.00--20.00
6023	Duo Candlestick	4.00----6.00
4143	6" Footed Vase	5.00----7.00
4143	7½" Ftd. Vase	6.00----8.00

*BUTTERCUP DESIGN
PLATE ETCHING No. 340
Made in Crystal

6030	10 oz. Goblet	7.00--10.00
6030	10 oz. Low Goblet	6.00----8.00
6030	6 oz. Saucer Champagne	6.00----8.00
6030	6 oz. Low Sherbet	3.00----5.00
6030	3½ oz. Cocktail	7.00--10.00
6030	3½ oz. Claret-Wine	7.00--10.00
6030	1 oz. Cordial	7.00--10.00
6030	4 oz. Oyster Cocktail	5.00----8.00
6030	5, 12 oz. Ftd. Tumbler	5.00----8.00
1769	Finger Bowl	2.00----4.00
6011	Ftd. Jug	35.00--45.00
2337	6", 7", 8", 9" Plate	2.00----8.00
2364	Crescent Plate	3.00----5.00
2364	11" Sandwich Plate	9.00--12.00
2364	14" Torte Plate	10.00--15.00
2364	16" Torte Plate	15.00--20.00
2350½—Footed Cup		3.00----5.00
2350	Saucer	2.00----3.00
2350½—Ftd. Sugar		5.00----8.00
2350½—Ftd. Cream		5.00----8.00
2350	8" Pickle	3.00----4.00
2350	11" Celery	4.00----6.00
2364	6" Baked Apple	3.00----5.00
2083	Salad Dressing Bottle	12.00--16.00
2586	Sani-Cut Syrup	15.00--20.00
2364	Shaker	3.00----5.00
2364	2-Part Relish	3.00----5.00
2364	3-Part Relish	9.00--12.00
2364	Mayonnaise, Plate & Ladle	9.00--12.00
2364	Mayonnaise	5.00----8.00
2364	Mayonnaise Plate	2.00----4.00
2364	Cheese & Cracker	10.00--15.00
2364	Ftd. Cheese	3.00----5.00
2364	11" Cracker Plate	8.00--10.00
2364	Handled Lunch Tray	8.00--12.00
2364	9", 10½" Salad Bowl	9.00--12.00
6030	5" Comport	6.00----8.00
2364	8" Comport	9.00--12.00
2364	Candy Box & Cov.	10.00--15.00
2364	Cigarette Holder	3.00----5.00
2364	Individual Ash Tray	2.00----3.00
2364	13" Fruit Bowl	10.00--15.00
2364	12" Lily Pond	10.00--15.00
2364	12" Bowl, Flared	10.00--15.00
2594	10" Handled Bowl	10.00--15.00
6023	9" Ftd. Bowl	15.00--20.00
2324	4" Candlestick	3.00----5.00
2324	6" Candlestick	4.00----6.00
2594	5½" Candlestick	5.00----8.00
2594	Trindle Candlestick	8.00--12.00
6023	Duo Candlestick	5.00----7.00
2614	10" Vase	10.00--14.00
4143	6" Ftd. Vase	5.00----8.00
4143	7½" Ftd. Vase	6.00----9.00
6021	6" Ftd. Bud Vase	3.00----5.00

*ROMANCE DESIGN
PLATE ETCHING No. 341
Made in Crystal

6017	9 oz. Goblet	7.00--10.00
6017	6 oz. Saucer Champagne	7.00--10.00
6017	6 oz. Low Sherbet	3.00----5.00
6017	3½ oz. Cocktail	7.00--10.00
6017	4 oz. Claret	7.00--10.00
6017	3 oz. Wine	7.00--10.00
6017	¾ oz. Cordial	7.00--10.00
6017	4 oz. Oyster Cocktail	7.00--10.00
6017	5, 9, 12 oz. Ftd. Tumbler	5.00----8.00
766	Finger Bowl	2.00----4.00
6011	Ftd. Jug	35.00--45.00
2337	6", 7", 8", 9" Plate	2.00----8.00
2364	11" Sandwich Plate	10.00--12.00
2364	14", 16" Torte Plate	12.00--20.00
2350½—Ftd. Cup		3.00----5.00
2350	Saucer	2.00----3.00
2350½—Ftd. Sugar		5.00----8.00
2350½—Ftd. Cream		5.00----8.00
2364	8" Pickle	3.00----5.00
2364	11" Celery	4.00----6.00
2364	6" Baked Apple	3.00----5.00
2364	8" Rim Soup	4.00----6.00
2364	2, 3-Part Relish	4.00--10.00
2364	Shaker	3.00----5.00
2364	Mayonnaise, Plate & Ladle	9.00--12.00
2364	Mayonnaise	5.00----8.00
2364	Mayonnaise Plate	2.00----4.00
2364	8" Comport	7.00----9.00
2364	Cheese & Cracker	10.00--15.00
2364	10½" Ornamental S. Bowl	12.00--15.00
2364	Handled Lunch Tray	9.00--12.00
2364	9" Ornamental S. Bowl	10.00--12.00
2364	9" 4 Pc. Salad Set	20.00--25.00
	Consisting of:	
	2364 9" Salad Bowl	
	2364 11" Sandwich Plate	
	2364 Salad Fork & Spoon (wood)	
2364	10½" 4 Pc. Salad Set	25.00--30.00
	Consisting of:	
	2364 10½" Salad Bowl	
	2364 14" Torte Plate	
	2364 Salad Fork & Spoon (wood)	
2364	Crescent Salad Plate	2.00----3.00
2666	1 Qt. Pitcher	10.00--15.00
6023	Duo Candlestick	5.00----7.00
2470	10" Ftd. Vase	10.00--15.00
2660	8" Flip Vase	10.00--12.00
2364	13" Bowl	10.00--15.00
2364	12" Lily Pond	10.00--15.00
2364	12" Bowl, Flared	10.00--15.00
2594	10" Handled Bowl	10.00--15.00
2324	4" Candlestick	3.00----5.00
2594	5½" Candlestick	4.00----6.00
2594	Trindle Candlestick	8.00--12.00
6023	Duo Candlestick	5.00----7.00
2364	Ftd. Cheese	3.00----5.00
2364	11" Cracker Plate	8.00--10.00
2364	Handled Lunch Tray	8.00--12.00
2364	10½" Salad Bowl	10.00--12.00
2364	9" Salad Bowl	9.00--12.00
2364	Fork & Spoon, Wood	1.00----2.00
4132	Ice Bowl	10.00--15.00
6030	5" Comport	8.00--10.00

Matching service discontinued in 1977.

2364	8" Comport (2400)	8.00--12.00
2364	Candy Box & Cover	10.00--15.00
2364	Cigarette Holder	3.00----5.00
2364	Individual Ash Tray	2.00----3.00
2364	13" Fruit Bowl	10.00--15.00
2364	12" Lily Pond	10.00--15.00
2364	12" Bowl, Flared	10.00--15.00
2594	10" Handled Bowl	12.00--15.00
2596	11" Oblong Shallow Bowl	12.00--16.00
6023	9" Ftd. Bowl	15.00--20.00
2324	4" Candlestick	3.00----5.00
2594	5½" Candlestick	5.00----8.00
2594	Trindle Candlestick	8.00--12.00
2596	5" Candlestick	4.00----6.00
6023	Duo Candlestick	5.00----7.00
2470	10" Vase	8.00--10.00
2614	10" Vase	10.00--14.00
2619½—6", 7½", 9½" Vase, G. B.		8.00--12.00
4121	5" Vase	6.00----8.00
4143	6" Ftd. Vase	7.00----9.00
4143	7½" Ftd. Vase	8.00--10.00
6021	6" Ftd. Bud Vase	3.00----5.00

CUTTING No. 700
FORMAL GARDEN DESIGN
SQUARE BASE
Made in Ebony Base—Crystal Bowl

4120	Goblet	8.00--10.00
4120	High Sherbet	6.00----8.00
4120	7 oz. Low Sherbet	3.00----5.00
4120	5 oz. Low Sherbet	3.00----4.00
4120	3½ oz. Cocktail	8.00--10.00
4120	2 oz. Whiskey	8.00--10.00
4120	5, 10, 13, 16 oz. Tumbler	6.00----9.00
4121	Finger Bowl	2.00----4.00
2419	6", 7", 8" Sq. Plate	2.00----6.00
2350½—Ftd. Cup		3.00----5.00
2419	Saucer	2.00----3.00
2350	After Dinner Cup	2.00----4.00
2419	After Dinner Saucer	2.00----3.00

Made in Solid Crystal

4020	Goblet	5.00----8.00
4020	High Sherbet	4.00----6.00
4020	7 oz. Low Sherbet	3.00----4.00
4020	5 oz. Low Sherbet	2.00----3.00
4020	3½ oz. Cocktail	5.00----8.00
4020	2 oz. Whiskey	5.00----8.00
4020	5, 10, 13, 16 oz. Tumbler	3.00----6.00
4021	Finger Bowl	2.00----4.00

CUTTING No. 701
TAPESTRY DESIGN—SQUARE BASE
Made in Crystal

4020	Goblet	5.00----8.00
4020	High Sherbet	4.00----6.00
4020	5, 7 oz. Low Sherbet	3.00----4.00
4020	3½ oz. Cocktail	5.00----8.00
4020	2 oz. Whiskey	5.00----8.00
4020	5, 10, 13, 16 oz. Tumbler	3.00----6.00
4021	Finger Bowl	2.00----4.00
2419	6", 7", 8" Sq. Plate	2.00----6.00
2350½—Ftd. Cup		2.00----4.00
2419	Saucer	2.00----3.00
2350	After Dinner Cup	2.00----4.00
2419	After Dinner Saucer	2.00----3.00

CUTTING No. 702—COMET DESIGN
Made in Solid Crystal

4020	Goblet	6.00----8.00
4020	High Sherbet	4.00----6.00
4020	5, 7 oz. Low Sherbet	3.00----4.00
4020	3½ oz. Cocktail	6.00----8.00
4020	2 oz. Whiskey	6.00----8.00
4020	5, 10, 13, 16 oz. Tumbler	3.00----6.00
4021	Finger Bowl	2.00----4.00
4020	Ftd. Jug	20.00--25.00
4020	Sugar	4.00----6.00
4020	Cream	4.00----6.00
2419	6", 7", 8" Plate	2.00----5.00
2419	Ftd. Cup	2.00----4.00
2419	Saucer	2.00----3.00
2419	After Dinner Cup	2.00----4.00
2419	After Dinner Saucer	2.00----3.00
2430	8" Vase	12.00--15.00

Made in Ebony Base—Crystal Bowl

4120	Goblet	8.00--10.00
4120	High Sherbet	5.00----7.00
4120	5, 7 oz. Low Sherbet	4.00----6.00
4120	3½ oz. Cordial	8.00--10.00
4120	2 oz. Whiskey	8.00--10.00
4120	5, 10, 13, 16 oz. Tumbler	6.00----9.00
4121	Finger Bowl	3.00----4.00
4120	Ftd. Jug	25.00--35.00
4120	Sugar	5.00----7.00
4120	Cream	5.00----7.00

CUTTING No. 703
NEW YORKER DESIGN
1931—1944
Solid Crystal
Green Base with Crystal Bowl
Not in Fostoria Book

4020	Goblet	8.00--10.00
4020	High Sherbet	6.00----8.00
4020	7 oz. Low Sherbet	2.00----4.00
4020½—4 oz. Cocktail		8.00--10.00
4020	2 oz. Whiskey	8.00--10.00
4020	5, 10, 13, 16 oz. Ftd. Tum	6.00----9.00
4021	Finger Bowl	2.00----4.00
4020	Ftd. Jug	20.00--30.00
4020	Ftd. Sugar	4.00----6.00
4020	Ftd. Cream	4.00----6.00
4020	Decanter	15.00--25.00
2419	6", 7", 8" Plate (Crys. only	2.00----4.00

ROYAL GARDEN DESIGN
CUTTING No. 704
Solid Crystal—Solid Topaz
1931—1933
Not in Fostoria Book

2433	12" Bowl "A"	20.00--25.00
2433	3" Candlestick	6.00----8.00
2433	6" Tall Comport	8.00--12.00
2430	11" Bowl	10.00--15.00
2430	9½" Candlestick	8.00--12.00
2394	12" Bowl "A"	15.00--20.00
2394	2" Candlestick	4.00----6.00
2443	6" Ice Tub	12.00--16.00
2447	Duo Candlestick	8.00--12.00
4107	12" Vase	10.00--15.00

4108	6″ Vase	8.00--10.00
2430	8″ Vase	9.00--12.00
2419	Handled Lunch Tray	12.00--15.00
2375	10″ Cake Plate	10.00--15.00
2430	½ lb. Candy Jar & Cover	15.00--20.00

BARCELONA DESIGN
CUTTING No. 705
Solid Rose—Solid Azure
1931—1933
Not in Fostoria Book

2297	12″ Bowl "A"	15.00--20.00
2324	4″ Candlestick	5.00----7.00
4100	8″ Vase	10.00--14.00
2430	8″ Vase	10.00--14.00
2287	11″ Handled Lunch Tray	10.00--15.00
2430	7″ Jelly	6.00----8.00
2394	6″ Bowl	8.00--10.00
2375	7″ Comport	8.00--12.00
2331	3 Candy Box & Cover	12.00--16.00
2375	Large Dessert	8.00--12.00
2375	10″ Cake Plate	8.00--12.00
2375	Lemon Dish	5.00----7.00
2375	Bon Bon	5.00----7.00
2375	Sweetmeat	5.00----7.00
2375	Whip Cream	5.00----7.00
2375½—Ftd. Sugar		6.00--10.00
2375½—Ftd. Cream		6.00--10.00

CUTTING No. 707
STAUNTON DESIGN—ROCK CRYSTAL
and
CUTTING No. 708
NAIRN DESIGN—ROCK CRYSTAL

6004	9 oz. Goblet	5.00----8.00
6004	5½ oz. High Sherbet	4.00----6.00
6004	5½ oz. Low Sherbet	2.00----4.00
6004	3 oz. Cocktail	5.00----8.00
6004	4 oz. Claret	5.00----8.00
6004	2½ oz. Wine	5.00----8.00
6004	4½ oz. Oyster Cocktail	5.00----7.00
6004	2½, 5, 9, 12 oz. Ftd. Tumb.	4.00----6.00
869	Finger Bowl	2.00----4.00
2283	6″ Finger Bowl Plate, R/O	2.00----3.00
2283	7″, 8″ Plate, R/O	3.00----5.00
2451	Ice Dish	4.00----6.00
2451	Ice Dish Plate	4.00----6.00
2470½—10½″ Bowl		15.00--20.00
2470½—5½″ Candlestick		5.00----8.00

CUTTING No. 709
YORK DESIGN—ROCK CRYSTAL
and
CUTTING No. 710
BRISTOL DESIGN—ROCK CRYSTAL
and

CUTTING No. 711
INVERNESS DESIGN
—ROCK CRYSTAL
1933—1936
Not in Fostoria Book

6007	10 oz. Goblet	5.00----8.00
6007	5½ oz. High Sherbet	4.00----6.00
6007	5½ oz. Low Sherbet	3.00----5.00
6007	3½ oz. Cocktail	5.00----8.00
6007	4 oz. Ciaret	5.00----8.00
6007	3 oz. Wine	5.00----8.00

6007	1 oz. Cordial	5.00----8.00
6007	4½ oz. Oyster Cocktail	5.00----8.00
6007	2, 5, 9, 12 oz. Ftd. Tumb.	3.00----6.00
869	Finger Bowl	2.00----4.00
2283	6″ Finger Bowl Plate, R/O	2.00----3.00
2283	7″ Plate, R/O	2.00----4.00
2283	8″ Plate, R/O	3.00----5.00
2451	Ice Dish	3.00----5.00
2451	Ice Dish Plate	3.00----5.00
2440	13″ Torte Plate	15.00--20.00
2470	10″ Cake Plate	10.00--15.00
2470	6″ Tall Comport	9.00--12.00
2470	12″ Bowl	27.00--30.00
2470	5½″ Candlestick	6.00----8.00

CUTTING No. 712
WATERBURY DESIGN—ROCK CRYSTAL

6000	10 oz. Goblet	5.00----8.00
6000	6 oz. High Sherbet	4.00----6.00
6000	6 oz. Low Sherbet	4.00----6.00
6000	3½ oz. Cocktail	4.00----6.00
6000	3 oz. Wine	4.00----6.00
6000	4 oz. Oyster Cocktail	4.00----6.00
6000	12 oz. Ftd. Tumbler	4.00----6.00
6000	5 oz. Ftd. Tumbler	3.00----5.00
869	Finger Bowl	2.00----4.00
2283	6″ Finger Bowl Plate, R/O	2.00----3.00
2283	7″, 8″ Plate, R/O	3.00----5.00
2451	Ice Dish	3.00----5.00
2451	Ice Dish Plate	3.00----5.00
2453	7½″ Lustre	10.00--18.00
2424	8″ Bowl, Regular	15.00--20.00

CUTTING No. 713
EATON DESIGN—ROCK CRYSTAL
and
CUTTING No. 714
OXFORD DESIGN—ROCK CRYSTAL

6007	10 oz. Goblet	5.00----8.00
6007	5½ oz. High Sherbet	4.00----6.00
6007	5½ oz. Low Sherbet	3.00----5.00
6007	3½ oz. Cocktail	5.00----8.00
6007	4 oz. Claret	5.00----8.00
6007	3 oz. Wine	5.00----8.00
6007	1 oz. Cordial	5.00----8.00
6007	4½ oz. Oyster Cocktail	5.00----8.00
6007	2, , 9, 12 oz. Ftd. Tumb.	3.00----6.00
869	Finger Bowl	2.00----4.00
2283	6″ Finger Bowl Plate, R/O	2.00----4.00
2283	7″, 8″ Plate R/O	3.00----5.00
2451	Ice Dish	4.00----6.00
2451	Ice Dish Plate	3.00----5.00
2451	Tomato Juice Liner (N. C.)	1.00----2.00
2451	Crab Meat Liner (Not Cut)	1.00----2.00
2451	Fruit Cocktail Liner (N.C.)	1.00----2.00
2440	Ftd. Sugar	4.00----6.00
2440	Ftd. Cream	4.00----6.00
2440	13″ Torte Plate	15.00--20.00
2400	6″ Comport	6.00----8.00
2419	5 Part Relish	8.00--10.00
2430	½ lb. Candy & Cover	8.00--12.00
2470½—10½″ Bowl		10.00--15.00
2470½—5½″ Candlestick		6.00----8.00
2482	Trindle Candlestick	10.00--12.00
2467	7½″ Vase	9.00--12.00
2472	Duo Candlestick	8.00--10.00
2470	Lemon Dish	3.00----4.00
2470	Bon Bon	3.00----4.00
2470	Sweetmeat	3.00----4.00

| 2470 | Cake Plate | 8.00--10.00 |
| 2481 | 11" Oblong Bowl | 10.00--15.00 |

CUTTING No. 715
CARLISLE DESIGN
--ROCK CRYSTAL
1933—1936
Not in Fostoria Book
and

CUTTING No. 716
CANTERBURY DESIGN
—ROCK CRYSTAL
1933—1936
Not in Fostoria Book
and

CUTTING No. 717
MARLBORO DESIGN—ROCK CRYSTAL

6008	10 oz. Goblet	5.00----8.00
6008	5½ oz. High Sherbet	4.00----6.00
6008	5½ oz. Low Sherbet	3.00----5.00
6008	3¾ oz. Cocktail	5.00----8.00
6008	4 oz. Wine	5.00----8.00
6008	1 oz. Cordial	5.00----8.00
6008	5 oz. Oyster Cocktail	5.00----8.00
6008	5, 9, 12 oz. Ftd. Tumbler	4.00----6.00
869	Finger Bowl	2.00----4.00
2283	6" Finger Bowl Plate R/O	2.00----3.00
2283	7", 8" Plate, R/O	3.00----5.00
2451	Ice Dish	3.00----5.00
2451	Ice Dish Plate	3.00----5.00
2440	Ftd. Sugar	4.00----6.00
2440	Ftd. Cream	4.00----6.00
2364	16" Plate	15.00--20.00
2400	6" Comport	6.00----8.00
2470	Lemon Dish	3.00----5.00
2470	Bon Bon	3.00----5.00
2470	Sweetmeat	3.00----5.00
2470	Cake Plate	8.00--10.00
2470½—10½" Bowl	10.00--15.00
2470½—5½" Candlestick	6.00----8.00
2472	Duo Candlestick	8.00--10.00
2482	Trindle Candlestick	10.00--12.00
2440	7" Vase	9.00--12.00
4107	9" Vase	10.00--15.00

CUTTING No. 718
DONCASTER DESIGN—ROCK CRYSTAL
and

CUTTING No. 719
LANCASTER DESIGN
—ROCK CRYSTAL
1933—1936
Not in Fostoria Book

6009	9 oz. Goblet	5.00----8.00
6009	5½ oz. Saucer Champagne	4.00----6.00
6009	5½ oz. Low Sherbet	3.00----5.00
6009	3¾ oz. Cocktail	5.00----8.00
6009	3¾ oz. Claret-Wine	5.00----8.00
6009	1 oz. Cordial	5.00----8.00
6009	4¾ oz. Oyster Cocktail	5.00----8.00
6009	5, 9, 12 oz. Ftd. Tumbler	4.00----6.00
869	Finger Bowl	2.00----4.00
2337	6", 7", 8" Plate	2.00----4.00
2400	6" Comport	6.00----8.00
2440	13" Torte Plate	15.00--20.00
4112	8½" Vase	10.00--14.00
2470½—10½" Bowl	10.00--15.00
2470½—5½" Candlestick	6.00----8.00

CUTTING No. 720
NOTTINGHAM DESIGN
—ROCK CRYSTAL
1933—1935
Not in Fostoria Book
and

CUTTING No. 721
BUCKINGHAM DESIGN
—ROCK CRYSTAL
1933—1935
Not in Fostoria Book

6009	9 oz. Goblet	5.00----8.00
6009	5½ oz. High Sherbet	4.00----6.00
6009	5½ oz. Low Sherbet	3.00----5.00
6009	3¾ oz. Cocktail	5.00----8.00
6009	3¾ oz. Claret-Wine	5.00----8.00
6009	1 oz. Cordial	5.00----8.00
6009	4¾ oz. Oyster Cocktail	5.00----8.00
6009	5, 9, 12 oz. Ftd. Tumbler	4.00----6.00
869	Finger Bowl	2.00----4.00
2337	6", 7", 8" Plate	2.00----5.00
2400	6" Comport	6.00----8.00
4112	8½" Vase	10.00--14.00
2470½—10½" Bowl	10.00--15.00
2470½—5½" Candlestick	6.00----8.00

CUTTING No. 722
WELLINGTON DESIGN—ROCK CRYSTAL
and

CUTTING No. 722½
LEICESTER DESIGN
—ROCK CRYSTAL
1933—1935
Not in Fostoria Book
and

CUTTING No. 723
WESTMINSTER DESIGN—ROCK CRYSTAL

6010	9 oz. Goblet	5.00----8.00
6010	5½ oz. High Sherbet	4.00----6.00
6010	5½ oz. Low Sherbet	3.00----5.00
6010	4 oz. Cocktail	5.00----8.00
6010	4½ oz. Claret-Wine	5.00----8.00
6010	1 oz. Cordial	5.00----8.00
6010	5½ oz. Oyster Cocktail	5.00----8.00
6010	5, 9, 12 oz. Ftd. Tumbler	4.00----6.00
869	Finger Bowl	2.00----4.00
2337	6", 7", 8" Plate	2.00----4.00
2400	6" Comport	6.00----8.00
2470	10" Vase	12.00--15.00
2470½—10½" Bowl	10.00--15.00
2470½—5½" Candlestick	6.00----8.00

CUTTING No. 725
MANHATTAN DESIGN—ROCK CRYSTAL
and
CUTTING No. 726
METEOR DESIGN
Made in Solid Crystal
and
CUTTING No. 727
NATIONAL DESIGN
Made in Solid Crystal
and
CUTTING No. 728
EMBASSY DESIGN
Made in Solid Crystal

4024	11½ oz. Goblet	4.00----6.00
4024	10 oz. Goblet	4.00----6.00
4024	6½ oz. Saucer Champagne	3.00----5.00

4024	5½ oz. Sherbet	2.00----4.00
4024	4 oz. Cocktail	4.00----6.00
4024	3½ oz. Rhine Wine	4.00----6.00
4024	3½ oz. Wine	4.00----6.00
4024	2 oz. Sherry	4.00----6.00
4024	1 oz. Cordial	4.00----6.00
4024	4 oz. Oyster Cocktail	4.00----6.00
4024	2, 5, 8, 12 oz. Ftd. Tumb.	3.00----5.00
4024	5" Comport	4.00----6.00
701	12 oz. Tumb., Sham, Plain	3.00----5.00
701	10 oz. Tumb., Sham, Plain	3.00----5.00
1184	7 oz. O.F. Cocktail, Sham, Pl	2.00----4.00
887	1¼ oz. Whiskey	3.00----5.00
869	Finger Bowl	2.00----4.00
6011	Ftd. Jug	20.00--30.00
6011	Ftd. Decanter	15.00--20.00
2337	6", 7", 8" Plate	2.00----5.00
2337	11" Plate	9.00--12.00
4024	10" Ftd. Bowl	10.00--14.00
4024	6" Candlestick	4.00----6.00

CUTTING No. 729—ROCKET DESIGN
Made in Solid Crystal
and
CUTTING No. 730—WHIRPOOL DESIGN
Made in Solid Crystal
and
CUTTING No. 731—CELESTIAL DESIGN
Made in Solid Crystal

6011	10 oz. Goblet	4.00----6.00
6011	5½ oz. Saucer Champagne	3.00----5.00
6011	5½ oz. Low Sherbet	2.00----4.00
6011	3 oz. Cocktail	4.00----6.00
6011	4½ oz. Rhine Wine	4.00----6.00
6011	4½ oz. Claret	4.00----6.00
6011	3 oz. Wine	4.00----6.00
6011	2 oz. Sherry	4.00----6.00
6011	2 oz. Creme de Menthe	4.00----6.00
6011	1 oz. Cordial	4.00----6.00
6011	1 oz. Brandy	4.00----6.00
6011	4 oz. Oyster Cocktail	4.00----6.00
6011	5, 10, 13 oz. Ftd. Tumbler	3.00----5.00
6011	2 oz. Ftd. Whiskey	4.00----6.00
6011	Ftd. Jug	20.00--30.00
6011	Ftd. Decanter	15.00--20.00
795	5½ oz. Hol. Stem Champ.	4.00----6.00
863	5 oz. Hol. Stem Champ. C/F	4.00----6.00
906	Brandy Inhaler	6.00----8.00
1769	Finger Bowl	2.00----4.00
701	10, 12 oz. Tumb., Sham, Pl.	2.00----4.00
1184	7 oz. O.F. Cocktail, Sham, Pl.	1.00----3.00
887	1¼ oz. Whiskey, Sham, Plain	2.00----3.00
4122	1½ oz. Whiskey, Sham, Plain	2.00----3.00
2337	6", 7", 8" Plate	1.00----4.00
4024	10" Ftd. Bowl	10.00--15.00
4024	6" Candlestick	4.00----6.00

CUTTING No. 732—SEAWEED DESIGN
Made in Solid Crystal
and
CUTTING No. 733—MARQUETTE DESIGN
ROCK CRYSTAL

4024½	11 oz. Goblet	4.00----6.00
4024	10 oz. Goblet	4.00----6.00
4024	6 oz. Saucer Champagne	3.00----5.00
4024	5½ oz. Sherbet	4.00----6.00
4024	4 oz. Cocktail	4.00----6.00
4024	3½ oz. Rhine Wine	4.00----6.00
4024	3½ oz. Claret	4.00----6.00

4024	2 oz. Sherry	4.00---6.00
4024	1 oz. Cordial	4.00---6.00
4024	4 oz. Oyster Cocktail	4.00---6.00
4024	2, 5, 8, 12 oz. Ftd. Tumbler	3.00---5.00
4024	5" Comport	4.00---6.00
869	Finger Bowl	2.00---4.00
701	10, 12 oz. Tumb., Sham, Pl.	3.00---5.00
1184	7 oz. O.F. Cocktail, Sham, Pl.	2.00---4.00
887	1¼ oz. Whiskey, Sham, Pl.	2.00---3.00
4122	1½ oz. Whiskey, Sham, Pl.	2.00---3.00
6011	Ftd. Jug	20.00--30.00
6011	Ftd. Decanter	15.00--20.00
2337	6", 7", 8" Plate	1.00---4.00
4024	10" Ftd. Bowl	10.00--15.00
4024	6" Candlestick	4.00---6.00
795	5½ oz. Hol. Stem Champ.	4.00---6.00
863	5 oz. Hol. Stem Champ.	4.00---6.00
906	Brandy Inhaler	6.00---8.00

CUTTING No. 734—PLANET DESIGN
Made in Solid Crystal
and
CUTTING No. 735
SHOOTING STARS DESIGN
Made in Solid Crystal

6011	10 oz. Goblet	4.00----6.00
6011	5½ oz. Saucer Champagne	3.00----5.00
6011	5½ oz. Low Sherbet	2.00----4.00
6011	3 oz. Cocktail	4.00----6.00
6011	4½ oz. Rhine Wine	4.00----6.00
6011	4½ oz. Claret	4.00----6.00
6011	3 oz. Wine	4.00----6.00
6011	2 oz. Sherry	4.00----6.00
6011	2 oz. Creme de Menthe	4.00----6.00
6011	1 oz. Cordial	4.00----6.00
6011	1 oz. Brandy	4.00----6.00
6011	4 oz. Oyster Cocktail	4.00----6.00
6011	2, 5, 10, 13 oz. Ftd. Tumbler	3.00----5.00
6011	Ftd. Jug	20.00--30.00
6011	Ftd. Decanter	15.00--20.00
795	5½ oz. Hol. Stem Champ.	4.00----6.00
863	5 oz. Hol. Stem Champ., C/F	4.00----6.00
906	Brandy Inhaler	6.00----8.00
1769	Finger Bowl	2.00----4.00
701	10, 12 oz. Tumb., Sham, Pl.	2.00----3.00
1184	7 oz. O.F. Cocktail, Sham, Pl.	1.00----3.00
887	1¼ oz. Whiskey, Sham, Pl.	2.00----3.00
4122	1½ oz. Whiskey, Sham, Pl.	2.00----3.00
2337	6", 7", 8" Plate	1.00----4.00
4024	10" Ftd. Bowl	10.00--12.00
4024	6" Candlestick	4.00----6.00

DIRECTOIRE DESIGN
CUTTING No. 736
Made in Solid Crystal
and
CUTTING No. 737 QUINFOIL DESIGN
Made in Solid Crystal

6011	10 oz. Goblet	4.00----6.00
6011	5½ oz. Saucer Champagne	3.00----5.00
6011	5½ oz. Low Sherbet	2.00----4.00
6011	4½ oz. Rhine Wine	4.00----6.00
6011	3 oz. Cocktail	4.00----6.00
6011	4½ oz. Claret	4.00----6.00
6011	3 oz. Wine	4.00----6.00
6011	2 oz. Sherry	4.00----6.00
6011	2 oz. Creme de Menthe	4.00----6.00
6011	1 oz. Brandy	4.00----6.00
6011	4 oz. Oyster Cocktail	4.00----6.00

6011	2, 10, 13 oz. Ftd. Tumbler	3.00----5.00
1769	Finger Bowl	2.00----4.00
6011	Ftd. Decanter	20.00--30.00
2518	Decanter	15.00--20.00
2518	Cocktail Shaker	20.00--25.00
701	12 oz. Tumbler, Sham.	1.00----2.00
701	10 oz. Tumbler, Sham	1.00----2.00
1185	O. F. Cocktail, Sham	2.00----3.00
2518	Whiskey	1.00----3.00
795	Hollow Stem Champagne	2.00----4.00
906	Brandy Inhaler	3.00----6.00
2337	6'', 7'', 8'' Plate	1.00----4.00
2400	6'' Comport	5.00----7.00
2350½	Ftd. Sugar	3.00----5.00
2350½	Ftd. Cream	3.00----5.00
319	Bar Bottle	8.00--12.00
4024	10'' Ftd. Bowl	10.00--15.00
4024	6'' Candlestick	4.00----6.00
4122	Whiskey, Sham	1.00----2.00
6011	Ftd. Jug	15.00--20.00
2518	5 oz. Wine	1.00----3.00

FESTOON DESIGN
CUTTING No. 738
and
ROCK GARDEN DESIGN
CUTTING No. 739
ROCK CRYSTAL

6012	10 oz. Goblet	5.00----8.00
6012	5½ oz. Saucer Champagne	4.00----6.00
6012	5½ oz. Low Sherbet	3.00----5.00
6012	4½ oz. Rhine Wine	5.00----8.00
6012	3 oz. Cocktail	5.00----8.00
6012	4½ oz. Claret	5.00----8.00
6012	3 oz. Wine	5.00----8.00
6012	2 oz. Sherry	5.00----8.00
6012	2 oz. Creme de Menthe	5.00----8.00
6012	1 oz. Cordial	5.00----8.00
6012	1 oz. Brandy	5.00----8.00
6012	4 oz. Ftd. Cocktail (Oyster)	5.00----8.00
6012	5, 10, 13 oz. Ftd. Tumbler	3.00----5.00
1769	Finger Bowl	2.00----3.00
701	12 oz. Tumbler, Sham	2.00----3.00
701	10 oz. Tumbler, Sham	2.00----3.00
1185	O. F. Cocktail, Sham	2.00----4.00
4122	1½ oz. Whiskey, Sham	1.00----2.00
6011	Ftd. Jug	20.00--30.00
6011	Ftd. Decanter	15.00--20.00
2525	Decanter	18.00--22.00
2337	6'', 7'', 8'' Plate	1.00----4.00
2400	6'' Comport	5.00----7.00
2364	16'' Plate	15.00--20.00
2440	13'' Plate	12.00--18.00
4117	Bubble Candy Jar & Cover	8.00--12.00
4024	10'' Ftd. Bowl	10.00--15.00
4024	6'' Candlestick	4.00----6.00
2470	10'' Vase	12.00--15.00
2350½	Ftd. Sugar	4.00----6.00
2350½	Ftd. Cream	4.00----6.00
863	Hollow Stem Champagne	2.00----4.00
319	Bar Bottle	8.00--12.00

CUTTING No. 740—RONDEAU DESIGN
ROCK CRYSTAL
and
CUTTING No. 741—WATERCRESS DESIGN
ROCK CRYSTAL

6012	10 oz. Goblet	5.00----8.00
6012	5½ oz. Saucer Champagne	4.00----6.00
6012	5½ oz. Low Sherbet	3.00----5.00

6012	4½ oz. Rhine Wine	5.00----8.00
6012	3 oz. Cocktail	5.00----8.00
6012	4½ oz. Claret	5.00----8.00
6012	3 oz. Wine	5.00----8.00
6012	2 oz. Sherry	5.00----8.00
6012	2 oz. Creme de Menthe	5.00----8.00
6012	1 oz. Cordial	5.00----8.00
6012	1 oz. Brandy	5.00----8.00
6012	4 oz. Ftd. Cocktail (Oyster)	5.00----8.00
6012	5, 10, 13 oz. Ftd. Tumbler	3.00----5.00
1769	Finger Bowl	2.00----3.00
863	5 oz. Hol. Stem Champ. C/F	3.00----5.00
701	10, 12 oz. tumbler, Sham	2.00----3.00
1185	O. F. Cocktail, Sham	2.00----4.00
4122	1½ oz. Whiskey, Sham	1.00----2.00
6011	Ftd. Jug	20.00--25.00
2525	Decanter	18.00--22.00
2525	Cocktail Shaker	20.00--25.00
2337	6'', 7'', 8'' Plate	1.00----4.00
2350½	Ftd. Sugar	4.00----6.00
2350½	Ftd. Cream	4.00----6.00
2364	16'' Plate	15.00--20.00
2440	13'' Torte Plate	12.00--18.00
2440	8½'' Oval Tray	4.00----6.00
2440	2 Part Mayonnaise	5.00----7.00
2440	2, 3 Part Hdld. Relish	5.00----7.00
2440	4½'' Hdld. Sweetmeat	3.00----4.00
2400	6'' Comport	5.00----7.00
2496	Trindle Candlestick	10.00--12.00
2472	Duo Candlestick	8.00--10.00
2470½	10½'' Bowl	10.00--15.00
4024	10'' Ftd. Bowl	10.00--15.00
4024	6'' Candlestick	4.00----6.00
2470	10'' Vase	12.00--15.00

CUTTING No. 743—HERALDRY DESIGN
Made in Solid Crystal

6012	10 oz. Goblet	3.00----5.00
6012	5½ oz. Saucer Champagne	3.00----5.00
6012	5½ oz. Low Sherbet	2.00----4.00
6012	4½ oz. Rhine Wine	3.00----5.00
6012	3 oz. Cocktail	3.00----5.00
6012	4½ oz. Claret	3.00----5.00
6012	3 oz. Wine	3.00----5.00
6012	2 oz. Sherry	3.00----5.00
6012	2 oz. Creme de Menthe	3.00----5.00
6012	1 oz. Cordial	3.00----5.00
6012	1 oz. Brandy	3.00----5.00
6012	4 oz. Ftd. Cocktail (Oyster)	3.00----5.00
6012	5, 10, 13 oz. Ftd. Tumbler	3.00----5.00
1769	Finger Bowl	2.00----3.00
6011	Ftd. Jug	15.00--25.00
701	10 oz. Tumb., Sham, Pl.	2.00----3.00
701	12 oz. Tumb., Sham, Pl.	2.00----3.00
1185	7 oz. O.F. Cocktail Pl.	1.00----3.00
2337	6'', 7'', 8'' Plate	1.00----4.00
2400	6'' Comport	5.00----7.00
2364	11'' Sandwich Plate	6.00----8.00
2364	14'' Torte Plate	9.00--12.00
2364	2 Part Relish	3.00----5.00
2364	3 Part Relish	3.00----5.00
2364	Shaker & Chrome Top ''C''	2.00----3.00
2666	Sugar	3.00----5.00
2666	Cream	3.00----5.00
2666	3 Pc. Ind. Sugar, Cm. & Tray	8.00--10.00
2364	9'' Salad Bowl	8.00--10.00
2364	12'' Bowl, Flared	8.00--10.00
2364	12'' Lily Pond	10.00--15.00
2324	4'' Candlestick	3.00----5.00
6023	Duo Candlestick	4.00----6.00

2666	Cup	2.00----3.00
2350	Saucer	1.00----2.00
2666	Pint Pitcher	8.00--10.00
2666	Quart Pitcher	8.00--10.00
2666	3 Pint Pitcher	10.00--12.00
2364	Mayonnaise, Plate & Ladle	4.00----6.00

CUTTING No. 742
ORBIT DESIGN—ROCK CRYSTAL
and
CUTTING No. 744—REGENCY DESIGN
Made in Solid Crystal

6012	10 oz. Goblet	3.00----5.00
6012	5½ oz. Saucer Champagne	3.00----5.00
6012	5½ oz. Low Sherbet	2.00----4.00
6012	4½ oz. Rhine Wine	3.00----5.00
6012	3 oz. Cocktail	3.00----5.00
6012	4½ oz. Claret	3.00----5.00
6012	3 oz. Wine	3.00----5.00
6012	2 oz. Sherry	3.00----5.00
6012	2 oz. Creme de Menthe	3.00----5.00
6012	1 oz. Cordial	3.00----5.00
6012	1 oz. Brandy	3.00----5.00
6012	4 oz. Ftd. Cocktail (Oyster)	3.00----5.00
6012	5, 10, 13 oz. Ftd. Tumbler	2.00----5.00
1769	Finger Bowl	1.00----3.00
6011	Ftd. Jug	15.00--20.00
701	10, 12 oz. Tumbl, Sham, Pl.	2.00----4.00
1185	7 oz. O.F. Cocktail, Plain	2.00----4.00
2337	6", 7", 8" Plate	1.00----4.00
2440	13" Torte Plate	10.00--15.00
2470½—10½" Bowl		10.00--14.00
2470	Duo Candlestick	4.00----6.00
2525	Decanter	15.00--20.00
2525	42 oz. Cocktail Shaker	20.00--25.00
2525½—30 oz. Cocktail Shaker		15.00--20.00
319	Bar Bottle	8.00--12.00
2550½—Ftd. Sugar		2.00----4.00
2550½—Ftd. Cream		2.00----4.00
2400	6" Comport	4.00----7.00

CUTTING No. 745
IVY DESIGN—ROCK CRYSTAL
and
CUTTING No. 746—GOSSAMER DESIGN
Made in Crystal

6012	10 oz. Goblet	4.00----6.00
6012	5½ oz. Saucer Champagne	4.00----6.00
6012	5½ oz. Low Sherbet	3.00----5.00
6012	4½ oz. Rhine Wine	4.00----6.00
6012	3 oz. Cocktail	4.00----6.00
6012	4½ oz. Claret	4.00----6.00
6012	3 oz. Wine	4.00----6.00
6012	2 oz. Sherry	4.00----6.00
6012	2 oz. Creme de Menthe	4.00----6.00
6012	1 oz. Cordial	4.00----6.00
6012	1 oz. Brandy	4.00----6.00
6012	4 oz. Ftd. Cocktail (Oyster)	4.00----6.00
6012	5, 10, 13 oz. Ftd. Tumbler	2.00----5.00
1769	Finger Bowl	2.00----4.00
6011	Ftd. Jug	15.00--25.00
701	10 oz. Tumb., Sham, Plain	2.00----4.00
701	12 oz. Tumb., Sham, Plain	2.00----4.00
1185	7 oz. O.F. Cocktail, Plain	2.00----4.00
2337	6", 7", 8" Plate	1.00----4.00
2400	6" Comport	5.00----7.00
2536	9" Handled Bowl	10.00--15.00
2535	5½" Candlestick	5.00----7.00

CUTTING No. 747
FANTASY DESIGN—ROCK CRYSTAL
and
CUTTING No. 748
ALLEGRO DESIGN—ROCK CRYSTAL

6013	10 oz. Goblet	5.00----8.00
6013	9 oz. Low Goblet	4.00----7.00
6013	6 oz. Saucer Champagne	4.00----7.00
6013	5 oz. Low Sherbet	3.00----5.00
6013	3½ oz. Cocktail	5.00----8.00
6013	4 oz. Claret	5.00----8.00
6013	3 oz. Wine	5.00--8.00
6013	1 oz. Cordial	5.00----8.00
6013	4 oz. Oyster Cocktail	5.00----8.00
6013	13 oz. Ftd. Tumbler	5.00----7.00
6013	5 oz. Ftd. Tumbler	3.00----5.00
6013	5" Comport	4.00---6.00
766	Finger Bowl, N/O	2.00----4.00
5000	Ftd. Jug	20.00--30.00
701	10, 12 oz. Tumb., Sham,	3.00----5.00
1184	7 oz. O. F. Cocktail,	2.00----4.00
2337	6", 7", 8" Plate	1.00----4.00
2533	9" Handled Bowl	15.00--20.00
2533	Duo Candlestick	8.00--10.00

CUTTING No. 749
CELEBRITY DESIGN—ROCK CRYSTAL
and
CUTTING No. 750
MEMORIES DESIGN—ROCK CRYSTAL

6000	10 oz. Goblet	5.00----8.00
6000	6 oz. High Sherbet	5.00----7.00
6000	6 oz. Low Sherbet	3.00----5.00
6000	3½ oz. Cocktail	5.00----8.00
6000	3 oz. Wine	5.00----8.00
6000	4 oz. Oyster Cocktail	5.00----8.00
6000	13 oz. Ftd. Tumbler	4.00----6.00
6000	5 oz. Ftd. Tumbler	4.00----6.00
869	Finger Bowl, Optic	3.00----4.00
5000	Ftd. Jug	25.00--30.00
701	10, 12 oz. Tumb., Sham, Pl.	3.00----5.00
1185	7 oz. L.F. Cocktail, Plain	3.00----5.00
2337	6", 7", 8" Plate	2.00----5.00
2337	11" Service Plate	6.00----8.00
2424	8" Bowl, Regular	8.00--12.00
2481	5" Candlestick	4.00----6.00

CUTTING No. 751—HEIRLOOM DESIGN
Fancy Pieces in Rock Crystal

2394	12" Bowl	15.00--20.00
2447	Duo Candlestick	8.00--10.00
2527	2 Light Candelabra, U.D.P.	20.00--25.00
2470	10" Vase	15.00--20.00
2514	5 Part Relish	15.00--20.00
2440	2 Part Relish	6.00----9.00
2440	3 Part Relish	7.00--10.00
2440	2 Part Oval Mayonnaise	6.00----9.00
2440	Oval Sauce Dish	8.00--10.00
2440	Oval Tray	8.00--10.00
2440	13" Torte Plate	15.00--20.00
2364	16" Plate	20.00--25.00

ENGRAVING No. 752
EVANGELINE DESIGN
Made in Solid Crystal

2364	16" Plate	20.00--25.00
2440	13" Torte Plate	15.00--20.00

2440	3 Part Relish	7.00--10.00
2440	2 Part Relish	6.00----9.00
2440	2 Part Mayonnaise	6.00----9.00
2440	6½" Oval Sauce Dish	6.00----8.00
2440	8½" Oval Tray	8.00--10.00
2440	Cake Plate	9.00--12.00
2440	Pickle	7.00--10.00
2440	Celery	8.00--11.00
2419	4 Part Relish	8.00--10.00
2419	5 Part Relish	10.00--12.00
2514	5 Part Relish	12.00--14.00
2470½—10½" Bowl		10.00--14.00
2472	Duo Candlestick	8.00--10.00
2482	Trindle Candlestick	9.00--12.00
2470	10" Vase	10.00--14.00
2467	7½" Vase	9.00--12.00

CUTTING No. 753 PINNACLE DESIGN
Solid Crystal—Optic
1935—1938
Not in Fostoria Book

660	9 oz. Goblet	3.00----5.00
660	5 oz. Saucer Champagne	2.00----4.00
660	5 oz. Low Sherbet	1.00----3.00
660	4 oz. Claret	3.00----5.00
660	2¾ oz. Wine	3.00----5.00
660	¾ oz. Cordial	3.00----5.00
660	3 oz. Cocktail	3.00----5.00
4095	5, 10, 13 oz. Ftd. Tumbler	1.00----4.00
869	Finger Bowl	1.00----3.00
2337	6", 7", 8" Plate	1.00----4.00

CUTTING No. 754—CAVENDISH DESIGN
Rock Crystal—Optic
and
CUTTING No. 755—PALMETTO DESIGN
Rock Crystal—Optic

6014	9 oz. Goblet	5.00----8.00
6014	5½ oz. Saucer Champagne	4.00----6.00
6014	5½ oz. Low Sherbet	3.00----5.00
6014	3½ oz. Cocktail	5.00----8.00
6014	4 oz. Claret	5.00----8.00
6014	3 oz. Wine	5.00----8.00
6014	1 oz. Cordial	5.00----8.00
6014	4 oz. Oyster Cocktail	5.00----8.00
6014	5, 9, 12 oz. Ftd. Tumbler	3.00----5.00
869	Finger Bowl	3.00----4.00
5000	Ftd. Jug	25.00--35.00
2337	6", 7", 8" Plate	2.00----6.00
2533	9" Handled Bowl	15.00--20.00
2533	Duo Candlestick	8.00--10.00
2470½—10½" Bowl		10.00--15.00
2472	Duo Candlestick	8.00--10.00

CUTTING No. 756—BOUQUET DESIGN
Rock Crystal—Optic
and
CUTTING No. 757—SOCIETY DESIGN
Rock Crystal—Optic

6013	10 oz. Goblet	5.00----8.00
6013	9 oz. Low Goblet	4.00----7.00
6013	6 oz. Saucer Champagne	4.00----7.00
6013	5 oz. Low Sherbet	4.00----6.00

6013	3½ oz. Cocktail	5.00----8.00
6013	4 oz. Claret	5.00----8.00
6013	3 oz. Wine	5.00----8.00
6013	1 oz. Cordial	5.00----8.00
6013	4 oz. Oyster Cocktail	5.00----8.00
6013	13 oz. Ftd. Tumbler	4.00----6.00
6013	5 oz. Ftd. Tumbler	3.00----5.00
6013	5" Comport	5.00----7.00
766	Finger Bowl	2.00----4.00
2337	6", 7", 8" Plate	2.00----6.00
2527	9" Ftd. Bowl	15.00--20.00
2527	2 Lt. Candelabra, U.D.P.	20.00--25.00

CUTTING No. 758—BORDEAUX DESIGN
Made in Solid Crystal—Optic
and
CUTTING No. 759—WEYLIN DESIGN
Made in Solid Crystal—Optic

6014	9 oz. Goblet	4.00----6.00
6014	5½ oz. Saucer Champagne	3.00----5.00
6014	5½ oz. Low Sherbet	2.00----4.00
6014	3½ oz. Cocktail	4.00----6.00
6014	4 oz. Claret	4.00----6.00
6014	3 oz. Wine	4.00----6.00
6014	1 oz. Cordial	4.00----6.00
6014	5, 9, 12 oz. Ftd. Tumbler	3.00----5.00
869	Finger Bowl	2.00----4.00
5000	Ftd. Jug	25.00--35.00
2337	6", 7", 8" Plate, Optic	2.00----5.00
2375	Ice Bucket	10.00--15.00
2400	6" Comport	6.00----8.00
2451	Ice Dish	3.00----5.00
2451	Ice Dish Plate	2.00----4.00
2470½—10½" Bowl		10.00--15.00
2472	Duo Candlestick	8.00--10.00
2470	10" Vase	10.00--15.00
4121	5" Vase	8.00--10.00
4128	5" Vase	8.00--10.00

CUTTING No. 760—WHEAT DESIGN
Made in Solid Crystal

2375	Ice Bucket	10.00--15.00
2496	Ice Bucket, Chrom. Handle	10.00--15.00
2440	Ftd. Sugar	3.00----5.00
2440	Ftd. Cream	3.00----5.00
2496	Individual Sugar	2.00----4.00
2496	Individual Cream	2.00----4.00
2440	8½" Pickle	4.00----6.00
2496	8" Pickle	4.00----6.00
2440	11½" Celery	6.00----8.00
2496	11" Celery	6.00----8.00
2440	10" Cake Plate	8.00--10.00
2496	10" Cake Plate, 2 Hdles.	8.00--10.00
2496	8½" Serving Dish, 2 Hdles.	8.00--10.00
2419	5 Part Relish	8.00--10.00
2496	2, 3, 4 Part Relish	4.00----8.00
2496	Cheese & Cracker	8.00--12.00
2496	5½" Comport	4.00----6.00
2496	6½" Tall Comport	5.00----7.00
2496	Jelly & Cover	9.00--12.00
2496	Sweetmeat	4.00----6.00
2496	3-Toed Tid Bit, Flat	5.00----7.00
2496	3-Toed Bon Bon	5.00----7.00
2496	3-Toed Nut Bowl	5.00----7.00
2496	3-Part Candy Box & Cover	8.00--12.00
2496	Oblong Sauce Dish	4.00----6.00
2496	Oblong Tray	4.00----6.00
2496	2 Part Mayonnaise	4.00----6.00
2496½—Mayonnaise & Plate		6.00----8.00

2496	14" Torte Plate	15.00--20.00
2496	10" Floating Garden	10.00--12.00
2496	10½" Handled Bowl	10.00--15.00
2496	12" Bowl, Fld.	12.00--17.00
2496	5½" Candlestick	3.00----5.00
2496	4" Candlestick	3.00----5.00
2496	Duo Candlestick	6.00----8.00
2496	Trindle Candlestick	8.00--10.00
2545	12½" "Flame" Oval Bowl	8.00--12.00
2545	"Flame" Duo Candlestick	6.00----8.00
2545	2 Lt. "Flame" Candelabra, B Prisms	20.00--30.00
2470	10" Vase	10.00--12.00

CUTTING No. 761—MELBA DESIGN
Made in Solid Crystal
and
CUTTING No. 762—CUMBERLAND DESIGN
Rock Crystal—Optic

6016	10 oz. Goblet	5.00----8.00
6016	6 oz. Saucer Champagne	3.00----5.00
6016	6 oz. Low Sherbet	2.00----4.00
6016	3½ oz. Cocktail	5.00----8.00
6016	4½ oz. Claret	5.00----8.00
6016	3¼ oz. Wine	5.00----8.00
6016	¾ oz. Cordial	5.00----8.00
6016	4 oz. Oyster Cocktail	5.00----8.00
6016	5, 10, 13 oz. Ftd. Tumbler	3.00----6.00
869	Finger Bowl	2.00----4.00
5000	Ftd. Jug	25.00--35.00
2337	6", 7", 8" Plate, Optic	2.00----5.00
2400	6" Comport	6.00----8.00
2470½—10½" Bowl		10.00--15.00
2472	Duo Candlestick	8.00--10.00

CUTTING No. 763—CYRENE DESIGN
Made in Solid Crystal
and
CUTTING No. 764—PIERRETTE DESIGN
Rock Crystal—Plain—Hand Polished

6012	10 oz. Goblet	3.00----5.00
6012	5½ oz. Saucer Champagne	3.00----5.00
6012	5½ oz. Low Sherbet	2.00----4.00
6012	3 oz. Cocktail	3.00----5.00
6012	4½ oz. Claret	3.00----5.00
6012	3 oz. Wine	3.00----5.00
6012	1 oz. Cordial	3.00----5.00
6012	4 oz. Oyster Cocktail	3.00----5.00
6012	5, 10, 13 oz. Ftd. Tumbler	2.00----4.00
1769	Finger Bowl	2.00----3.00
6011	Ftd. Jug	25.00--30.00
2337	6", 7", 8" Plate	2.00----5.00

CUTTING No. 765
MADRI GRAS DESIGN
Rock Crystal—Plain—Hand Polished

6011	10 oz. goblet	3.00----5.00
6011	5½ oz. Saucer Champagne	3.00----5.00
6011	5½ oz. Low Sherbet	2.00----4.00
6011	3 oz. Cocktail	3.00----5.00
6011	4½ oz. Claret	3.00----5.00
6011	3 oz. Wine	3.00----5.00
6011	1 oz. Cordial	3.00----5.00
6011	4 oz. Oyster Cocktail	3.00----5.00
6011	5, 10, 13 oz. Ftd. Tumbler	2.00----4.00
1769	Finger Bowl	2.00----3.00
6011	Ftd. Jug	25.00--30.00
2337	6", 7", 8" Plate	2.00----5.00

CUTTING No. 766—RIPPLE DESIGN
Made in Crystal
and
CUTTING No. 768
BRIDAL SHOWER DESIGN
Made in Crystal

6017	9 oz. Goblet	3.00----5.00
6017	6 oz. Saucer Champagne	3.00----5.00
6017	6 oz. Low Sherbet	2.00----4.00
6017	3½ oz. Cocktail	3.00----5.00
6017	4 oz. Claret	3.00----5.00
6017	3 oz. Wine	3.00----5.00
6017	¾ oz. Cordial	3.00----5.00
6017	4 oz. Oyster Cocktail	3.00----5.00
6017	5, 9, 12, 14 oz. Ftd. Tumb.	2.00----4.00
4132	4, 5, 7, 9, 12, 14 oz. Tumbler Sham	1.00----3.00
4132	7½ oz. O.F. Cocktail, Sham	1.00----3.00
4132	1½ oz. Whiskey, Sham	1.00----3.00
766	Finger Bowl	2.00----3.00
6011	Ftd. Jug	20.00--25.00
2337	6", 7", 8" Plate	1.00----4.00
2350½—Ftd. Sugar		2.00----4.00
2350½—Ftd. Cream		2.00----4.00
2545	12½" "FLame" Oval Bowl	8.00--12.00
2545	"Flame" Duo Candlestick	6.00----8.00
2545	2-Lt. "Flame" Candelabra	20.00--25.00

CUTTING No. 767—BEACON DESIGN
Rock Crystal

6017	9 oz. Goblet	4.00----6.00
6017	6 oz. Saucer Champagne	3.00----5.00
6017	6 oz. Low Sherbet	2.00----4.00
6017	3½ oz. Cocktail	4.00----6.00
6017	4 oz. Claret	4.00----6.00
6017	3 oz. Wine	4.00----6.00
6017	¾ oz. Cordial	4.00----6.00
6017	5, 9, 12, 14 oz. Ftd. Tumb.	3.00----6.00
4132	4, 5, 7, 9, 12, 14 oz. Tumbler Sham	2.00----5.00
4132	7½ oz. O. F. Cocktail, Sham	2.00----4.00
4132	1½ oz. Whiskey, Sham	2.00----4.00
4132	Decanter & Stopper	10.00--15.00
4132	Ice Bowl	8.00--10.00
766	Finger Bowl	2.00----4.00
6011	Ftd. Jug	20.00--25.00
2337	6", 7", 8" Plate	2.00----5.00
2496	Ftd. Sugar	3.00----5.00
2496	Ftd. Cream	3.00----5.00
2496	Individual Sugar	2.00----4.00
2496	Individual Cream	2.00----4.00
2496	3-Pc. Ind. Sugar & Cream St.	8.00--12.00
	Consisting of—	
	2496 Individual Sugar	
	2496 Individual Cream	
	2496½—6½" S. & C. Tray	
2496	8" Pickle	3.00----5.00
2496	11" Celery	4.00----6.00
2496	10" Cake Plate, 2 Hdls.	6.00----9.00
2496	8½" Serving Dish, 2 Hdls.	6.00----9.00
2496	5½" Comport	5.00----7.00
2496	6½" Tall Comport	6.00----8.00
2496	3-Toed Tid Bit, Flat	4.00----6.00
2496½—6½" S. & C. Tray		3.00----5.00
2496	8" Oblong Tray	4.00----6.00
2496	Oblong Sauce Dish	4.00----6.00
1496	2-Part Mayonnaise	4.00----6.00
2496½—Mayonnaise, Plate & Ladle		5.00----7.00
2496	3-Part Relish	6.00----8.00
2496	2-Part Relish	6.00----8.00

2496	Sweetmeat	4.00----6.00
2496	Ice Bucket, Chrom. Hdl.	10.00--12.00
2496	14'' Torte Plate	14.00--18.00
2496	Cheese & Cracker	10.00--14.00
2496	Ftd. Cheese	2.00----5.00
2496	Cracker Plate	6.00----9.00
2496	12'' Bowl, Flared	12.00--17.00
2496	10½'' Handled Bowl	10.00--15.00
2496	4'' Candlestick	4.00----6.00
2496	5½'' Candlestick	4.00----6.00
2496	Duo Candlestick	5.00----7.00
2496	Trindle Candlestick	6.00----8.00
2545	12½'' ''Flame'' Oval Bowl	8.00--12.00
2545	''Flame'' Duo Candlestick	6.00----8.00
2545	2-Lt. ''Flame'' Candelabra, B Prisms	20.00--25.00

CUTTING no. 769—PUSSYWILLOW DESIGN
Rock Crystal

4132	5, 9, 12, 14 oz. Tumb., Sham	2.00----4.00
4132	7½ oz. O.F. Cocktail, Sham	2.00----3.00
4132	1½ oz. Whiskey, Sham	2.00----3.00
4132	Decanter & Stopper	10.00--15.00
4132	Ice Bowl	8.00--10.00
2337	7'' Plate	2.00----4.00

CUTTING No. 770—ATHENIAN DESIGN
Made in Crystal

6011	10 oz. Goblet	3.00----5.00
6011	5½ oz. Saucer Champagne	3.00----5.00
6011	5½ oz. Low Sherbet	2.00----4.00
6011	3 oz. Cocktail	3.00----5.00
6011	4½ oz. Claret	3.00----5.00
6011	3 oz. Wine	3.00----5.00
6011	1 oz. Cordial	3.00----5.00
6011	4 oz. Oyster Cocktail	3.00----5.00
6011	5, 10, 13 oz. Ftd. Tumb.	2.00----4.00
1769	Finger Bowl	2.00----3.00
4132	5, 9, 12, 14 oz. Tumb., Sham	2.00----4.00
4132	7½ oz. O.F. Cocktail, Sham	2.00----3.00
4132	1½ oz. Whiskey, Sham	2.00----3.00
4132	Decanter & Stopper	10.00--15.00
4132	Ice Bowl	8.00--10.00
2337	7'' Plate	2.00----4.00

CUTTING No. 771—FEDERAL DESIGN
Made in Crystal
and
CUTTING No. 772—TULIP DESIGN
Rock Crystal

6019	10 oz. Goblet	4.00----6.00
6019	6½ oz. Sherbet	3.00----5.00
6019	3½ oz. Cocktail	4.00----6.00
6019	4½ oz. Claret	4.00----6.00
6019	3½ oz. Wine	4.00----6.00
6019	4¾ oz. Oyster Cocktail	4.00----6.00
6019	6 oz. Parfait	4.00----6.00
6019	12 oz. Ftd. Tumbler	3.00----5.00
6019	5 oz. Ftd. Tumbler	2.00----4.00
766	Finger Bowl	2.00----3.00
4132	5, 9, 12, 14 oz. Tumb., Sham	2.00----4.00
4132	7½ oz. O.F. Cocktail, Sham	1.00----3.00
4132	1½ oz. Whiskey, Sham	1.00----3.00
4132	Decanter & Stopper	10.00--15.00
4132	Ice Bowl	8.00--10.00
2337	6'', 7'', 8'' Plate	2.00----6.00
2496	10½'' Handled Bowl	10.00--15.00
2496	5½'' Candlestick	4.00----6.00

2430	7'' Jelly	3.00----5.00
2430	5½'' Mint	2.00----4.00
2430	11'' Bowl	9.00--12.00
2430	2'' Candlestick	3.00----4.00
2430	8'' Vase	6.00----9.00

CUTTING No. 773—RHYTHM DESIGN
Rock Crystal

4020	11 oz. Goblet	4.00----6.00
4020	7 oz. Saucer Champagne	4.00----6.00
4020	7 oz. Low Sherbet	3.00----5.00
4020	5 oz. Low Sherbet	2.00----4.00
4020	3 oz. Wine	4.00----6.00
4020	4 oz. Claret	4.00----6.00
4020	3 oz. Cocktail	4.00----6.00
4020½	4 oz. Cocktail	4.00----6.00
4020	5, 10, 13 oz. Ftd. Tumbler	3.00----5.00
4020	2 oz. Whiskey	2.00----4.00
4020	Ftd. Jug	20.00--25.00
4021	Finger Bowl	2.00----4.00
2419	7'', 8'' Plate	2.00----4.00

CUTTING No. 774—GOTHIC DESIGN
Rock Crystal

6020	9 oz. Goblet	4.00----6.00
6020	6 oz. Saucer Champagne	4.00----6.00
6020	6 oz. Low Sherbet	3.00----5.00
6020	5½ oz. Parfait	4.00----6.00
6020	3½ oz. Cocktail	4.00----6.00
6020	4½ oz. Claret	4.00----6.00
6020	3½ oz. Wine	4.00----6.00
6020	1 oz. Cordial	4.00----6.00
6020	4 oz. Oyster Cocktail	4.00----6.00
6020	5, 9, 12 oz. Ftd. Tumbler	3.00----5.00
869	Finger Bowl	2.00----4.00
5000	7 Ftd. Jug	25.00--30.00
2337	6'', 7'', 8'' Plate, Optic	2.00----5.00
2560	Ftd. Sugar	3.00----5.00
2560	Ftd. Cream	3.00----5.00
2400	6'' Comport	6.00----8.00
2560	Handled Bowl	15.00--20.00
2560	4½'' Candlestick	3.00----5.00
2560	Duo Candlestick	4.00----6.00
2430	11'' Bowl	10.00--15.00
2430	2'' Candlestick	3.00----5.00

CUTTING No. 775—KIMBERLEY DESIGN
Rock Crystal

6017	9 oz. Goblet	4.00----6.00
6017	6 oz. Saucer Champagne	3.00----5.00
6017	6 oz. Low Sherbet	2.00----4.00
6017	3½ oz. Cocktail	4.00----6.00
6017	4 oz. Claret	4.00----6.00
6017	3 oz. Wine	4.00----6.00
6017	¾ oz. Cordial	4.00----6.00
6017	4 oz. Oyster Cocktail	4.00----6.00
6017	5, 9, 12, 14 oz. Ftd. Tumb.	3.00----5.00
4132	4, 5, 7, 9, 12, 14 oz. Tumbler Sham	2.00----4.00
4132	7½ oz. O.F. Cocktail Sham	1.00----3.00
4132	1½ oz. Whiskey, Sham	2.00----3.00
4132	Decanter & Stopper	10.00--15.00
4132	Ice Bowl	8.00--10.00
766	Finger Bowl	2.00----4.00
6011	Ftd. Jug	20.00--25.00
2337	6'', 7'', 8'' Plate	2.00----5.00
2496	Ftd. Sugar	3.00----5.00

2496	Ftd. Cream	3.00----5.00
2496	Individual Sugar	3.00----4.00
2496	Individual Cream	3.00----4.00
2496	3 Pc. Ind. Sugar & Cream St.	8.00--10.00
	Consisting of—	
	2496 Individual Sugar	
	2496 Individual Cream	
	2496½—6½" S. & C. Tray	
2496	8" Pickle	3.00----5.00
2496	11" Celery	4.00----6.00
2496	10" Cake Plate, 2 handles	6.00----9.00
2496	8½" Serving Dish, 2 Hdls.	6.00----9.00
2496	5½" Comport	6.00----9.00
2496	6½" Tall Comport	7.00--10.00
2496	3-Toed Tid Bit, Flat	3.00----5.00
2496½—6½" S. & C. Tray		2.00----4.00
2496	8" Oblong Tray	3.00----5.00
2496	Oblong Sauce Dish	3.00----5.00
2496	2-Part Mayonnaise	3.00----5.00
2496½—Mayo. & Plate & Ladle		6.00----9.00
2496	3-Part Relish	6.00----8.00
2496	2-Part Relish	3.00----5.00
2496	Sweetmeat	3.00----5.00
2496	Ice Bucket, Chrom. Hdl.	8.00--10.00
2496	14" Torte Plate	12.00--16.00
2496	Cheese & Cracker	10.00--14.00
2496	Ftd. Cheese	3.00----5.00
2496	Cracker Plate	6.00----9.00
2496	12" Bowl, Flared	10.00--14.00
2496	10½" Handled Bowl	10.00--14.00
2496	4" Candlestick	3.00----5.00
2496	5½" Candlestick	4.00----6.00
2496	Duo Candlestick	4.00----6.00
2496	Trindle Candlestick	6.00----8.00
2545	12½" "Flame" Oval Bowl	8.00--12.00
2545	"Flame" Duo Candlestick	6.00----8.00
2545	2-Lt. "Flame" Candelabra, B Prisms	20.00--25.00
6020	9 oz. Goblet	4.00----6.00
6020	6 oz. Saucer Champagne	3.00----5.00
6020	6 oz. Low Sherbet	2.00----4.00
6020	5½ oz. Parfait	4.00----6.00
6020	3½ oz. Cocktail	4.00----6.00
6020	4½ oz. Claret	4.00----6.00
6020	3½ oz. Wine	4.00----6.00
6020	1 oz. Cordial	4.00----6.00
6020	4 oz. Oyster Cocktail	4.00----6.00
6020	5, 9, 12 oz. Ftd. Tumbler	3.00----5.00
869	Finger Bowl	2.00----4.00
5000	7 Ftd. Jug	25.00--30.00
2337	6", 7", 8" Plate, Optic	2.00----6.00
2560	Ftd. Sugar	3.00----5.00
2560	Ftd. Cream	3.00----5.00
2400	6" Comport	6.00----8.00
2560	Handled Bowl	15.00--20.00
2560	4½" Candlestick	3.00----5.00
2560	Duo Candlestick	5.00----7.00
2430	11" Bowl	10.00--15.00
2430	2" Candlestick	2.00----4.00
5100	10" Vase, Plain	8.00--10.00

CUTTING No. 776—*LAUREL DESIGN
Made in Crystal

6017	9 oz. Goblet	4.00----6.00
6017	6 oz. Saucer Champagne	3.00----5.00
6017	6 oz. Low Sherbet	2.00----4.00
6017	3½ oz. Cocktail	4.00----6.00
6017	4 oz. Claret	4.00----6.00
6017	3 oz. Wine	4.00----6.00
6017	¾ oz. Cordial	4.00----6.00

6017	4 oz. Oyster Cocktail	4.00----6.00
6017	5, 9, 12 oz. Ftd. tumbler	3.00----5.00
6019	10 oz. Goblet	4.00----6.00
6019	6½ oz. Sherbet	4.00----6.00
6019	3½ oz. Cocktail	3.00----5.00
6019	4½ oz. Claret	4.00----6.00
6019	3½ oz. Wine	4.00----6.00
6019	4¾ oz. Oyster Cocktail	4.00----6.00
6019	6 oz. Parfait	4.00----6.00
6019	12 oz. Ftd. Tumbler	3.00----5.00
6019	5 oz. Ftd. Tumbler	2.00----4.00
766	Finger Bowl	2.00----4.00
6011	Ftd. Jug	20.00--25.00
2337	6", 7", 8" Plate	2.00----5.00
2451	Ice Dish	4.00----6.00
2574	Ftd. Sugar	3.00----5.00
2574	Ftd. Cream	3.00----5.00
2574	Individual Sugar	2.00----4.00
2574	Individual Cream	2.00----4.00
2574	Olive	3.00----5.00
2574	Pickle	4.00----5.00
2574	Celery	4.00----6.00
2574	5" Comport	4.00----6.00
2574	Mayo. & Plate & Ladle	6.00----8.00
2574	Mayonnaise	3.00----5.00
2574	Mayonnaise Plate	2.00----4.00
2586	Sani Cut Server	9.00--12.00
2574	3-Part Relish	8.00--10.00
2574	Cake Plate	6.00----8.00
2574	Serving Dish	6.00----9.00
2574	Whip Cream	2.00----4.00
2574	Sweetmeat	2.00----4.00
2574	Lemon	2.00----4.00
2574	Bon Bon	2.00----4.00
2574	Ice Tub	5.00----8.00
2574	Ice Tongs, Chrom. (2510)	1.00----2.00
2574	9½" Handled Bowl	10.00--15.00
2574	4" Candlestick	3.00----5.00
6023	Ftd. Bowl	15.00--20.00
2527	2-Lt. Candelabra, U.D.P.	20.00--25.00
4148	2¼" Cigarette Holder	2.00----4.00
4148	2½" Individual Ash Tray	1.00----3.00
2324	6" Candlestick	4.00----7.00

CUTTING No. 777—RAYNEL DESIGN
Rock Crystal
and
CUTTING No. 778—LUCERNE DESIGN
Rock Crystal

6017	9 oz. Goblet	4.00----6.00
6017	6 oz. Saucer Champagne	3.00----5.00
6017	6 oz. Low Sherbet	2.00----4.00
6017	3½ oz. Cocktail	4.00----6.00
6017	4 oz. Claret	4.00----6.00
6017	3 oz. Wine	4.00----6.00
6017	¾ oz. Cordial	4.00----6.00
6017	4 oz. Oyster Cocktail	4.00----6.00
6017	5, 9, 12 oz. Ftd. Tumbler	3.00----5.00
766	Finger Bowl	2.00----3.00
6011	Ftd. Jug	20.00--25.00
4132	12 oz. Tumbler, Sham	2.00----4.00
4132	9 oz. Tumbler, Sham	2.00----4.00
4132	7½ oz. O. F. Cocktail, Sham	1.00----3.00
4132	5 oz. Tumbler, Sham	1.00----3.00
4132	1½ oz. Whiskey, Sham	1.00----3.00
4132	Decanter	10.00--15.00
4132	Ice Bowl	10.00--15.00
2337	6", 7", 8" Plate	2.00----5.00

Matching Service discontinued in 1977.

CUTTING No. 779—SOUTH SEAS DESIGN
Made in Crystal

4132	14 oz. Tumb. (Hands in Air)	2.00----4.00
4132	12 oz. Tumb. (Hands in Air)	2.00----4.00
4132½	9 oz. Scotch & Soda (Knee Lifted)	2.00----4.00
4132	9 oz. Tumb. (Knee Lifted)	2.00----4.00
4132	5 oz. Tumb. (Hands Out)	2.00----4.00
4132	C. F. Cocktail (Running)	2.00----4.00
4132	1½ oz. Whiskey (Hd. on Hip)	2.00----4.00
4132	Decanter (Hands Out)	15.00--20.00
4132	Ice Bowl (Running)	10.00--15.00

CUTTING No. 780—SERENADE DESIGN
Made in Crystal

4132	14 oz. Tumbler (Guitar)	2.00----4.00
4132	12 oz. Tumbler (Guitar)	2.00----4.00
4132½	9 oz. Scotch & Soda Trumpet	2.00----4.00
4132	9 oz. Tumbler (Trumpet)	2.00----4.00
4132	5 oz. Tumbler (Violin)	2.00----4.00
4132	O.F. Cocktail (Accordion)	2.00----4.00
4132	1½ oz. Whiskey (Base Drum)	2.00----4.00
4132	Decanter (Guitar)	15.00--20.00
4132	Ice Bowl (Accordion)	10.00--15.00

CUTTING No. 781—DRUM DESIGN
Made in Crystal

4139	5, 10, 12, 14, 16 oz. Tumb	2.00----5.00
4139	9 oz. Water Tumbler	2.00----4.00
4139	O. F. Cocktail	2.00----4.00
4139	Whiskey	2.00----4.00
4139	Decanter	15.00--20.00
4132	Ice Bowl	10.00--15.00

CUTTING No. 782—REGAL DESIGN
Rock Crystal

6024	10 oz. Goblet	4.00----6.00
6024	6 oz. Saucer Champagne	3.00----5.00
6024	6 oz. Low Sherbet	2.00----4.00
6024	3½ oz. Cocktail	4.00----6.00
6024	4½ oz. Claret	4.00----6.00
6024	3½ oz. Wine	4.00----6.00
6024	1 oz. Cordial	4.00----6.00
6024	4 oz. Oyster Cocktail	4.00----6.00
6024	5, 9, 12 oz. Ftd. Tumbler	3.00----6.00
869	Finger Bowl, Optic	2.00----4.00
5000	Ftd. Jug, Optic	25.00--30.00
2337	6", 7", 8" Plate, Optic	2.00----5.00

CUTTING No. 783—CHELSEA DESIGN
Rock Crystal

4020	11 oz. Goblet	3.00----5.00
4020	7 oz. Saucer Champagne	3.00----4.00
4020	7 oz. Low Sherbet	2.00----4.00
4020	5 oz. Low Sherbet	2.00----4.00
4020	4 oz. Claret	3.00----5.00
4020	3 oz. Wine	3.00----5.00
4020	3½ oz. Cocktail	3.00----5.00
4020½	4 oz. Cocktail	3.00----5.00
4020	5, 10, 13 oz. Ftd. Tumbler	2.00----4.00
4020	2 oz. Whiskey	3.00----4.00
4020	Ftd. Jug	20.00--25.00
4021	Finger Bowl	2.00----4.00
2419	7", 8" Plate	3.00----5.00

CUTTING No. 784—DRAPE DESIGN
Made in Crystal

6017	9 oz. Goblet	4.00----6.00
6017	6 oz. Saucer Champagne	3.00----5.00
6017	6 oz. Low Sherbet	2.00----4.00
6017	3½ oz. Cocktail	4.00----6.00
6017	4 oz. Claret	4.00----6.00
6017	3 oz. Wine	4.00----6.00
6017	¾ oz. Cordial	4.00----6.00
6017	4 oz. Oyster Cocktail	4.00----6.00
6017	5, 9, 12 oz. Ftd. Tumbler	3.00----5.00
766	Finger Bowl, Plain	2.00----4.00
6011	Ftd. Jug	25.00--30.00
2337	6", 7", 8" Plate, Plain	2.00----4.00

CUTTING No. 785— *CYNTHIA DESIGN
Made in Crystal

6017	9 oz. Goblet	4.00---6.00
6017	6 oz. Saucer Champagne	3.00----5.00
6017	6 oz. Low Sherbet	2.00----4.00
6017	3½ oz. Cocktail	4.00----6.00
6017	4 oz. Claret	4.00----6.00
6017	3 oz. Wine	4.00----6.00
6017	¾ oz. Cordial	4.00----6.00
6017	4 oz. Oyster Cocktail	4.00----6.00
6017	5, 9, 12 oz. Ftd. Tumbler	3.00----5.00
766	Finger Bowl, Plain	2.00----4.00
6011	Ftd. Jug	25.00--35.00
2337	6", 7", 8" Plate, Plain	2.00----5.00
2560	Ftd. Sugar	3.00----5.00
2560	Ftd. Cream	3.00----5.00
2560	Individual Sugar	2.00----4.00
2560	Individual Cream	2.00----4.00
2560	6½" Olive	3.00----5.00
2560	8¾" Pickle	4.00----5.00
2560	11" Celery	4.00----6.00
2560	Mayonnaise, Plate & Ladle	8.00--10.00
2560	Mayonnaise	3.00----5.00
2560	Mayonnaise Plate	2.00----4.00
2560	Mayonnaise Ladle	1.00----2.00
2560	2-Part Mayonnaise	3.00----5.00
2560	2-Part Mayo. w/2 Ladles	4.00----7.00
2560	2 Part Relish	3.00----5.00
2560	3, 4, 5 Part Relish	5.00----9.00
2560	2 Part Salad Bowl	10.00--12.00
2560	11½" Hdld. Lunch Tray	8.00--10.00
2560	3 oz. Ftd. Oil & Stopper	10.00--12.00
2560	Serving Dish	8.00--10.00
2560	Hdld. Muffin Tray	8.00--10.00
2560	Whip Cream	3.00----4.00
2560	Sweetmeat	3.00----4.00
2560	Lemon	3.00----4.00
2560	Bon Bon	3.00----4.00
2560	3-Toed Bon Bon	3.00----5.00
2560	3-Toed Tid Bit	3.00----5.00
2560	14" Torte Plate	12.00--16.00
2560	Cheese & Cracker	10.00--14.00
2560	Cheese	4.00----6.00
2560	Cracker	6.00----8.00
2560	Ice Bucket, Chrom. Hdl.	8.00--10.00
2560	Ice Tongs, Chrom.	1.00----2.00
2560	6" Comport	8.00--10.00
2560	11½" Bowl, Crimped	10.00--15.00
2560	13" Fruit Bowl	10.00--15.00
2560	Handled Bowl	10.00--15.00
2560	4½" Candlestick	4.00----6.00
2560½	4" Candlestick	4.00----6.00
2560	Duo Candlestick	6.00----8.00
2567	7½" Ftd. Vase	15.00--20.00
5100	10" Vase	12.00--16.00

**Matching Service discontinued in 1977.*

2560	10:" Hdld. Cake Plate . .	8.00--10.00
2560	Cup	3.00----5.00
2560	Saucer	2.00----3.00
2666	1 Qt. Pitcher	10.00--15.00

CUTTING No. 786
DOLLY MADISON DESIGN—Rock Crystal

6023	9 oz. Goblet	4.00----6.00
6023	6 oz. Saucer Champagne	3.00----5.00
6023	6 oz. Low Sherbet	2.00----4.00
6023	3¾ oz. Cocktail	4.00----6.00
6023	4 oz. Claret-Wine	4.00----6.00
6023	1 oz. Cordial	4.00----6.00
6023	4 oz. Oyster Cocktail . .	4.00----6.00
6023	5, 9, 12 oz. Ftd. Tumbler	3.00----5.00
766	Finger Bowl	2.00----4.00
846	2 oz. Sherry	4.00----6.00
6023	5" Comport	5.00----7.00
833½	—5, 8, 10, 12, 14 oz. Tumbler, Sham	2.00----4.00
833½	—1½ oz. Whiskey, Sham	1.00----3.00
833½	—7 oz. O.F. Cocktail, Sham	1.00----3.00
4132	Decanter & Stopper	12.00--15.00
6011	Ftd. Jug	20.00--25.00
2574	6", 7", 8" Plate (Not Cut)	1.00----2.00
6023	Ftd. Bowl	10.00--15.00
2324	6" Candlestick	4.00----7.00

CUTTING No. 787—PILGRIM DESIGN
Rock Crystal

6023	9 oz. Goblet	4.00----6.00
6023	6 oz. Saucer Champagne	3.00----5.00
6023	6 oz. Low Sherbet	2.00----4.00
6023	3¾ oz. Cocktail	4.00----6.00
6023	4 oz. Claret-Wine . . .	4.00----6.00
6023	1 oz. Cordial	4.00----6.00
6023	4 oz. Oyster Cocktail . .	4.00----6.00
6023	5, 9, 12 oz. Ftd. Tumbler	3.00----5.00
766	Finger Bowl	2.00----4.00
6011	Ftd. Jug	25.00--30.00
2574	6", 7", 8" Plate	2.00----5.00
2574	9" Plate	4.00----6.00
2574	Ftd. Cup	2.00----4.00
2574	Saucer	2.00----3.00
2574	Ftd. Sugar	4.00----6.00
2574	Ftd. Cream	4.00----6.00
2574	Individual Sugar	3.00----5.00
2574	Individual Cream	3.00----5.00
2574	6" Olive	3.00----5.00
2574	8" Pickle	4.00----6.00
2574	10½" Celery	4.00----6.00
2574	5" Comport	6.00----9.00
6023	5" Comport	7.00--10.00
2574	Mayo. & Plate & Ladle . .	8.00--12.00
2574	Mayonnaise	4.00----6.00
2574	Mayonnaise Plate	3.00----5.00
2574	4¼ oz. Oil, Ground Stop.	12.00--15.00
2586	Sani Cut Server	10.00--15.00
2574	14" Torte Plate	12.00--16.00
2574	3-Part Relish	6.00----8.00
2574	10" Cake Plate	6.00----8.00
2574	8½" Serving Dish	5.00----7.00
2574	Sweetmeat	2.00----4.00
2574	Whip Cream	2.00----4.00
2574	Lemon	2.00----4.00
2574	Bon Bon	2.00----4.00

Matching service discontinued in 1977.

2574	Ice Tub	8.00--10.00
2574	Ice Tongs, Chrom. (2510)	1.00----2.00
2574	9½" Handled Bowl . . .	8.00--12.00
2574	4" Candlestick	3.00----5.00
6023	Footed Bowl	10.00--15.00
2324	6" Candlestick	4.00----6.00
2574	12" Bowl, Flared . . .	12.00--17.00
2574	13" Fruit Bowl	15.00--20.00
2567	6" Footed Vase	8.00--12.00
2567	7½" Footed Vase . . .	10.00--14.00
2567	8½" Footed Vase . . .	12.00--16.00

CUTTING No. 788—CHIPPENDALE DESIGN
Rock Crystal

6023	9 oz. Goblet	4.00----6.00
6023	6 oz. Saucer Champagne	3.00----5.00
6023	6 oz. Low Sherbet	2.00----4.00
6023	3¾ oz. Cocktail	4.00----6.00
6023	4 oz. Claret-Wine	4.00----6.00
6023	1 oz. Cordial	4.00----6.00
6023	4 oz. Oyster Cocktail . .	4.00----6.00
6023	5, 9, 12 oz. Ftd. Tumbler	3.00----5.00
766	Finger Bowl	2.00----4.00
6011	Footed Jug	25.00--30.00
2337	6", 7", 8" Plate	2.00----5.00
6023	Footed Bowl	10.00--15.00
2324	6" Candlestick	4.00----6.00

CUTTING No. 789—SUFFOLK DESIGN
Rock Crystal
and
CUTTING No. 790—HAWTHORN DESIGN
Rock Crystal
and
CUTTING No. 791—GEORGIAN DESIGN
Rock Crystal

6025	10 oz. Goblet	3.00----5.00
6025	6 oz. Sherbet	2.00----4.00
6025	3½ oz. Cocktail	3.00----5.00
6025	4 oz. Claret-Wine	3.00----5.00
6025	1 oz. Cordial	3.00----5.00
6025	4 oz. Oyster Cocktail . .	3.00----5.00
6025	5, 12 oz. Footed Tumbler	2.00----4.00
1769	Finger Bowl	2.00----3.00
6011	Footed Jug	20.00--25.00
2574	6", 7", 8" Plate (Not Cut)	1.00----2.00
6023	Footed Bowl	10.00--15.00
2324	6" Candlestick	4.00----6.00

CUTTING No. 792—CATHEDRAL DESIGN
Rock Crystal
and
CUTTING No. 793—SPIRE DESIGN
Rock Crystal

6023	9 oz. Goblet	4.00----6.00
6023	6 oz. Saucer Champagne	3.00----5.00
6023	6 oz. Low Sherbet	2.00----4.00
6023	3¾ oz. Cocktail	4.00----6.00
6023	4 oz. Claret-Wine . . .	4.00----6.00
6023	1 oz. Cordial	4.00----6.00
6023	4 oz. Oyster Cocktail . .	4.00----6.00
6023	5, 9, 12 oz. Ftd. Tumbler	3.00----5.00
6023	5" Comport	5.00----7.00
766	Finger bowl	2.00----4.00
6011	Ftd. Jug	20.00--25.00
2337	6", 7", 8" Plate	2.00----5.00
6023	Ftd. Bowl	10.00--15.00
2324	6" Candlestick	4.00----6.00

CUTTING No. 794—INGRID DESIGN
Made in Crystal
and
CUTTING No. 795—PAPYRUS DESIGN
Made in Crystal
and
CUTTING No. 796—LYRIC DESIGN
Made in Crystal

892	11 oz. Goblet	4.00----6.00
892	7 oz. Saucer Champagne	3.00----5.00
892	6 oz. Low Sherbet	2.00----4.00
892	4 oz. Cocktail	4.00----6.00
892	4 oz. Claret	4.00----6.00
892	3 oz. Wine	4.00----6.00
892	1 oz. Cordial	4.00----6.00
892	4½ oz. Oyster Cocktail	4.00----6.00
892	5, 12 oz. Ftd. Tumbler	3.00----5.00
1769	Finger Bowl	2.00----3.00
6011	Footed Jug	20.00--25.00
2337	6", 7", 8" Plate	2.00----5.00
6023	Ftd. Bowl	10.00--15.00
2324	6" Candlestick	4.00----6.00

CUTTING No. 797—DAPHNE DESIGN
Rock Crystal

2424	12" Plate	12.00--16.00
2424	Mayo. & Plate & Ladle	15.00--20.00
2424	Mayonnaise	8.00--12.00
2424	Mayonnaise Plate	5.00----8.00
2424	Sweetmeat	8.00--10.00
2424	Candy Jar & Cover	15.00--20.00
2424	Cigarette Box & Cover	10.00--15.00
2424	Ash Tray	2.00----4.00
2424	11½" Fruit Bowl	15.00--20.00
2424	8" Bowl, Regular	15.00--20.00
2424	9½" Bowl, Flared	15.00--20.00
2424	3½" Candlestick	6.00----8.00
2424	7½" Ftd. Urn, Regular	20.00--25.00
2424	6½" Ftd. Urn, Flared	20.00--25.00

CUTTING No. 798—CHRISTINE DESIGN
Made in Solid Crystal

892	11 oz. Goblet	3.00----5.00
892	7 oz. Saucer Chapagne	3.00----4.00
892	6½ oz. Low Sherbet	2.00----4.00
892	4 oz. Cocktail	3.00----5.00
892	4 oz. Claret	3.00----5.00
892	3 oz. Wine	3.00----5.00
892	1 oz. Cordial	3.00----5.00
892	4½ oz. Oyster Cocktail	3.00----5.00
892	5, 12 oz. Ftd. Tumbler	2.00----4.00
1769	Finger Bowl	2.00----4.00
6011	Ftd. Jug	20.00--25.00
2337	7", 8" Plate	2.00----4.00
6023	Ftd. Bowl	10.00--15.00
6023	Duo Candlestick	5.00----7.00

CUTTING No. 799—*MULBERRY DESIGN
Rock Crystal
and
CUTTING No. 800—SELMA DESIGN
Rock Crystal
and
CUTTING No. 803—RHEIMS DESIGN
Rock Crystal

6026	9 oz. Tall Goblet	4.00----6.00

**Matching service discontinued in 1977.*

6026	9 oz. Low Goblet	3.00----5.00
6026	6 oz. Saucer Champagne	3.00----5.00
6026	6 oz. Low Sherbet	2.00----4.00
6026	4 oz. Cocktail	4.00----6.00
6026	4½ oz. Claret-Wine	4.00----6.00
6026	1 oz. Cordial	4.00----6.00
6026	4 oz. Ftd. Cocktail	4.00----6.00
6026	5, 13 oz. Ftd. Tumbler	2.00----4.00
869	Finger Bowl	2.00----3.00
5000	Ftd. Jug	20.00--25.00
2337	7", 8" Plate, Optic	3.00----5.00
2545	12½" Oval Bowl	10.00--15.00
2545	4½" Candlestick	4.00----6.00
6023	Ftd. Bowl	10.00--15.00
6023	Duo Candlestick	6.00----8.00

CUTTING No. 801—BRIGHTON DESIGN
Rock Crystal

and

**CUTTING No. 802
WENTWORTH DESIGN**
Rock Crystal
Not in Fostoria Book

(1940—1942)

6023	9 oz. Goblet	4.00----6.00
6023	6 oz. Saucer Champagne	3.00----5.00
6023	6 oz. Low Sherbet	2.00----4.00
6023	3¾ oz. Cocktail	4.00----6.00
6023	4 oz. Claret-Wine	4.00----6.00
6023	1 oz. Cordial	4.00----6.00
6023	4 oz. Oyster Cocktail	4.00----6.00
6023	5, 9, 12 oz. Ftd. Tumbler	3.00----6.00
6023	5" Comport	4.00----6.00
766	Finger Bowl	2.00----4.00
6011	Footed Jug	20.00--25.00
2337	7", 8" Plate	3.00----5.00
2574	9½" Hdld. Bowl	10.00--15.00
2574	Duo Candlestick	6.00----8.00

CUTTING No. 804—SALON DESIGN
Made in Crystal
and
CUTTING No. 805—ALOHA DESIGN
Made in Crystal
and
CUTTING No. 806—CADENCE DESIGN
Rock Crystal

6027	10 oz. Goblet	4.00----6.00
6027	5½ oz. Saucer Champagne	3.00----5.00
6027	5½ oz. Low Sherbet	3.00----4.00
6027	3½ oz. Cocktail	4.00----6.00
6027	4 oz. Wine	4.00----6.00
6027	1 oz. Cordial	4.00----6.00
6027	4 oz. Oyster Cocktail	4.00----6.00
6027	5, 12 oz. Ftd. Tumbler	3.00----5.00
4021	Finger Bowl	2.00----4.00
6011	Footed Jug	20.00--25.00
2337	7", 8" Plate, Plain	2.00----4.00
2364	12" Lily Pond	10.00--15.00
6023	Duo Candlestick	6.00----8.00

CUTTING No. 807—COVENTRY DESIGN
Rock Crystal

2364	10½" Salad Bowl	20.00--30.00

2364	14" Torte Plate	30.00--40.00
2364	16" Torte Plate	30.00--40.00
2364	13" Fruit Bowl	20.00--30.00
2364	12" Lily Pond	20.00--30.00
6023	Duo Candlestick	10.00--15.00
2324	6" Candlestick	10.00--12.00
2596	7½" Square Bowl	15.00--20.00
2596	11" Oblong Shallow Bowl	20.00--25.00
2596	5" Candlestick	8.00--10.00
2567	7½" Ftd. Vase	20.00--25.00
2567	8½" Ftd. Vase	20.00--30.00
2577	6" Vase	20.00--25.00
2577	8½" Vase	15.00--20.00
4126½—11" Ftd. Vase		20.00--25.00
4132½—8" Vase		20.00--25.00
4143½—6" Ftd. Vase		15.00--20.00
4143½—7½" Ftd. Vase		20.00--25.00

ROCK CRYSTAL SMOKING ACCESSORIES

2306	3 pc. Smoker Set	5.00----8.00
	Cutting No. 811	
2306	3" Ash Tray	1.00----2.00
2306	3½" Ash Tray	1.00----3.00
2306	4" Ash Tray	2.00----3.00
4148	2¼" Cigarette Holder Blown	2.00----4.00
	Laurel Design Cutting No. 776	
	Top Diameter 2"	
4148	2½" Individual Ash Tray	1.00----2.00
	Laurel Design Cutting No. 776	
2427	Oblong Cigarette Box & Cov.	5.00----8.00
	Cutting No. 810—Lgth. 7",	
	Ht. 2¼", Width 3-1/8", Each	
	side holds 35 Cigarettes	
2427	Oblong Cigarette Box & Cov.	5.00----8.00
	Cutting No. 809, Lgth. 7",	
	Ht. 2¼", Width 3-1/8", Each	
	side holds 35 Cigarettes	
2427	Oblong Ash Tray	2.00----4.00
	Cutting No. 809, Lgth 3½",	
	Width 2¾"	
2550½—Oblong Cig. Box & Cover		4.00----6.00
	Cutting No. 808, Ht., 2-1/8",	
	Lgth. 4¾", Wt. 3-3/8"	
2550	Round Ash Tray	1.00----2.00
	Cutting No. 808, Diameter 3¼"	
2427	Oblong Cigarette Box & Cov.	5.00----8.00
	Cutting No. 808, Lth. 7",	
	Ht. 2¼", Wt. 3-1/8", Each	
	side holds 35 cigarettes	
2427	Oblong Ash Tray.	1.00----2.00
	Cutting No. 808, Lth. 3½",	
	Width 2¾"	
2516	Ash Tray, Cut. No. 808	2.00----4.00
	Ht. 2-1/8", Diameter 5"	

CUTTING No. 812—CHALICE DESIGN
Made in Crystal

6029	9 oz. Goblet	2.00----4.00
6029	6½ oz. Saucer Champagne	2.00----4.00
6029	3½ oz. Cocktail	2.00----4.00
6029	4 oz. Claret	2.00----4.00
6029	3 oz. Wine	2.00----4.00
6029	1 oz. Cordial	2.00----4.00
6029	4½ oz. Oyster Cocktail	2.00----4.00
766	Finger Bowl (Cut 786)	1.00----2.00
833½	12, 14 oz. Tumb. (Cut 786)	2.00----4.00
846	2 oz. Sherry (Cut 786)	2.00----4.00
863	2 oz. Hol. Stem. Champ. C.F.	2.00----4.00

CUTTING No. 813—SAYBROOKE DESIGN
Rock Crystal with a Full Cut & Polished Stem

6029	9 oz. Goblet	4.00----6.00
6029	6½ oz. Saucer Champagne	3.00----5.00
6029	3½ oz. Cocktail	4.00----6.00
6029	4 oz. Claret	4.00----6.00
6029	3 oz. Wine	4.00----6.00
6029	1 oz. Cordial	4.00----6.00
6029	4½ oz. Oyster Cocktail	4.00----6.00
766	Finger Bowl	2.00----3.00
6011	Footed Jug	20.00--25.00
2337	6", 7", 8" Plate	2.00----5.00

CUTTING No. 814—*CHRISTIANA DESIGN
Rock Crystal
and

CUTTING No. 816—GADROON DESIGN
Made in Crystal

6030	10 oz. Goblet	4.00----6.00
6030	10 oz. Low Goblet	3.00----5.00
6030	6 oz. Saucer Champagne	3.00----5.00
6030	6 oz. Low Sherbet	2.00----4.00
6030	3½ oz. Cocktail	4.00----6.00
6030	3½ oz. Claret-Wine	4.00----6.00
6030	1 oz. Cordial	4.00----6.00
6030	4 oz. Oyster Cocktail	4.00----6.00
6030	5, 12 oz. Ftd. Tumbler	3.00----5.00
1769	Finger Bowl	2.00----4.00
6011	Footed Jug	20.00--25.00
2337	7", 8" Plate	3.00----5.00
6023	9" Footed Bowl	8.00--12.00
6023	Duo Candlestick	6.00----8.00

CUTTING No. 815 ** HOLLY DESIGN
Made in Crystal

6030	10 oz. Goblet	5.00----8.00
6030	10 oz. Low Goblet	4.00----6.00
6030	6 oz. Saucer Champagne	3.00----5.00
6030	6 oz. Low Sherbet	2.00----4.00
6030	3½ oz. Cocktail	5.00----8.00
6030	3½ oz. Claret-Wine	5.00----8.00
6030	1 oz. Cordial	5.00----8.00
6030	4 oz. Oyster Cocktail	5.00----8.00
6030	12 oz. Ftd. Tumbler	4.00----6.00
6030	5 oz. Ftd. Tumbler	4.00----6.00
1769	Finger Bowl	2.00----4.00
6011	Footed Jug	20.00--30.00
2337	6", 7", 8" Plate	2.00----5.00
2364	Cigarette Holder	2.00----4.00
2364	Ind. Ash Tray	1.00----2.00
6023	9" Footed Bowl	10.00--15.00
6023	Duo Candlestick	6.00----8.00
2364	11" Sandwich Plate	6.00----8.00
2364	14" Torte Plate	8.00--12.00
2364	2-Part Relish	4.00----6.00
2364	3-Part Relish	6.00----8.00
2364	Large Shaker & Chrome Top "B"	3.00----4.00
2364	Shaker & Chrom. Top "C"	3.00----4.00
2350½—Sugar		4.00----6.00
2350½—Cream		4.00----6.00
2666	3 pc. Ind. S. & C. & Tray	6.00--10.00
2666	Individual Sugar	2.00----4.00
2666	Individual Cream	2.00----4.00
2364	Handled Lunch Tray	6.00----9.00

Matching service discontinued in 1977.

**Open stock today in stemware only.*

2350½	Cup	2.00----4.00
2350	Saucer	2.00----3.00
2666	1 Quart Pitcher	10.00--14.00
2364	Mayo. & Plate & Ladle	6.00----9.00
2364	8" Pickle	3.00----4.00
2364	9" Salad Bowl	6.00----8.00
2364	12" Bowl, Flared	10.00--12.00
2364	12" Lily Pond	10.00--12.00
2364	13" Fruit Bowl	10.00--12.00
2324	4" Candlestick	2.00----4.00
2364	Mayonnaise	4.00----6.00
2364	Mayonnaise Plate	2.00----3.00
2364	Cheese & Cracker	8.00--12.00
2364	Footed Cheese	2.00----4.00
2364	11" Cracker Plate	6.00----8.00
6030	5" Comport	6.00----9.00
2364	8" Comport	7.00--10.00
2324	6" Candlestick	4.00----6.00
2619½	6" Vase, Ground Bottom	6.00----8.00
2619½	7½" Vase, Gd. Bottom	8.00--10.00
2619½	9½" Vase, Gd. Bottom	10.00--12.00
2364	5" Fruit	2.00----4.00
2364	6" Baked Apple	2.00----4.00
2364	8" Rim Soup	2.00----4.00
2364	11" Celery	3.00----5.00
2364	16" Torte Plate	10.00--15.00
2337	9" Dinner Plate	3.00----5.00
2364	10½" Salad Bowl	8.00--12.00

CUTTING No. 817
MOUNT VERNON DESIGN—*Made in Crystal*

6031	10 oz. Goblet	3.00----5.00
6031	10 oz. Low Goblet	3.00----5.00
6031	6 oz. Saucer Champagne	3.00----5.00
6031	6 oz. Low Sherbet	2.00----4.00
6031	3½ oz. Cocktail	3.00----5.00
6031	3½ oz. Claret-Wine	3.00----5.00
6031	1 oz. Cordial	3.00----5.00
6031	4 oz. Oyster Cocktail	3.00----5.00
6031	5, 12 oz. Ftd. Tumbler	2.00----5.00
1769	Finger Bowl	2.00----3.00
6011	Footed Jug	20.00--25.00
2337	6", 7", 8" Plate	2.00----5.00
2364	13" Fruit Bowl	10.00--15.00
6023	Duo Candlestick	6.00----8.00

CUTTING No. 818—FORMALITY DESIGN
Made in Crystal
and
CUTTING No. 819—GREEK KEY DESIGN
Made in Crystal

6032	9 oz. Goblet	3.00----5.00
6032	6 oz. Saucer Champagne	3.00----5.00
6032	6 oz. Low Sherbet	2.00----4.00
6032	3½ oz. Cocktail	3.00----5.00
6032	3½ oz. Wine	3.00----5.00
6032	4½ oz. Claret	3.00----5.00
6032	4 oz. Oyster Cocktail	3.00----5.00
6032	1 oz. Cordial	3.00----5.00
6032	5, 13 oz. Ftd. Tumbler	2.00----4.00
766	Finger Bowl	2.00----3.00
6011	Footed Jug	20.00--25.00
2337	6", 7", 8" Plate	2.00----4.00
2596	11" Oblong Shallow Bowl	8.00--10.00
2596	5" Candlestick	3.00----5.00

CUTTING no. 820*WAKEFIELD DESIGN
Rock Crystal

6023	9 oz. Goblet	6.00---8.00
6023	6 oz. Saucer Champagne	5.00----7.00
6023	6 oz. Low Sherbet	4.00---6.00
6023	3½ oz. Cocktail	6.00----8.00
6023	4 oz. Claret-Wine	6.00----8.00
6023	1 oz. Cordial	6.00----8.00
6023	4 oz. Oyster Cocktail	6.00----8.00
6023	5, 12 oz. Ftd. Tumbler	3.00----5.00
766	Finger Bowl	4.00---6.00
6011	Footed Jug	35.00--45.00
2337	6", 7", 8" Plate	4.00----6.00
2364	12" Lily Pond (Cut 807)	10.00--15.00
6023	Duo Candlestick (C. 807)	8.00--10.00
2567	7½" Ftd. Vase (Cut 807)	8.00--12.00

CARVING No. 1—WATERFOWL DESIGN
Made in Crystal—Heavy Bottom

4132	14 oz. Tumbler (Crane)	2.00----5.00
4132	12 oz. Tumbler (Crane)	2.00----5.00
4132½	9 oz. Scotch & Soda (Duck)	2.00----5.00
4132	9 oz. Tumbler (Swan)	2.00----5.00
4132	5 oz. Tumbler (Duck)	2.00----5.00
4132	O.F. Cocktail (Goose)	2.00----5.00
4132	1½ oz. Whiskey (Gull)	2.00----5.00
4132	Decanter (Gull)	12.00--18.00
4132	Ice Bowl (Goose)	10.00--14.00
2391	Lge. Cig. Bx. & Cov. (Swan)	6.00----8.00
2550	Round Ash Tray (Swan)	2.00----3.00
2337	7" Plate (Swan)	3.00----4.00

CARVING No. 2—SKI DESIGN
Made in Crystal—Sham Bottom

4139	5, 10, 12, 14, 16 oz. Tumb.	2.00----5.00
4139	9 oz. Water Tumbler	2.00----4.00
4139	O. F. Cocktail	2.00----4.00
4139	Whiskey	2.00----4.00
4132	Decanter	12.00--18.00
4132	Ice Bowl	10.00--14.00
2391	Lge. Cig. Box & Cover	6.00----8.00
2550	Round Ash Tray	2.00----3.00
2337	7" Plate	3.00----4.00

CARVINGS

Colonial Design Carving No. 5 26/1 Candle Lamp w/2545 2" "Flame" Candlestick, Ht. 7"	12.00--15.00
Aztec Design Carving No. 6 1895½—10" Vase	9.00--12.00
Carnival Design Carving No. 7 4128½—5" Vase	8.00--10.00
Yachting Design Carving No. 8 4132½—8" Vase	10.00--15.00
Skater Design Carving No. 9 4132½—8" Vase	10.00--15.00
Stallion Design Carving No. 10 2567—7½" Vase	10.00--15.00

CARVING No. 12
MORNING GLORY DESIGN
Made in Crystal

2337	7" Plate	4.00----6.00
2337	8" Plate	5.00----7.00

**Matching service discontinued in 1976.*

2364	14" Torte Plate	9.00--12.00
2364	16" Torte Plate	10.00--15.00
2419	Cake Plate	8.00--12.00
2364	11" Sandwich Plate	8.00--12.00
2364	Mayo. & Plate & Ladle	8.00--10.00
2364	Mayonnaise	3.00----5.00
2364	Mayonnaise Plate	3.00----5.00
2364	Cheese & Cracker	10.00--12.00
2364	11" Cracker Plate	8.00--10.00
2364	9, 10½" Salad Bowl	10.00--14.00
4132	Ice Bowl	10.00--15.00
2427	Cigarette Box & Cover	8.00--12.00
2427	Oblong Ash Tray	1.00----2.00
2516	Ash Tray	2.00----4.00
315	7" Bowl	8.00--10.00
315	9" Bowl	12.00--15.00
2364	12" Lily Pond	8.00--10.00
2364	13" Fruit Bowl	8.00--12.00
2364	12" Bowl, Flared	8.00--12.00
2596	11" Oblong Shallow Bowl	8.00--10.00
6023	Footed Bowl	15.00--25.00
2324	6" Candlestick	4.00----6.00
2596	5" Candlestick	3.00----5.00
6023	Duo Candlestick	6.00----8.00
2577	5½" Wide Vase	8.00--10.00
2577	6", 8½" Vase	8.00--12.00
2591	15" Vase	15.00--25.00
4126½—11" Ftd. Vase		10.00--12.00
4128½—5" Vase		6.00----8.00
4132½—8" Vase		10.00--15.00
4143½—6", 7½" Ftd. Vase		8.00--10.00
5100	10" Vase	10.00--14.00
2364	Handled Lunch Tray	10.00--15.00
2618	4" Square Ash Tray	3.00----5.00

CARVING No. 13—BROCADE DESIGN
Made in Crystal

2424	12" Plate	12.00--15.00
2424	Mayo. & Plate & Ladle	12.00--18.00
2424	Mayonnaise	6.00----9.00
2424	Mayonnaise Plate	5.00----8.00
2424	Sweetmeat	5.00----8.00
2424	Candy Jar & Cover	12.00--18.00
2424	5" Comport	6.00----9.00
2424	5" Comport & Cover	12.00--15.00
2424	Cigarette Box & Cover	6.00----8.00
2424	Ash Tray	1.00----2.00
2516	Ash Tray	2.00----4.00
2424	8" Bowl, Regualr	10.00--12.00
2424	9½" Bowl, Flared	12.00--15.00
2424	11½" Fruit Bowl	12.00--15.00
2424	Duo Candlestick	6.00----8.00
2424	3½" Candlestick	4.00----6.00
2424	7½" Ftd. Urn, Reg.	10.00--15.00
2424	6½" Ftd. Urn, Flared	10.00--15.00
2424	5½" Ftd. Urn, Reg.	8.00--12.00
2424	5" Ftd. Urn, Flared	8.00--12.00

CARVING No. 15—19th HOLE DESIGN
Made in Crystal—Heavy Bottom

4132	12 oz. Tumbler "Driving"	2.00----4.00
4132½—9 oz. S & S "Exploding"		2.00----5.00
4132	5 oz. Tumbler "Exploding"	2.00----4.00
4132	O.F. Cocktail "Putting"	2.00----4.00
4132	Whiskey "Approaching"	2.00----4.00
4132	Ice Bowl, "Putting"	10.00--12.00
4132	Decant. & Stop. "Driving"	15.00--20.00
2391	Lge. Cig. Bx. & Cov. "Driv."	6.00----8.00
2427	Obg. Ash Tray, "Putting"	2.00----4.00
2419	Sq. Ash Tray "Approching"	2.00----3.00

CARVING no. 16—HOLLYHOCK DESIGN
Made in Crystal

4126½—11" Vase		15.00--20.00
1895½—10" Vase		12.00--18.00
5100	10" Vase	15.00--20.00

CARVING No. 17—NARCISSUS DESIGN
Made in Crystal

2577	6" Vase	12.00--15.00
4126½—11" Vase		15.00--20.00
4143½—6" Ftd. Vase		8.00--10.00
4143½—7½" Ftd. Vase		10.00--14.00

CARVING No. 18—TIGER LILY DESIGN
Made in Crystal

4132	5" Vase (Ice Bowl)	10.00--14.00
2577	6" Vase	12.00--15.00
2577	5½" Wide Vase	12.00--15.00

CARVING No. 19
LILY OF THE VALLEY DESIGN
Made in Crystal

4143½—7½" Ftd. Vase		10.00--15.00
4143½—6" Ftd. Vase		8.00--10.00
2568	9" Ftd. Vase	15.00--20.00
4132½—8" Vase		15.00--20.00

CARVED DECORATIVE GROUP

4116½—5" Ball-Bubble Baby		10.00--12.00
	Carving 28	
2577	5½" Wd. Vase Greyhound	12.00--15.00
	Carving 25	
315	9" Bowl Archer	12.00--15.00
	Carving 24	
2577	8½" Vase Dolphin	15.00--20.00
	Carving 27	
4132½—8" Vase Three Geese		15.00--20.00
	Carving 26	

CARVING No. 34—HUNT DESIGN
Made in Crystal

4146	9 oz. Scotch & Soda	3.00----5.00
4146	4 oz. Cocktail	3.00----5.00
4146	1 oz. Cordial	3.00----5.00
4146	3 Piece Set, Nested	9.00--15.00

TOY DESIGN—DECORATION 620

4146	9 oz. Scotch & Soda Ht.3-1/8"	3.00----5.00
4146	4 oz. Cocktail, Ht. 2½"	3.00----5.00
4146	1 oz. Cordial, Ht. 1½"	3.00----5.00
2306	4" Ash Tray	3.00----4.00
2306	3½" Ash Tray	3.00----4.00
2306	3" Ash Tray	3.00----4.00
2306	2¾" Ash Tray	3.00----4.00

NIGHTMARE DESIGN
DECORATION 621

4146	9 oz. S. & S., Ht. 3-1/8"	3.00----5.00
4146	4 oz. Cocktail, Ht. 2½"	3.00---5.00
4146	1 oz. Cocktail, Ht. 1½"	3.00----5.00
2306	4" Ash Tray	3.00----4.00
2306	3½" Ash Tray	3.00---4.00
2306	3" Ash Tray	3.00----4.00

2306 2¾'' Ash Tray 3.00----4.00

CARVED SMOKING ACCESSORIES

4148 2¼'' Cig. Holder, Blown 2.00----5.00
  Horse carving 35—Top Diam. 2''
4148 2½'' Ind. Ash Tray . . . 3.00----4.00
  Blown Horse, Carving 35
4148 2¼'' Cig. Holder, Blown 2.00----5.00
  Elephant Carving 36—Top
  Diameter 2''
4148 2½'' Ind. Ash Tray 3.00----4.00
  Blown Elephant, Carving 36
4148 2¼'' Cig. Holder, Blown 2.00----5.00
  Rooster Carving 37, Top
  Diameter 2''
4148 2½'' Ind. Ash Tray . . . 3.00----4.00
  Blown, Rooster Carving 37
2427 Oblong Cig. Box & Cover 6.00----9.00
  Snow Crystal, Carving 42, Lgt. 7'',
  Ht. 2¼'', Wdt. 3-1/8'', Each
  side holds 35 cigarettes
2427 Oblong Cig. Box & Cover 6.00----9.00
  Gros Point Carving 43, Lt. 7'',
  Ht. 2¼'', Wdt. 3-1/8''
  Each side holds 35 Cigarettes
2427 Oblong Ash Tray Snow Crys 2.00----4.00
  Carving 42, Lt. 3½'',
  Width 2¾''
2516 Ash Tray Chanticleer
  Carving 41 . . . . . 3.00----5.00
  Ht. 2-1/8'' Diameter 5''
2427 Oblong Ash Tray . . . 2.00----4.00
  Gros Point Carving 43, Lt. 3½'',
  Width 2¾''
2427 Oblong Cig. Box & Cover 6.00----9.00
  Lyre Carving 30, Lt. 7'', Ht. 2¼'',
  Width 3-1/8'', Each side
  holds 35 Cigarettes
2427 Oblong Ash Tray 2.00----4.00
  Lyre Carving 30, Lt. 3½'',
  Width 2¾''
2516 Ash Tray Throughbred . . 3.00----5.00
  Carving 40, Ht. 2-1/8'', Diameter
  5''

CORNUCOPIA

2364 13'' Fruit Bowl, Ht. 2¾'' 15.00--20.00
2364 12'' Lily Bowl, Ht. 2¼'' 10.00--15.00
6023 Duo Candlestick, Ht. 5½'' 6.00----9.00
  Spread 6''
2364 14'' Torte Plate 18.00--22.00
2364 16'' Torte Plate 20.00--25.00
2577 8½'' Vase 9.00--12.00

STARS & BARS DESIGN

2596 Cigarette Box & Cover . . 8.00--10.00
  Lt. 4'', Width 3½''
  Capacity 25 cigarettes
2596 4'' Sq. Ash Tray 3.00----4.00
2596 11'' Obg. Shal. Bowl, Ht. 2'' 10.00--12.00
2596 5'' Candlestick 6.00----8.00
2596 7½'' Sq. Bowl, Ht. 2½'' . . 6.00----8.00

SPECIAL CARVINGS

2577 6'' Vase, Polar Bear 10.00--15.00
  Carving 29

2577 6'' Vase, U.S.A. Map . . 10.00--15.00
  Carving 44
4143½—6'' Ftd. Vase 10.00--15.00
4143½—7½'' Ftd. Vase, Spread
  Eagle, Carving 32 . . 15.00--20.00
2591 15'' Vase, Heron Carv. 31 25.00--35.00
2577 8½'' Vase, Banner Carv. 45 10.00--15.00

DEER DESIGN
CUTTING A, B, C, D
Made in Crystal

4132 14 oz. Tumb. H. B. 3.00----5.00
4132 12 oz. Tumb. H. B. 2.00----4.00
4132½—9 oz. Scotch & Soda, H.B. 2.00----4.00
4132 9 oz. Tumb. H. B. 2.00----4.00
4132 5 oz. Tumb. H. B. 2.00----4.00
4132 7½ oz. O.F. Cocktail, H.B. 2.00----4.00
4132 1½ oz. Whiskey, H.B. . . 2.00----4.00
4132 Decanter & Stopper 15.00--20.00
4132 Ice Bowl 10.00--12.00

GOLD LACE & ITALIAN LACE DESIGN
DECORATION no. 514
Made in Crystal
All Over Etching with Gold Edge

2496 Ftd. Sugar 5.00----7.00
2496 Ftd. Cream 5.00----7.00
2496 8'' Pickle 6.00----8.00
2496 11'' Celery 8.00--10.00
2496 5½'' Comport 10.00--12.00
2496 6½'' Oblong Sauce Dish 6.00----8.00
2496 8'' Oblong Tray 8.00--10.00
2496 6½'' 2 Part Mayonnaise . . 6.00----8.00
2496 3 Part Relish 12.00--15.00
2496 2 Part Relish 8.00--10.00
2496 Sweetmeat 8.00--10.00
2496 10'' Cake Plate, 2 Hdls. . . 12.00--15.00
2496 14'' Torte Plate 15.00--18.00
2496½ Mayo. & Plate & Ladle . . 12.00--15.00
2496 Cheese & Cracker 15.00--18.00
2496 Hdld. Nappy, Flared . . 5.00----7.00
2496 Hdld. Nappy, Sq. 5.00----7.00
2496 Hdld. Nappy, 3-Cor. . . 5.00----7.00
2496 3-Part Candy Box & Cover 18.00--22.00
2496 Duo Candlestick 10.00--12.00
2496 5½'' Candlestick 8.00--10.00
2545 ''Flame'' Duo Candlestick 12.00--15.00
2545 4½'' ''Flame'' Candlestick 6.00----8.00
2545 12½'' ''Flame'' Oval Bowl 15.00--18.00
2496 12'' Bowl, Flared 15.00--18.00
2545 10'' Vase 15.00--18.00
2467 7½'' Vase 9.00--12.00

ADDITIONAL LINES

With our bit of extra space this year we're reprinting a few additional lines not published before. These items, made circa 1927 - 1929 in colors, did not get printed in the Fostoria book because they fell on catalog pages showing duplicates of pieces already shown in other years.

2352—Candle.
Also made in orchid.
Not made in ebony.

2063—Candle.
Not made in ebony.

2464—Ice Jug
Capacity ½ Gal.
Height 6¾ in.

2299—Candle.

2299—Clock.

2299—Candle.

Fostoria Glass Company, Moundsville, West Virginia, Jan. 1, 1939

614
Shaker, F. G. T.
Height 3 in.

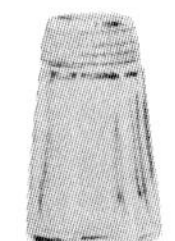

713½—Shaker, F. G. T.
Height 3 in.

800—Shaker, F. G. T.
Height 2½ in.

2111—Shaker, F. G. T.
Height 2⅛ in.

2374—Individual Nut

2521—Bird
For Salt or Almonds

2513
Individual Almond

2306—4 Piece Smoker Set

2515—Ash Tray
Diameter 3 in.

2391—Large Cigarette and Cover
Length 4¾ in.—Width 3½ in.
2391—Small Cigarette and Cover
Length 3½ in.—Width 2¾ in.

2566—Fish Ash Tray
Diameter 5¼ in.

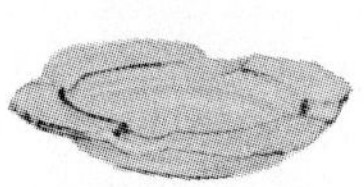

2419—Ash Tray
4 in. Square

2538—Place Card
Holder. Also used for Nut
Dish or Ash Tray
Height 2¾ in.

DESIGN PATENT NO. 102743

Place Card Holder
in Use

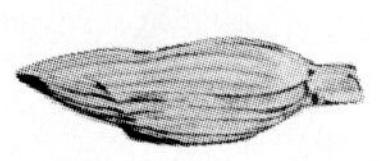

2520—Ash Tray
Length 4½ in.

Fostoria Glass Company, Moundsville, West Virginia, Jan. 1, 1939

1185—8 oz.
Old Fashioned Cocktail
Sham
Height 3½ in.

1184—7-oz.
Old Fashioned Cocktail
Sham.   Height 3⅜ in.

1184—7-oz.
Old Fashioned Cocktail
Narrow Optic
Height 3⅜ in.

889
5 oz. Whiskey Sour,
Plain
Height 3½ in.

4115—3 oz. Footed Cocktail
Height 3⅛ in.
2492—Fish Canape
Length 8½ in.

4115—3 oz. Ftd. Cocktail
Height 3⅛ in.
4115½—4 oz. Ftd. Cocktail
Height 3¾ in.

887
1¾-oz. Whiskey, Sham.
Height 2⅛ in.

887—2½ oz. Whiskey
Height 2¼ in.

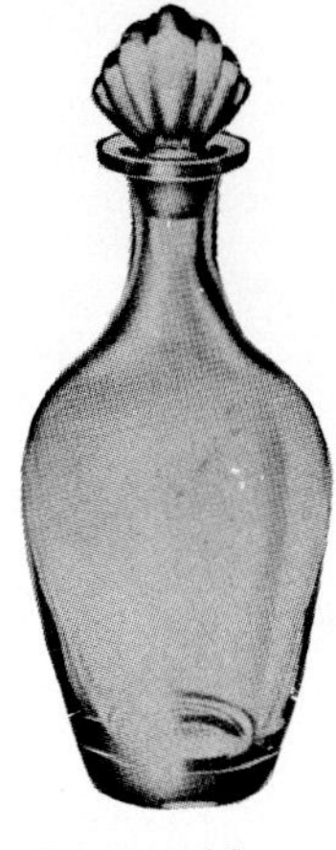

4132—Decanter and Stopper
Capacity 24 oz.
Height 9¾ in.

4132—Ice Bowl
Height 4¾ in.
Top Diameter 6 in.

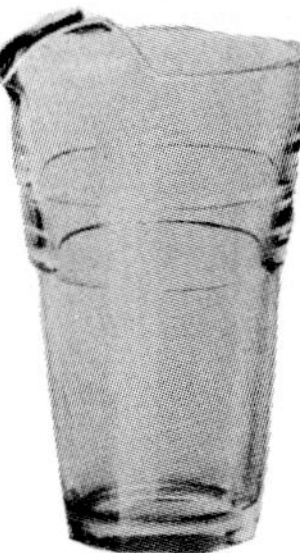

2524—Cocktail Mixer
Capacity 21 oz.
Height 6½ in.

Fostoria Glass Company, Moundsville, West Virginia, Jan. 1, 1939

2561—Bath Bottle
Height 5¼ in.
Capacity 6¾ oz.

2561½—Bath Bottle, W.M.
Height 5¼ in.
Capacity 6¾ oz.

2562½—Bath Bottle, W.M.
Height 5 in.
Capacity 6½ oz.

2562—Bath Bottle
Height 5 in.
Capacity 6½ oz.

Gold Band Decoration
2562—Bath Bottle
2562½—Bath Bottle, W.M.

Silver Mist Decoration
2562—Bath Bottle
2562½—Bath Bottle, W.M.

Silver Mist Decoration
2561—Bath Bottle
2561½—Bath Bottle, W.M.

Carved Decoration
2561—Bath Bottle
2561½—Bath Bottle, W.M.

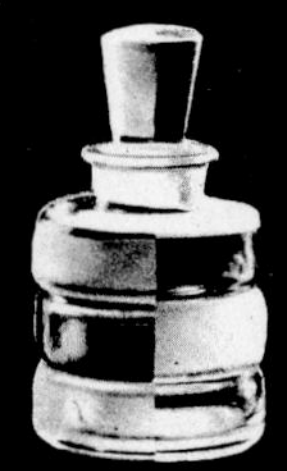

Carved Decoration
2562—Bath Bottle
2562½—Bath Bottle, W.M.

HEIRLOOM PATTERN

Made in Yellow, Blue, Pink, Green, Opal and Bittersweet

1002/834	20 in. Vase
1229/757	6 in. Bud Vase
1515/208	10 in. Bowl
1515/270	15 in. Oblong Bowl
1515/279	16 in. Oval Centerpiece
1515/311	10 in. Candle Vase
1515/364	16 in. Large Epergne
	Consisting of:
	1 - 1515/312 9 in. Epergne Vase
	1 - 1515/413 16 in. Epergne Bowl
1515/827	11 in. Vase
2183/168	7 in. Bowl
2183/311	Flora Candle
2183/415	10 in. Flower Float
2570/575	17 in. Plate
2720/126	Basket
2720/168	6½ in. Crinkle Bowl
2720/170	Square Florette
2720/191	8½ in. Star Bowl
2726/311	Candleholder
2727/202	9 in. Square Bowl
2727/557	11 in. Plate
2727/231	11 in. Shallow Bowl
2727/239	11 in. Bowl, Crimped
2727/550	8 in. Plate
2727/152	6 in. Hanky Bowl
2727/155	6 in. Square Bowl
2728/751	4½ in. Handled Vase
2728/807	9 in. Pitcher Vase
2728/827	11 in. Winged Vase
2729/135	Bon Bon
2729/540	10 in. Oval Bowl
2730/255	12 in. Oval Centerpiece
2730/319	6 in. Candle
2730/364	12 in. Small Epergne
	Consisting of:
	1 - 2730/254 12 in. Epergne Bowl
	1 - 2730/319 7 in. Epergne Vase

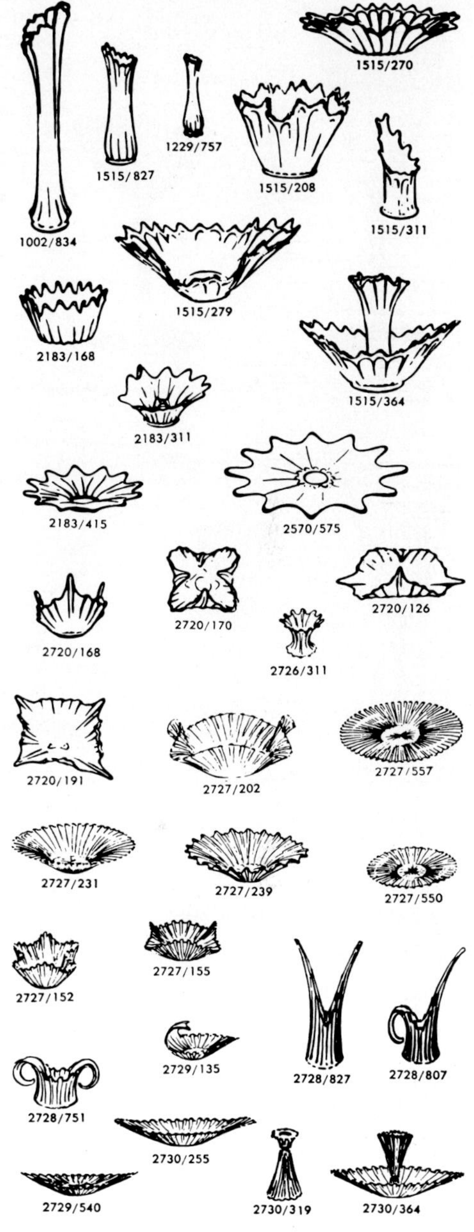

5098—9 oz. Goblet
Height 8¼ in.

5098—6 oz. Saucer Champagne
Height 6 in.

5098—6 oz. Low Sherbet
Height 4⅛ in.

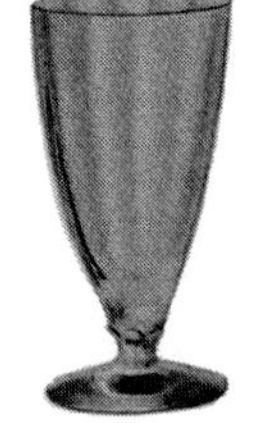

5098—6 oz. Parfait
Height 5¼ in.

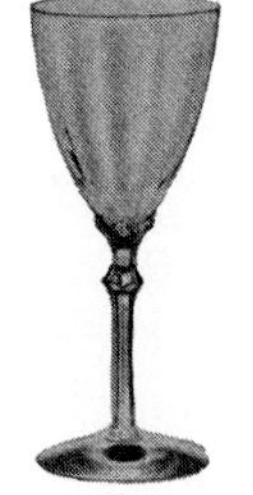

5098—4 oz. Claret
Height 6 in.

5098—2½ oz. Wine
Height 5⅜ in.

5098—3 oz. Cocktail
Height 5⅛ in.

5098—¾ oz. Cordial
Height 3⅞ in.

5098—5 oz. Oyster
Cocktail
Height 3¾ in.

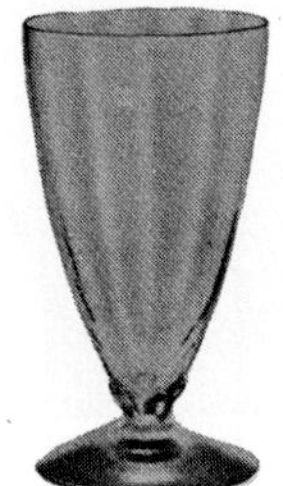

5098—12 oz. Footed Tumbler
Height 6 in.

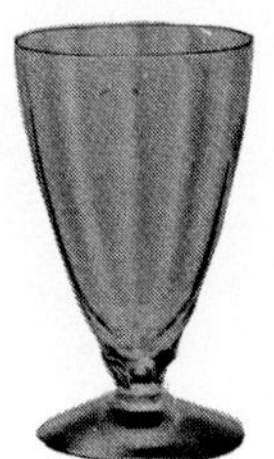

5098—9 oz. Footed Tumbler
Height 5¼ in.

5098—5 oz. Footed Tumbler
Height 4⅜ in.

5098—2½ oz. Footed
Tumbler
Height 2⅞ in.

Fostoria Glass Company, Mounasville, West Virginia, Jan. 1, 1936

NEW STEM SECTION

I've researched and prepared this new section to help identify, at a glance, the numerous Fostoria stems made through the years.

The goblet is the piece illustrated, but other pieces were made as well, as illustrated by the #5098 line on the opposite page.

All stem lines were made in crystal plus the colors as noted. But you may find them made in other Fostoria colors — it was very difficult to research them fully.

Documenting this information proved so valuable that I went right on researching through 1978. Part 1, below, shows all stems from 1900 to 1942, the date with which the FOSTORIA book concludes. Part 2, following that, covers the 1942-1978 period.

PART 1: 1900-1942

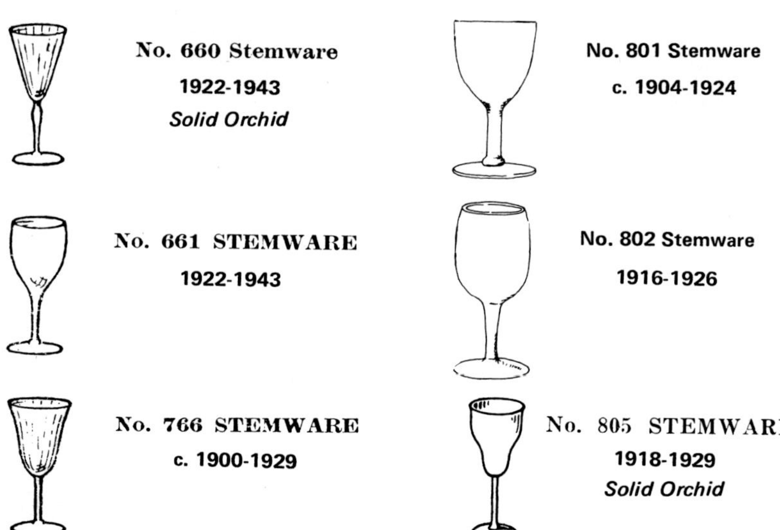

No. 660 Stemware
1922-1943
Solid Orchid

No. 801 Stemware
c. 1904-1924

No. 661 STEMWARE
1922-1943

No. 802 Stemware
1916-1926

No. 766 STEMWARE
c. 1900-1929

No. 805 STEMWARE
1918-1929
Solid Orchid

No. 826 Stemware
1916-1924

No. 879 STEMWARE
1916-1924

No. 858 STEMWARE
1904-1930

No. 880 STEMWARE
c. 1900-1928

No. 863 STEMWARE
1910-1928

No. 882 Stemware
1913-1924

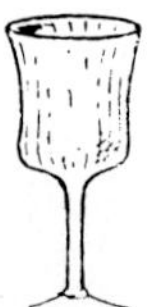

No. 867½ STEMWARE
1916-1926

No. 890 LINE
1929-1942

*Solid Green, Rose,
Burgundy*

No. 869 LINE
1925-1938
*Solid Amber,
Green, Blue*

No. 891 LINE
1933-1938
Topaz

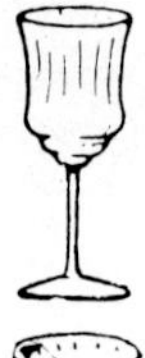 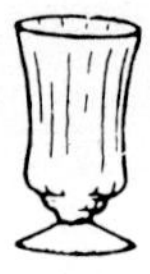 

No. 870 LINE
1921-1942
*Solid Amber, Green,
Rose, Blue*

NORDIC PATTERN
No. 892 Line
1929-1943

No. 877 LINE
1927-1942
*Solid Amber, Green,
Orchid, Azure.
Empire Green, Regal Blue*

No. 4020 LINE
1929-1943
*Rose, Topaz Wisteria
Bowl
Amber, Green, Ebony
Base*

VICTORIAN PATTERN
No. 4024 LINE
1934-1943
Empire Green
Burgunday, Regal
Blue Bowl

No. 5082 STEMWARE

1924-1943
Solid Green
Green, Rose, Azure
Bowl
Amber, Green, Blue
Base

No. 4095 FOOTED WARE
1923-1929
Solid Green,
Amber, Green, Rose Bowl
Amber, Green, Blue Base

No. 5083 STEMWARE
1925-1932
Solid Green
Amber, Green, Blue
Base

No. 5008 Stemware

c. 1904-1921

No. 5093 LINE
1926-1940
Solid Amber, Green,
Blue
Rose, Azure Bowl
Amber, Green, Blue
Base

No. 5025 Stemware

c. 1900-1933

Amber, Green, Rose
Bowl

No. 5097 LINE
1927-1943
Amber, Green, Rose,
Orchid Bowl
Amber, Green Base

No. 5050 STEMWARE
1918-1924

No. 5098 LINE
1928-1950
Amber, Green, Rose,
Topaz, Azure, Wisteria
Bowl.

AMERICAN LADY PATTERN
No. 5056 LINE
1933-1973
Empire Green, Burgundy,
Regal Blue Bowl

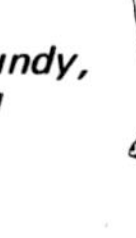
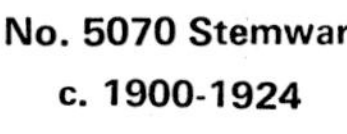

No. 5099 LINE
1928-1943
Green, Rose,
Topaz, Azure, Wisteria
Bowl

No. 5070 Stemware
c. 1900-1924

No. 6000 LINE
1932-1943
Solid Amber,
Green, Topaz

NO. 6002 LINE

1931-1933

Rose, Topaz Bowl
Green, Ebony Base

NO. 6010 LINE

1932-1940

NO. 6003 LINE

1932-1943

Green, Topaz Bowl
Wisteria Base

**NEO CLASSIC
PATTERN**
NO. 6011 LINE
1934-1964

Burgundy, Regal Blue Bowl
Amber, Ruby Base

NO. 6004 LINE
1934-1943

Green, Wisteria Base

**WESTCHESTER
PATTERN**
NO. 6012 LINE
1936-1970

Empire Green
Burgundy, Regal Blue Bowl

NO. 6005 LINE

1934-1943

Green, Topaz Base

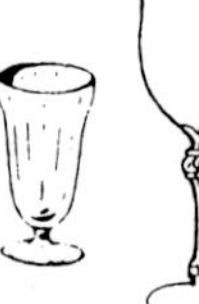

NO. 6013 LINE

1936-1948

Burgundy, Ruby,
Regal Blue Bowl

NO. 6007 LINE

1934-1943

Green, Topaz, Wisteria
Bowl
Amber Base

NO. 6014 LINE

1936-1958

Topaz, Azure Bowl

NO. 6008 LINE

1934-1943

Topaz, Wisteria Bowl

NO. 6016 LINE

1936-1978

Azure Bowl

SCEPTRE PATTERN
NO. 6017 LINE
1938-1976
Topaz, Azure
Bowl
Plain Gold Band

NO. 6009 LINE

1934-1957

Amber, Rose Bowl

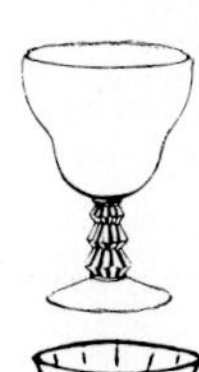 

RONDEL PATTERN
No. 6019 LINE
1938-1943
Topaz, Azure Bowl

NIAGARA PATTERN
No. 6026/2 Line
1940-1976

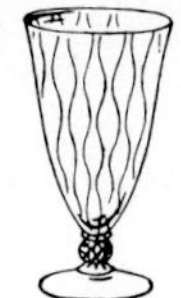

MELODY PATTERN
No. 6020 Line
1940-1957

ENVOY PATTERN
No. 6027 Line
1940-1957

COLFAX PATTERN
No. 6023 Line
1940-1976 M.A.

CHALICE DESIGN
No. 6029 Line
1941-1944

CELLINI PATTERN
No. 6024 Line
1940-1975 M.A.

ASTRID PATTERN
No. 6030 Line
1942-1978 M.A.

CABOT PATTERN
No. 6025 Line
1940-1958

WAVEMERE PATTERN
No. 6030/3 Line
1942-1943

No. 6025/1 Line
1940-1943

No. 6031 Line
1942-1957

GREENBRIER PATTERN
No. 6026 Line
1940-1976 M.A.

TEMPO PATTERN
No. 6032 Line
1942-1950

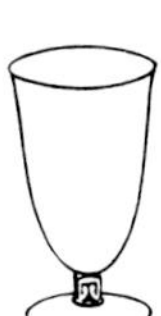

PART 2: 1942-1978

S.B.M. — Still being made in 1978

M.A. — Matching Available in 1978
S.B.M. — Still being made in 1978

MADEMOISELLE PATTERN
No. 6033 Line
1949-1972

COURTSHIP PATTERN
No. 6051½ Line
1956-1976-78 M.A.

RUTLEDGE PATTERN
No. 6036 Line
1951-1977

MOON RING PATTERN
No. 6052 Line
1954-1965

SILVER FLUTES PATTERN
No. 6037 Line
1949-1972

CONTINENTAL PATTERN
No. 6052½ Line
1956-1973

CAPRI PATTERN
No. 6045 Line
1952-1965

MARILYN PATTERN
No. 6055 Line
1954-1977

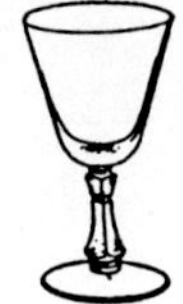

WINDSOR PATTERN
No. 6049 Line
1952-1965

RHAPSODY PATTERN
No. 6055½ Line
1955-1973

RINGLET PATTERN
No. 6051 Line
1954-1965

DIADEM PATTERN
No. 6056 Line
1954-1965

CHALICE PATTERN
No. 6059 Line
1955-1965

VICTORIA PATTERN
No. 6068½ Line
1957-1971

CONTOUR PATTERN
No. 6060 Line
1955-1977

PRELUDE PATTERN
No. 6071 Line
1957-1970

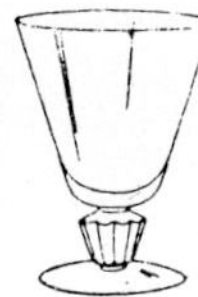

LYRIC PATTERN
No. 6061 Line
1955-1965

CELESTE PATTERN
No. 6072 Line
1957-1974

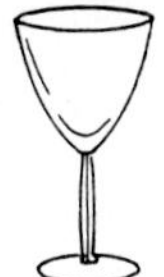

PATRICIAN PATTERN
No. 6064 Line
1956-1971

ENCHANTMENT PATTERN
No. 6074 Line
1958-1965

ELEGANCE PATTERN
No. 6064½ line
1956-1971

NORDIC PATTERN
No. 6077 Line
1958-1965

SYMPHONY PATTERN
No. 6065 Line
1956-1971

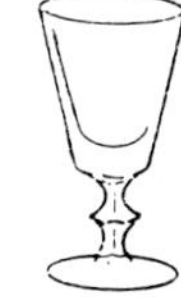

KENT PATTERN
No. 6079 Line
1958-1971

PURITAN PATTERN
No. 6068 Line
1957-1971

FASCINATION PATTERN
No. 6080 Line
1958-1978 S.B.M.

EMBASSY PATTERN
No. 6083 Line
1959-1973

SHERATON PATTERN
No. 6097 Line
1961-1978 S.B.M.

PETITE PATTERN
No. 6085 Line
1959-1978 M.A.

VOGUE PATTERN
No. 6099 Line
1961-1976

VESPER PATTERN
No. 6086 Line
1959-1965

DEBUTANTE PATTERN
No. 6100 Line
1962-1978 S.B.M.

CHATEAU PATTERN
No. 6087 Line
1959-1970

CRYSTAL TWIST PATTERN
No. 6101 Line
1962-1971

ORLEANS PATTERN
No. 6089 Line
1960-1977

SILHOUETTE PATTERN
No. 6102 Line
1963-1978 S.B.M.

PRISCILLA PATTERN
No. 6092 Line
1960-1978 S.B.M.

GLAMOUR PATTERN
No. 6103 Line
1964-1978 S.B.M.

STOCKHOLM PATTERN
No. 6093 Line
1960-1969

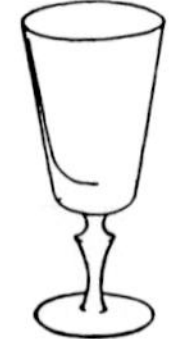

JEFFERSON PATTERN
No. 6104 Line
1964-1973

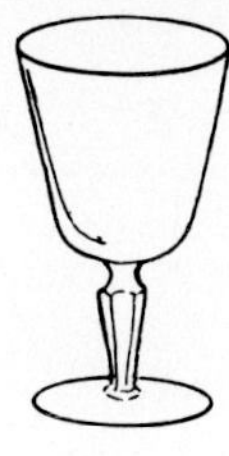

BERKSHIRE PATTERN
No. 6105 Line
1966-1974

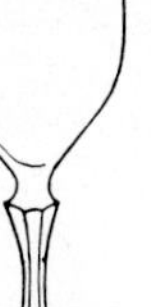

ILLUSION PATTERN
No. 6111 Line
1969-1978 S.B.M.

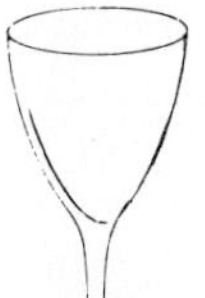

CELEBRITY PATTERN
No. 6106 Line
1966-1971

SILVER TRIUMPH PATTERN GOLDEN TRIUMPH PATTERN
No. 6112 Line
1969-1973

INSPIRATION PATTERN
No. 6107 Line
1966-1971

VERSAILLES DESIGN
No. 6113 Line
1969-1972

PRECEDENCE PATTERN
No. 6108 Line
1967-1975

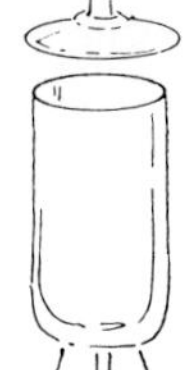

VENTURE PATTERN
No. 6114 Line
1969-1971

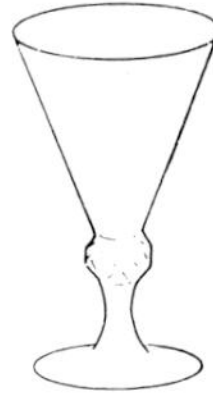

EXETER PATTERN
No. 6109 Line
1967-1971

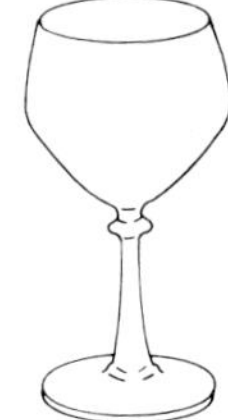

CONTRAST PATTERN ELOQUENCE PATTERN
NO. 6120 LINE
1971-1978 M.A.

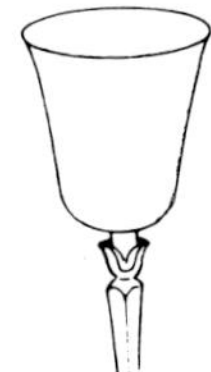

PROMISE PATTERN
No. 6110 Line
1967-1978 M.A.

SPHERE PATTERN
No. 6121 Line
1971-1973

SOMMELIER COLLECTION

1970-1974

6115/34

6116/35

6117/36

6118/37

6119/38

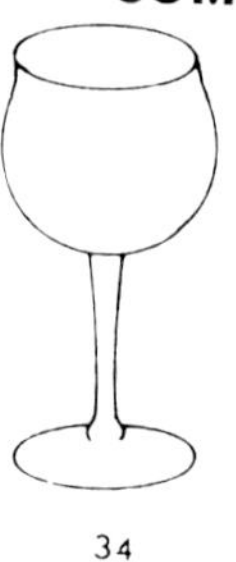

34

35

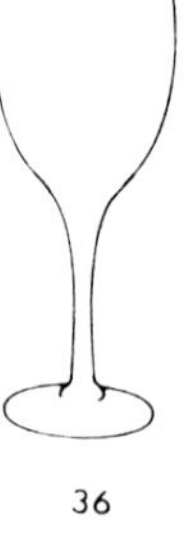

36

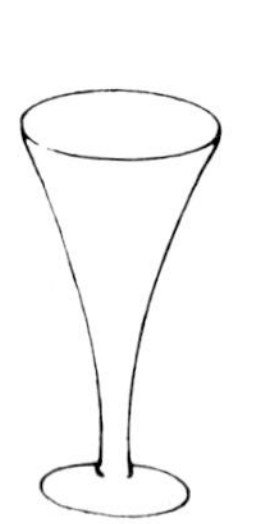

37

38

BISCAYNE PATTERN
No. 6122 Line
1971-1974

PRINCESS PATTERN
No. 6123 Line
1972-1978 S.B.M.

SPLENDOR PATTERN
No. 6124 Line
1972-1974

DISTINCTION PATTERN
No. 6125 Line
1972-1978 S.B.M.

THE PRESIDENT'S HOUSE
No. 7780 Line
1972-1974

VISION PATTERN
No. 3008 Line
1972-1974

CORSAGE PLUM PATTERN
WIMBLEDON PATTERN
No. 6126 Line
1974-1978 S.B.M.

FESTIVE PATTERN
No. 6127 Line
1975-1978

Index